Philosophy for an Ending World

Philosophy for an Ending World

TIM MULGAN

OXFORD
UNIVERSITY PRESS

Great Clarendon Street, Oxford, OX2 6DP,
United Kingdom

Oxford University Press is a department of the University of Oxford.
It furthers the University's objective of excellence in research, scholarship,
and education by publishing worldwide. Oxford is a registered trade mark of
Oxford University Press in the UK and in certain other countries

© Tim Mulgan 2024

The moral rights of the author have been asserted

All rights reserved. No part of this publication may be reproduced, stored in
a retrieval system, or transmitted, in any form or by any means, without the
prior permission in writing of Oxford University Press, or as expressly permitted
by law, by licence or under terms agreed with the appropriate reprographics
rights organization. Enquiries concerning reproduction outside the scope of the
above should be sent to the Rights Department, Oxford University Press, at the
address above

You must not circulate this work in any other form
and you must impose this same condition on any acquirer

Published in the United States of America by Oxford University Press
198 Madison Avenue, New York, NY 10016, United States of America

British Library Cataloguing in Publication Data
Data available

Library of Congress Control Number: 2023945239

ISBN 9780192856173

DOI: 10.1093/9780191946479.001.0001

Printed and bound by
CPI Group (UK) Ltd, Croydon, CR0 4YY

Links to third party websites are provided by Oxford in good faith and
for information only. Oxford disclaims any responsibility for the materials
contained in any third party website referenced in this work.

Contents

Acknowledgements — vii
Prologue: Life at Humanity's End — ix
Introduction — xiii
Cast of Characters — xxxiii

1. First Debate: Pessimism for a Post-Cataclysm World: The Meaning of Life in the Face of Oblivion — 1

2. Second Debate: Religion for a Post-Cataclysm World — 49

3. Lecture One: Introducing Multigenerationalism — 82

4. Lecture Two: Introducing Procreative Ethics — 113

5. Lecture Three: Weinberg's Contractualist Procreative Ethic — 144

6. Lecture Four: Collective Consequentialist Procreative Ethics — 169

7. Lecture Five: Moral Progress, Transformation, and Imaginativeness — 199

8. Lecture Six: Post-Cataclysm Utopias — 215

9. Third Debate: Virtual Endings and Digital Futures — 249

    Conclusion: Lessons from an Ending World — 291

Bibliography — 293
Index — 303

Acknowledgements

I presented earlier versions of the ideas in this book to seminars at the Universities of St Andrews, Auckland, Glasgow, Reading, and Southampton, at workshops at Concordia University and the University of Reading, at the International Society for Utilitarian Studies conference at Karlsruhe Institute of Technology in July 2018, and at the Pacific Division meeting of the American Philosophical Association in San Francisco in April 2023. I am very grateful to audiences at all these venues for many helpful comments and suggestions.

I am very grateful to several anonymous readers for Oxford University Press for their detailed, forthright, and insightful comments on both the proposal and the draft manuscript; to Peter Momtchiloff for his advice and encouragement over several iterations of this project; and to Susan Frampton and Ethiraju Saraswathi for turning my Word document into a book.

I started writing this book in late 2019, when the end of the world was a merely theoretical concern. In hindsight, writing a book about the end of the world was not the best project during a global pandemic. I thank the (former) New Zealand Government for keeping me alive, and my bubble companions Janet McLean and Margaret Bedggood for keeping me sane.

I dedicate this book to the memory of three dear friends and colleagues who died while I was writing it, and from whom I learnt so much, both about philosophy and about other things that matter more: Sarah Broadie, Peter Clark, and Katherine Hawley.

Prologue: Life at Humanity's End

In the beginning, it was merely an anomaly. A strange phenomenon in a distant corner of our galaxy, of interest only to astrophysicists. As its true nature was revealed, it became the Cataclysm—an explosion of an unprecedented kind, sending out waves of destruction that destabilise all complex molecules in their path. These 'omega rays'—as they were soon christened—travel slower than the speed of light. So we can see what they do. The omega rays will not reach us for two hundred years. But when they do, all life on Earth will end.

Most people's initial reaction was some (not very coherent) combination of incredulity, morbid fascination, and despair. For a while, nothing seemed worth doing, everyday life seemed pointless. But when things settled down, as things always do, people's considered reactions fell into a number of broad categories:

1. *Denial:* In a culture where all science is contested and everyone has their own 'alternative facts', it was inevitable that some people would dismiss the Cataclysm as a hoax. The usual suspects were rounded up—unspecified 'elites', the Chinese military, the US military, astrophysicists jealous of the funding given to climate science (another hoax, of course). Maverick astrophysicists were in hot demand on chat shows, talkback radio, and the less discerning corners of the web.
2. *Despair:* Some people sank into despair—concluding that, without an indefinite human future, life was not worth living now. As a short-term or intermittent reaction, this was very common. But—perhaps surprisingly—long-term despair has been much less common. Of course, some projects really did become pointless. (The bottom immediately dropped out of the market for paying exorbitant sums of money to have your body cryogenically frozen in the hope that distant future people would have nothing better to do than bring you back to life.) But most people eventually found some way to reorient their lives in the shadow of the Cataclysm.
3. *Literal Escapism:* Some optimists accepted the Cataclysm, but poured all their energy into finding ways to ensure the survival of life on Earth. Two hundred years is a long time. Perhaps, if we start thinking now, we might devise some shield or deflector to protect our solar system from omega rays' destructive impact. Surely, given the stakes, this is the most important task humanity has ever faced?

4. *Metaphorical Escapism:* Self-styled 'realists', implicitly conceding that the Cataclysm robbed their lives of genuine meaning, sought refuge in unashamedly meaningless activities such as video games, extreme sports, reality television re-runs, and so on.
5. *Hedonism:* Others acted similarly, but with a very different rationale. Hedonists—in the philosophical sense—argued that the Cataclysm changed nothing. Pleasure was still good and pain was still bad. Egoist hedonists sought their own pleasure, while utilitarian hedonists sought—as ever—to maximise the net balance of pleasure over pain. The foreshortened horizon of the Cataclysm gives us less scope to promote pleasure and alleviate pain. But these tasks are no less valuable in themselves. (After all, most people's predictable impact on the global net balance of pleasure over pain has never extended much beyond their own lifetime. So why would imminent extinction make any practical difference at all?)
6. *Intensification:* Many people found the meaning in their lives intensified rather than diminished. The Cataclysm disrupted all our expectations, changing the moral landscape in ways we could never have predicted. But this is hardly the first such disruption humanity has faced, even if it will be the last. Civilizations have collapsed, traditional ways of life have become impossible, worldviews have been overturned, the Universe has turned out to be not quite as we imagined, every individual has always had to face their own death, and so on. Yet everyday human life has always simply carried on. While we now paint on a smaller canvas, we can still strive to achieve the best possible world. Eliminating poverty, building just societies, curing preventable disease, minimising unnecessary non-human suffering, and generally making life go better for people and animals still inspire many people. Indeed, these goals have a new urgency. It really is now or never.
7. *Supernatural Transcendence:* Many people sought solace in religion or other supernatural or transcendent sources of meaning. Doomsday cults sprang up, and existing fundamentalist sects scoured sacred texts for predictions of the Cataclysm. But more rational religious responses have also thrived. If meaning and purpose could no longer be found in the secular human future in this world, perhaps they could be found in contemplation of the divine, or care for one's immortal soul. Alongside existing religions, new non-human-centred supernatural worldviews have emerged. Unable to reconcile the imminent destruction of all life on Earth with the traditional idea that God cares for individual human lives, many now conclude that the cosmos is best interpreted as unfolding according to some higher plan where humanity is simply irrelevant.

Are these reactions any less reasonable than analogous responses in the optimistic affluent Pre-Cataclysm world? (What actually motivated those people to spend their lives as they did? Reading the twittering records of that lost age, it often is hard to tell!) Trying to make the world go better for the next two centuries is not an obviously pointless goal. Indeed, if that isn't a worthwhile goal, then what is?

Our Cataclysm-overshadowed world has seen the birth of new philosophical concerns and questions. Creative artists who work in temporal media—novelists, composers, singers, storytellers—have always known the importance of a good ending: no good thing lasts forever, don't outstay your welcome. Individuals, cultures, institutions, religions, empires, linguistic communities, ethnic groups, family lines, and societies have often faced the same sobering challenge: 'We always knew this wouldn't last forever. It is about to end. How do we ensure that it ends well, appropriately, fittingly?' The human story is coming to an end. Most of us think this is a pity. We would have liked it to last a bit longer. But such is life. We must now ask how it should end.

One popular, if somewhat frivolous, analogy compares our present generation to the writers of a cult TV series whose network has just announced that our next season will be the last. We cannot hope to reverse this decision. Our only concern is to end our story in the best possible way.

One new pressing question, of course, is when the human future should end. The Cataclysm sets an upper bound, but we might choose to bring human history to a close sooner—most obviously by deciding not to bring any more children into the world. Procreative choices look very different in our foreshortened world.

In some ways, life in our ending world resembles the post-apocalyptic dystopias so popular in pre-Cataclysm fiction. But in other ways, it is closer to pre-Cataclysm fantasies of a post-scarcity future. While time is now a very scarce resource, everything else is much less scarce than ever before—because it no longer has to last into the indefinite future. Why not party like there's no tomorrow when there isn't?

Introduction

0.1 A New Thought Experiment

This book explores the following imaginary scenario:

The Ending World: Scientists are agreed on the following grim facts. A cataclysmic event in a distant corner of the galaxy, caused by hitherto unknown physical processes, has produced a deadly new kind of cosmic rays that are spreading throughout the galaxy. These 'omega rays' will pass through our solar system two hundred years from now. Fortunately, omega rays travel slower than the speed of light, so we can observe their impact on other star systems. Unfortunately, that impact is very negative. Omega rays destroy everything in their path. When omega rays hit, in two centuries' time, life on earth will be extinguished. There is no way to avoid this, nor can we hope to outrun the omega rays. (Although they travel slower than light, omega rays travel much faster than any feasible mode of human interstellar travel.) Humanity thus faces an extinction that is imminent and unavoidable, but not immediate.

The book explores philosophy within this slowly ending world. I imagine philosophers living in this imaginary future, absorbing the discovery that humanity has only two centuries to live, and then trying to make philosophical sense of their unprecedented situation. I present transcripts of imaginary philosophical debates and lectures within the ending world. I adopt the perspective of these 'Post-Cataclysm' philosophers (as they dub themselves) to help us imagine their world from the inside. I have chosen the mix of dialogues and lectures because, while I do not want to prescribe one specific future philosophy, I do want to explore one distinctive approach in more detail. My primary goal, however, is to persuade readers that the ending world is worth exploring, whether or not they share my own particular views about where that exploration might lead.

Why think about this scenario? And why think about it in this way? More bluntly, why did I write this book, and why should you read it?

The ending world is both a provocative thought experiment and a challenging possible future. And exploring it *from within*—adopting the perspective of philosophers living *in* that ending world—helps us to get the most out of our thought experiment, to evaluate it as a possible future, to discover what we owe to future people who might inhabit such a future, and to explore how we might justify ourselves to them. A central question throughout the book is whether we could equip our descendants to flourish in an ending world, even if we cannot imagine flourishing there ourselves.

0.2 Why a New Thought Experiment?

A good thought experiment aids our conceptual understanding. Many thought experiments also highlight the role of implicit empirical assumptions in our philosophical thinking. We are often influenced by contingent claims that we take for granted, but which could, in principle, turn out to be false. Thought experiments also often prize apart things that typically go together. To take two examples: Robert Nozick's famous experience machine thought experiment—the basis for my final debate on virtual futures—asks whether pleasure is sufficient for well-being when it is completely isolated from its usual effects;[1] and Derek Parfit's non-identity arguments—a central topic in my series of lectures on procreative ethics—ask whether person-affecting harm is necessary for wrongdoing when it diverges entirely from separate impersonal value.[2] Similarly, in our everyday lives, we take it for granted that humanity faces an indefinite future. What difference would it make if we suddenly discovered that it did not? What might we learn about *our own present values* by imagining away the human future?

The ending world is worth exploring because it is an interesting and distinctive thought experiment. I defend its *distinctiveness* in Section 0.4, by contrasting it with other imaginary tales of human extinction. The rest of the book defends the claim that it is interesting.

0.3 Why Think about Possible Futures?

My ending world is not merely imaginary. It is also somewhere our own descendants might live. This book therefore contributes to a broader project that imagines how people might live in a variety of possible futures, and then asks (1) how we should equip those people to best inhabit those futures, and (2) how we could answer to them if we do not.[3]

Why should we think about possible futures? In particular, why should we care what future people might think? Throughout this book, I argue that people in a possible ending future will find this or that ethical view or philosophical position more or less plausible or useful than we do. Even if you agree that the ending world *is* a possible future, and even if you accept all my speculations about the ethical and/or philosophical beliefs of its inhabitants, why should you care? What impact should future people's beliefs have on our *current ethical or philosophical thinking*?

---

[1] Nozick, *Anarchy, State, and Utopia*, pp. 42–45.   [2] Parfit, *Reasons and Persons*, pp. 351–379.
[3] I explore possible futures in *Ethics for a Broken World*; 'Ethics for Possible Futures'; 'Utilitarianism for a Broken World'; 'How Should Utilitarians Think about the Future?'; 'Answering to Future People'; 'Moral Imaginativeness, Moral Creativity and Possible Futures'; 'Corporate Agency and Possible Futures'; *Utilitarianism*; 'From Brad to Worse: Rule Consequentialism and Undesirable Futures'.

Imagining the future of ethics is not merely an interesting intellectual exercise. It is also an essential part of our own exploration of our current obligations to future people. In particular, thinking about possible futures from the inside helps us to appreciate the *urgency* of our obligations to future people, provides a deeper understanding of the *content* of those obligations, and gives us new resources to *meet* those obligations.

We cannot possibly consider all *possible* futures, nor all possible reactions within any given future. Imaginary debates among morally eccentric individuals living in possible-but-vanishingly-unlikely futures would have little value. And my very specific ending world scenario does contain its own implausible details! However, a simplified, specific scenario that is very unlikely in itself can still be useful *because it represents a broad class of futures that is collectively quite likely*.

Some possible futures are more ethically significant than others. If we are risk-averse, or if we give priority to the interests of the worst-off, then we should pay disproportionate attention to futures whose inhabitants are worse-off than ourselves, even if more optimistic futures are equally likely.[4] If we are designing or re-engineering our moral outlooks or institutions, then we should also pay disproportionate attention to scenarios where our influence on future people's moral beliefs might have the greatest impact.[5]

We should focus on futures that are *credible*, *unsettling*, and *worrying*: futures that might happen, that destabilise the presuppositions of our current ethical thinking, and that raise significant new ethical challenges for future people.

The selection of possible futures to explore is thus driven by philosophical and normative considerations, as much as practical ones. We seek, not necessarily the most likely possible futures, but the most revealing or disturbing ones. And we seek *representative* possible futures, not precise predictions. Like philosophers' thought experiments, these 'possible futures' are simplified scenarios that teach important lessons.

My ending world represents a much broader set of all futures where humanity faces imminent extinction. And that broader set of futures is *not* too unlikely. Ending worlds also intersect in interesting ways with *other* important possible futures. These include futures broken by climate change (or other catastrophe) where our affluent way of life is no longer available; post-scarcity futures where resource constraints are removed; and virtual or digital futures where people escape a harsh or unpalatable 'real world' by escaping into experience machines or uploading themselves into computers.[6]

---

[4] Mulgan, *Ethics for a Broken World*; 'Ethics for Possible Futures'.
[5] Mulgan, 'Ethics for Possible Futures'; 'How Should Utilitarians Think about the Future?'
[6] Mulgan, 'Ethics for Possible Futures'; 'How Should Utilitarians Think about the Future?'; 'Corporate Agency and Possible Futures'.

Reflecting on possible futures brings home the *urgency* of future ethics. Imagining future ethical challenges reinforces the *importance and inescapability* of our obligations to future people—especially when we imagine futures that are worse than the present. This is why we must focus on *worrying* futures.

Up until the late twentieth century, most moral and political philosophers focused primarily on obligations to contemporaries and/or people in the near future. Obligations to the distant future were seldom discussed. Philosophers set the distant future aside for three main reasons: *optimism, similarity,* and *convergence.* They assumed (1) that future people will be better-off than present people; (2) that the future will resemble the present in most morally relevant ways; and (3) that the interests of present and future people largely converge.

Environmental crises and other recent developments have undermined this optimistic picture. We now recognise that future people might be worse-off than ourselves; that they might inhabit very unfamiliar futures; and that their interests might conflict with our own. Future ethics is central to contemporary ethics.

In my book *Ethics for a Broken World* and elsewhere, I explore the outlook of philosophers inhabiting a future broken by climate change, where a chaotic climate makes life precarious, each generation is worse-off than the last, it is no longer possible to meet everyone's basic needs, and our affluent way of life is no longer an option.[7]

This broken future is *credible*. No-one can reasonably be confident it won't happen. It involves no outlandish claims, scientific impossibilities, or implausible expectations about human behaviour. Climate change—or some other disaster—might produce a broken future. We do not know exactly what harms climate change will cause. But we do know it may very well cause significant and lasting harm. And climate change is not the only route to a broken world. (Other routes include technological catastrophe, financial collapse, or global pandemic.)

The credibility of the broken future undermines the three complacent presumptions of optimism, similarity, and convergence. In a broken future, people are (by definition) worse-off than ourselves; their moral challenges differ from our own; and both the likelihood and the severity of the broken future may depend on *present* choices. In particular, we might be able to mitigate *future* brokenness by making significant *present* sacrifices. Present and future interests thus conflict—and one key task for future ethics is to balance these competing interests.

My *ending* future is worth exploring, in part, because it has much in common with this broken future. A theme of this book is that people living in an ending future face new challenges of intergenerational conflict—and declining well-being and meaningfulness—as humanity nears its end. In particular, I argue that the ability of the *last* human generation to truly flourish without any successors of

---

[7] Mulgan, *Ethics for a Broken World*; 'Utilitarianism for a Broken World'; 'Answering to Future People'.

their own depends, in large part, on the social, ethical, philosophical, and imaginary resources that we bequeath to them.

Reflecting on possible futures in the abstract highlights the urgency of future ethics. Imagining the reactions *of future people* adds something more. Asking how future people, and especially future philosophers, might evaluate our moral legacy to them gives our future ethics a *second-personal dimension*.[8] The idea of justifying ourselves to future people is common in everyday language. (We often pause to ask what our descendants will think of us.) Future-directed second-personalism gives our obligations to distant future people *the same felt moral urgency* as our obligations to our contemporaries—enabling future interests to compete with present interests when the two conflict. Without future-directed second-personalism, the abstractly described future is too easily trumped by the directly encountered present. One sign that we have balanced competing intra- and inter-generational obligations fairly is that we are confident that we could justify ourselves equally well *to both present and future people.*

Once we recognise the importance and inescapability of future ethics, we must then ask what our obligations to future people actually *are*, and how we might *meet* them. As well as helping us to recognise both the urgency of future ethics and the need to justify ourselves to future people, imagining possible futures also transforms our understanding of the content of future ethics.

Any plausible future ethic includes obligations regarding future people's well-being, flourishing, and quality of life. Other things equal, we should strive to leave future people as well-off as possible. And perhaps we are *obliged* to leave them reasonably well-off and/or no worse-off than ourselves. We should also strive to enable future people to live meaningful and morally decent lives. If our descendants must choose between individual flourishing and intergenerational injustice, then we have failed them—even if they end up 'flourishing' (in some non-moral sense) in immoral ways.

We naturally judge any new possible future against our own present values, priorities, and accounts of well-being. We ask whether we would like to live there ourselves. But what if future people themselves would reasonably have different values, or even a different ethical outlook altogether? We cannot simply assume that is what is good, important, or meaningful for us would work equally well for future people. More specifically, we cannot determine what is valuable for future people without knowing *what they will value*. Some theories of well-being, of course, *identify* what is good for *anyone* with *whatever* they value (or desire, or would desire under ideal conditions, or...). But our reason to imagine future ethical outlooks is not contingent on such extreme subjectivism. Not even the most thoroughgoing objectivist will deny that, *as a matter of fact*, whether or not someone flourishes is partly dependent on whether they value what they get.

---

[8] cf. Darwall, *The Second-Person Standpoint*; Mulgan, 'Answering to Future People'.

Therefore, we cannot determine whether a possible future is good or bad for its inhabitants without imagining that future clearly from their perspective. We must imagine possible futures *from the inside*.

Our legacy to future people includes, not only the physical infrastructure, cultural capital, and environmental conditions we leave behind, but also the moral outlook(s) we teach directly to our immediate descendants and thereby indirectly bequeath to later generations. This is arguably our most important legacy to the future. Our present choices influence, not only the future that people will inhabit, but how they will regard—and evaluate—that future.

One urgent task of future ethics is to prepare future people, especially our own immediate descendants, for the new moral challenges they might face. Insofar as their flourishing depends on *their* moral ideas, it depends on *our* moral legacy. We must develop and bequeath a moral outlook that will enable future people to flourish. We must therefore ask how competing moral outlooks would actually work *for them*.

Our ultimate goal is to bequeath a *temporally robust* moral philosophy: one that provides the inhabitants of a broad range of credible futures with the conceptual resources they need to recognise, confront, and hopefully avoid the particular threats that are most salient to them. At the very least, we must not bequeath an ethic that leaves future people unable to recognise the most worrying threats, prevents them from addressing them, or leads them into avoidable despair.

I argue elsewhere that broken futures are particularly disturbing because our current moral outlook is not fit for purpose there.[9] If we allow future people to inherit a broken future, and then bequeath our own unrealistic and unattainable affluent morality, then we will have done them a double disservice.

A theme of this book is that the *ending* future is disturbing in exactly the same way. Insofar as our current moral outlook attaches significance to the indefinite human future—making present meaning contingent on our connection to future generations—then bequeathing that outlook is simply a recipe for despair and disappointment in an ending world. Can we do better? Are there moral outlooks that would enable future people to flourish in an ending world?

Reflecting on possible futures has a broader impact on contemporary ethics, beyond our obligations to future people. Whenever we encounter another group whose ethical outlook differs from our own, we naturally ask what, if anything, *we* should borrow from that alternative outlook. Imagining the *future* of ethics promises a similar source of ethical enrichment.

Imaginary thought experiments highlight the *conceptual* contingency of our current ethical beliefs. Imagining possible *futures* highlights their *historical* contingency. Reimagining contemporary philosophy from the point of view of future

---

[9] Mulgan, *Ethics for a Broken World*; 'Utilitarianism for a Broken World'; 'Answering to Future People'.

philosophers promises the same benefits of distance and perspective that we gain from studying past philosophers in their historical and social context. In both cases, we learn to see *our own ethical worldview* from the outside. The fact that actual past people did, or actual future people might, see the world very differently may make us less confident that we have got things right.

Of course, we cannot time travel and simply help ourselves to some superior future ethic. We cannot go beyond the limits of our own ethical imagination. But that imagination itself is improved by reflection on possible future perspectives. I return to themes of moral progress, moral transformation, and moral imaginativeness throughout the book—especially in my lectures on multigenerationalism.

0.4 Why This Thought Experiment?

My ending world is designed to be both a challenging new thought experiment, and a credible, unsettling, and worrying possible future. The rest of this book argues that the ending world is challenging, interesting, worrying, and unsettling. In this section, I argue that it is both original and credible.

In my ending world, humanity faces an extinction that is *unavoidable* and *imminent*, but *not immediate*. This raises three immediate questions.

1. Why *human extinction*?
2. Why *unavoidable* extinction?
3. Why *imminent-but-not-immediate* extinction? (Why the two-hundred-year delay?)

Philosophers should think about threats of human extinction for two reasons. First, it is increasingly widely acknowledged that such threats are plausible and non-negligible.[10] Second, ethical theories that cope with comparisons between different *inhabited* futures may struggle to cope with choices between an inhabited future *and an empty future*.[11]

Two existing philosophical literatures already engage with human extinction. On one side, a growing interdisciplinary discussion asks how we should think about *risks* of human extinction—and especially how much we should be prepared to sacrifice to reduce those risks. This literature on 'existential risks' explicitly

---

[10] On the importance of existential risks, see, e.g., Bostrom, 'Existential Risk as a Global Priority'; Bostrom and Cirkovic, *Global Catastrophic Risks*; Ord, *The Precipice*. For a more sceptical view, see Schuster and Woods, *Calamity Theory*.

[11] My inspiration here is Derek Parfit's influential arguments that theories that work in Same People Choices don't necessarily cope well with Different People Choices, and that theories that work in Same Number Choices don't necessarily cope well with Different Number Choices (Parfit, *Reasons and Persons*, pp. 351–441).

addresses possible futures, not just imaginary thought experiments. Indeed, it has a clear *real-world* agenda—arguing that a greater share of present resources (time, intellectual attention, research funding, political capital, philanthropic spending) should be devoted to thinking about how to prevent human extinction.

A second philosophical literature asks *why* human extinction would be bad. In two recent books, Samuel Scheffler explores a *doomsday scenario* where the world will be destroyed thirty days after my death, and an *infertility scenario* where everyone on earth becomes infertile and the present generation know they will be the last.[12] Scheffler conjectures 'that most of us would find the prospect of humanity's imminent extinction unbearably depressing'.[13] He argues that this 'afterlife conjecture' reveals the importance, for our everyday projects and lives, of the assumption 'that others will continue to live after I have died'.[14]

Avoidable and immediate extinction are already on the philosophical agenda. I depart from the existential risk literature by making extinction unavoidable; and I depart from Scheffler by moving extinction from the immediate future into the near future.

Why make extinction unavoidable? When I began thinking about human extinction, I did address the costs of *avoiding* extinction. I used a different thought experiment where we *can* escape imminent human extinction, but only at a very high present cost. In this Starship Choice scenario, when omega rays render the Earth uninhabitable, humanity can escape imminent extinction by sending a small group of pioneers on a long journey (lasting several generations) to a distant exo-planet where the human story might continue. We can *either* accept imminent extinction *or* escape to the stars.[15]

I used this *disjunctive* thought experiment to explore the contrast between contractualism and consequentialism. Launching generation starships is bad for most people who are currently alive; but it (hopefully) enables many more people to live in the further future. Indeed, we can construct imaginary cases where not launching starships would be better *for everyone who ever lives*, even though launching them would produce *much greater total future welfare*. Contractualists then *cannot* launch starships—no matter how great the potential payoff; while consequentialists *must* launch—no matter how low the probability of success or how great the present cost.[16] I then asked whether contractualists and consequentialists can moderate their positions and meet somewhere in the middle.

---

[12] Scheffler, *Death and the Afterlife*; *Why Worry about Future Generations*.
[13] Scheffler, *Why Worry about Future Generations*, p. 42.
[14] Scheffler, *Death and the Afterlife*, p. 15.
[15] Mulgan, 'What Exactly Is Wrong with Human Extinction?' This thought experiment is inspired by the 'Generation Starship' sub-genre of speculative fiction: for a history, see Caroti, *The Generation Starship in Science Fiction*.
[16] The Starship Futures case thus challenges to Parfit's argument that (the best form of) rule-consequentialism delivers the same set of moral principles as (the best forms of) both Scanlonian and Kantian Contractualism (Parfit, *On What Matters*, volume one, pp. 244–253).

I still think this Starship Choice scenario is worth thinking about. I plan to return to it in future work. However, I no longer believe this is the best place to *begin* a philosophical examination of human extinction. To understand the values at stake in extinction vs escape *choices*, we need to *first* think through the stay-at-home alternative. If humanity really did have only two centuries left, what might those centuries be like?

Even a very small chance of escaping extinction is distracting. In the existential risk literature, total utilitarians argue that, given the potential astronomical amount of future well-being at stake, even the smallest reduction in the probability of imminent human extinction justifies any (finite) present cost;[17] while, in most fictional tales of human extinction, the hero, almost by definition, is the obtuse person who simply refuses to accept that extinction is unavoidable and then (absurdly) succeeds in preventing it.[18] Therefore, I remove those distractions by eliminating the possibility of escape altogether—with one significant exception. In my final debate on virtual futures, I do explore the possibility of a *digital* future where a digital version of human civilisation could endure for very many generations, thanks to the faster pace of digital 'life' (Section 9.10).

The existing literature largely takes it for granted that human extinction is bad.[19] The existential threat literature is dominated by optimistic total utilitarians who assume that future human lives will (on balance) be worth living; while Scheffler's starting point is the intuitive repugnance of human extinction, which he then seeks to *explain*.

By contrast, in my ending world, the removal of *any* possibility of escape forces us to address the prior question whether human extinction really *is* a tragedy to be avoided at (almost) any cost. Perhaps we should instead devote our resources to the different challenge of ensuring that, when it *does* arrive, human extinction is not so bad after all.

I concede that any assumption of *certainty* about extinction is very artificial—as is any other presumption of certainty about the future. And removing any possibility of escape *does* remove some of the most interesting and urgent ethical questions about extinction. However, every philosophical thought experiment side-lines some questions *in order to highlight others*. And a specific scenario that

---

[17] See, e.g., Beckstead, *On the Overwhelming Importance of Shaping the Far Future*. There is an obvious connection here to long-termism—the view that our over-riding current ethical priority should be to positively influence the far distant human future. For different perspectives, see, e.g., Torres, 'Against Longtermism'; MacAskill, *What We Owe the Future*; C. Adams, Crary, and Gruen, 'Future-Oriented Effective Altruism: What's Wrong with Longtermism?' I return to long-termism briefly in my discussion of digital futures in Section 9.10. However, for the most part, my concerns in this book are tangential to this fast-moving topical debate.

[18] Consider two examples: (1) In Neal Stephenson's novel *Seveneves*, the survival of humanity relies on a series of 'coincidences' that could most charitably be described as 'impossible'; (2) while P. D. James's *The Children of Men* is the model for Scheffler's tale of (unavoidable) universal infertility, the actual *plot* revolves around an inexplicable opportunity to avoid extinction.

[19] One important recent exception is Crisp, 'Pessimism about the Future'.

is itself incredible can represent a broader range of possible futures that are (collectively) very credible. My ending world is not plausible. But future people might face unavoidable extinction. Indeed, this is almost certain. While it may seem unlikely, something analogous to my scenario is more-or-less inevitable. Desperate transhumanist fantasies notwithstanding, humanity will eventually become extinct sooner or later. *Someone* will inhabit an ending world. Extinction cannot be *avoided*. It can only be *postponed*.[20]

In our world, where humanity apparently enjoys an indefinite future, it is easy to forget the inevitability of extinction, because the last human generation is lost in the mists of (future) time. In my ending world, where the last human generation would be (at most) our near descendants, humanity's inevitable mortality is much harder to ignore.

I conclude that unavoidable extinction is worth exploring. But Scheffler has already put unavoidable *immediate* human extinction on the philosophical agenda. Why add my thought experiment to Scheffler's? Why talk about a *slowly* ending world? What does the extra two hundred years *add*?

I argue that my *slowly* ending world has several advantages over Scheffler's immediate endings—both as a thought experiment, and as a credible possible future.

The shift to a slowly ending world helps to *clarify* our intuitive reactions to human extinction. Immediate extinction is bad in too many, too obvious ways. Scheffler highlights the significance of the implicit assumption that there will be *some* future generations: some future people whose culture, traditions, values, and projects are connected to, and descended from, our own. It is not hard to see why the denial of *this* assumption—the removal of *any* cultural descendants—might be very de-stabilising. In my *slowly* ending world, by contrast, the disruption to present projects is much less obvious. Two hundred years is quite a long time. How many of our present activities will leave *any* discernible trace in two centuries' time? We don't think about distant future people in our daily lives. So why should their absence matter to us?

The slowly ending world thus offers a more compelling test case for Scheffler's claims about the importance of future generations, precisely *because* self-interested prudential reasons are *less* prominent. We *could* simply ignore the prospect of human extinction in two centuries. (Arguably, most present people *do* ignore this possibility!) And yet it seems—at least to me, and to many other people with whom I have discussed this thought experiment—that the removal of the more distant human future would be very de-stabilising *in its own right*. If so, how can we explain this?

A second advantage is that my slowly ending world contains future generations. In Scheffler's two scenarios, by definition, there are no future people.

---

[20] cf. Johnston, 'Is Life a Ponzi Scheme?'; Section 1.5 below.

People mourn the loss of the human future, but they do not otherwise think about intergenerational ethics. By contrast, if we imagine the *start* of the ending world—when humanity still has two hundred years to run—then present people still have obligations *to future people*—namely, people who will live closer to humanity's end, and especially those living in the last human generation. Indeed, people at the *start* of the ending world must decide whether or not there will (or should) *be* future generations. Could we permissibly create new people if we knew they would inherit an ending world—and that their prospects for a human future would be even more constrained than our own? Can early generations in an ending world ensure that life is *meaningful* for their own descendants—and especially for the last human generation who must handle *immediate* human extinction? Could they hope to build a just society—or to rectify historical or environmental injustice—in two hundred years?

Suppose we agree with Scheffler that *for us* meaning, well-being, and making sense of our projects and traditions all require future generations who will continue those projects and traditions. One vital question *within* the ending world is whether our dependence on future generations is an *essential feature of the human condition* or merely a *contingent feature of the way we have been raised or acculturated*.

Unlike Scheffler's doomsday and infertility scenarios, the slowly ending world thus opens the door to a position I call *multigenerationalism*—where the best way to find *meaning* in the ending world is to embark on projects spanning several generations that only come to fruition long after the present generation are gone. More formally, I identify multigenerationalism with the following two claims introduced in Lecture One:

1. *Basic Multigenerational Claim*: People living at the start of a slowly ending world should devote themselves to initiating terminal intergenerational projects (which I dub 'multigenerational projects').
2. *Reorientation Claim*: People living at the start of a slowly ending world should devote themselves to initiating a particular kind of multigenerational project that aims to reorient our current, inherited, future-dependent traditions and practices so that they remain fit for purpose even at humanity's end.

A theme of the book is that, in an ending world, these multigenerational projects are morally permissible only if they somehow transform the moral landscape—enabling the last human generation to find meaning in their truncated present in ways that our generation could not.

I explore multigenerationalism at considerable length. Unsurprisingly, it is the main focus of my three lectures on multigenerationalism (Lectures One, Five, and Six). It is also a background theme of my three procreative ethics lectures

(Lectures Two, Three, and Four), which are delivered by a proponent of multigenerationalism, and serve to illustrate one central argument for multigenerationalism. I believe multigenerationalism is the most distinctive new ethical approach in an ending world.

Scheffler's primary interest is the role that future generations play in our *present actual evaluative lives*. His doomsday and infertility scenarios highlight the importance *to us* of future generations. For Scheffler, the plausibility or likelihood of his scenarios is largely irrelevant. Conceivability is sufficient for his purposes. Scheffler does not claim that any future generation is likely to encounter such scenarios. So it is no objection to Scheffler's project that his doomsday scenario—in particular—is quite implausible. (How could I possibly know that, whenever I die, the world will end thirty days after my death?)

By contrast, adding the two-century time-frame gap before inevitable human extinction renders my thought experiment *a more plausible possible future*. My slowly ending world is a place where future people *might actually live*. It might happen. Humanity might well face a genuine extinction threat *at some point in the next two hundred years*. Our descendants might face real threats of imminent-but-not-immediate extinction. We must strive to develop and leave behind a moral code that will enable future people to cope with such threats.

I do not claim that my particular slowly ending world is the only imminent extinction scenario worth exploring. We could reintroduce the possibility of escaping extinction, at various different present costs, and ask which costs are worth paying; or we could imagine that *non-human nature* will continue after humanity's demise, to focus attention on our long-term environmental obligations and reasons (for instance, in Scheffler's infertility scenario, the disease that causes human infertility may not infect other species); or we might introduce intelligent extra-terrestrial beings who will escape the Cataclysm that dooms humanity—and ask whether the last humans might find meaning by communicating with them. I return to extra-terrestrial life in my religion debate (Section 2.3.2), and I explore ecological issues in my final lecture on multigenerational utopias (Section 8.4). However, for the sake of simplicity, I otherwise set these alternatives aside, and suppose that the Cataclysm that dooms us also spells the end of all life.

0.5 Plan of the Book

The book consists of transcripts of an imaginary philosophy conference within the ending world. Imaginary Post-Cataclysm philosophers explore our 'Pre-Cataclysm' philosophy—tailored to a world facing an indefinite human future. They ask how this Pre-Cataclysm philosophy might apply in their new situation.

I imagine my symposium occurring at the very start of the slowly ending world, when inevitable human extinction lies two hundred years in the future.

My Post-Cataclysm philosophers explore a wide range of philosophical topics, to illustrate the many ways that the loss of the indefinite human future might affect philosophical thinking. The book contains a mix of debates and lectures. To provide continuity throughout the different topics in the book, all three debates feature the same six participants, while the lectures are all delivered by one of those participants.

Chapter One. 'First Debate: Pessimism for a Post-Cataclysm World: The Meaning of Life in the Face of Oblivion'

The book opens with a debate on Post-Cataclysm pessimism that sets the scene for everything that follows. Pessimism is a perennial philosophical worry. Is life worth living? Can human lives be meaningful? Is a connection to something beyond this life—such as the human future—essential for a meaningful, worthwhile human life? Pessimists argue that life is either meaningless or not worth living.

My First Debate's central character is a *Post-Cataclysm Pessimist*, who argues that losing the indefinite human future is sufficient to *make* life meaningless or not worth living. I contrast Post-Cataclysm pessimism with *last generation pessimism*, where life becomes meaningless only in the last generation. Can earlier generations (in a slowly ending world) enjoy meaningful lives if they know that life will soon become meaningless? Or does last generation pessimism lead inevitably to Post-Cataclysm pessimism? (Section 1.5).

Following Scheffler, I focus on future-dependent *meaning*. Scheffler argues that even our most present-directed projects presuppose an ongoing background of traditions, values, or relationships that extend into the future. *Last Generation Pessimists* insist that the loss of *all* future-dependent meaning makes life meaningless at humanity's end. My Post-Cataclysm Pessimist extends this critique, arguing that future-dependent meaning is lost even earlier, because our current (Pre-Cataclysm) values require an *indefinite* human future.

This debate pits the Post-Cataclysm Pessimist against five opponents. The *Perennial Pessimist* argues that life has always been meaningless. Imminent extinction doesn't change anything. It only makes the absurdity of human existence harder to avoid. The *Presentist* finds sufficient meaning in present pleasures and achievements, or in care and compassion for the suffering of others. The *Multigenerationalist* takes a middle-road. On the one hand, they agree with Scheffler that *for us* meaning, well-being, and making sense of our projects and traditions all require future generations—future descendants who will continue those projects and traditions. The Multigenerationalist therefore agrees with Last

Generation Pessimists that, if *we* were the last generation, then our lives would be meaningless. Meaning *is* lost in Scheffler's doomsday and infertility scenarios. On the other hand, the Multigenerationalist rejects Post-Cataclysm pessimism. They insist that the loss of future-directed meaning is a *contingent feature of the way we have been raised or acculturated*, rather than an *essential feature of the human condition*. People living at the *start* of the ending world could raise *new generations* for whom meaning, well-being, and value were not dependent on the existence of any (further) future people.

The final two characters are the *Theist*, who argues that meaningful human lives require a connection to divine reality—something that is unaffected by the Cataclysm; and the *Escapist*, who argues that we should devote all our energies to trying to find ways to escape imminent extinction—no matter how unlikely that may be. These last two characters take a back seat in this debate. The four principal participants (Post-Cataclysm Pessimist, Perennial Pessimist, Presentist, and Multigenerationalist) share a secular, naturalist worldview. They seek meaning in human life within the familiar, natural, physical universe. Theism, supernatural meaning, and the consolations of religion are set aside for now.

The Post-Cataclysm Pessimist argues that future-dependent meaning *matters*. They draw inspiration from a variety of previous philosophers. These include: Scheffler's work on the relationship between values and traditions (Section 1.4); Jonathan Lear's work on radical hope—which links present meaning to future moral transformation (Section 1.6); nineteenth-century German pessimism, especially the now largely forgotten Eduard von Hartmann, who argued that, in a world of suffering, meaning can only be found in future cultural progress (Section 1.7); and Mark Johnston's argument that good people literally 'live on' in future generations (Section 1.8). The Post-Cataclysm Pessimist argues that *all* secular replacements for a personal afterlife—all hopes to 'live on in the ongoing rush of humanity', as J. S. Mill put it—collapse in the face of imminent extinction.[21]

The Post-Cataclysm Pessimist deploys these Pre-Cataclysm resources to argue that life cannot be meaningful in an ending world, and especially in the last generation; while the Multigenerationalist instead deploys them to reimagine future-dependent traditions in new ways; and the Presentist objects that both sides over-estimate the significance of future-dependent meaning in the first place.

Chapter Two. 'Second Debate: Religion for a Post-Cataclysm World'

My Second Debate asks how the Cataclysm impacts on familiar debates between theism and atheism. It features the same participants as the First Debate. The lead

---

[21] See, e.g., Lear, *Radical Hope*; Beiser, *Weltschmerz* on Hartmann; Johnston, *Surviving Death*; and the works cited in the First Debate in Chapter One.

characters are now the Theist who believes in the God of traditional Western monotheism, and two atheist opponents who reject all gods, supernatural beings, and supernatural explanations. The Post-Cataclysm Pessimist insists that the Cataclysm strengthens the case for atheism, while the Presentist argues that we have never needed God to make our lives meaningful. In a brief appearance in the final section, the Multigenerationalist remains agnostic—suggesting that imminent human extinction should prompt us to explore alternatives to atheism and theism, including my own *ananthropocentric purposivism*, where the universe has a purpose, but human beings are completely irrelevant or incidental to that purpose.[22]

The debate has two main parts. First, the Theist argues that the Cataclysm breathes new life into one familiar (or notorious!) set of arguments for belief in God and personal immortality—variously known as Kantian, moral, pragmatic, or practical arguments (Section 2.2). In the face of imminent human extinction, we can only live meaningful lives by positing God, objective value, and personal immortality. Therefore, it is reasonable for us to believe in these things. The Post-Cataclysm Pessimist agrees that the loss of the indefinite human future is devastating for secular attempts to render life meaningful. However, they deny that theist leaps of faith are ever reasonable. We should simply accept that life has become meaningless. The Presentist replies instead that we don't need either God or the human future to make human lives meaningful, and therefore that moral arguments don't get off the ground.

The Post-Cataclysm Pessimist then argues that the Cataclysm *strengthens* the philosophical case for atheism—supporting atheist arguments from evil and scale and weakening theist cosmological and teleological arguments (Section 2.3). The Cataclysm is simply not the kind of thing that an omnipotent benevolent God would permit. The Theist replies that the Cataclysm has no significant impact on any of these familiar debates. Along the way, the participants explore connections between cosmic purpose and objective value, and the significance of extraterrestrial life.

Chapter Three. 'Lecture One: Introducing Multigenerationalism'

The heart of the book is a series of six lectures delivered by my Multigenerationalist character. The first lecture introduces multigenerationalism—explaining what it is, why it is credible, and how it is defended. Multigenerationalism claims that, in a slowly ending world, the present generation should devote themselves to initiating terminal intergenerational projects, especially those that aim to reorient

---

[22] I develop ananthropocentric purposivism in *Purpose in the Universe*; 'Beyond Theism and Atheism'; 'Could We Worship a Non-Human-Centred Impersonal Cosmic Purpose?'

current future-dependent traditions and practices in ways that enable those traditions and practices to still provide meaning even in the last generation.

Multigenerationalism is a thesis in *normative ethics*—a claim about what people ought to do in a particular situation. While it is *related* to claims about meaningfulness, value, obligations, and reasons, multigenerationalism is *distinct* from those other claims. This lecture explores a range of particular arguments for multigenerationalism. Two key arguments are based on meaningfulness and procreative permissibility. My Multigenerationalist argues that multigenerational projects and reorientations are necessary if *anyone* in my slowly ending world is to enjoy a meaningful life, and that procreation is only permissible if such projects succeed. Multigenerational projects are also something that we owe *to other people*—and especially to past and future people—because intergenerational cooperation is necessary for anyone's life to be meaningful.

Chapters Four, Five, and Six. Lectures Two, Three, and Four: Post-Cataclysm Procreative Ethics

Over three lectures, the Multigenerationalist next explores procreative ethics in an ending world. My ending world differs from Scheffler's *immediate* extinction scenarios because the first generation is not necessarily the last. Present people can create future people. But is this permissible? In particular, is it permissible to create a last generation who cannot have children of their own?

Procreative permissibility is especially important for the Multigenerationalist. While the Presentist and the Theist seek solace in the present or in God, and the Post-Cataclysm Pessimist argues that no solace can be found, the Multigenerationalist grounds *present meaning* in collaborations with future people. Multigenerational projects are permissible *only if* procreation is permissible.

However, while procreative ethics is vital to the case for multigenerationalism, it is also of much wider interest. I have therefore endeavoured to write standalone lectures whose central arguments do not presuppose my imaginary lecturer's multigenerationalist agenda.

Most contemporary (Pre-Cataclysm) philosophical procreative ethicists share a broad commitment to procreative liberty. People should be *morally* free to decide whether, when, how often, with whom, and in what ways they will have children. I ask whether our commitment to procreative liberty could survive in an ending world, where it is challenged both by anti-natalists (who insist that procreation is now forbidden) and by 'pro-natalists' (who argue that, in an uncertain world of impending extinction, future procreative *obligations* are the only reliable way to ensure that enough people have children).

Many justifications for procreative liberty cite the importance *to potential parents* of the parent–child relationship, the project of raising a child, or the decision whether to include these procreative goods in one's life in the first place. *Ex hypothesi*, people in the *penultimate* generation cannot create children who can enjoy these goods themselves. Post-Cataclysm procreative liberals thus face a dilemma. The more we emphasise the value of procreative projects to potential parents, the more we highlight the disvalue of the resulting child's life. Imminent human extinction thus breathes new life into familiar Pre-Cataclsym anti-natalist arguments.

After a brief overview of our contemporary Pre-Cataclysm procreative ethics (Sections 4.2 and 4.3), the lectures explore four particular approaches, and apply them to the ending world. I have chosen four approaches that illustrate the breadth of procreative ethics: Elizabeth Harman's harm-based approach (Section 4.4), Melinda Roberts's person-affecting consequentialism (Section 4.5), Rivka Weinberg's contractualism (Chapter Five), and my own collective consequentialist future ethics (Chapter Six).[23]

Another theme of the lectures is that permissible procreation, in an ending world, requires active cooperation with future people—and not merely passive promotion of their well-being. This has important implications for multigenerationalism, which are explored in the final two lectures (Chapters Seven and Eight).

The Multigenerationalist argues that procreative freedom is most plausible in the ending world if we can both (a) remove the harm of lost future-directed meaning altogether; and also (b) ensure that the last generation are no worse-off than previous generations. They then argue that multigenerationalism alone can meet these two demanding conditions—because it offers the last generation the opportunity to join with earlier generations in bringing the human story to a satisfactory conclusion.

I seek to remain agnostic between competing accounts of procreative ethics—and especially between consequentialism and non-consequentialism. Because it relies on the voluntary cooperation of all future people, multigenerationalism cannot commit itself to any procreative ethical principle that future people might reasonable reject. (Otherwise, they might refuse to create further future people—thereby bringing intergenerational cooperation to an abrupt end.) I therefore argue that multigenerationalism is consistent with, and supported by, both traditions in procreative ethics. I also explore overlaps between the best Pre-Cataclysm versions of both consequentialism and non-consequentialism.

---

[23] See, e.g., Harman, 'Can We Harm and Benefit in Creating?'; Roberts, 'A New Way of Doing the Best We Can'; Weinberg, *The Risk of a Lifetime*; Mulgan, *Future People*; and other works cited in Lectures Two, Three, and Four.

Chapter Seven. 'Lecture Five: Moral Progress, Transformation, and Imaginativeness'

In their fifth lecture, the Multigenerationalist argues that multigenerationalism is feasible and distinctive. This lecture draws on Pre-Cataclysm work on moral progress—especially on Allen Buchanan and Russell Powell's evolutionary defense of the possibility of moral progress; on Jonathan Lear's influential *Radical Hope*—a philosophical reflection on the life of the Crow leader Plenty Coups, who led his people into a future where their whole way of life no longer made sense; on recent work in environmental philosophy; and on my own earlier work on moral imaginativeness and possible futures.[24] Against both progressive opponents who claim that future moral transformation is unnecessary, and conservative opponents who dismiss it as impossible, my Multigenerationalist argues that multigenerationalism's claims about moral progress, moral imaginativeness, and moral transformation are all credible—given our knowledge of human nature, and of past moral transformations.

Drawing on their procreative ethics lectures, the Multigenerationalist argues that future moral transformation is necessary, not only for multigenerationalists, but for everyone in an ending world who wants to permissibly create a new generation.

Chapter Eight. 'Lecture Six: Post-Cataclysm Utopias'

In their final lecture, my Multigenerationalist explores a diverse range of Post-Cataclysm multigenerational utopias—ranging from ambitious final generation utopias based on John Rawls's liberal egalitarianism (Section 8.2) and Robert Nozick's libertarianism (Section 8.3); to ecological utopias designed to give non-human nature a good ending (Section 8.4); to pluralist religious utopias encompassing a wide range of religious experiments (Section 8.5). These utopias are inspired, in part, by the difficulties of imagining a coherent *intergenerational* utopia. If a perfectly just society can only last a single generation, then perhaps the true utopia can only exist at humanity's end. Earlier generations can then find life meaningful only by working together to pave the way for this short-lived just world.

Chapter Nine. 'Third Debate: Virtual Endings and Digital Futures'

My third and final debate explores experience machines, virtual reality, and the value of connections to reality, freedom, and other people. Should the last humans

---

[24] Buchanan and Powell, *The Evolution of Moral Progress*; Lear, *Radical Hope*; Mulgan, 'How Should Utilitarians Think about the Future?'; Mulgan, 'Moral Imaginativeness, Moral Creativity and Possible Futures'.

abandon the real world altogether and spend their entire lives plugged into Nozickean experience machines that perfectly simulate any possible human experience?[25] The participants from previous debates return. The Presentist defends a virtual world—arguing that hedonist defenses of virtuality remain powerful, while familiar objections lose their force after the Cataclysm. The Post-Cataclysm Pessimist replies that the deficiencies of virtual worlds are *more* apparent in an ending world, because people are more aware of the importance of connections to reality, other people, and the human future. The Theist defends a virtual world as the best place to connect to divine reality—a necessary condition for a meaningful Post-Cataclysm life. In particular, theists who favour Idealism, Neoplatonism, and other *transcendent* metaphysical views argue that empirical 'reality' itself is a pale reflection of *true* reality—and therefore no better than an experience machine (Section 9.6). In the final section, the Escapist returns to argue that a *digital* future offers our only hope of a truly meaningful life—precisely because the faster pace of digital 'life' enables us to restore the lost human future (Section 9.10).

The Multigenerationalist replies that, given the complexities involved, people living at the start of a slowly ending world cannot hope to answer these questions themselves. Their best option is to launch an open-ended multigenerational project designed to enable the last humans to construct whatever world (virtual, non-virtual, digital, or whatever) is best for them. While the present generation cannot flourish in a virtual or digital world, perhaps their descendants could.

The book ends with a brief conclusion, where I bring together the main themes of the book, and draw lessons for our own non-ending-world philosophy.

0.6 How to Read the Book

Unsurprisingly, I hope all readers will carefully read the whole book. However, individual readers will naturally be more interested in some topics than others. Whatever your interests, I strongly suggest starting with the opening debate on Post-Cataclysm pessimism, which sets the scene for everything that follows (Chapter One). If you are particularly interested in religious themes, then you should read Chapter Two—as well as Section 8.5 in the final lecture on Post-Cataclysm utopias (Chapter Eight); and Section 9.6 in the virtual and digital futures debate (Chapter Nine). Conversely, if you have no interest in alternatives to atheism, then the religion debate can be skipped (Chapter Two). The heart of the book is a cumulative argument for multigenerationalism. To understand what that argument is all about, you should read the introductory lecture on

---

[25] Nozick, *Anarchy, State, and Utopia*, pp. 42–45.

multigenerationalism (Chapter Three). If you are particularly interested in procreative ethics, then the three lectures on that topic are relatively self-contained and can be read on their own (Chapters Four, Five, and Six). Conversely, if you are not interested in procreative ethics, those three chapters can be skipped without compromising the overall argument. The three lectures on multigenerationalism are designed to be read in order (Chapters Three, Seven, and Eight). Chapters Seven and Eight both build on Chapter Three; and Chapter Seven builds on Chapter Eight. Finally, the virtual and digital futures debate can be read on its own—although it does bring together themes from all earlier chapters (Chapter Nine).

Philosophy for an Ending World. Tim Mulgan, Oxford University Press. © Tim Mulgan 2024.
DOI: 10.1093/9780191946479.001.0001

Cast of Characters

The Perennial Pessimist argues that life has always been meaningless. Imminent extinction doesn't change anything. It only makes the absurdity of human existence harder to avoid. In the ending world, it is simply more apparent to more people that life has always been meaningless.

- The Perennial Pessimist plays a significant role in the First Debate on Pessimism, and makes brief appearances in the other two debates.

The Post-Cataclysm Pessimist argues that losing the indefinite human future is sufficient to make life meaningless and not worth living. Before the Cataclysm, life was meaningful for some people. After the Cataclysm, life is meaningless for everyone—because human meaning is dependent on inherited traditions and values that presuppose an indefinite human future.

- The Post-Cataclysm Pessimist is the principal character in the First Debate on Pessimism, and plays a significant role in the other two debates.

The Last Generation Pessimist argues that life (only) becomes meaningless in the last generation.

- The Last Generation Pessimist is a silent character who does not appear in the book. They are mentioned by the Post-Cataclysm Pessimist, who argues that, if life will be meaningless in the last generation, then life is already meaningless for earlier generations in the ending world.

The Presentist argues that, after the Cataclysm, present-focused activities based on present pleasures, non-future-dependent achievements, and compassion for the suffering of others are sufficient to render life worth living, meaningful, and morally satisfactory for most people even in the last generation. If life was acceptable before the Cataclysm, then it is still acceptable afterwards. Imminent human extinction alone cannot tip the balance.

- The Presentist plays a significant role in all three debates.

The Multigenerationalist argues that people living at the start of the ending world should devote themselves to initiating terminal intergenerational projects, especially those that aim to reorient current future-dependent traditions and practices in ways that enable those traditions and practices to still provide meaning even in the last generation. This character treads a middle-road between pessimism and presentism. They agree with the Post-Cataclysm Pessimist that, if the present generation were the last, then their lives would be pointless. However, they reply that present people could raise new generations for whom meaning, well-being, and value were not dependent on the existence of any (further) future people.

- The Multigenerationalist features in all three debates. They also deliver the six lectures on multigenerationalism (Lectures One, Five, and Six) and procreative ethics (Lectures Two, Three, and Four).

The Theist argues that true meaning flows, not from the secular human present or future, but from appropriate connections to divine reality. Human meaningfulness is therefore not affected by the Cataclysm. The Theist also argues that the Cataclysm strengthens the philosophical case for theism by strengthening moral, prudential, or Kantian meaning-based arguments for both God and immortality.

- The Theist is the principal character in the Second Debate on religion. They also appear in the other two debates.

The Escapist argues that people living at the start of an ending world should devote all their energies to trying to escape imminent extinction by uploading themselves into digital realms where the human future could last a subjectively long time, as this is the only way to preserve values and traditions that presuppose an indefinite human future.

- The Escapist plays a minor role in the first two debates, and then closes the Third Debate on Virtual and Digital Futures.

1
First Debate

Pessimism for a Post-Cataclysm World: The Meaning of Life in the Face of Oblivion

Perennial Pessimist: For pessimists, *the* fundamental philosophical question is whether life is *ever* worth living. Unsurprisingly, our Post-Cataclysm world has seen a resurgence of philosophical interest in pessimism. For perennial pessimists, this reflects greater awareness of timeless truths about the human condition. It is now more apparent to more people that life has *always* been meaningless.

Post-Cataclysm Pessimist: By contrast, *Post-Cataclysm* pessimists believe that imminent human extinction *itself* has undermined human meaning. Pessimist arguments were not persuasive before the Cataclysm. But they are now. Life used to be meaningful, at least for some people. But it has now *become* meaningless for everyone.

Theist: Many people find meaning in their relationships with God. Does your pessimism presuppose atheism? Or do you deny that even God could provide meaning *in our Post-Cataclsym world*?

Post-Cataclysm Pessimist: As an atheist, I don't think God would help. And I also think the philosophical case for atheism is stronger now than it was before the Cataclysm. However, as our Second Debate focuses on religion, I will set God aside here. My present opponents are *secular optimists*, who believe that life can still be meaningful and worthwhile in our Post-Cataclysm world—even without gods, afterlives, or any other supernatural reality.

In this debate, I will present a variety of arguments for Post-Cataclysm pessimism. First, however, we must establish what pessimism in general, and Post-Cataclysm pessimism in particular, actually claims.

1.1 What Is Post-Cataclysm Pessimism?

Post-Cataclysm Pessimist: 'Pessimism' means many different things to different people, both within philosophy and beyond. Every pessimist claims that human life is *bad*. I begin with a taxonomy of pessimisms, designed to highlight what is distinctive in our Post-Cataclysm world.[1]

Our first question is: Bad *for whom?* Pessimism has three main possible scopes:

- *Universal*: Every human life is bad. 'The quality of human life is…actually quite appalling.… While some lives are better than others, none are (non-comparatively and objectively) good.'[2]
- *Majority*: While some human lives are acceptable, most are bad.
- *Too many*: While some (perhaps even most) human lives are acceptable, too many are bad.

To make our debate interesting, I defend *universal* Post-Cataclysm pessimism. After the Cataclysm, *all* human lives are bad.

Our next question concerns *temporal scope*. All pessimists *agree* that human life is now bad. But pessimists *disagree* whether things have *always* been bad, or whether they used to be better. Actually, there are *three* salient positions:

- *Perennial pessimism*: Human life has always been (and always will be) bad. What makes it bad is either essential to the human condition or endemic in any possible human society.
- *Modernity pessimism*: Human life used to be acceptable, but irreversible historical change has made it bad. Humanity's lost innocence cannot be regained.
- *Future pessimism*: Some Pre-Cataclysm environmental philosophers were pessimistic *only about the future*. Human life is not bad *yet*. But it will soon *become irreversibly bad* due to catastrophic climate change, ocean acidification, run-away artificial intelligence, nuclear winter, population pressure, and so on.

Presentist: Of course, environmental future pessimism no longer bites, because there is no (long-term) human future! Perhaps we should be *less* pessimistic than previous generations.

Multigenerationalist: This is also a central claim of the ambitious multigenerationalism that I will defend in my later lectures!

Post-Cataclysm Pessimist: However, instead of *environmental* future pessimism, we now have a new kind of future pessimism. For *Post-Cataclysm* pessimists, the Cataclysm is *the* decisive moment in human history. Life was not bad before,

---

[1] My discussion of pessimism owes most to Beiser, *Weltschmerz*; Benetar, *Human Predicament*; Dienstag, *Pessimism*; and Van der Lugt, *Dark Matters*.

[2] Benatar, *Human Predicament*, pp. 66–67.

but it is bad now. We reject both *perennial* pessimism and *standard* modernity pessimism. (Modernity began well before anyone was aware that the world was ending.)[3] Instead, the previous divide between modernity pessimism and future pessimism evolves into a new divide between Post-Cataclysm pessimism and last generation pessimism. *Post-Cataclysm pessimism* says that life is bad now. The loss of the indefinite human future is both sufficient and necessary.[4] *Last generation pessimism* says that life will be bad *only in the last generation*. The loss of *all* future generations is sufficient to make life bad.

Last generation pessimism can be exclusive or inclusive. Exclusive last generation pessimism says that life is *only* meaningless at the end, and not before. The loss of *all* future generations is *necessary*, as well as sufficient. Inclusive last generation pessimism leaves open whether life is also meaningless before the end. Hereafter, unless otherwise stated, I will use 'last generation pessimism' inclusively. It is the *sufficient* condition that is more interesting.

We return to the complex relationship between (inclusive) last generation pessimism and Post-Cataclysm pessimism in Section 1.2.

Perennial Pessimist: Pessimists who reject both Post-Cataclysm pessimism and last generation pessimism insist that life is bad *even if humanity enjoys an indefinite future*. We can distinguish two distinct views here. *Perennial pessimism proper* says that human life is bad because of its intrinsic features; and therefore that life would still be bad even if humanity endured forever. By contrast, *finite pessimism* says that life is bad *only because* humanity will one day become extinct. The real problem is not immediate or imminent extinction, but *eventual extinction*.

Post-Cataclysm Pessimist: We next ask what *standard* pessimists use to judge human lives as good or bad. While pessimists offer many particular standards, one overarching divide is between *meaning* and *well-being*. Pessimists can object *either* that life is meaningless (empty, pointless, banal) *or* that it has negative well-being (painful, insufferable). Some pessimists combine these two complaints: life is both meaningless and painful. But the two complaints can come apart—life could be pleasant but pointless, or painful but meaningful. Pessimists often use the generic phrase 'a life not worth living', which is ambiguous between meaning and well-being.

We can also distinguish *whole life* standards—where individual goods and bads can be traded-off against one another—and *specific* standards. The latter come in

---

[3] In other imaginary scenarios, post-Cataclysm pessimism could be a *variant* of modernity pessimism—especially if imminent human extinction results from human activity. Life is bad because modernity (inevitably) leads to imminent human extinction.

[4] More precisely, post-Cataclysm pessimism argues that the loss of the indefinite human future is both necessary and sufficient—*when combined with other ineliminable features of human life*. Perhaps imminent extinction would not undermine the flourishing of angels or ants. But it does undermine *human* flourishing.

two varieties. *Essential good pessimists* claim that, whatever the overall balance of goods over bads, a person's life is bad if it *lacks some essential good*. (Putative essential goods include: freedom, self-respect, knowledge of God, engagement in meaningful work, non-alienated relationships with other people and/or non-human nature, a sense of purpose, the ability to live a morally decent life without entirely sacrificing one's own well-being or personal projects, and so on.) By contrast, *unacceptable bad pessimists* claim that, whatever the overall balance of goods and bads, a person's life is bad if it *contains some unacceptable bad*. (Putative unacceptable bads include: slavery, lack of meaningful autonomy, chronic disease, disability, agony, mortality, and so on.) Essential good and unacceptable bad accounts are often inter-translatable: the lack of an essential good is *itself* an unacceptable bad.

A classic whole life well-being standard is *hedonism*, where pleasures and pains are weighed against one another across the person's life. A classic specific good meaning standard is *existential pessimism*, where life is meaningless due to the absence of God and/or objective values.

Some pessimist standards can apply to *either* meaning *or* well-being. For instance, *preference pessimism* says life is bad because the balance of desire-frustration over desire-satisfaction is negative; while *objective pessimism* says life is bad either because the balance of objective goods over objective bads across a whole life is negative, or because some specific objective good is missing, or because some specific objective bad is present. Preference and objective good are popular philosophical accounts *of well-being*.[5] My life goes well if I get what I want, or if I enjoy objective goods. But some pessimists instead combine hedonism *about well-being* with a preference-based or objective measure *of meaning*. Life can then be bad either (a) because it contains more pain than pleasure; or (b) because it lacks some (essential) desired or desirable thing.

Another distinct kind of pessimist standard is *moral*. Life could be bad because either (a) it is simply impossible to live a morally satisfactory life; or (b) living morally is not compatible with living well or meaningfully. For instance, living a pleasant or meaningful life may require resources (time, money, attention) that one is *morally* obliged to devote to other people's more urgent needs. In principle, well-being and meaning standards can both incorporate morality—living morally might itself be necessary for a flourishing or meaningful human life. However, for analytical purposes, it is sometimes useful to separate morality from well-being and meaning.

---

[5] For overviews of current debates about well-being, see Crisp, 'Well-Being'; Moore, 'Hedonism'; Bradley, 'Objective Theories of Well-Being'; Crisp, 'Hedonism Reconsidered'; Feldman, *Pleasure and the Good Life*; Heathwood, 'Subjective Theories of Well-Being'. My discussion is also influenced by Adams, *Finite and Infinite Goods*; Bradford, *Achievement*; Kraut, *The Quality of Life*; Mawson, *God and the Meaning of Life*; Metz, *God, Soul and the Meaning of Life*; Nozick, *The Examined Life*, pp. 104–118; Parfit, *Reasons and Persons*, Appendix J; Tollefsen, 'Experience Machines, Dreams, and What Matters'.

Perennial Pessimist: Some Pre-Cataclysm pessimist standards naturally suggest *perennial* pessimism. If what makes life bad is human mortality, the absence of moral facts, or the non-existence of God, then life has *always* been bad. The Cataclysm makes no difference. Nor is hedonism likely to justify *Post-Cataclysm* pessimism. Why should the balance of pleasure over pain suddenly become negative simply because humanity will die out in two hundred years?

Post-Cataclysm Pessimist: This is one place where the difference between Post-Cataclysm pessimism and last generation pessimism could be relevant. Future lives cut short by human extinction will be bad in purely hedonist terms—especially if omega rays hit when you are very young. But I agree that the impact of imminent-*but-not-immediate* human extinction must be more indirect. And even in the last generation, the primary burden is a loss of *meaning*, not a loss of pleasure.

Post-Cataclysm pessimism is most plausible if our standard is meaning-based and specific. Life is meaningless due to *the absence of specific essential goods*. The Cataclysm undermines one easily ignored essential good, which I call 'future-dependent meaning'. This can be cashed-out in several overlapping ways: connection to future generations, engagement in long-term project or traditions, the open human future, and so on. This meaning pessimism then *indirectly* grounds *well-being* pessimism. Many people in our Post-Cataclysm world are *unhappy* because they mourn the loss of future-dependent *meaning*.

I distinguish between future-*directed* projects and future-*dependent* meaning. Drawing on work by Scheffler discussed later, Post-Cataclysm pessimism claims that many projects that are not obviously future-directed are nonetheless future-dependent—because they derive their meaning *for us* from their connections to the (indefinite) human future (Section 1.4).

Before I conclude my introduction, I will now briefly address three other relevant philosophical controversies:

1. *Subjective versus objective*: Can a person's life be bad, even though they think it is good? (or vice versa)
2. *Harm and knowledge*: Can I be harmed by events or facts of which I am unaware? Can my friend's betrayal reduce my well-being and/or the meaning of my life if I never discover it? If I derive comfort from my religious beliefs, does it matter that they are false?
3. *Posthumous harm*: Can I be harmed by *post-mortem events*? Can things that happen after my death make my life go better or worse?

These three questions intersect. *Unknown* events are the most common test case between subjectivism and objectivism; while *post-mortem* events are the ultimate test case. One popular solution combines subjectivism about well-being with objectivism about meaning.[6] Post-mortem events make my life less meaningful, even though they cannot affect my happiness.

We naturally ask whether the real harm the Cataclysm inflicts *on us* is the *fact* that humanity faces imminent extinction, or *our knowledge of that fact*. Suppose human extinction *is* imminent, but people never discover this. Are they harmed by the (unknown) fact that there is no human future? Are they *also* harmed by their own *ignorance*? Is blissful ignorance harmful *in itself*? Did the scientists who rushed to publish news of the Cataclysm do the right thing?

Multigenerationalist: These questions are especially significant if we want to create *new* generations in our Post-Cataclysm world. *We* all know about the Cataclysm. We cannot remove that knowledge by swallowing a pill. But our as-yet-unborn descendants need not know. We could—at least in principle—hide knowledge of imminent human extinction from future generations. Would that be good for them? Would it make their lives more or less meaningful?

Post-Cataclysm Pessimist: While these questions of knowledge and ignorance are interesting, I strive to remain neutral. Therefore, I focus on our actual situation: the Cataclysm is real and we know about it.

Posthumous harms are less easily sidestepped. This philosophical debate quickly reaches an impasse.[7] Sceptics presume that posthumous harms are logically impossible—and then reject any account of well-being or meaning that permits them; while defenders cite intuitively compelling cases of post-humous harm (real or imaginary) to defeat any account that *cannot* permit them! Sceptics and defenders also typically disagree about wider philosophical questions. Most obviously, disagreement about posthumous harms tracks disagreement about the broader category of 'unfelt harm'. If you cannot be harmed by anything that doesn't affect your experiences, then you cannot be harmed by events after your death.

Theist: As someone who believes in a personal afterlife, I find it very easy to believe that people can be harmed after death—and by events that affect their post-mortem experiences!

Post-Cataclysm Pessimist: Point taken. I am following the philosophical debate over 'posthumous harm'—which first equates death with non-existence, and *then*

---

[6] cf. Wolf, *Meaning in Life and Why It Matters*. For an overview of current debates about meaning in life, see Metz, 'The meaning of life'. My discussion is particularly influenced by Adams, *Finite and Infinite Goods*, pp. 373–389; Bradford, *Achievement*; Clark, *Plotinus*; Hare, *The Moral Gap*, chapter three; Mawson, 'Recent work on the Meaning of Life and Philosophy of Religion'; Mawson, *God and the Meaning of Life*; Metz, *Meaning in Life*; Metz, *God, Soul and the Meaning of Life*; Parfit, *Reasons and Persons*, Appendix J; Nozick, *The Examined Life*, pp. 104–118; Tollefsen, 'Experience Machines, Dreams, and What Matters'.

[7] For overviews of the debate about posthumous harm, see Luper, 'Death'—section 6 'Posthumous Harm'; Luper, 'Retroactive Harms and Wrongs'; Boonin, *Dead Wrong*; Keller, 'Posthumous Harm'; Kraut, *The Quality of Life*, pp. 139–144.

asks whether or not the no-longer-existent dead person retains interests in the world of the living. Ideally, I would like to remain agnostic about that question.

Multigenerationalist: I return to posthumous harms several times in my later lectures. I argue that it is surprisingly difficult to remain agnostic. In our Post-Cataclysm philosophy, we must take sides (Sections 3.6, 3.7, 6.3.2, 6.3.4, 9.5).

Post-Cataclysm Pessimist: For the moment, however, I will just set these controversies aside, and return to my exposition of Post-Cataclysm pessimism. Suppose we agree that human life is bad. How should we *respond* to this discovery? Pre-Cataclysm pessimism offers five main responses: suicide, anti-natalism, withdrawal, activism, and compassion. *Suicidal* pessimists argue that suicide is the only rational response to pessimism.

Presentist: That is obvious. If life is bad, then surely you *should* end it. If there are living pessimists, then they can't really believe their own gloomy claims!

Post-Cataclysm Pessimist: This objection is unfair. Suicide is one *understandable* response to the unpleasant realities of human life. But many pessimists deny it is the only response or the most rational. The prominent Pre-Cataclysm pessimist Benatar argued that the idea of a *life not worth living* is ambiguous between a life that is *not worth starting* and a life that (having been started) is *not worth continuing*.[8] While all human lives are not worth starting, some lives are worth continuing—because an early death merely increases the number of frustrated desires and thwarted projects in the person's life. Human life is a trap that you cannot escape: 'one's death obviously does not solve the problem of one's mortality'.[9] Life is bad—but you don't necessarily make it *better* by cutting it short.

Presentist: If pessimism doesn't entail suicide, how should we respond?

Post-Cataclysm Pessimist: *Anti-natalists* argue that it is wrong to create a new person whose life will (predictably) be bad. *Withdrawal* pessimists, regarding all human activity as essentially futile, recommend ironic detachment from the world. *Activist* pessimists agree that *grand schemes* for human improvement are hopeless. Instead of withdrawing, however, they engage with the world—often to combat the dangerous influence of *optimists*. Finally, *compassionate* pessimists agree that *all* attempts to improve human circumstances are futile. However, instead of withdrawing, they seek to comfort others. We can make human lives *less* bad, even if we cannot make them *worth living*.

Pessimists have typically favoured anti-natalism. It is particularly wrong to bring a child into a Post-Cataclysm world. Our present generation should be the last human generation.

---

[8] Benatar, *Human Predicament*, p. 242.   [9] Benatar, *Human Predicament*, p. 163.

Multigenerationalist: I will discuss anti-natalism, its relations with pessimism, and its plausibility in our Post-Cataclysm world in my lectures on procreative ethics (Section 4.3.1).

Post-Cataclysm Pessimist: Apart from anti-natalism, there is no distinctive *Post-Cataclysm* pessimist response. We variously recommend despair, withdrawal, activism, and compassion. Our distinctive views concern our *reasons* for pessimism, not our response to it.

To sum up, Post-Cataclysm pessimism makes three main claims:

- *Meaning is possible*: Human projects, activities, and lives can be meaningful in some situations.
- *Pre-Cataclysm meaning*: The projects, activities, and lives of (at least some) people living before the Cataclysm *were* meaningful. Our immediate predecessors could live meaningful lives—and some of them did. (Or, at least, they *thought* they did—and they would have been right if the Cataclysm had not been about to intervene.)
- *No meaning after the Cataclysm*: The projects, activities, and lives of *all* people living after the Cataclysm *cannot be* meaningful. This last claim is deliberately and provocatively strong. It is obvious that *some* sources of meaning have disappeared. And many agree that life is *less* meaningful now. Post-Cataclysm pessimism goes further: *because of the Cataclysm*, a meaningful life is now *impossible*.

Perennial Pessimists: Post-Cataclysm pessimism faces opposition from both directions. *Perennial* pessimists agree that there is no meaning after the Cataclysm, but we deny that the Cataclysm *makes* life meaningless. Despair is a frivolous response *to the Cataclysm*. True philosophical pessimism is grounded in essential features of the human condition. Life was never acceptable; it is no *less* acceptable now; and imminent human extinction is a consummation devoutly to be wished. Only a shallow person would mourn the loss of the pointless, absurd, agonising human future.

Alternatively, if we adopt the more moderate position that I earlier dubbed 'finite pessimism', we might agree that human extinction makes life meaningless—but then still insist that the Cataclysm makes no difference, because *eventual* human extinction is sufficient for meaninglessness, and eventual human extinction was always inevitable.

Presentist: Conversely, secular optimists will agree with your first two claims, and reject the third. Meaning can *still* be found in our Post-Cataclysm world, and perhaps even in the last generation. While the Cataclysm is disappointing, it doesn't (or shouldn't) have the profound impact that Post-Cataclysm pessimists claim. If life was bad before the Cataclysm, then it is probably still bad. But if life was acceptable before, then it is probably still acceptable. Imminent human extinction alone cannot tip the balance. As a presentist, of course, I think present-directed activities are sufficient.

Multigenerationalist: While, as a multigenerational secular optimist, I would argue that our generation can only enjoy meaningful lives via *future-directed* multigenerational projects.

Perennial Pessimist: But what about the *last* generation? They cannot possibly get future-dependent meaning from any multigenerational project.

Multigenerationalist: My lectures offer a very long answer to that question! The short answer is that the primary goal of any multigenerational project is to transform our inherited sources of future-dependent meaning so that something analogous *is* available to the last generation. How that works, and whether it even makes sense, is the central theme of my last two lectures.

Presentist: Strictly speaking, optimists need not deny that life is now *worse* than before the Cataclysm. However, ambitious optimists argue instead that life is actually *better* now. For instance, some presentists argue that the distant future was always more a source of anxiety than hope. We are better off without it!

Multigenerationalist: Similarly, I would argue that the shorter time-frame makes possible a new set of more valuable multigenerational projects. A realistic Post-Cataclysm utopia is better than anything the Pre-Cataclysm world could offer. I return to multigenerational Post-Cataclysm utopias in my final lecture.

1.2 From Last Generation Pessimism to Post-Cataclysm Pessimism

Post-Cataclysm Pessimist: The relationship between Post-Cataclysm pessimism and last generation pessimism is central to my case for Post-Cataclysm pessimism. Unless there is something particularly good about living at the very end, *Post-Cataclysm* pessimism implies last generation pessimism. If life is bad throughout our Post-Cataclysm world, then it is bad at the end. The more interesting question is whether last generation pessimism implies (or at least supports) Post-Cataclysm pessimism. If life will be bad in the last generation, can we infer that life is already bad now?

A *bridging argument* has last generation pessimism as a premise, and Post-Cataclysm pessimism as its conclusion. Bridging arguments can be either direct or evidential. In a *direct* argument, last generation pessimism *makes* Post-Cataclysm pessimism true. Things are bad now *because* they will be bad later. In an *evidential* argument, the fact that things will be bad later is (prima facie) evidence that things are already bad now. For instance, if whatever makes life bad at humanity's end is already present, but in a less obvious way, then we can infer that life is already bad.

Bridging arguments have a simple structure:

1. *Last generation pessimism*: Life is bad in the last human generation.
2. *Conditional premise*: If life is bad in the last generation, then life is bad in every generation in our Post-Cataclysm world.
3. *Post-Cataclysm pessimism*: Therefore, life is bad now.

This argument is trivially valid, and has only two premises. We can therefore categorise opponents of Post-Cataclysm pessimism by their responses to those premises.

1. Presentists and multigenerationalists sidestep the conditional premise by rejecting last generation pessimism. Life is not bad in the last generation. Presentists reject last generation pessimism *tout court*; while multigeneralists deny that life *must* be meaningless in the last generation *whenever that generation lives*.
2. Exclusive last generation pessimists reject the conditional premise. Although life will be meaningless at the end, it is not meaningless *for us*.
3. Perennial pessimists endorse the two premises and the conclusion. But they dismiss the bridging argument as irrelevant. Life is bad at the end, and throughout our Post-Cataclysm world—but only because life is always bad.
4. Finite pessimists also accept both premises and the conclusion. But they insist that the bridging argument succeeds *no matter when human extinction occurs*. If life is bad at the end, then life has always been bad.

Post-Cataclysm pessimists who endorse a bridging argument thus have *three* main tasks. To defeat presentism, multigenerationalism, and (exclusive) last generation pessimism, we must defend both premises. In addition, to defeat finite pessimism, we must demonstrate that the analogous argument did *not* go through *before the Cataclysm*.

Bridging arguments are a powerful tool. However, Post-Cataclysm pessimists are not wedded to them. We can also offer independent arguments that establish Post-Cataclysm pessimism without mentioning the last generation.

I will now defend Post-Cataclysm pessimism from a variety of philosophical perspectives. In each case, we ask whether we can derive (a) an *independent* argument for Post-Cataclysm pessimism; (b) a *direct* argument for last generation pessimism; or (c) a *bridging* argument from last generation pessimism to Post-Cataclysm pessimism.

1.3 Utilitarian Despair

Post-Cataclysm Pessimist: Premature human extinction is the ultimate tragedy. The loss of all those future human lives—all that future human well-being—is unimaginably bad. Utilitarians—and especially total utilitarians—are particularly susceptible to the thought that the Cataclysm must transform optimists into pessimists. Compared with the vast galaxy-spanning, multi-billion-year canvas imagined by Pre-Cataclysm effective altruist, long-termist, billionaire 'philanthropists', any Post-Cataclysm project is bound to seem puny, insignificant, not worth doing. Why bother acting when so little is at stake?

Presentist: I completely disagree. Fantasies about the distant future were only ever a sideline to the real utilitarian business of promoting pleasure and alleviating suffering in the present. Very few Pre-Cataclysm people—even very few utilitarians—made very-long-term-well-being-promotion their life's work. Any loss of meaning suffered by that tiny group has no broader significance.

The discovery of imminent human extinction may disappoint. (Alternatively, if one was less optimistic about the very distant future, it may be a relief.) But no one has any grounds for *despair*. Despair is perhaps psychologically understandable, but not philosophically justified.

The idea of *utilitarian* despair is also inconsistent. Very few Pre-Cataclysm optimists about the very far distant future were pessimists about either the present or the near future. If distant future well-being will be overwhelmingly positive, then presumably life is (on average) worth living *now*. But if present lives are worth living, then the rational response is a more modest kind of *optimism*, not pessimism.

Utilitarians should not despair. And *non-utilitarians*, for whom the loss of flourishing future lives is less significant, have even less reason to worry. Why should the non-existence of possible future people upset us? We need a better reason to believe that imminent extinction undermines *present* meaning.

Escapist: I agree that utilitarians should not despair, but for a quite different reason. I don't agree that the Cataclysm renders long-termist, existential-risk-reducing, expected-utility-maximising utilitarianism redundant. Many Pre-Cataclysm total utilitarians argued that, given the potentially astronomical amount of future well-being at stake, even the smallest reduction in the probability of imminent human extinction justifies any (finite) present cost.[10] Of course, their default alternative

---

[10] On the importance of existential risks, see, e.g., Bostrom, 'Existential Risk as a Global Priority'; Bostrom and Cirkovic, *Global Catastrophic Risks*; Ord, *The Precipice*. For a more sceptical view, see Schuster and Woods, *Calamity Theory*. On the broader 'longtermist' claim that our over-riding current ethical priority should be to positively influence the far distant human future, see Beckstead, *On the Overwhelming Importance of Shaping the Far Future*; MacAskill, *What We Owe*

was an indefinite human future containing potentially enormous total future well-being. In our situation, where we face a very high likelihood of imminent extinction, the same total utilitarian logic favours maximising *any* chance of escaping that imminent extinction. I say 'very high likelihood' rather than 'certainty' quite deliberatively. Real life is never as neat as any philosopher's thought experiment. There is always *some* chance that the current scientific consensus about the future is mistaken—especially when it concerns the future of human technological innovation and ingenuity. Even if we grant that the Cataclysm is as bad as it seems—and I am not here to question that!—it is still possible that some as-yet-unimaginable future technology *might* enable our descendants to escape it by stepping into parallel dimensions or alternative universes, jumping onto faster-than-light generation starships, or uploading themselves into digital realms where the human future would last a *subjectively* long time because digital persons 'live' so much faster than biological ones.[11]

In short: I think a consistent total utilitarian, seeking to maximise expected total future well-being, should put all their eggs in the escape basket. And I do believe that this endeavour provides adequate present meaning—even if success if vanishingly unlikely.

Presentist: I find it hard not to regard this as a *reductio ad absurdum* of longtermism, or total utilitarianism, or expected utility maximisation—or all of the above! Surely it is crazy to put all our energy into desperate projects that have virtually no chance of success? The expected-value-maximisation approach obviously delivers *very* irrational results when faced with very small probabilities. No sane individual has ever even tried to follow that approach in those cases. Why not simply abandon this weird utilitarian obsession?

Escapist: The sanity of escapism depends on the alternatives. If perennial pessimism is correct, then all human endeavours are pointless. But if *Post-Cataclysm* pessimism is correct—if human meaning is incoherent without an indefinite human future—then escapism represents our only chance of enjoying a meaningful life. Therefore, it is not an irrational choice. Similarly, if one were truly convinced that God was the only possible route to human meaning, then it would not

---

the Future. For critical discussion of longtermism, see c. Adams, Crary, and Gruen, 'Future-Oriented Effective Altruism: What's Wrong with Longtermism?'; Torres, 'Against Longtermism'.

[11] On generation starships, see Mulgan, 'What Exactly Is Wrong with Human Extinction?' For history of this sub-genre of speculative fiction, see Caroti, *The Generation Starship in Science Fiction*. There is a huge literature on digital futures—and on the nature, agency, consciousness, and value of digital beings. Chalmers, *Reality+* is a very readable, up-to-date overview of philosophical issues. My thinking about digital futures is especially indebted to Agar, *Humanity's End*; Agar, 'On the Prudential Irrationality of Mind Uploading'. For general philosophical discussion, see Blackford and Broderick, *Intelligence Unbound*; Bostrom, *Superintelligence*; and Hauskeller, *Better Humans?*, pp. 115–132. I have discussed digital futures briefly in Mulgan, 'How Should Utilitarians Think about the Future?' section 8; 'Moral Philosophy, Superintelligence, and the Singularity'. On the idea that digital beings live 'faster' than biological humans, see Bostrom, *Superintelligence*, pp. 53–54.

be irrational to put all one's eggs into the theist basket—even if one regarded God's existence as extremely unlikely!

Presentist: I think the stark choice between despair and desperate escapism can be avoided. Things are not that bad. We don't need to gamble on very unlikely sources of meaning—because everyday human activities are sufficient.

Multigenerationalist: My own response to the escapist challenge is less simple. I agree that we don't currently have available any sufficient source of present meaning—we need to construct something new. But I would argue that escapism is only a plausible contender if it is multigenerational—a project of escape must spread across several generations. And I would *then* argue that escapism is not the most plausible multigenerational option. We have alternative strategies that offer a *higher* likelihood of delivering present and (near) future meaning—and especially a higher likelihood of meaning in the last generation—than pinning our hopes on some as-yet-unimaginable future escape. This is true even if the latter (escapist) option would maximise expected total future well-being. As I argue at greater length in my lectures on procreative ethics, I think even consequentialists have sound reasons to reject both total utilitarianism and the maximisation of expected value (Section 6.3.4).

Escapist: There is a lot more to be said here. We will return to this topic several times, especially in our debate on virtual futures—because I regard the *digital* future as the most philosophically challenging form of escapism.

1.4 Scheffler on Tradition, Reason, and the Future

Post-Cataclysm Pessimist: In *Death and the Afterlife*, Samuel Scheffler explores two thought experiments. In the *doomsday scenario,* you (somehow) know that human history will end thirty days after your death. In the *infertility scenario,* some mysterious disease renders everyone on earth unable to have children, and people must suddenly adjust to the realisation that they belong to the last human generation.

Scheffler conjectures 'that most of us would find the prospect of humanity's imminent extinction unbearably depressing'.[12] He calls this claim 'the afterlife conjecture', because it reveals the importance, for our everyday projects and lives, of an *afterlife* where 'others will continue to live after I have died'.[13]

Theist: Of course, Scheffler's 'afterlife' is a pale secular imitation of the real thing. He dismisses the *personal* afterlife of traditional religion as both unlikely and

---

[12] Scheffler, *Why Worry about Future Generations*, p. 42.
[13] Scheffler, *Death and the Afterlife*, p. 15.

insufficient. I reply that Scheffler's this-worldly afterlife was never an adequate substitute for the 'real thing'. And after the Cataclysm, any hope for any kind of afterlife must come from God. We return to *that* question in our religion debate (Section 2.2).

Post-Cataclysm Pessimist: Scheffler's afterlife requires future *generations*, not merely future *people* or future rational beings: 'What is in question is the future of a chronological *succession* of generations, each produced causally, in the familiar way, by the one preceding it.'[14] Underlying this interest in future generations is a recognition of the importance of *traditions*: 'human practices whose ongoing purpose is to preserve what is valued beyond the lifespan of a single individual'.[15] Because they extend into the future, traditions require future successors: 'We think of our successors as people who will share our values, and ourselves as having custodial responsibility for the values that will someday be theirs.'[16] Future rational aliens might inherit the Earth after our civilisation is extinct. And our present activities might affect their well-being. (We might leave behind resources they could use, or toxic waste that would harm them.) But they would not be *our future generations* in Scheffler's sense.[17]

Scheffler's central claim is that 'our capacity to find value in our activities here and now is more dependent than we realise on the implicit assumption that human life will continue long after we ourselves have died'.[18] On one level, this is a counterfactual psychological prediction: if the infertility or doomsday scenario were to occur, then *as a matter of fact* people would respond in a particular way. Scheffler cites the disturbing impact of universal human infertility in P. D. James's novel *The Children of Men*: 'Without the hope of posterity... for our race, if not for ourselves, without the assurance that we being dead yet live, all pleasures of the mind and senses sometimes seem to me no more than pathetic and crumbling defences shored against our ruin.'[19]

Scheffler offers no empirical evidence for this *psychological* conjecture. He freely admits that his talk of 'our attitudes' begins with himself: 'I mean to be characterising my own attitudes and the attitudes of any other people who share them, however numerous those people happen to be.'[20] However, Scheffler's attitudes are not idiosyncratic. Many Pre-Cataclysm commentators found Scheffler's predictions very plausible.

Presentist: Although, as we'll see, not everyone was quite so pessimistic.

---

[14] Scheffler, *Why Worry about Future Generations*, p. 15.
[15] Scheffler, *Death and the Afterlife*, p. 33.   [16] Scheffler, *Death and the Afterlife*, p. 33.
[17] Scheffler, *Death and the Afterlife*, p. 214, footnote 13.
[18] Scheffler, *Why Worry about Future Generations*, p. 41.
[19] James, *The Children of Men*, p. 9; quoted in Scheffler, *Death and the Afterlife*, p. 41.
[20] Scheffler, *Death and the Afterlife*, p. 18.

Post-Cataclysm Pessimist: Scheffler's main interest is in *diagnosis* and *justification*, rather than prediction. He argues that his afterlife conjecture is both 'a convincing empirical prediction about how people would react' and 'a normatively *reasonable* response'.[21] The fact that people would (probably) respond to the infertility or doomsday scenarios with despair tells us something important about *those people's values*. Insofar as we would share that response, and insofar as we think it is rationally *justified*, we thus learn something important about *our own values*.

Scheffler argues that 'our' intuitive response to his scenarios (a) 'supports a non-experiential interpretation of our values';[22] (b) brings out the significance of ongoing traditions; and demonstrates that our interest in future generations is neither (c) purely egoistic[23] nor (d) purely consequentialist.[24] And he argues that all these reactions are justified.

Presentist: Some projects—where the human future is clearly essential—are obviously threatened in Scheffler's doomsday and infertility scenarios: conducting an experiment that is the first stage of a decades-long plan to discover a cure for cancer; laying the foundations for a building that will take several generations to build; training a new generation of teachers who will have no one to teach; and so on. Reasons associated with these projects clearly lose their normative force in Scheffler's scenarios. We can all concede Scheffler's claims about activities with a long-term goal-oriented structure, and about 'meliorative research' aimed at benefiting future individuals or communities.[25] But, of course, that doesn't get us very far. Many other projects are *not* undermined by the Cataclysm in these obvious ways.

Post-Cataclysm Pessimist: Scheffler argues that meliorative research, in particular, 'adds up to a very sizeable human enterprise'.[26] So conceding even that much might take us a surprisingly long way. But I concede your main point. Scheffler is interesting primarily because he goes beyond the obvious impacts of immediate human extinction: 'Many [seemingly intra-generational and/or temporally unextended] individual activities have among their good-making features the specific feature of belonging to an ongoing practice or process that is itself valuable.'[27] More ambitiously still, Scheffler suggests that the very activity of valuing may itself be threatened in his scenarios: 'We need humanity to have a future for the very idea that things matter to retain a secure place in our conceptual scheme.'[28]

---

[21] Scheffler, *Death and the Afterlife*, p. 188.
[22] Scheffler, *Death and the Afterlife*, p. 21.
[23] Scheffler, *Why Worry about Future Generations*, p. 54.
[24] Scheffler, *Death and the Afterlife*, p. 21.
[25] Scheffler, *Why Worry about Future Generations*, pp. 44, 46.
[26] Scheffler, *Why Worry about Future Generations*, p. 46.
[27] Scheffler, *Why Worry about Future Generations*, p. 48.
[28] Scheffler, *Death and the Afterlife*, p. 60.

Presentist: That sounds implausibly strong. Surely value would not simply evaporate?

Post-Cataclysm Pessimist: Scheffler's position is not that extreme. He is not arguing that 'nothing at all would matter to us or that the concept [of value] would simply disappear'.[29] Instead, he argues only that, in the absence of his afterlife, 'our competent deployment of the concept of something's mattering would be destabilised and rendered insecure'.[30] We would not know how to go on valuing.

Presentist: Why not?

Post-Cataclysm Pessimist: Scheffler argues that a commitment to the persistence of our values is part of what it is for them to be *our values*.[31] He draws here on his own earlier account of value: 'Valuing something, in my view, involves a complex syndrome of attitudes and dispositions, including... a disposition to treat considerations pertaining to the thing as providing one with reasons for action in relevant deliberative contexts.... Valuing something involves more than just believing that it is valuable.... it involves, in addition, a kind of *attachment to* or, alternatively, a kind of *investment in* or *engagement with* that thing.'[32] This attachment is destabilised if we know that the valued thing cannot persist into the future.

Presentist: Suppose we grant all this. How exactly do Scheffler's controversial claims ground an argument for *Post-Cataclysm pessimism*?

Post-Cataclysm Pessimist: My argument has two stages. I first use Scheffler to argue that human life *would* lose its meaning in his two scenarios. I then argue that, while there are significant differences between our Post-Cataclysm world and Scheffler's scenarios, they are insufficient to rescue meaning for us. If meaning is lost with *immediate* human extinction, then it is also lost when human extinction is only *imminent*.

I do not claim that Scheffler himself would find our Post-Cataclysm world meaningless—or that he would expect *us* to find it meaningless. Rather, I take his observations as a starting point, and then argue that, *in our Post-Cataclysm world, every actual life (present or future) falls short of the threshold necessary for a meaningful* life.

I go beyond Scheffler in two ways. First, Scheffler only discusses immediate extinction. So *any* extension to our Post-Cataclysm world is a leap he does not make. Second, Scheffler himself focuses, not on either meaning or well-being, but on *reasons*. He never directly claims that life is *meaningless* in his doomsday or infertility scenarios—still less that it is not worth living.

---

[29] Scheffler, *Death and the Afterlife*, p. 183. [30] Scheffler, *Death and the Afterlife*, p. 183.
[31] Scheffler, *Death and the Afterlife*, p. 60.
[32] Scheffler, *Why Worry about Future Generations*, p. 88; cf. Scheffler, 'Valuing'; Scheffler, 'The Normativity of Tradition'.

Indeed, Scheffler isn't really interested in the ongoing reality of *life* in his two scenarios at all. His primary interest is to explore the hidden presuppositions of *his own reasons*—and those of his Pre-Cataclysm readers. He argues that *those* reasons would lose their force in his imaginary scenarios—and therefore that their actual normative force has *always* depended on the easily overlooked presupposition that there will be future generations who continue our present traditions.

The pervasive role of ongoing human traditions in our motivations, reasons, and experiences of value explains why immediate extinction is so disruptive. Even such present-focused (and even seemingly *ephemeral*) activities as playing music or performing a play occur within an ongoing tradition. These activities subtly presuppose the existence of *future participants* in that tradition. This is why they seem hollow once those future generations are removed.

Presentist: So Scheffler's emphasis on *tradition* is crucial for your Scheffler-inspired defense of Post-Cataclysm pessimism?

Post-Cataclysm Pessimist: Yes. I think it is. In particular, the loss of tradition-based reasons is the main threat to meaning for *early* generations in our Post-Cataclysm world. Most people's lives derive their meaning from tradition-based projects that no longer matter *enough*. Pessimism is not (as perennial pessimists suppose) the only rational response to the human condition per se. But it is the most rational response in our Post-Cataclysm world. Our inherited traditions presuppose, not only *some afterlife*, but also an *indefinite human future*.

Post-Cataclysm pessimists can use Scheffler to defend all three components of their case: an argument for last generation pessimism; a defense of the conditional premise in the bridging argument; and an independent argument for Post-Cataclysm pessimism.

First, even though Scheffler himself does not directly address overall lifetime meaning, his discussion clearly supplies an argument for last generation pessimism. A life without meaningful values certainly suggests a pessimist diagnosis! And Scheffler's original commentators *do* ask whether life is meaningful in his scenarios.[33]

Second, Scheffler's later discussion of the many ways that future generations matter to the present generation supports the conditional premise of the bridging argument.[34] If my life is built around projects that connect me to future generations, then (to say the least) the knowledge that *their* lives will be bad must reduce the value of those projects *to me*. A moral theory that recognises the importance of Scheffler's many intergenerational connections will not sanction *indifference* to the fate of future generations. If we accept last generation pessimism, then we can reject Post-Cataclysm pessimism only if our interests are divorced

---

[33] Frankfurt, 'How the Afterlife Matters'; Wolf, 'The Significance of Doomsday'.
[34] Scheffler, *Why Worry about Future Generations?*

from the interests of future people—if we can flourish despite knowing that our descendants will not. But this is precisely what Scheffler denies. I will return to this Scheffler-inspired bridging argument in Section 1.5.

Finally, Scheffler grounds an independent argument for Post-Cataclysm pessimism that doesn't cite the specific plight of the last generation. The real damage, even in Scheffler's infertility scenario, is the loss of the *indefinite* human future. Our values, traditions, projects, relationships, and so on, do not simply presuppose that there will be *some* future generations. Rather, they assume that there will be *many*. Perhaps not infinitely many, but certainly indefinitely many—and definitely more than two hundred years' worth.

Presentist: I doubt that. Two centuries is a *long* time. Few actual projects—indeed, few actual traditions—last two hundred years. How many current values or traditions are that old? Most sports, cultures, nations, religions, or philosophical traditions are much more recent.

Post-Cataclysm Pessimist: I agree that many particular projects and specific traditions presuppose neither two hundred years of past participants, nor an equivalent future duration. But the background framework of human civilisation—the practice of inventing and pursuing particular practices, the tradition of developing particular traditions—is certainly far older than two hundred years, and arguably does presuppose a lot more than two hundred years to come.

Perennial Pessimist: I agree that life is meaninglessness in Scheffler's doomsday and infertility scenarios. And Scheffler may be correct that future-dependent reasons are central *to our values*. But 'our values' were always an inadequate replacement for the genuine cosmic values that either disappeared from our evaluative repertoire with the death of God or never existed at all. Future-dependent reasons were never sufficient for meaningful or worthwhile human life, so their loss is neither here nor there. The significance of Scheffler's scenarios is psychological or epistemic—they force us to realise the (perennial) emptiness of human existence.

Post-Cataclysm Pessimist: I would reply that, *with* an indefinite human future, Scheffler's future-dependent reasons *would be* sufficient for a meaningful life. But I don't think Scheffler adds much to that familiar debate between perennial pessimism and Post-Cataclysm pessimism. I suggest that we focus instead on three other significant opposing positions: presentism, multigenerationalism, and first of all *finite* pessimism.

Perennial Pessimist: Personally, I think the finite pessimist argument is redundant. But I do think it is valid. I would argue that your Scheffler-inspired case for Post-Cataclysm pessimism extends to any situation where humanity faces *eventual* extinction. If we care about future generations, and if *some* future generation must confront immediate extinction, then shouldn't we be worried about their fate no matter how far ahead they lie? But then this Scheffler-inspired argument for pessimism was already compelling *before* the Cataclysm.

Post-Cataclysm Pessimist: Scheffler himself addresses this challenge. Scheffler argues that, as a matter of fact, our values, practices, and traditions *do* make sense, even though we believe in eventual human extinction; while they would *not* make sense if we discovered that extinction is immediate. Post-Cataclysm pessimism adds that they also do not make sense if extinction is imminent rather than immediate. Post-Cataclysm pessimism claims both (a) that the Pre-Cataclysm argument for finite pessimism fails; and (b) that the parallel Post-Cataclysm argument for Post-Cataclysm pessimism succeeds. Imminent extinction is problematic in a way that eventual extinction is not.

Perennial Pessimist: What is the difference?

Post-Cataclysm Pessimist: Scheffler begins with psychology. Most people are *not* worried about the heat death of the universe, whereas immediate extinction *would* upset them. Many people have plans, desires, and activities that explicitly presume that humanity will not immediately go extinct. By contrast, no sane person's actual life projects are undermined by the heat death of the universe.

Perennial Pessimist: But psychology is not enough. The real philosophical question is whether these reactions are justified.

Post-Cataclysm Pessimist: Yes. But Scheffler's insight is that, while psychology is not an infallible guide to eternal moral truth, it is a reliable indicator of our values. We all know about the heat death of the universe—just as each of us knows about our own individual mortality. I know that I will die, and that humanity will eventually become extinct. Yet this common knowledge of individual mortality and eventual extinction does *not* cause (most of) us to lose faith in our values, projects, and traditions—partly because those values, projects, and traditions are not philosophically dependent either on personal immortality or on humanity living for ever.

By contrast, we can imagine people whose values and traditions *did* presume an infinite human future, just as we can imagine possible values that presuppose personal immortality. (Indeed, we don't need to *imagine* these possibilities. Human history offers many examples of both.) The former values would collapse on the discovery of eventual human extinction, while the latter would be destabilised by a loss of faith in personal immortality. But 'our' values are immune to *these* crises, because the relevant disappointments are common knowledge—and have been for a long time.

Perennial Pessimist: I would question this inference from (a) 'X is common knowledge' to (b) 'our values and traditions do not implicitly presuppose not-X'.

Perhaps we are simply self-deceived. Or perhaps our ancestors *did* believe not-X, and we have not yet completely emancipated our inherited values and traditions from this presupposition. (The continuing appeal of transhumanist fantasies of personally escaping the heat death of the universe, and other irrational religions, testifies to an underlying refusal to *really internalise* one's own mortality.)

This finite pessimist argument is not imaginary. The discovery that the universe must eventually end *is* unsettling. Why *doesn't* this knowledge undermine present meaning? Why should it matter *when* the end will come? After all, a venerable philosophical tradition argues that meaning, value, and purpose *do* require some *permanent* foundation.[35] If one seeks this permanent foundation in the physical universe, and especially in the human future, then one will be very disappointed.

Theist: I agree entirely! The inadequacy of secular alternatives to theism's divine sources of eternal meaning is a central theme of our religion debate.

Post-Cataclysm Pessimist: Scheffler can reply that, while individual mortality and eventual extinction are *individually* upsetting, they do not threaten our values—because those values have evolved to accommodate these individually distressing facts. Some people do succumb to despair—either at their own mortality or at humanity's eventual extinction. But most do not, because we find solace in finite future-dependent meaning.

This brings us back to the familiar debate between pessimist and optimist perspectives *on everyday human life*. My Scheffler-inspired Post-Cataclysm pessimism is optimistic about everyday life, but agrees with Scheffler that this optimism is undermined *by immediate (or imminent) extinction*.

Presentist: I am much more optimistic. I insist that present-focused activities are sufficient to render life worth living, meaningful, and morally satisfactory for most people even in the last generation. Life is worth living—and meaningful— even in Scheffler's extreme doomsday and infertility scenarios. A fortiori, it can be meaningful in our Post-Cataclysm world.

After all, my opponent here is the *Post-Cataclysm pessimist*, not Scheffler himself. In principle, presentists could accept Scheffler's original claims, and then deny your more ambitious extensions. Even if future-dependent reasons are as significant as Scheffler claims, our remaining reasons are still sufficient for a

---

[35] cf. Mulgan, *Purpose in the Universe*, pp. 307–308. On the relationship between meaningfulness, God, and personal immortality, see Adams, *Finite and Infinite Goods*, pp. 373–389; Hare, *The Moral Gap*, chapter three; Mawson, 'Recent Work on the Meaning of Life and Philosophy of Religion'; Mawson, *God and the Meaning of Life*; Metz, 'Meaning in Life'; Metz, 'The Meaning of Life', section 2.2: 'Soul-Centered Views'; Metz, *Meaning in Life*, part two: 'Supernaturalist Theories of Meaning in Life', pp. 75–161; Metz, *God, Soul and the Meaning of Life*. I discuss immortality and meaningfulness myself in Mulgan, *Purpose in the Universe*, chapter ten, especially pp. 307–322.

meaningful life. After all, Scheffler himself concedes that some reasons still retain their full force, even in his scenarios.[36]

Post-Cataclysm Pessimist: However, Scheffler also argues that non-future-presupposing reasons are very narrow. A life containing *only* those reasons might be minimally 'meaningful'—but it is hardly very rich or enjoyable.

Presentist: I agree. Presentism is probably on stronger ground if it pushes back against Scheffler's original claims. Drawing on Scheffler's original opponents, notably Frankfurt and Wolf, as well as on earlier philosophers, most presentists extend our extinction-immune present-focused reasons beyond what Scheffler would admit.[37]

Post-Cataclysm Pessimist: What exactly do you mean by 'present-focused'?

Presentist: Presentists highlight activities that are available (a) to the present generation; (b) within this present life; and (c) without any connections to future generations. These present-focused activities are sufficient. There is no need for future-directed or future-presupposing activities, future generations, or any other kind of afterlife. To defeat *last-generation* pessimism—and find meaning even in Scheffler's infertility scenario—I insist that present-focused activities are sufficient *even if one has no connections to any future people*. Therefore, our set of sufficient present-focused activities does *not* include caring for the present needs of one's own children or anyone else in the next generation. Of course, these activities are very important to many people. But the crucial point is that a life with no children, no descendants, and no future generations can be meaningful.

Post-Cataclysm Pessimist: Can you say more about what these sufficiently meaningful present-focused activities actually *are*?

Presentist: I argue that, together, three sets of present-focused activities are sufficient for a meaningful life:

1. *Hedonist*: Activities devoted to my own present pleasure.
2. *Achievement*: Non-future-dependent achievements.
3. *Compassion*: Compassion for the suffering of others, and relieving the *present* suffering of present people.

For instance, among Scheffler's own original commentators, Frankfurt argues that the value of immediate pleasure is independent of future-dependent traditions; while Wolf highlights the importance of compassion as a source of meaning.[38]

---

[36] 'Obvious exceptions might include such things as relief from extreme pain' (Scheffler, *Death and the Afterlife*, p. 54).
[37] Frankfurt, 'How the Afterlife Matters'; Wolf, 'The Significance of Doomsday'.
[38] Frankfurt, 'How the Afterlife Matters'; Wolf, 'The Significance of Doomsday'.

These are not second-best options that people only consider after future-dependent alternatives have collapsed. On the contrary, they were always among the most choice-worthy options for human beings, even when Scheffler's future-dependent tradition-based alternatives were also on the table. Even in the last generation, therefore, a flourishing human life, filled with perennially choice-worthy enjoyment, achievement, and compassion, is widely available—whether we interpret 'flourishing' in terms of well-being, or meaning, or morality.

Alongside the desirability of present-focused activities, presentists also highlight the unreliability, uncertainty, untrustworthiness, and fragility of all future-dependent sources of well-being, meaning, or moral purpose—citing familiar philosophical debates about the vulnerability of secular meaning, the fragility of goodness, the cluelessness of consequentialism, and so on.[39]

Presentism can be more or less ambitious. *Exclusive* presentists insist that *only* present-focused activities provide meaning: the loss of the human future is no loss at all. *Ambitious* presentists argue that, even if future-dependent activities can provide *some* meaning, their loss is easily outweighed by additional present-focused activities. *Modest* presentists insist that, while the loss of future-dependent activities *reduces* meaning, our remaining present-focused activities are nonetheless sufficient.

Some presentists concede that Scheffler may be correct about *our* values, but only because the post-Christian philosophy we have inherited from our immediate Pre-Cataclysm predecessors in the secular, liberal, affluent West is singularly unsuited to our Post-Cataclysm world. Earlier philosophies offer more robust values that we can borrow instead. In particular, Hellenist philosophers, living in a time of disruption and powerlessness, sought to make human flourishing and happiness immune to the physical world's fickle disappointments. Stoicism eschews future-dependent values because they cannot reliably be known, acquired, or achieved; while Epicureans focus on present pleasures because these alone are certain.[40] More generally, as Kraut emphasises, ancient philosophers privileged reliable internal goods over unreliable external ones: 'It was widely accepted in antiquity that "internal" goods—the ones that reside in the soul, the ones we are conscious of—are the only goods, or that little else has value. That is the view not only of Plato and Aristotle, but of the Epicureans, the Stoics, and Plotinus.'[41]

Post-Cataclysm Epicureans, Stoics, Sceptics, and Cynics each argue that their favourite School offers our best hope for a happy life in the face of imminent human extinction. Ancient philosophy thus supplements the arguments of Scheffler's

---

[39] See, e.g., Metz, *Meaning in Life*, especially part two; Nussbaum, *The Fragility of Goodness*; and Lenman, 'Consequentialism and Cluelessness'.
[40] For an overview of these ancient philosophical schools, see Cooper, *Pursuits of Wisdom*.
[41] Kraut, *The Quality of Life*, p. 82.

original presentist opponents. For the wise, the discovery that there are no future generations is a relief, because it removes hubristic future-dependent temptations.

Our current 'crisis of meaning' thus has a deflationary historical explanation. Ancient philosophy offered three main promising alternatives to pessimism: Stoic duty-focused resignation, Epicurean present-focused hedonism, and Platonic reliance on transcendent values. Unfortunately, over the next two millennia, the metaphysically extravagant Platonist option won the day, albeit in a Christian form. Nineteenth-century crises of faith then replaced faith in transcendent value with *faith in the human future*. As this latter faith cannot survive the Cataclysm, we must revisit Platonism's original opponents, and embrace presentism.

Perennial pessimists have always derided secular optimists for their faith in our ability to predict, control, or improve the future. Presentists agree. We also reject grandiose fantasies where humanity masters the galaxy in the very far distant future. The present generation cannot find our salvation in the secular human future. We must find sufficient meaning in the present.

Presentism thus collapses the gap between our Post-Cataclysm world and Scheffler's shorter scenarios. If the present is not sufficient unto itself, then *no possible* human future is meaningful.

Post-Cataclysm Pessimist: This suggests that presentists are really *pessimists*—at least about the future.

Presentist: I agree that presentism problematises the standard dichotomy between pessimists and optimists. In ordinary language, 'pessimism' and 'optimism' both concern *the future*. But *philosophical* pessimism also rejects the present. Presentists are not philosophical pessimists in this sense. But we are equally wary of optimistic predictions of future improvement, or any other present reliance on the future. We are optimists about the present human condition, but not necessarily about the future.

Post-Cataclysm Pessimist: I reply that the loss of the indefinite human future is different *in kind* from other threats to secular optimism. *Uncertainty* about the future is not the same as losing the future altogether. In Scheffler's terms, our tradition-based values can accommodate the future's uncertainty, but not its absence.

Presentist: I'm not sure how much dialectical progress we can make here. How can we adjudicate this debate between Scheffler, on the one side, and Frankfurt, Wolf, Stoics, and Epicureans on the other side? How can we adjudicate the perennial debate between presentists and pessimists? It is easy to grant that future-dependent meaning has *some* significance to us. (With the exception of exclusive presentists, everyone agrees on that!) But judging exactly *how* significant it is—and whether it is essential for a meaningful life—is much harder. Perhaps we just reach intuitive bedrock—where clashing positions reflect different reasonable ways to weigh competing values?

Multigenerationalist: I agree that it is difficult to advance the debate in its own terms. Multigenerationalists seek philosophical progress in a different direction. We tread a middle-road between pessimism and presentism. We agree with Scheffler about *our* need for future generations. We also concede that meaning *is* lost in Scheffler's doomsday and infertility scenarios. If we were the last human generation, then our lives would be pointless. But we deny that meaning is *necessarily* lost in our Post-Cataclysm world. We can create a meaningful existence for a *later* last human generation—and this multigenerational goal *also confers meaning on our present lives*. We thus seek a reply to Scheffler that concedes that future-dependent meaning is central *to our present values*.

Presentists argue that *we* could revive the lost worldviews of pre-Christian Stoics or Epicureans, and reorient our own lives entirely around present-focused pleasures, achievements, or compassion. I agree that this could be done. But I very much doubt that we could do it *in the present generation*. The necessary reorientation is only possible if a new generation is raised in new values and traditions. Only future people—with new values and a new outlook—could possibly be fully satisfied with the present.

1.5 Ponzi Arguments

Post-Cataclysm Pessimist: One specific class of bridging arguments exploits the fact that the present generation are always directly responsible for the existence of the next generation, and therefore indirectly responsible for the existence of all later generations. If the last generation suffer a special burden, then we are at least indirectly responsible for their plight.

These arguments draw an analogy between human procreation and continuing a Ponzi scheme. Roughly, a Ponzi scheme is a seemingly legitimate investment scheme where each 'generation' of investors can only recoup its initial losses by recruiting a new generation of investors. Eventually, the scheme collapses, and the last generation of investors lose everything.[42]

Consider two Pre-Cataclysm philosophical Ponzi-based arguments:

1. *Johnston's Ponzi Challenge to Scheffler.* In a review of Scheffler's *Death and the Afterlife*, Mark Johnston argued that it is odd to argue from the

---

[42] The details of actual Ponzi schemes are not strictly relevant. As we'll see, one important distinction is between (a) schemes that leave *all* participants (except the founder) worse-off, and where recruiting new members only 'cuts one's losses'; and (b) schemes where most participants benefit from the scheme, *except* for those who are last in.

premise that it is undesirable to belong to the last human generation to the conclusion that we ought to continue the human story.[43] We cannot remove the burden of last-generation-hood. We can only avoid it for ourselves *by passing it down the line to some unspecified future generation.* Isn't this is the moral equivalent of continuing a Ponzi scheme?

2. *Benatar's Ponzi Pessimism.* Benatar argued that human procreation is *always* a Ponzi scheme.[44] It is better not to be in the scheme at all, but once you are in the scheme you can reduce your losses by recruiting others. Life is never worth living, but having children of your own makes *your* life less undesirable. Although everyone's life is bad, the last generation suffer a special burden. Each generation can shift *that* burden by creating successors. But this is obviously morally dubious.

Johnston is *not* a pessimist. He uses his Ponzi analogue to challenge Scheffler's claims about future-dependent meaning. Benatar *is* a pessimist, but not a *Post-Cataclysm* pessimist. While the last generation suffers a *greater* burden, every generation already has a bad life. Benatar's Ponzi analogy helps explain *why* we continue to procreate despite the awfulness of human life.[45]

To separate the different possible roles of a Ponzi analogy, consider an imaginary *unending* case. Infinitely many human generations each create a next generation. There is no last generation. The burden of last-generation-hood is forever deferred. In this scenario, the Ponzi argument for Post-Cataclysm pessimism collapses, as does Johnston's Ponzi objection to Scheffler. But Benetar's Ponzi analogy still bites. Every generation imposes the unacceptable burden of human existence on its own children *to avoid the additional burden of last-generation-hood* for themselves.

Post-Cataclysm pessimists agree that it is wrong to inflict the last generation burden on a new generation. We also claim: (1) that this burden makes life bad for the new generation; and (2) that *imposing* that burden on a new generation makes life bad *for the present generation*. (Neither Johnston nor Benatar is committed to these two further claims.) Our Ponzi argument is *only* a bridging argument. It presupposes last generation pessimism, and then derives Post-Cataclysm pessimism.

Presentist: I can see the analogy. But what exactly is your Ponzi *argument* for Post-Cataclysm pessimism?

Post-Cataclysm Pessimist: We begin with a simple model containing two generations: penultimate and last. The *penultimate generation* can either be the last

---

[43] Johnston, 'Is Life a Ponzi Scheme?' [44] Benatar, *The Human Predicament*, p. 208.
[45] For Benatar, human life thus resembles Parfit's Hell examples—which Parfit presents in the context of a *reductio ad absurdum* of average utilitarianism (Parfit, *Reasons and Persons*, pp. 406–409).

generation, or create a new generation who must be the last. (The phrase 'penultimate generation' is thus not strictly accurate, as the whole point is that these people might be the last humans. But I hope the idea is clear enough.) *Ex hypothesi*, the burden falling on the last generation is sufficient to make life meaningless. The last generation cannot enjoy meaningful lives. Therefore, no one in the penultimate generation can have children who enjoy meaningful lives; and the penultimate generation collectively cannot be followed by a new generation enjoying meaningful lives.

Can the penultimate generation nonetheless enjoy meaningful lives *themselves*? If they do not procreate, then they belong to the last generation. *Ex hypothesi*, their lives are meaningless. They can only enjoy meaningful lives if they create a new generation whose lives, in turn, are not meaningful. But this does not seem very meaningful either. Imposing an insufferable burden on your own children also makes your own life meaningless.

This Ponzi bridging argument builds on the Scheffler-inspired case for last generation pessimism. Life is meaningless in the last generation *because* it lacks future-dependent meaning. The penultimate generation can pursue *some* future-directed projects. But any *meaningful* future-directed project aims at, or presupposes, future generations whose lives are themselves meaningful. Therefore, the penultimate generation cannot enjoy future-dependent *meaning*, because their future-directed projects cannot be meaningful *to them*.

If the penultimate generation did create a new generation, their own lives would be unhappy, meaningless, and morally deficient—because they have imposed meaningless lives on their own children. The *knowledge* that they have done this makes them *miserable*; the *fact* that they have done this renders their central life projects *meaningless*; and the *wrongness* of what they have done renders their life *morally indefensible* (and therefore either meaningless or unhappy).

This very simple two-generation bridging argument is compelling. *If* we accept last generation pessimism, and *if* we accept Scheffler's explanation for it, *then* we cannot avoid penultimate pessimism.

Post-Cataclysm pessimism then generalises this argument to cases involving several possible future generations. We consider two generalisations. The first is an inductive argument, based on Nozick's zipper argument against Locke's proviso on just acquisition.[46]

Multigenerationalist: As it happens, I will be returning to Nozick's original argument in my final lecture (Section 8.3.3). But perhaps you could summarise your analogous argument?

---

[46] Nozick, *Anarchy, State, and Utopia*, p. 176; cf. Mulgan, *Ethics for a Broken World*, p. 49. I owe the name 'zipper argument' to Gosseries, 'What Do We Owe the Next Generation(s)?'

Post-Cataclysm Pessimist: *Ex hypothesi*, the last generation (generation N) cannot enjoy meaningful lives. The penultimate generation (N–1) cannot create a new generation who enjoy meaningful lives, and therefore cannot enjoy meaningful lives of their own, as we have just seen. Now consider the *third-last* generation (N–2). They know that their own children (N–1) will face an impossible choice between (a) shouldering the last generation burden themselves; and (b) shifting it onto their own children (N). Therefore, N–2 face an equally impossible choice between (a) shouldering the last generation burden themselves; and (c) imposing an impossible choice on their own children. Therefore, the third-last generation cannot enjoy meaningful lives either. But now consider the *fourth*-last generation (N–3). And so on. The argument 'zips' back to the first generation (ourselves) who also cannot enjoy meaningful lives.

The alternative generalisation is a *direct* Ponzi argument. It simply says that life is meaningless for *any* generation who must choose between (a) shouldering the last generation burden themselves; and (b) *passing it down the line to some future generation*. More formally:

1. *Last generation pessimism*: The last-generation burden makes life meaningless for that generation.
2. *Conditional premise*: If a burden makes life meaningless, then imposing that burden on someone else makes your life meaningless too.
3. *Hard choice premise*: Our only present options are to shoulder the last generation burden ourselves, or to shift it onto some future generation.
4. *Post-Cataclysm pessimism*: Whatever we do, our lives will be meaningless. (From 1, 2, and 3 by disjunction elimination).

The main challenge for the direct Ponzi argument is to establish its conditional premise. Why is my life meaningless if I shift the last generation burden on to some (potentially quite distant) future generation? My answer cites Scheffler-inspired future-dependent meaning. Any meaningful future-directed project presupposes, not only some future generations, but a series of future generations who *all* enjoy meaningful lives. Two hundred years is not so long that the last generation is lost in the mists of (future) time. We can visualise all the intermediate generations. Once we realise that life will soon become meaningless, we lose faith in all our future-directed projects.

Any successful Ponzi argument removes any *moral* difference between imminent and immediate human extinction. We have a greater number of *physical* options than people in Scheffler's infertility scenario. We *could* create new people. However, our *morally acceptable* options are as limited as theirs. If human extinction is imminent, then it must *become* immediate. But immediate extinction makes life meaningless. Therefore, life is already meaningless.

Ponzi arguments have two possible conclusions: either pessimism or anti-natalism. As a pessimist anti-natalist, I conclude both that life is meaningless (pessimism) and that we cannot permissibly create a new generation (anti-natalism). However, while pessimism and anti-natalism are mutually supporting, they can come apart. We could have anti-natalism without pessimism, where you are not permitted to impose the last generation burden, even if it does not make life meaningless. Alternatively, we could have pessimism without anti-natalism, where it is permissible to create a new generation whose lives are meaningless—*if* the cost to you of *not* procreating is sufficiently high.

Multigenerationalist: I return to anti-natalism, and the moral dimension of Ponzi analogies, in my lectures on procreative ethics (Section 4.3.1).

Perennial Pessimist: Of course, I can accept the Ponzi bridging argument, because I don't think it establishes *Post-Cataclysm* pessimism per se. Instead, if it succeeds, it establishes *finite* pessimism. After all, your argument says nothing new. The inevitability of the last generation burden has always made life meaningless *for every generation*. Imminent extinction merely forces us to acknowledge what has always been true. Your inductive zipper argument, like Nozick's original, goes through for any finite value of N; while the conditional premise of your direct argument applies to any generation in any world where humanity is not immortal. This was Johnston's original point against Scheffler. Scheffler's claims about the plight of the last generation zipped back to condemn present meaning even before the Cataclysm.

Post-Cataclysm Pessimist: Unsurprisingly, I disagree. I think we can reasonably distinguish Post-Cataclysm pessimism from finite pessimism, blocking the Ponzi argument for the latter. Presentist and multigenerational strategies *did* work before the Cataclysm. But they do *not* work in our Post-Cataclysm world. We no longer have sufficient time to re-imagine our values and traditions, and we cannot separate present meaning from *near-future* burdens as easily as from distant future burdens. The Ponzi argument fails to grip when inevitable extinction is sufficiently distant. But it does grip us.

Presentist: Presentists, of course, reject last generation pessimism. So the Ponzi argument doesn't worry us. Exclusive presentists reject the very idea of a last generation burden; while more moderate presentists, who admit there is some last generation burden, deny that it makes life meaningless. If there is no last generation burden at all, then all Ponzi arguments collapse, because the original analogy no longer applies. Milder last generation burdens do generate *some* Ponzi puzzles, especially in relation to procreative permissibility. But these milder burdens do not justify pessimism. All presentists insist that life is meaningful without any next generation, and without any procreation. So the dilemma at the heart of the Ponzi argument does not move us.

Post-Cataclysm Pessimist: This presentist reply does not really address the *bridging* argument. It merely rejects the starting point—which leads us back to ground we covered earlier (Section 1.4).

Multigenerationalist: I address those puzzles in my procreative ethics lectures (Sections 4.3.1, 5.2.1, 5.2.4, and 6.3.3). My response to the Ponzi argument is more nuanced, like my response to last generation pessimism itself. I reject *unconditional* last generation pessimism. I concede that, if *we* were the last generation, then our lives would be meaningless—for exactly the reasons that Scheffler suggests. But this vulnerability is a *contingent feature of the way we have been raised or acculturated*, rather than an *essential feature of the human condition*. We could raise *a new generation* who were not so vulnerable to the loss of future generations.

I reject your framing of the Ponzi analogy. There is no *constant* last generation burden. Rather, the burden of last-generation-hood is variable, and it depends on the values and traditions we bequeath to later generations. We can diminish that burden, and perhaps even eliminate it altogether. In your direct argument, I would reject the hard choice premise. Our present options are *not* limited to shouldering and shifting. We can escape the burden of last-generation-hood ourselves *without transferring that same burden to anyone else*. We can pass on a burden that is either eliminated or (at least) greatly reduced.

Post-Cataclysm Pessimist: Of course, multigenerationalism makes ambitious claims.

Multigenerationalist: Yes it does. And I defend those claims at length throughout my later lectures. For the moment, to motivate my exploration of multigenerationalism, I think it is worth pausing to ask *why* Ponzi arguments were largely ignored before the Cataclysm. Many Pre-Cataclysm philosophers—and non-philosophers—were well aware that life might look very bleak and disorienting at humanity's end. After all, Pre-Cataclysm speculative fiction abounded with apocalyptic scenarios. Everyone knew that they *might* be exposing their very distant descendants to a very grim fate. The Ponzi argument was available to everyone. But it did not catch on.

Perennial Pessimist: I diagnose familiar human moral and epistemic failings. Pre-Cataclysm people lacked the imagination to see that they were wronging distant future people. We simply see this more clearly.

Post-Cataclysm Pessimist: I disagree. Discounting the distant future is not necessarily either an epistemic or a moral failing. Perhaps it *is* reasonable to treat obligations to contemporaries and near-future people as more urgent than obligations to distant future people. It is clearly wrong to give one's children meaningless lives, or to impose this burden on near descendants. But it is not obviously wrong to shift the same burden onto distant future people.

Perennial Pessimist: I just don't see that. I regard temporal impartiality as a central moral ideal. Discounting the distant future, simply because it is *distant*, is never permissible.

Post-Cataclysm Pessimist: One obvious justification for discounting the distant future is uncertainty. We *know* that our near descendants *will* face immediate extinction *within the next two centuries*. Pre-Cataclysm people had very little idea when extinction would strike, or what life might be like when it did.

Multigenerationalist: However, when it comes to justifying temporal discounting, the only uncertainty that really *matters* is uncertainty about the fate of the last generation, not uncertainty about when they will live. And this is where multigenerationalism enters the picture. I begin with my own diagnosis of the lack of interest in Ponzi arguments before the Cataclysm. I suspect that Pre-Cataclysm philosophers rejected last generation pessimism, perhaps unconsciously, because they hoped that the last generation would *not* face meaningless lives. If pressed, some would have based their optimism on future improvements in living standards that would compensate for the loss of future-dependent meaning, while others put their faith in some distant-future reorientation of values that would enable the last generation to *embrace* their place at humanity's end. We can no longer rest content with vague faith in the distant future. We must replace Pre-Catalysm implicit hope with explicit plans to realise the necessary improvement or reorientation over the next two centuries. Multigenerationalists embrace this task. We claim that present people should devote ourselves to initiating terminal intergenerational projects (which I dub 'multigenerational projects'). These projects last several generations and are designed to end. As I argue later, one argument for this claim is that we can only find our own lives meaningful by devoting ourselves to multigenerational cooperation with future people.

1.6 Lear on Intelligibility, Cultural Devastation, and Radical Hope

Post-Cataclysm Pessimist: In *Radical Hope*, Jonathan Lear recounts the moral journey of the Crow chief Plenty Coups who led his tribe through the loss of their traditional hunting grounds in the late nineteenth and early twentieth centuries.[47] Lear interprets Plenty Coups as re-imagining the traditional Crow virtue of courage. What counted as courage in a world dominated by tribal warfare no longer makes sense *either* against the overwhelming military force of the US Army

---

[47] Lear, *Radical Hope*. See also Baker, 'Vulnerabilities of Morality'; Dreyfus, 'Comments on Jonathan Lear's *Radical Hope*'; Sherman, 'The Fate of a Warrior Culture'; Lear, 'Response to Hubert Dreyfus and Nancy Sherman', and Lear, *Imagining the End*.

(where military opposition can only bring futile destruction) *or* in the post-conquest world of the reservation (where traditional warfare is mere pointless criminality).

Lear's book is in two parts. The first explores the philosophical nature of the loss suffered by the Crow, while the latter explores Plenty Coups' response to that loss. Lear dubs these two phenomena 'intelligibility loss' and 'radical hope' respectively. Post-Cataclysm pessimists borrow Lear's idea of intelligibility loss.

Multigenerationalist: By contrast, Lear's positive concept of radical hope inspires multigenerational optimism, as I'll explain in my fifth lecture (Sections 7.1, 7.2).

Post-Cataclysm Pessimist: I will first explain what Lear *means* by intelligibility loss, before asking whether the loss of the human future fits the bill. We can then ask how optimists might respond.

Lear argues that, following the loss of their traditional way of life—based around buffalo hunting, nomadic existence, and inter-tribal warfare—the Crow suffered a loss of *intelligibility*. Particular activities that were imbued with meaning and served as ethical paradigms no longer made sense.

Presentist: In what sense is this a loss of *intelligibility*?

Post-Cataclysm Pessimist: I find it helpful to distinguish three kinds of activities: foundational, ritual, and mundane.[48] The Crow's *foundational* activities are the three pillars of their traditional way of life: hunting, nomadism, and warfare. These activities structure the Crow world. As I read Lear, these foundational activities remained *intelligible*. We can identify present actions that would count as hunting buffalo or waging war on a neighbouring tribe. However, the three pillars were no longer live options, once the US government imposed *and enforced* bans on inter-tribal warfare, buffalo hunting, and nomadic lifestyles.

The loss of *intelligibility* concerns, not the foundational activities themselves, but *other* practices that presuppose them. Intelligibility loss is most obvious for *ritual* activities. Lear's two main examples are dancing the Sun Dance and planting a coup-stick. The Sun Dance was a prayer-filled ritual asking God's help in winning military victory. The planting of coup-sticks was central to Crow warrior life: 'The paradigmatic use of a coup-stick was for a warrior to mark a boundary.... A fundamental principle of warrior honour was this: If in battle a warrior stuck his stick in the ground, he must not retreat...[he] must hold his ground or die losing his coup-stick to the enemy.'[49] Coup-sticks thus provided the Crow with a paradigm of courage in battle. They also played the crucial function (especially in

---

[48] These are my terms, not Lear's. The tripartite division is artificial, and a bit clumsy, but it is helpful if we want to apply Lear's analysis to other cases.

[49] Lear, *Radical Hope*, p. 13, drawing on Linderman, *Plenty-Coups*, p. 54; and Lowie, *The Crow Indians*, p. 184.

a nomadic community) of marking the limits of Crow territory—'a boundary across which a non-Crow enemy must not pass'.[50]

On the reservation, no one could plant a coup-stick or dance the Sun Dance. Why not? After all, unlike warfare or hunting, these ritual activities were *not* prohibited. The necessary *physical actions* could still be performed. Consider the Sun Dance. The dance was not banned; there were places where people could dance; and many living people remembered how the dance was performed. Nothing prevented the Crow from (literally) 'going through the motions' of the Sun Dance. But no one did. Performing *those physical acts* would no longer count as dancing the Sun Dance—because *those* physical acts only constitute *that* meaning-imbued dance within the broader context of a lost traditional way of life whose foundational activities (nomadism, buffalo hunting, and intertribal warfare) *are* now physically impossible: 'The Sun Dance...is not something that can intelligibly be performed now. At best, one could perform "it" as a nostalgic gesture: an acted-out remembrance of things past.'[51] Similarly, 'The very physical movements that, at an earlier time, would have constituted a brave act of counting coups are now a somewhat pathetic expression of nostalgia.'[52]

The loss of intelligibility is practical, not theoretical. Crow living on the reservation could still make *theoretical* sense of their previous way of life. Plenty Coups had no difficulty understanding his *past* actions in terms of traditional Crow values. Planting coup-sticks had not become unthinkable. It had instead ceased to be a live *practical* option in the present.

Presentist: That seems obvious. A dance—or a prayer—for success in war no longer makes sense if one no longer wages war. Intelligibility loss for specific ritual activities is hardly news.

Post-Cataclysm Pessimist: Like Scheffler, Lear is interesting because he goes beyond the obvious. Intelligibility loss is not limited to specific activities explicitly associated with war or hunting. Lear argues, much more provocatively, that the collapse of their traditional way of life drained meaning from *all* Crow activities— even the most mundane everyday chores. Crow ethics took its paradigms of virtue from the three pillars (hunting, nomadism, warfare). Bravery *outside of war* is analogous to bravery in warfare. Without the latter, the former is unintelligible.

Lear himself poses the obvious question: 'But what about simple acts like cooking a meal? People continued to prepare meals on the reservation. Why doesn't that count as something happening?'[53] Lear replies that a Crow woman preparing a meal, in the Crow traditional way of life, would have described what she was doing as "I'm getting my husband and family ready for tomorrow's battle." In other words, 'She is preparing a meal, but she identifies the act by locating it in a

---

[50] Lear, *Radical Hope*, p. 13.   [51] Lear, *Radical Hope*, p. 37.
[52] Lear, *Radical Hope*, p. 32.   [53] Lear, *Radical Hope*, p. 39.

larger scheme of purposefulness.'⁵⁴ More generally, 'Every meal was in effect the cooking-of-a-meal-so-that-those-who-ate-it-would-be-healthy-to-hunt-and-fight.'⁵⁵ In traditional Crow life, 'everything counted either as hunting or fighting or as preparing to hunt and fight.'⁵⁶ On the reservation, where hunting and fighting are no longer possible, nothing can count as any of those things. Nothing is intelligible. Recounting his own life story, when Plenty Coups reaches the points where the Crow settled on the reservation, he said only, 'after that, nothing happened'. Similarly Pretty Shield, a Crow woman, said, 'I am living a life I don't understand.'⁵⁷

On the reservation, nothing people *used* to do is intelligible, because the way of life that gave it meaning has been lost; and therefore nothing anyone can do *now* can count as continuing what they used to do. 'One sign...that there has been a genuine loss of intelligibility is that *the agents themselves* cannot see how to take up the concepts of their past and project them into their futures. This is what it is to take seriously the Crows' own sense of loss of intelligibility.'⁵⁸

Presentist: I would still question the crucial final step in your argument. I am happy to grant intelligibility loss for specific ritual activities, but not for mundane ones. Surely a community that loses its traditional way of life can still find meaning in everyday human activities. How do you defend that much stronger claim?

Post-Cataclysm Pessimist: My Lear-inspired argument for Post-Cataclysm pessimism is simple. Intelligibility loss leads to meaninglessness; and this is what has happened *to us*.

1. The loss of the indefinite future leads to widespread intelligibility loss.
2. Widespread intelligibility loss renders life meaningless.
3. Therefore: Life is meaningless in our Post-Cataclysm world.

The Crows' inherited ethical thinking presupposed their traditional way of life. *Our* inherited ethical thinking presupposes the indefinite human future. All our activities derive their meaning from that future. Once the human future is removed, nothing we used to do remains intelligible.

As with Scheffler, I draw on Lear to provide three things: (a) an argument for last generation pessimism; (b) an argument for the conditional premise in a bridging argument from last generation pessimism to Post-Cataclysm pessimism; and (c) an independent argument for Post-Cataclysm pessimism.

Presentist: Let's begin with the last generation. What would Lear say about Scheffler's scenarios?

---

⁵⁴ Lear, *Radical Hope*, p. 39. ⁵⁵ Lear, *Radical Hope*, p. 40. ⁵⁶ Lear, *Radical Hope*, p. 40.
⁵⁷ Lear, 'Response to Hubert Dreyfus and Nancy Sherman', p. 91.
⁵⁸ Lear, 'Response to Hubert Dreyfus and Nancy Sherman', p. 91 [italics in original].

Post-Cataclysm Pessimist: That is easy. The loss of the *entire* human future surely *does* constitute cultural devastation on a par with North American colonisation.

Presentist: But Lear's Crow example is very different from Scheffler's scenarios. The Crow traditional way of life did not collapse because anyone ceased to believe in its values. Rather, its foundational activities became *practically* impossible, because they were forcibly prohibited by the US government. Our loss of the human future is quite different. No one in the last generation will be prevented— either by circumstances or any outside agency—from continuing their previous way of life. If anything is lost in Scheffler's scenarios, it is people's *faith* in their traditional way of life.

Post-Cataclysm Pessimist: I agree that the cases are different. But I think the differences support my argument, rather than weakening it. Following Scheffler, we can see our traditional way of life as grounded in future-dependent meaning. We can then—perhaps artificially—identify *our* foundational activities in explicitly future-directed terms: 'preserving our society into the future', 'keeping my family going', 'maintaining and bequeathing our traditions', and so on. These are not as clear-cut as Lear's three pillars of Crow life. But they play an analogous role.

Presentist: I'm not sure that is the right analogy. I think a closer analogy to our present situation might be the loss of intelligibility that follows the *theoretical* collapse of a religious worldview. There is a difference between (a) the cessation of a religious practice because it is physically impossible; and (b) the cessation of a religious practice because practitioners no longer believe in it. Lear himself cites the destruction of the Temple in Jerusalem as an example of intelligibility loss of the first kind.[59] But our situation is closer to the second—and that kind of loss is *not* an insurmountable problem.

Post-Cataclysm Pessimist: I agree that the analogy between Lear's Crow and Scheffler's scenarios is not perfect. But I still insist that Lear's broad notion of *practical unintelligibility* applies to both cases. If I no longer believe in God, then nothing I can now do would count as *worshipping God*—even though I remember exactly how I *used* to worship and I can still 'go through the motions'. Similarly, although people in the last generation could continue their 'traditional' lifestyle, many particular activities *within* that way of life will be unintelligible, because they no longer make *future-dependent* sense. This is one way to cash out Scheffler's diagnosis of his own scenarios. People in the last generation can still go through the motions. They can still *say* that they are building a school, developing a long-term plan, teaching philosophy, or even doing philosophy. But these daily activities no longer make sense as moves in a familiar future-dependent way of

---

[59] Lear, *Radical Hope*, p. 163.

life. The physical actions can still be performed, but nothing could now count as *doing that thing*.

Presentist: As with Scheffler, I want to push back against this wholesale rejection of everyday activities. Even if they previously derived *some* meaning from (now lost) future-dependent traditions, our everyday activities still make *present-focused* sense—as ways to nurture and comfort our fellow human beings.

In other words, even if the last generation suffer *some* intelligibility loss, that loss is not sufficiently widespread to justify last generation *pessimism*. Lear's original commentators raise an analogous objection. They question the warrior-privileging ethical perspective that regards *all* of Crow traditional life as preparatory to *male* hunting and warfare, and therefore downgrades 'everyday' (often feminine) pursuits.[60] Even if women—and others excluded from the warrior paradigm—internalised this perspective, they might still (eventually) experience its disappearance as a liberation rather than a calamity. Unglamourous everyday Crow life did continue, and many people did find life meaningful, even after the three pillars collapsed. Why can't the last generation do the same?

Post-Cataclysm Pessimist: This brings us to another difference between Lear's Crow example and our Post-Cataclysm world—a difference that strengthens the case for last generation pessimism. The Crow claim that 'after this, nothing happened' sounds paradoxical to us *because a great deal did happen*. The Crow adapted to a *new* life based on settled farming rather than nomadic hunting. They could borrow from a different culture whose foundational activities were not dependent on the Crow's three pillars. (This was not a coincidence, of course. The incompatibility between farming and nomadism was one reason why the US government banned the *Crow's* foundational activities.) Many Crow individuals eventually found meaning by blending this new culture with their own traditions. By contrast, no one in the last generation has any non-future-dependent *alternative*.

Presentist: I am not persuaded that *all* our inherited activities *are* future-dependent. However, even if they were, and even if the last generation therefore did suffer universal intelligibility loss, alternatives would still be available. Other human traditions are less future-dependent than ours. The last generation could borrow intelligible activities *from less future-fixated communities*.

In other words, we can—and must—do what the Crow did. We can look beyond our own traditional way of life—emphasising marginalised non-future-dependent strands in our own cultural inheritance, or borrowing them from other cultures. Human beings can flourish without faith in the human future. Present-focused activities are sufficient without any broader narrative to render them 'intelligible'. Intelligibility loss does not justify *pessimism*.

---

[60] Baker, 'Vulnerabilities of Morality'; Sherman, 'The Fate of a Warrior Culture', pp. 77–79; cf. Lear's response in Lear, 'Response to Hubert Dreyfus and Nancy Sherman', pp. 88–91.

Multigenerationalist: I draw very different lessons from Lear. I agree that intelligibility loss is a real threat to both well-being and meaning, and that it is hard to imagine a community recovering intelligibility within a generation. Intelligibility loss does ground *last generation* pessimism. However, the principal message of the *second* half of Lear's book is that the story of Plenty Coups—and the Crow in general—is one of hopeful optimism, despite its opening chapter of cultural devastation. Looking back, *later* generations would certainly *not* describe Plenty Coups' post-traditional life as meaningless. Plenty Coups recognised the loss of *traditional* intelligibility, and lead his people on the path to a new meaning.

Lear's Plenty Coups embodies *radical hope*. Plenty Coups hoped that his successors would flourish—even though he could not even imagine the standard against which that future flourishing might be judged. The Crow story demonstrates that *multigenerational* recovery of intelligibility is possible. The Crow have forged a new intelligibility that is *not* dependent on their traditional way of life. The three pillars have not been restored, but things can now happen again.

Lear's contrast between intelligibility loss and radical hope explains why last generation pessimism does *not* imply Post-Cataclysm pessimism. In Scheffler's *immediate* extinction scenarios, there is no time to create new sources of intelligibility. Because intelligibility depends on a way of life, it can only be restored as new ways of life develop. Radical hope must be *multigenerational*. Even if life remains unintelligible to us, and our near descendants, it may become intelligible for later generations. We cannot assume, in advance, that two hundred years is not sufficient. (After all, the Crow arguably began to find new intelligibility in a much shorter time-frame.)

Post-Cataclysm Pessimist: But if things are unintelligible *now*, doesn't that justify pessimism for the present generation?

Multigenerationalist: Not necessarily. The *prospect* of future intelligibility is sufficient, if not for present intelligibility, then at least for *present meaning*. Plenty Coups' hope that his descendants would find new meaning was sufficient both to motivate him to continue a life that he could not understand *and to give that life meaning*. Radical hope is an antidote to pessimism. 'What radical hope is opposed to is a certain form of despair: namely, the attitude that the current understanding of the good exhausts all that is worth hoping for.'[61]

We can now separate two distinct things that happen in Scheffler's infertility scenario. First, humanity faces immediate extinction. Second, the present generation have just discovered this. Discovery and extinction occur together, leaving no time to adjust. In our Post-Cataclysm world, *our* generation discovers imminent extinction, but some *later* generation must face it. Neither generation faces

---

[61] Lear, 'Response to Hubert Dreyfus and Nancy Sherman', p. 86.

the double-whammy of discovery and (immediate) extinction. And it is this double-whammy that makes Scheffler's scenarios so unpalatable, by eliminating the possibility of radical hope.

Post-Cataclysm Pessimist: I remain sceptical. Our situation is different from Plenty Coups'. His radical hope was based on reconfiguring marginalised values within his own tradition, integrating them into practices borrowed from Western civilisation, and building a new future based on values that he himself could not imagine. We do not have time to do anything analogous. Radical hope may be *necessary* for present meaning. But is it *sufficient*? Can we reasonably put our faith in a future we cannot even imagine?

Multigenerationalist: There are no guarantees. Plenty Coups' hope is *radical*, because present meaning rests on uncertain future developments that present generations cannot even imagine. Multigenerationalism makes an analogous leap of faith—built on the radical hope that future people will develop some new source of meaning that may be unintelligible to us. I explore this search throughout my lectures.

1.7 Hartmann's Pessimist Optimism

Post-Cataclysm Pessimist: Another inspiration for Post-Cataclysm pessimism, from a very different philosophical tradition, is Eduard von Hartmann (1842–1906).[62] Philosophical pessimism flourished in Germany in the late-nineteenth century, when rapid social change and religious doubt fuelled debate about the pointlessness of human life. Characteristically, the German language has a specific word to describe the resulting mood: *weltschmerz* [literally "world pain"], which 'signifies a mood of weariness or sadness about life arising from the acute awareness of evil and suffering'.[63]

While Schopenhauer is now the most famous German pessimist, Hartmann was arguably more famous *at the time*. Indeed, one reviewer in 1880 described him as 'the best known, the most important, and the most discussed among the German philosophers of the present'.[64] One explanation of his broad appeal is that Hartmann 'seemed to offer not only a more rigorous and systematic pessimism than Schopenhauer, but also a kinder and gentler version, one which combines pessimism about human happiness with optimism about cultural progress'.[65] Many of his contemporaries—especially those without independent fortunes who

---

[62] My discussion of Hartmann, and German pessimism more generally, draws on Beiser, *Weltschmerz*; and Dienstag, *Pessimism*.
[63] Beiser, *Weltschmerz*, p. 1. [64] Beiser, *Weltschmerz*, p. 122.
[65] Beiser, *Weltschmerz*, p. 123.

had to actually work to survive—found Schopenhauer's ironic detachment from the ills of the world neither congenial nor helpful. Those who could not afford to despise the world found Hartmann more palatable.

I should warn you that my 'reading' of Hartmann takes many liberties. I am *not* engaged in historical scholarship! I am more interested in what Hartmann can *teach us* than in what he *originally meant*.[66]

Hartmann argues that modern philosophy leads inevitably to pessimism about individual well-being. We cannot be happy in this life, and the *supernatural* afterlife of traditional theism is absurd. If we seek our own individual happiness, we are doomed to disappointment and frustration.

Hartmann describes this side of his own philosophy as 'eudemonic pessimism'. Hartmann's pessimist standard is hedonist: (i) every human life contains more pain than pleasure, more suffering than happiness; and (ii) this cannot be changed. No possible future cultural achievement, technological advance, social innovation, or moral improvement could eliminate the greatest sources of human misery: 'sickness, ageing, dependence on the will of others, sexual frustration, and hunger'.[67]

Perennial Pessimist: In short, Hartmann is a *perennial* pessimist about well-being measured in hedonist terms—not a *Post-Cataclysm* pessimist.

Post-Cataclysm Pessimist: Yes. Regarding well-being, Hartmann is a perennial pessimist. But there is another side to Hartmann. He is *not* a pessimist about *meaning*. Life is not meaningless. Even if we cannot be happy, 'we can still find value...through striving for cultural achievement and moral improvement'.[68] Hartmann thus combines his eudemonic pessimism with what he calls 'evolutionary optimism': while 'happiness is unattainable in this life...we can make moral and cultural progress in history'.[69] Indeed, for Hartmann, the discovery of eudemonic pessimism *drives* evolutionary optimism: 'It is only when we are ready to renounce the illusion that we can achieve happiness in this life, that we are fully ready to devote ourselves to our moral ideals.'[70] These two sides of Hartmann represent his debts to two German predecessors: 'if Schopenhauer represents the pessimistic side of Hartmann's system, Hegel represents its optimistic side.'[71]

For Hartmann, the alleviation of suffering is not one of the goals, ends, or purposes of human cultural evolution. History does not aim at individual happiness. Progress is not measured in hedonist terms, so there is no reason to expect progress to improve happiness.

---

[66] My reading of Hartmann is also necessarily second-hand. His main writings are not available in English translation, and therefore I am entirely reliant on secondary sources, notably Beiser, *Weltschmerz*.
[67] Beiser, *Weltschmerz*, p. 155.
[68] Beiser, *Weltschmerz*, p. 135.
[69] Beiser, *Weltschmerz*, p. 136.
[70] Beiser, *Weltschmerz*, p. 157.
[71] Beiser, *Weltschmerz*, p. 143.

Presentist: This suggests that Hartmann's idea of 'progress' is very different from our own.

Post-Cataclysm Pessimist: Yes. Indeed, modern liberal democrats will find Hartmann's *substantive* political agenda 'shocking'.[72] Inspired by a brutal reading of the Darwinian notion of the survival of the fittest, Hartmann was an archconservative, fiercely loyal to the not-altogether-morally-admirable Bismarck regime in Prussia. As Beiser sums up, 'war, competition, inequality, exploitation, colonisation—all these lead to the unhappiness of the great majority of people; but that, Hartmann insists, is the price that we have to pay for evolution and the development of culture.'[73] This is the dark side of Hartmann's eudemonic pessimism. Life is inevitably bleak for individuals—so any additional individual suffering is a small price to pay for cultural progress. The alleviation of suffering, the removal of inequality, the introduction of democratic accountability, and other utilitarian, liberal, hedonist goals are simply no part of the *point* of human cultural progress.

Presentist: This is a hard view to sell today!

Post-Cataclysm Pessimist: Of course. Hartmann's allegiance to the Prussian state explains both why he was very popular in the 1870s, and why he was then more-or-less irrelevant after World War I. Hartmann's philosophy was tied to a particular cultural world. When that world ceased to exist, he ceased to be read.

Philosophically, Hartmann's particular combination of eudemonic pessimism and evolutionary optimism posits a *very* sharp divide between our standards of (a) individual welfare and (b) cultural progress. For Hartmann, a culture can flourish even if everyone is very unhappy and most people are oppressed. Indeed, this is the *only* way that *any* culture can ever flourish. At best, cultural progress *might* reduce human suffering—but even that is neither required nor guaranteed. Cultural progress is just not *about* individual flourishing. Hartmann's 'optimism' is thus at odds with the individualist and welfarist tendencies of Pre-Cataclysm liberal political philosophy, where cultural progress is largely *defined* in terms of individual flourishing.

Presentist: What can this outmoded view contribute to *our* debate?

Post-Cataclysm Pessimist: Post-Cataclysm pessimists draw a negative lesson from Hartmann's case. The Cataclysm forever undermines *any* attempt to combine eudemonic pessimism with social, cultural, or evolutionary optimism. We can no longer believe that human history is progressive—because there is no future into which *anything* could 'progress'. While few Pre-Cataclysm philosophers shared Hartmann's actual political agenda, or were aware of his work at all, many did find meaning in social activism aimed at improving conditions in the long-term.

---

[72] Beiser, *Weltschmerz*, p. 160. [73] Beiser, *Weltschmerz*, p. 161.

Indeed, Derek Parfit, a Pre-Cataclysm philosopher who otherwise has little in common with Hartmann, expressed a similar hope that the distant human future might retrospectively outweigh past human misery enough to make the human story worthwhile overall:

> If we are the only rational beings in the Universe... it matters even more whether we shall have descendants or successors during the billions of years in which that would be possible. Some of our successors might live lives and create worlds that, though failing to justify past suffering, would have given us all, including those who suffered most, reasons to be glad that the Universe exists.[74]

In our Post-Cataclysm world, social activism can only be very short term. And such modest short-term activism cannot outweigh eudemonic or hedonist pessimism.

Presentist: So Hartmann grounds an argument for Post-Cataclysm pessimism *about meaning?*

Post-Cataclysm Pessimist: Yes. If Hartmann's diagnosis of the human condition is correct, then meaning *was* possible before the Cataclysm, but it is no longer possible now.

Presentist: Of course, this argument presumes a tight connection between meaning and *progress*.

Post-Cataclysm Pessimist: If we accept Hartmann's combination of eudemonic pessimism and supernatural atheism, then future social progress is the only route to meaning. Hartmann, as I interpret him, suggests that my contribution to the future of human cultural progress can deliver meaning for me even though, from the point of view of welfare, life is irredeemably bad. As a Post-Cataclysm pessimist, I would add that, whatever compensation Hartmann's future cultural progress might have offered *before* the Cataclysm, it is clearly insufficient in our Post-Cataclysm world. For one thing, the fact of the Cataclysm falsifies Hartmann's Hegelian optimism. The world is not progressing toward the self-realisation of the Absolute.

Presentist: That is hardly news. Very few people ever took that Hegelian story seriously.

Post-Cataclysm Pessimist: Setting metaphysics aside, even if *some* progress is possible in two hundred years, it cannot be sufficient to provide meaning *in the face of Hartmann's pessimistic diagnosis of the human condition*. While some grand

---

[74] Parfit, *On What Matters*, volume three, p. 437.

historical narrative *might* outweigh the sheer miserableness of human existence, the much less exalted goal of making things a little better over two centuries is no adequate substitute.

Hartmann and Scheffler are very different philosophers. Scheffler would reject eudemonic pessimism, hedonism, and an approach to individual flourishing that focuses exclusively on well-being; while his substantive accounts of political, social, and individual reasons are very different from Hartmann's. But Scheffler and Hartmann both emphasise the importance—*for a meaningful existence for anyone living in their respective societies*—of connections to future generations.

Hartmann definitely supports both last generation pessimism and Post-Cataclysm pessimism. If there will be no further human generations, then there can be virtually no future progress—and certainly not enough to make up for present misery. And meaning is equally unavailable at the *start* of our Post-Cataclysm world, because human progress cannot possibly be completed in two hundred years.

Perennial Pessimism: I would reply that human progress could *never* be brought to completion in *any finite* number of generations. Immediate or imminent extinction is unnecessary. *Eventual* extinction is enough to derail Hartmann's evolutionary optimism.

Post-Cataclysm Pessimist: I disagree. For Hartmann's purposes, the Hegelian sweep of history need not be infinite, or even indefinite, or even very long. Sufficient progress could be made—if only there were enough future generations. But the Cataclysm rules this out.

Multigenerationalist: I would then turn that reply back *against* Post-Cataclysm pessimism. Cynical critics have long suggested that, for Hegel, human history reaches its apotheosis in the nineteenth-century Prussian state.[75] If so, two hundred years is ample time for the consummation of human progress. More generally, if faith in future human progress was sufficient to outweigh Hartmann's eudemonic pessimism before the Cataclysm, then sufficient progress ought to be possible in two hundred years.

Perennial Pessimist: From the opposite direction, anyone who values human well-being must reject the very idea behind Hartmann's original 'optimism'. Future cultural progress was never an adequate compensation for the brutality and unfairness of human life. Indeed, many perennial pessimists, inspired by Schopenhauer's rejection of Hegel, are suspicious of the very idea of cultural *progress*. The Cataclysm thus changes nothing.

---

[75] Perhaps the most notorious example is Russell, *History of Western Philosophy*, book three, chapter twenty-two.

Presentist: On this point, presentists and perennial pessimists have something in common. I would reject both Hartmann's eudemonic pessimism and his grandiose reliance on 'progress'. Meaning can be found—can only be found, has always been found—in less grandiose projects that are not threatened by imminent human extinction or the collapse of metaphysical castles in the air. Alleviating suffering, reducing inequality, and promoting happiness remain worthy goals. Hartmann neatly illustrates why the loss of an indefinite human future is actually a *good* thing: it undermines future-obsessed blindness to present miseries.

As we saw in relation to both Scheffler and Lear, while present-focused activities may be less glamorous than future-directed ones, they are also both (a) more resilient; and (b) sufficient in their own right for a meaningful life. Hartmann fails at the first step. Even in the last generation, without any hope for a human future, sufficient meaning is available.

Multigenerationalist: Like the Post-Cataclysm pessimist, I too find Hartmann inspiring—but in a very different way. I think the very transience of Hartmann's fame is part of his appeal. A philosophy so closely tied to a particular place and time that it cannot survive more than a few generations is exactly what we now need! No one now wants to 'return' to Bismarck's Prussia—whatever that would mean today. But we can still adapt Hartmann's blend of pessimism and optimism to our own times—seeking meaning in collective activities that are not (only) devoted to the promotion of happiness.

Of course, I am also less pessimistic than Hartmann about our future prospects for improving human well-being. Few multigenerationalists would endorse any kind of evolutionary optimism in the face of eudemonic pessimism. We prefer more hopeful readings. While I agree with Hartmann that human progress cannot eliminate suffering, I do think we *can* make some progress in *reducing* human suffering, as well as achieving greater cultural and moral perfection.[76] If we start with a more optimistic baseline—if we reject pessimism about well-being—then Hartmann offers resources that multigenerationalists could borrow.

Another, even more radical reading, takes Hartmann's optimism in yet another direction—one that he himself would not have encouraged. Religious or metaphysical interpreters of Hartmann argue instead that his notion of future cultural progress was never plausible on any modern secular (i.e., post-Hegalian) interpretation. The only progress that can reliably deliver meaning is metaphysical, supernatural, or religious progress. In other words, Hartmann *needs* Hegel—or some other supernatural story. Hartmann explicitly sought a new religion to overcome both the spiritual poverty of materialist atheism and the out-of-date metaphysics and morality of traditional theism. But his outlook is still more religious than many later philosophers. It is always anachronistic to pigeon-hole a

---

[76] Beiser, *Weltschmerz*, p. 150.

philosopher using the taxonomy of a later age. However, in the categories of early twenty-first-century analytic philosophy, Hartmann's post-Hegelian metaphysic is probably closer to theism than atheism. In particular, Hartmann inspires ananthropocentric (non-human-centred) purposivists, who embrace his religious vision of a rational universe progressing toward a goal divorced from individual human happiness.[77] By separating progress and happiness so completely, Hartmann points toward a cosmic purpose that is entirely non-human-centred. I expand on alternatives to both theism and atheism, and their connection to multigenerationalism, in the final section of our religion debate (Section 2.4), and in my discussion of ecological and religious utopias in my final lecture (Sections 8.4, 8.5.2).

1.8 The Collapse of Secular Immortality

Post-Cataclysm Pessimist: Immanuel Kant famously argued that we are rationally required to hope that we inhabit a morally coherent and fundamentally just universe.[78] Kant himself notoriously concludes that we must postulate freedom, personal immortality, and the existence of God. While few philosophers go so far as Kant, many are attracted to the thought that meaningful, morally coherent human lives require some reasonable hope that our universe is not completely morally incoherent.

Scheffler and Hartmann, in their very different ways, continue this broadly post-Kantian search for secular hope. Unfortunately, the Cataclysm undermines the best secular alternatives to supernatural personal immortality. If we find the latter implausible, then we must embrace Post-Cataclysm pessimism.

We return to Kantian 'moral' arguments in our religion debate (Section 2.2) and our virtual futures debate (Section 9.6.3). To introduce the basic themes, I will now sketch one argument for Post-Cataclysm pessimism, based on the failure of secular optimist replies to Kant.

One secular analogue of Kantian hope is J. S. Mill's memorable metaphor of hoping to live on 'in the ongoing rush of mankind'. Mill, in turn, was inspired by Comte's earlier remark that 'He who has left great results acquires in others a

---

[77] cf. Mulgan, *Purpose in the Universe*.
[78] On Kant's original moral arguments, see, e.g., White, *Commentary*, pp. 267–269; Sullivan, *Immanuel Kant's Moral Theory*, pp. 142–144; Beach, 'The Postulate of Immortality in Kant: To What Extent Is It Culturally Conditioned?'; Guyer, *Kant*, chapter six: 'Freedom, Immortality, and God: The Presuppositions of Morality'; Irwin, *The Development of Ethics*, volume three, chapter seventy-one, sections 975 to 980; Rossi, 'Kant, Immanuel: Philosophy of Religion'. On moral, practical, or Kantian arguments more generally, see Hare, *The Moral Gap*, chapter three on Moral Faith; Bishop, *Believing by Faith*; Chignell, 'Belief, ethics of'; Adams, 'Moral Faith'; Adams, *Finite and Infinite Goods*, pp. 373–389. I discuss moral arguments myself in Mulgan, *Purpose in the Universe*, pp. 301–322.

subjective immortality, so that the work of his life is perpetuated and even extended.'[79] While Mill was surely speaking metaphorically, some philosophers (perhaps including Comte) interpret this idea of living on in future humanity *literally*.

The search for *literal personal* secular survival requires a radical re-interpretation of conventional ideas about personal identity. Philosophers have offered many competing accounts of personal identity over time—competing stories about what makes me the same person I was yesterday: continuity of memory, psychological continuity and connectedness, bodily continuity, brain identity, animal identity, and many others. By contrast, non-supernatural literal survivalists typically identify my self with *my concerns*. Concern-based accounts of personal identity were especially popular among the nineteenth-century British Idealists. Bernard Bosanquet even presented this account as the commonsense view: 'No one will much object to an identification of the self in the main with the things we mainly care for.'[80]

Presentist: That sounds pretty far-fetched to me.

Post-Cataclysm Pessimist: Perhaps. However, the widespread use of thought experiments to settle questions about personal identity arguably supports some concern-based account. Our reactions to imaginary tales don't unearth any deep metaphysical reality. But they *do* reveal what *we* care about. In tele-transportation, fission, or body-swap tales, I am really asking not 'Is it me?' but 'Do I care?' If these thought experiments *also* reveal our views about personal identity, then the two must be closely linked.

Presentist: Suppose I accept all this—for the sake of argument. How does it support Post-Cataclysm pessimism?

Post-Cataclysm Pessimist: On a concern-based account, if I care about things outside myself, and if those things continue after my death, then their persistence *is* my survival. I can thus survive the death of my body. And, if I care about the right things, I may even enjoy personal *immortality*. One possibility, suggested by Bosanquet's own discussion, is that if I cease to care about my individual personality, and come to identify myself with the Absolute, then I will achieve post-mortem survival *via unity with the Absolute*.

Presentist: As with Hartmann, that is not much help if one rejects the underlying post-Hegelian metaphysics.

Post-Cataclysm Pessimist: Other Pre-Cataclysm secular concern-based theorists develop non-Hegelian alternatives. One example is Mark Johnston's *Surviving*

---

[79] Comte, *System of Positive Polity*, quoted in Mill, 'Auguste Comte and Positivism', p. 342.
[80] Bosanquet, *The Value and Destiny of the Individual*, p. 260; cf. Mander, *British Idealism*, pp. 382–391.

Death. Johnston builds a Kantian case for a secular alternative to traditional supernatural personal immortality, based on a literal version of Mill's striking metaphor. According to Johnston, personal identity is constituted by a certain kind of concern for future personalities. Most of us feel this special concern only (or primarily) for those future personalities that occur in *this* body, or contain apparent memories of *this* personality. But this limited pattern of concern is a contingent weakness, a moral failing. A *good person* would feel *the very same concern* for *all* future personalities. And therefore the good person would live on in all of them.

Presentist: Any particular story about concern can be deployed either as a *substitute* for personal survival, or an *interpretation* of it. The former is much less controversial. I come to believe that personal identity is not what *matters*. I transcend self-concern, and therefore I care less about my own survival. Future-directed concern for others thus *replaces* selfish concern for my post-mortem fate. This is a familiar theme in Pre-Cataclysm utilitarianism, especially among those influenced by Parfit.[81] Similarly, Scheffler suggests that his collective afterlife is *more valuable to us* than personal immortality would be.[82]

Post-Cataclysm Pessimist: Johnston goes further than either Parfit or Scheffler. He offers a concern-based *interpretation* of personal survival, where I literally live on *in others*. By identifying with future people, I live on in them. Johnston promises to 'explain how a good person quite literally survives death.'[83]

Theist: This secular replacement falls short of what *theists* need. It cannot deliver personal *immortality* unless humanity endures *forever*. Nor can Johnstonian survival ground a satisfactory theodicy. Many innocent sufferers of horrendous evil are not Johnstonian good people. There is no consolation here for the child who suffers horrendous evil and then dies before she can even begin to 'radically transform her patterns of self-concern'. Animal victims of horrendous evil fare even worse, as they are completely unable to adopt the good person's pattern of concern.

Post-Cataclysm Pessimist: Johnston never claims to offer a theodicy, to deliver personal immortality, or to replicate all the roles filled by the supernatural afterlife. Johnston's goal is much less ambitious. 'The constraint that I take myself to be under [is] to show that there is something in death that is better for the good than for the bad.... To the extent that they are good the good can see through death, and as a result death is less of a threat to them.'[84]

---

[81] Parfit, *Reasons and Persons*, pp. 321–347. [82] Scheffler, *Death and the Afterlife*, p. 72 ff.
[83] Johnston, *Surviving Death*, p. 15. [84] Johnston, *Surviving Death*, pp. 13–14.

Presentist: Johnston's accounts of both personal identity and goodness are highly controversial. For one thing, it is not obvious that Johnston's ingenious solution really captures the attitude of the good person. To be more precise, I wonder whether *all* good people *must* conform to his model—or whether Johnston's picture is just one (rather eccentric) way to be good. Does the good person have to *extend* their self-concern to others? Why couldn't they instead *replace* self-concern with some alternative pattern of concern for others that does not involve identification? Surely the latter would be equally praiseworthy? Indeed, it might be more praiseworthy, because it offers the possibility of genuine self-sacrifice. Is there anything morally deficient about a utilitarian good person who gives the interests of others exactly equal weight in their *practical* deliberations, even though they still care more deeply about their own interests? But this good person will *not* live on in others.[85]

Another problematic implication of Johnston's view is that the degree to which death is better for the good person than for the bad person depends, inter alia, on (a) whether or not there exist (in distant galaxies) extra-terrestrial beings whose interests matter; (b) whether or not those extra-terrestrials flourish; and (c) whether or not a particular good person identifies with the interests of *those* beings. But that sounds like a *reductio ad absurdum* of Johnston's view!

Post-Cataclysm Pessimist: I'm not asking you to endorse all the details of Johnston's view. I make only two claims:

1. There is *something* to Johnston's thought that, without *some* hope that we inhabit 'a universe in which the cries of great injustice to be punished, and the cries of great sacrifice in the name of the good to be rewarded, do not just echo in the void',[86] morality is an irrational and ridiculous farce: 'absent final justice, obedience to the moral law may simply turn the just into fodder for the predatory unjust'.[87]
2. Any consolation Johnston could have offered *before the Cataclysm* is now lost. Johnston himself concedes that his naturalist alternative offers *no consolation* to the last generation of good humans.[88] The good can only survive death by living on in others *if there will be future people*. The Cataclysm destroys this hope.

Presentist: Of course, that only gets you to last generation pessimism. So long as there may be *some* future good people, death is still better for the good than for the bad.

---

[85] cf. Mulgan, 'Review of Johnston'; Mulgan, *Purpose in the Universe*, pp. 301–303.
[86] Johnston, *Surviving Death*, p. 10.   [87] Johnston, *Surviving Death*, p. 12.
[88] Johnston, *Surviving Death*, pp. 376–377.

Post-Cataclysm Pessimist: Yes, but while Johnston offers *some* consolation to earlier generations in our Post-Cataclysm world, this is much less than the consolation available *before the Cataclysm*. (The maximum number of possible future people is now miniscule compared to what Johnston's contemporaries thought they could look forward to.) And things get progressively worse as we near humanity's end. We therefore have both a compelling new argument for last generation pessimism, and a very strong independent argument for Post-Cataclysm pessimism. Like Scheffler, Johnston also supplies a new argument for the conditional premise of the bridging argument from last generation pessimism to Post-Cataclysm pessimism. If last generation pessimism is true, then the last generation live miserable or meaningless lives. The fact that one's goodness enables one to 'live on' through such future lives doesn't seem like much of a consolation. The more the good person cares for *those* future good people, the worse-off that good person will be.

Perennial Pessimist: Perennial pessimists simply deny that Johnston's consolation was ever an adequate replacement for personal survival—let alone personal immortality. Some will reject his account of personal identity, others his account of goodness, others his optimistic presumption that this level of concern for others is even psychologically *possible* for any ordinary human being.

Presentist: Presentists get off the bus much earlier. We simply reject the initial Kantian set-up. We do not accept that the injustice of the universe is any real threat to our well-being, to the normative force of our obligations to care for one another, or to our search for meaning. Our universe is morally incoherent. So what? That is unfortunate, but we just have to live with it. We are not rationally required to hope for a just universe. We are only required to help one another as best we can in this bleak, uncaring, pointless universe. We are adults who must confront reality, not children to be comforted by fictions where good inevitably triumphs over evil in the end. The loss of Johnstonian consolation is disappointing, but it should not plunge us into despair.

Multigenerationalist: By contrast, while I don't agree with all the details, I find Johnston's consolation inspiring. Suppose Johnston is correct that personal identity is (or *could be*) constituted by patterns of self-concern. *Our* present patterns of self-concern are both self-interested *and future-directed*. Suppose I am not initially a good person. I care what will happen to me in the future. Johnston's good person redirects their self-concern impersonally into the future. They care equally about all (good) future personalities. It is a very difficult psychological question whether human beings could be trained—en masse—to redirect their self-concern in this way. My alternative *multigenerational* question is whether human beings could instead be trained to redirect the *temporality* of their self-concern. Could I identify myself, not only with *future* good people, but also with all the good people who have lived *before*? If so, the last generation of good people might conquer death by caring as much about past human flourishing as about future flourishing. Can I live on in the 'ongoing rush of mankind' even *after* it has rushed past?

Presentist: One obvious difference is that the past is unchangeable, whereas the future is not. I can't *do* anything in response to my concern for past people.

Multigenerationalist: But surely this metaphysical difference—if it *is* a real difference—is irrelevant. For Johnston, a present good person could still live on through future good people even in a deterministic universe without genuine free will, or a four-dimensional universe where the arrow of time was an illusion. (For all anyone knows, present good people *do* inhabit such universes.) Johnston's consolation does not depend on any *causal* link between the present good person and future good people. But then I *could* in principle identify with past good people just as much as future good people.

Presentist: If this temporal redirection is possible, then presumably even the egoist can find some consolation *in their own past*. This threatens Johnston's claim that death offers more to the good person than to the bad.

Multigenerationalist: Not quite. There is a still a very significant difference. The bad person may live on in their own past. But the good person can live on in *everyone's* past. So the good person still comes out ahead.

We should remember the dialectical context. If we allow Kantian practical arguments, then what matters is reasonable hope, not belief based on the balance of probabilities. Humanity may ultimately fail to escape death by transcending both self and time. But is it irrational to hope? I return to all these questions throughout my lectures (Sections 3.1, 3.6, 3.7, 6.3.2, 6.3.4, 9.5).

Theist: Of course, theists argue that the best source of consolation is God. And we take up *that* issue in our next debate.

2
Second Debate
Religion for a Post-Cataclysm World

Theist: In this debate, we turn from atheist pessimism to theism. For the committed theist, the previous debate is largely beside the point. Of course, *atheists* should despair—because the Cataclysm highlights the inadequacy of their secular sources of meaning. But theists believe that true meaning flows, not from the secular human present or future, but from appropriate connections to divine reality—from right relationship with God. And *that* source of meaning is unaffected by the Cataclysm.

Theists are not completely unaffected by imminent human extinction. We don't simply ignore it. For us, as for everyone else, the Cataclysm is a profoundly unsettling development. But it doesn't plunge us into despair. Life is still meaningful in the same way as it always was. Theists still continue to seek right relationship with God, live according to a divine plan, value other people (and non-human nature) as images of God, and look forward to a post-mortem reward.

Our debate has four sections. I begin by asking how the Cataclysm influences the content of theism, for those who remain committed to belief in God (Section 2.1). More ambitiously, I then argue that the Cataclysm strengthens the practical philosophical case for theism by strengthening moral, prudential, or Kantian meaning-based arguments for both God and immortality (Section 2.2).

Post-Cataclysm Pessimist: I then reply that, on the contrary, the Cataclysm weakens the case for theism in two key ways: it shows that this is not the kind of universe that a perfect benevolent God would create, and it undermines traditional explanatory arguments for the existence of God by showing that this universe is not so remarkable that its existence cannot be accepted as a brute fact (Section 2.3).

Multigenerationalist: Finally, I briefly argue that the Cataclysm motivates the urgent exploration of alternatives to both theism and atheism—an exploration that must itself be multigenerational (Section 2.4). This sets the scene for my later lectures—especially Section 8.5.2.

2.1 What Should Theists Make of the Cataclysm?

Theist: Suppose the Cataclysm does not make us lose faith in God. Our commitment to theism is as strong as before. What *other* impacts might the Cataclysm have?

For theists, as for everyone else, the Cataclysm puts things in perspective, makes everything seem more urgent, and renders many specific projects pointless. I can no longer serve God or my neighbours by laying the foundations for the eventual curing of cancer in three hundred years' time, or by helping to design a wonderful new Cathedral that will take centuries to build. Like secular optimists, when it comes to the *content* of our projects, theists divide between presentists and multigenerationalists—between those who find meaning in present-focused activities, and those who seek to reorient previously open-ended future-directed activities to bring them to a suitable end within two hundred years. In many cases, atheists and theists pursue the same projects—with the principal difference that, for the theist, all meaning is *ultimately* grounded in divine reality. On a day-to-day basis, that makes less difference than you might expect. Just as they did before the Cataclysm, many actual theists share the secular goals of actual atheists. We also seek to alleviate suffering, comfort the dying, fight injustice, build a just society, live in harmony with nature, and so on. Our actual pursuit of these joint goals is therefore transformed as much (or as little) by the Cataclysm as it is for atheists.

Some theists who previously thought their vocation lay in longer-term projects have had to rethink God's plan for their lives. This can be *very* unsettling. But it is hardly a new kind of problem. And while it is individually unsettling, it is not a theoretical problem for theism.

What has not changed, for all theists, is the ultimate grounding of meaning. All human meaning is grounded in God—either directly (because God is the ultimate standard and source of all values) or indirectly (because the person's relationship with God is what makes their particular projects meaningful). Like atheists, theists have lost particular future-directed projects. Unlike atheists, theists have no reason to lose faith in the projects that remain. And theists trust that their remaining projects are both meaningful and sufficient.

Beyond these platitudes, I don't think there is much we can say in general. Outside of a philosophy seminar, no actual person is simply 'a theist' *period*. Actual theists worship actual God(s) within actual religious traditions whose actual practices are guided by very specific historical traditions and particular revelations. One obvious Post-Cataclysm resource is that many theist religions have apocalyptic, eschatological, end-times traditions which obviously shape believers' responses to the Cataclysm. Insofar as the End is not unexpected, theists already have tools to respond to it.

The Cataclysm is less significant for theists than for atheists. It doesn't undermine our ultimate ground of meaning. And it doesn't remove what is most important. We have always believed that our true home—and God's true kingdom—is not of this world. The end of *this physical world* is neither here nor there. If you had told the first Christians that the world would end early in the third millennium, they would have been very surprised (and not a little disappointed) to learn that it would last so long!

More radically, some theists treat the Cataclysm as a vital new insight into God's plan—not only for the universe, but for us. Timing is everything. The Cataclysm has happened *after* we had acquired the scientific competence to see it coming, but *before* we had any feasible means of escape. God wants us to know that the end is nigh. The Cataclysm gives us time to repent—*and also time to mend our ways*. (*Immediate* extinction would have taught the different, harsher lesson that we should have repented earlier!) God wants us to know that we must bring things to a good end. But God wants us to discover this without direct divine revelation.

Multigenerationalist: This line of argument supports multigenerational optimism. This-worldly human events and achievements *do* matter, and two hundred years must be enough time to do something worthwhile. (Otherwise, why would God give us any advance warning at all?) We must put our house in order before it is too late.

Theist: Of course, many theists read *that* injunction in terms of individual spiritual repentance, conversion to the correct religion (whatever that might be), or in other religious terms—not in terms of larger intergenerational endeavours.

Multigenerationalist: Yes, but other theists unite with secular multigenerational utopians—arguing that God has left us sufficient time to finally make *this world* just. Similarly, *ecological* theists, joining with secular ecological utopians, argue that God is giving us the time to repair the damage, and rectify the wrongs, we have inflicted on non-human nature—another multigenerational project. And *virtualist* theists argue that the true utopia is a virtual future where humans seek communion with God without the distractions of a doomed physical world—yet another multigenerational project! I return to all these projects in Section 2.4 and in later lectures (Sections 8.4, 8.5.2, 9.6).

Theist: On the other hand, not all theists agree that the Cataclysm is meant to teach us anything. Theists don't have to regard the Cataclysm as a message from God. Many theists reject the whole idea of reading specific divine lessons into particular events. The Cataclysm simply reminds us that God is inscrutable, and teaches us not to put hubristic faith in human reasoning. We should stick to our assigned tasks, rather than second-guessing the divine plan.

Many theists draw a broader ethical lesson. The Cataclysm reminds us that God is not a consequentialist, and therefore that consequentialism cannot be the correct account of human morality either. In particular, the Cataclysm clearly demonstrates that God is not a long-termist effective altruist consequentialist.

Escapist: Not so fast. I would argue instead that, if there is a God, then, by forcing us to concentrate on the next 200 years, God is urging us to develop a digital utopia—the only possible future that is consistent with the grandeur of God! I pick up that idea in our final debate on virtual futures (Section 9.10).

Theist: Whatever our ethical theory, all theists insist that we should focus on our duty to God and to one another, on following the rules that God has given us, on developing the virtues that God has guided us to via moral exemplars—and *not* on the long-term consequences of our actions. These non-consequentialist aspects of morality are *not* undermined by the Cataclysm, because (contra Scheffler) they have always derived their reason-giving force—their ability to lend meaning to human lives—not from any ongoing fragile human tradition, but from the eternal reality of God.

Presentist: As an atheist, I think this is all beside the point, because God does not exist.

Post-Cataclysm Pessimist: I agree. And, as I argue in Section 2.3, the Cataclysm makes God's non-existence even more obvious than before!

Theist: Whereas I think exactly the opposite. The Cataclysm makes belief in God even more compelling—which brings us to our next topic.

2.2 How the Cataclysm Supports Theism

Theist: I said earlier that, for the committed theist, the previous debate was irrelevant. But that is not quite true. On the contrary, it strengthened my conviction that the Cataclysm actually supports theism. I agree with the Post-Cataclysm pessimist that, *if* we confine ourselves to the secular human world, *then* the Cataclysm renders life meaningless. I reply, so much the worse for the secular human world!

To parallel our earlier debates, I imagine a *Post-Cataclysm theist*—someone who was agnostic before the Cataclysm and is then converted to theism because of the Cataclysm. This is not my own view. I already found theism quite plausible before the Cataclysm. But I do think the Cataclysm adds a new and decisive argument—one that should persuade an open-minded agnostic.

My argument draws on the Kantian tradition of moral or practical arguments. These arguments claim that, when theoretical reason fails to answer a question, and practical reason demands a particular answer, then we can reasonably posit the necessary belief for the purposes of our practical deliberations.[1]

I deliberately elide two Kantian arguments: for God and Immortality. Actual theists typically believe in both God and Immortality. God makes human immortality possible; while we need immortality to reconcile God's benevolence with earthly suffering. Some moral arguments focus on God; others on an immortal soul. Some philosophers separate the arguments; while others argue that they stand or fall together.[2] I sidestep these controversies.[3] I assume that secular optimism—and Post-Cataclysm pessimism—reject both God and Immortality. So my argument succeeds, in this dialectical context, if it establishes either God or Immortality. Both God and Immortality play the same role—offering something eternal beyond the human present that (a) survives the Cataclysm; and (b) grounds human meaning.

The basic Post-Cataclysm theist argument is simple:

1. *Theoretical possibility*: There is no compelling theoretical case against theism. No evidential, explanatory, metaphysical, scientific, or other argument rules out theism.

Many practical arguments deploy much stronger versions of this premise. For instance, Kant himself argued that theoretical reason leaves all questions of God and immortality entirely open—and it is only then that practical reason enters the picture. By contrast, I think practical arguments still make sense even when theoretical reason has something to say—so long as theoretical reason does not decisively settle the question.

2. *Conditional premise*: If there is no compelling case against theism, and if theism is essential for a meaningful life, then it is reasonable to believe in theism.

Again, stronger versions are available. For instance, Kant himself argues that belief in Freedom, God, and Immortality is necessary for the intelligibility of the

---

[1] On Kant's original moral arguments, see, e.g., White, *Commentary*, pp. 267–269; Sullivan, *Immanuel Kant's Moral Theory*, pp. 142–144; Beach, 'The Postulate of Immortality in Kant: To What Extent Is It Culturally Conditioned?'; Guyer, *Kant*, chapter six: 'Freedom, Immortality, and God: The Presuppositions of Morality'; Irwin, *The Development of Ethics*, volume three, chapter seventy-one, sections 975 to 980; Rossi, 'Kant, Immanuel: Philosophy of Religion'. On moral, practical, or Kantian arguments more generally, see Hare, *The Moral Gap*, chapter three on Moral Faith; Bishop, *Believing by Faith*; Chignell, 'Belief, ethics of'; Adams, 'Moral Faith'; Adams, *Finite and Infinite Goods*, pp. 373–389. I discuss moral arguments myself in Mulgan, *Purpose in the Universe*, pp. 301–322.

[2] Metz, 'Meaning in Life'.

[3] I also sidestep many other controversial questions, including the following: What is the afterlife like? Does theism need pre-existence as well as afterlife? Must the afterlife be personal? Must it be *eternal*?

very idea of practical deliberation. By contrast, I think the loss of sufficient meaningfulness can also motivate a moral argument. Much depends on when we permit practical leaps of faith—when is it reasonable to leap beyond our evidence for practical, moral, or pragmatic reasons?

> 3. *Pre-Cataclysm alternatives*: Before the Cataclysm, belief in God or Immortality was *not* essential for a meaningful life—because the secular future provided a plausible alternative route to sufficient meaning.
> 4. *No Post-Cataclysm alternatives*: By contrast, after the Cataclysm, belief in God or Immortality *is* essential for a meaningful life—because the removal of the indefinite human future undermines the only plausible secular routes to a meaningful life.
> 5. *Reasonable theism*: Therefore, it is reasonable to believe in God and/or Immortality after the Cataclysm, even if it was not reasonable to do so before the Cataclysm.

This modest formulation leaves open the possibility that there were many other plausible Pre-Cataclysm arguments for theism—and that those arguments remain plausible today. It merely insists that, while considerations of meaningfulness left the question open before the Cataclysm, they now decisively favour theism.

The style of argument is familiar, and I think it is successful. The argument goes through if we accept all four premises.

Presentist: That's a big 'if'!

Theist: Of course. But note that my Post-Cataclysm theist argument borrows its third and fourth premises from the Post-Cataclysm pessimist arguments of our previous debate. All pessimists accept my fourth premise. They agree that, after the Cataclysm, there are no satisfactory secular routes to a meaningful life. And *Post-Cataclysm* pessimists also endorse my third premise. Unlike perennial pessimists, they think that secular meaning *was* available before the Cataclysm. While some pessimists reject the very idea of a meaningful human life, *Post-Cataclysm* pessimists cannot.

Post-Cataclysm Pessimist: I'm sure we will disagree about a lot of that! But before we discuss the argument, can you say a bit more about how it is meant to work *in practice*?

Theist: Imagine an agnostic person who is unsure whether or not God exists. Before the Cataclysm, they find sufficient meaning in future-directed projects whose meaning is grounded, following Scheffler, in ongoing human traditions stretching indefinitely into the future. This person therefore has no need to worry too much about whether or not God exists. Unfortunately, the Cataclysm deprives *this* person of both their current meaningful projects and the background story that gives those projects meaning.

The theist now says to this person, 'Don't despair! Your Pre-Cataclysm projects are gone, along with their Pre-Cataclysm source of meaning. But you can replace them with new projects whose meaning is grounded, not in the human future, but in God. Therefore, a reasonable leap of faith to belief in God would allow you to construct a new meaningful life.'

Now consider a different person, who built their meaningful Pre-Cataclysm life around present-focused projects—but who grounded the *meaning* of those projects in ongoing human traditions à la Scheffler. Before the Cataclysm, this person also had no reason to worry about God's existence. After the Cataclysm, things are not so good. This person's projects remain available, but they have lost faith in them.

The theist says to *this* person, 'Don't despair! God provides an alternative, more secure, source of meaning for your existing present-focused projects. Therefore, a reasonable leap of faith to belief in God would allow you to continue to find your Pre-Cataclysm life meaningful.'

Theism offers each of these imaginary people something closer to what they have lost than any atheist alternative could offer. Atheists and agnostics are attracted to future-directed projects, and to future-dependent meaning, because they need to find meaning by connecting themselves to *something* beyond their own present lives. God offers the same kind of meaning, only more securely. In particular, God offers *transcendent* meaning that is completely unaffected by the Cataclysm.

Post-Cataclysm Pessimist: I do accept your third and fourth premises. And I am happy to grant, at least for the sake of the present argument, that, if God and Immortality were credible, then they might provide sufficient alternative meaning. But I do not accept the conjunction of your first two premises. Personally, I would reject both premises. I think there is a decisive case against theism. Indeed, I will argue in Section 2.3 that the case against theism is much stronger after the Cataclysm.

Theist: I agree that a committed atheist—someone who thinks theism is hopeless—is unlikely to find my argument very interesting. Just as the committed theist who finds *atheism* hopeless would have been impatient during our previous debate. My argument presupposes that our universe is *religiously ambiguous*.[4] Theism and atheism are both reasonable interpretations of the available evidence—competing credible ways to read our cosmos. We therefore cannot

---

[4] On religious ambiguity, see McKim, 'On Religious Ambiguity'; Mulgan, *Purpose in the Universe*, pp. 8–13; 261–279.

expect knockdown arguments or conclusive proofs, but rather a recalibration of the delicate Pre-Cataclysm balance between competing considerations.

In any event, we return to the independent credibility of theism in the next section. For the sake of argument, I therefore suggest we take my first premise as common ground—at least for now.

Post-Cataclysm Pessimist: Setting aside the question of theism's theoretical credibility, I simply don't find any moral, practical, or Kantian argument intelligible. You can't help yourself to theoretical claims just because they are practically useful! I reject all comforting 'leaps of faith'. I agree with Sidgwick's caustic verdict on Kant:

> I am so far from feeling bound to believe for purposes of practice what I see no ground for holding as a speculative truth, that I cannot even conceive the state of mind which these words seem to describe, except as a momentary, half-willful irrationality, committed in a violent access of philosophic despair.[5]

If life is meaningless without God and Immortality—and if we lack sufficient theoretical, evidential, explanatory, or empirical reasons to believe that God exists and/or that we are immortal—then we must accept that our lives are meaningless. We are alone in a cold, uncaring, dying, purposeless universe. We have always known this. The Cataclysm just brings it home. Before the Cataclysm, we could seek meaning in the human future. Now we cannot. Therefore, we must now accept that life is meaningless.

Theist: Practical, moral, or Kantian arguments are very controversial. Many theists regard them as an inadequate substitute for real faith, revelation, or robust metaphysical argument. We should know that our Redeemer lives—not just posit this as a necessary practical precondition for the possibility of deliberation (whatever that means). I prefer to see revelation, theoretical reason, and practical argument as three independent supports for theism. Some theists are persuaded by experience, or by metaphysical or explanatory argument, or they just find themselves believing or trusting that God exists.[6] But it doesn't hurt to add that we *also* have compelling practical reasons, because we need God to escape despair.

Suppose you really did think both (a) that a meaningful life is only possible if P; and (b) that our universe is ambiguous with respect to P—that P is an open possibility. Wouldn't it then make sense to endorse P—to internalise it,

---

[5] Sidgwick, *The Methods of Ethics*, book four, chapter six, p. 507.
[6] cf. Plantinga's argument that belief in God can be 'properly basic'—and therefore it can be reasonable to believe in God without any direct evidence or argument (Plantinga, *Warranted Christian Belief*, pp. 167–198).

presuppose it, adopt it as a practical presupposition, make a leap of faith to it, embark on a doxastic venture, train yourself to believe that p, and so on?[7]

Recall my imaginary person whose actual projects are present-focused and self-contained—but who only finds those projects *meaningful* if they are grounded in something beyond the human present. To keep going, that person needs some *hope* in something beyond the present. Before the Cataclysm, the human future offered that hope. After the Cataclysm, only God can. So this person relies on a hope that God exists. Does that amount to *belief in God*? I don't know. I think that what really *matters* is that, without any hope, this person would not find their own present-focused projects worth doing. And I don't think they are being irrational.

There was a huge Pre-Cataclysm literature on the credibility of leaps of faith, doxastic ventures, or practical arguments. I don't think the Cataclysm adds much to the substance of those debates. I will say a bit more soon about why I think leaps of faith are not irrational. But first I'd like to move on to my main claim. I think the Cataclysm gives these familiar Pre-Cataclysm debates *a new significance*—because it raises the likelihood that belief in God and Immortality *is* necessary for a meaningful life.

Presentist: This brings us to your third and fourth premises. Perhaps you could explain your arguments for them?

Theist: I won't summarise the many Pre-Cataclysm moral arguments for God and/or Immortality.[8] I merely sketch three of them:

1. *Morally coherent universe argument.* We can only lead meaningful lives if we believe that we inhabit a *morally coherent* universe where personal fulfilment and moral obligation are not incompatible, and where virtue is not routinely unrewarded. This clearly doesn't happen in this life. Therefore, our universe is morally coherent only if a benevolent God presides over a just afterlife.
2. *Significant difference argument.* Unless I make some significant difference to the universe, my life is in vain. Given the vast (perhaps infinite) size of the cosmos, no finite earthly contribution could ever be significant *from the point of view of the universe*. An infinite contribution is required. But only an immortal being could make an infinite contribution. Therefore, my life is in vain unless I am immortal.

---

[7] The notion of a 'doxastic venture' is from Bishop, *Believing by Faith*.
[8] For further discussion, and references to specific arguments, see Mulgan, *Purpose in the Universe*, pp. 307–308. On the relationship between meaningfulness, God, and personal immortality in general, see Mawson, 'Recent Work on the Meaning of Life and Philosophy of Religion'; Mawson, *God and the Meaning of Life*; Metz, 'Meaning in Life'; Metz, 'The Meaning of Life', section 2.2 'Soul-Centered Views'; Metz, *Meaning in Life*, part two: 'Supernaturalist Theories of Meaning in Life', pp. 75–161; Metz, *God, Soul and the Meaning of Life*.

3. *Transcendent connection argument*: My life is meaningless unless I connect to something eternal beyond this physical world. This can only happen if either (a) I enjoy some connection to God; or (b) I am immortal.

In short, our human lives are meaningless and/or morally incoherent if we do not either survive death or ground our projects in God.

Presentist: Unsurprisingly, I don't agree. And I don't see where the Cataclysm comes in. Moral coherence, significant difference, and transcendent connection are clearly impossible standards for *any* secular project to meet. So how could the loss of the human *future* make any difference?

Theist: Some theists would agree that only God (and/or an immortal life) could possibly offer any worthwhile meaning. At the other end, some atheists insist that present-focused human activities are sufficient. My intermediate position, which I share with the Post-Cataclysm pessimist, makes two claims. (1) A meaningful human life *does* demand something beyond the human present—some connection to a greater whole that already transcends, not only my present life, but also my present concerns. However, (2) this transcendent source of meaning does *not* have to be eternal or supernatural.

In other words, I think the Pre-Cataclysm arguments for God and/or Immortality over-reached. There *was* a serious this-worldly alternative that offered a sufficient amount of (broadly) the same kind of meaning. But that alternative is now lost.

The indefinite human future was always the obvious alternative for those who reject God and Immortality but recognise the need for transcendence. If this life is all we have, then our lives do seem flat and unprofitable. We need *something* beyond this life to give us hope and meaning. This thought is not peculiar to theism—it is shared by multigenerationalists, pessimists, and many others. Our previous debate explored several arguments that the human future is a substitute for God and/or Immortality. Scheffler, Hartmann, Johnston, and Mill all seek—more or less explicitly—to replace supernatural meaning with something as close as possible to it.

Presentist: Theists who emphasise personal *immortality* have always regarded *any* this-universe-based afterlife as inadequate—thanks to the inevitable eventual heat death of the universe. For *those* theists, the Cataclysm surely makes no difference!

Theist: Yes. But I have never found that objection persuasive. I think trillions of years *would* be long enough for cosmic justice, the best possible human approximation to perfect virtue, a cosmically significant contribution, or whatever else we want an eternal afterlife to provide. I'm not sure we can even *imagine* the difference between living for trillions of years and living forever. And *that* is why the

Cataclysm matters. Whether or not a trillion years is as good as eternity, two hundred years are not. And, of course, things are even worse for the *last* generation. They cannot transcend this life in this world at all.

Presentist: You talk a lot about 'transcendence'. What exactly is that?

Theist: I think we can usefully distinguish three senses of 'transcendent meaning'. In the strongest sense, meaning must be grounded in *something beyond the physical universe*—such as God, Platonic Forms, or Immortal Souls. In this sense, transcendent meaning is not available within any secular worldview. In the weakest sense, meaning only has to be grounded in something outside the individual's own life. In this sense, present-focused projects that involve other people provide some kind of 'transcendence'. In my present remarks, I am using a third, intermediate sense, where transcendent meaning requires something beyond the present human generation—but not necessarily beyond the physical universe entirely. Our generation as a whole seeks a meaning beyond ourselves. Before the Cataclysm, this kind of transcendent meaning was available *either* through intergenerational human connections *or* through connections to God. But after the Cataclysm, only God—or something else beyond the physical universe—can enable the last generation (in particular) to transcend itself.

Perennial Pessimist: I reject your argument for a different reason. I deny that either God or Immortality could make any difference. Life is intrinsically meaningless because the very idea of a 'meaningful life' is incoherent. Adding a God who created the whole pointless farce would not help.

Presentist: I take the opposite view. I reject the overblown implicit standard of meaningfulness at play here. If there is no God, then our lives are not *cosmically meaningful*. But so what? *Cosmic* meaningfulness is not necessary, attainable, helpful, or indeed intelligible. *Human* meaningfulness is another thing altogether. It does not rest on gods, cosmic purposes, or future lives. We are finite, physical creatures who must (and can) find meaning in present-focused activities: immediate pleasure, compassion for others, and goals that we can accomplish in this world within our own lifetime. If we strive for some 'meaning' beyond our reach, then we will be disappointed. But we can find more than enough that is worth doing—and worth living for—much closer to home.

I deny that the Cataclysm has robbed life of any kind of meaning that humans can enjoy. So your argument leaves me unmoved. I find present-focused secular activities sufficient for *human* meaning. I gave my reasons in the previous debate. Is there anything more to say?

Theist: I think there is more to say. Theists and atheists disagree all the way down. We disagree, not just about what sources of meaning are available, but also about how much meaning, or what kind of meaning, is necessary for a truly meaningful human life.

Consider an analogy inspired by cosmological arguments for theism. For materialist atheists, this physical universe is the whole of reality. Therefore, it is obviously something that can exist 'on its own'. Atheists regard this universe as the most solid thing imaginable—and are thus happy to accept the existence of this physical universe as a brute fact. Why shouldn't the most solid imaginable thing exist? By contrast, for theists the physical universe is fragile, contingent, transient, and ephemeral when compared to the transcendent, ultimate, eternal reality of God. It only exists at all because God consistently maintains it in being. Theists thus naturally regard the existence of such a fragile, contingent universe as crying out for explanation. I think this difference in perspective explains philosophers' different reactions to cosmological arguments better than almost anything else. This is also perhaps why *former* theists find such arguments intriguing in a way that people who have never taken theism seriously do not.

Post-Cataclysm Pessimist: We consider cosmological arguments in the next section. What is the connection to your moral argument?

Theist: I think a similar difference in perspective underlies debates about meaning. Theists' paradigm of a meaningful human life involves an eternal post-mortem communion with the divine; while atheists have never imagined anything beyond the secular physical world and its pursuits. It is no surprise that all theists find present-focused secular substitutes unsatisfying; while many atheists find them fully satisfactory.

Presentist: But then we just reach an impasse.

Theist: That depends how ambitious our moral argument is. My argument will not convince atheists who cannot imagine a better world. But it might convince agnostics, especially former theists or doubtful theists or others who have felt the need for something that transcends the present. And it will certainly reassure anyone whose faith in the secular human future has been destroyed by the Cataclysm and who cannot find sufficient meaning in the human present.

I have framed my Post-Cataclysm theist argument in terms of necessary conditions for a meaningful life. On those terms, I must claim that something outside the human present is *necessary* for every meaningful human life. A more modest argument would acknowledge that there are different kinds of meaning; but then insist both (a) that my intermediate 'transcendent meaning' that transcends the present generation is one very important kind of meaning; and (b) that after the Cataclysm *that* kind of meaning can only be founded in God or Immortality.

Presentist: But once you concede that other kinds of meaning are sufficient for a meaningful human life, your leap of faith loses all legitimacy. If I can enjoy a meaningful life without God, then why posit God simply to make *extra* kinds of meaning available?

Theist: I think personal history matters at this point. If your life is already built around non- transcendent meaning, then perhaps *you* have no reason to worry about God or Immortality. But my target audience is not the committed, satisfied, presentist atheist. It is rather the agnostic who built their Pre-Cataclysm life on future-dependent meaning—and who now seeks a new kind of transcendent meaning. For that person, the shift to purely present-dependent meaning may be too hard. A leap to God or Immortality is then not absurd, as it offers this person's only hope of retaining something like what they have lost.

In Pre-Cataclysm debates, the human future appears as a substitute for God or Immortality—offered to those who have lost faith in the latter. After the Cataclysm, the reverse is the case. God and Immortality is now a substitute for those who have lost faith in the human future!

Multigenerationalist: I see things differently. I agree with both the theist and the Post-Cataclysm pessimist that a meaningful human life demands *something* beyond the human present; and I agree that this kind of transcendent meaning *is* threatened by the Cataclysm. But I think we can find adequate substitutes in our abbreviated human future *without making supernatural leaps*. That is a central theme in my later lectures on multigenerationalism.

Personally, I am agnostic between theism and atheism. But I do think that if theism is to survive after the Cataclysm, then it needs a much more radical revision—and that this revision itself must be a multigenerational project. I return to *that* thought in Section 2.4 of this debate.

Post-Cataclysm Pessimist: As I said earlier, my response to Post-Cataclysm theism, apart from scepticism about the very idea of Kantian practical arguments, is to attack your first premise and deny religious ambiguity. And that brings us to our next section.

2.3 The New Case for Atheism

Post-Cataclysm Pessimist: I agree that, if theism were credible, then it would ground a reply to pessimism. If God exists, then human lives can be meaningful and worthwhile. And I concede that, *before* the Cataclysm, our universe was religiously ambiguous—theism was one credible view. However, the Cataclysm has tipped the balance decisively against theism.

The Cataclysm strengthens the case for atheism—and thus for Post-Cataclysm pessimism—in two general ways. First, the Cataclysm is not what we would expect to find in a universe that had been created by a benevolent, perfect God. Therefore, the Cataclysm strengthens atheist arguments from evil and scale—and/or it weakens theist replies to those arguments (Sections 2.3.1 and 2.3.2). Second, the Cataclysm reveals that our universe is much less remarkable, valuable, or astonishing than people thought before the Cataclysm. Therefore, the Cataclysm weakens theist cosmological or teleological arguments whose starting point is the claim that the existence of our universe cries out for explanation (Section 2.3.3).

Theist: I will reply as follows. First, if theism had a satisfactory reply to arguments from evil and scale before the Cataclysm, then it has one still. Second, even if the Cataclysm reveals our universe to be less valuable then Pre-Cataclysm people thought, it does not render our universe less *remarkable* in the sense that matters for the most plausible Pre-Cataclysm theist explanatory arguments.

2.3.1 A New and Unprecedented Evil

Post-Cataclysm Pessimist: Our overarching theme is *explanation*. Theism and atheism offer competing explanations of the existence and nature of the physical universe, and the fate of humans within it. I will focus on five Pre-Cataclysm explanatory arguments: two atheist arguments (evil and scale) and three theist arguments (cosmological, specific design, and fine-tuning).

We begin with the most familiar atheist argument—the argument from evil.[9] Atheists argue that this is not the universe a benevolent God would create. Our world contains evils that an omnipotent benevolent deity could and would prevent. The presence of such evils therefore logically contradicts (or at least provides strong evidence against) the claim that our world was created by God. The Cataclysm is clearly a natural evil on an unprecedented scale. Therefore, it strengthens the best Pre-Cataclysm arguments from evil. A benevolent omnipotent God might conceivably allow many bad things to befall humanity, but the Cataclysm is surely not one of them!

Theist: Although it is the obvious place to start, I think the argument from evil is irrelevant. The Cataclysm is not a new kind of evil, but merely a striking new *example*. It is especially salient *to us*, of course—but then the Lisbon earthquake was especially salient to the philosophers of 1755.

Either theism had an adequate accounting of existing evils before the Cataclysm or it did not. If not, then theism was already unacceptable. But if we already possess an otherwise adequate response (whether a *theodicy* that presents God's *actual* reasons for permitting evil, or a more modest *defense* that suggests God's *possible* reasons), then why *wouldn't* it cover the Cataclysm? Is imminent human

---

[9] cf. Mulgan, *Purpose in the Universe*, chapter eight, pp. 220–260. From the vast literature on evil, I have learnt most from Adams, *Horrendous Evils and the Goodness of God*; Bishop and Perszyk, 'The Normatively Relativized Argument from Evil'; Oppy, 'Arguments from Moral Evil'; Dougherty, *The Problem of Animal Pain*; and van Inwagen, *The Problem of Evil*.

extinction really the worst thing that has ever happened? Other species have gone extinct; there have been other mass extinction events; and many people have endured horrendous suffering, often at the hands of their fellow humans. Is the Cataclysm a greater *evil* than the Holocaust or other great atrocities?

The Cataclysm causes a vast number of very familiar evils—individual deaths, the destruction of specific projects, cultures, traditions, peoples, nations, etc. But if Pre-Cataclysm theism was credible, then it already accounted for all these kinds of evils. And the number of particular deaths and destructions that occurred in the aeons before the Cataclysm outnumbers the number who will die at the end.

Post-Cataclysm Pessimist: But the Cataclysm *is* a new evil in one vital respect. Alongside billions of individual deaths, and the loss of many individual cultures and traditions, it *also* causes the extinction of humanity per se.

Theist: I don't think human extinction bothers theists nearly as much as atheists. As I said earlier, theists and atheists see the world very differently. We often talk past each other—using the same words in different ways. For atheists, this physical universe is *the whole world*—it is all that there is. So of course its destruction—or at least the removal of all sentient life within it—strikes *atheists* as the worst thing imaginable. But for theists, this physical universe has never been the whole world, or even the most important part of it—neither for God *nor for us*. Human extinction is neither the end of conscious life nor the end of the human story.

Every plausible Pre-Cataclsym theodicy includes a *personal afterlife*. Theists have long realised that nothing in this physical universe could possibly explain, redeem, compensate, or justify the amount and distribution of suffering, injustice, and evil that we see in this life. If God's plan is just, then it must involve another life.

Obviously, its commitment to a personal afterlife raises the metaphysical costs of theism. For some, the price is too high. But there is a definite upside to theism's reliance on the afterlife. Once we grant a personal afterlife, the Cataclysm no longer deprives *anyone* of the future that really matters *to them*.

As I said earlier, some Post-Cataclysm theists argue that the Cataclysm teaches us a valuable new lesson about God's plans. In principle, the Cataclysm *could* then be justified even if it is a new and unprecedented kind of evil. Perhaps God needs this new evil to teach a new kind of lesson. After all, how *else* could God teach us that we must bring the human story to a good end soon?

Post-Cataclysm Pessimist: But then theists would be admitting that the Cataclysm makes *some* difference to arguments about evil and theodicy—which is what you denied earlier.

Theist: Yes. That is why I am reluctant to go down this path myself. I don't put any weight on this argument myself.

Post-Cataclysm Pessimist: I don't think theists can simply dismiss the Cataclysm as irrelevant to theodicy. Anecdotally, many people have lost faith in God—or gods or whatever else—thanks to our impending doom.

Theist: I concede that the Cataclysm has had a significant *psychological* impact. It *has* undermined some people's faith in God. Some former theists can no longer believe that everything that happens is part of some greater plan. But that psychological impact cuts both ways. As I argued in Section 2.2, while some have lost religious faith, many more have lost *secular faith*. And theists have greater intellectual resources to cope with this loss than many atheists do.

In short, I agree that evil-based challenges to theism remain powerful. And perhaps more people are more focused on those challenges since the Cataclysm. But that is partly because more people now *want* to believe in God—for reasons I set out in the previous section. The Cataclysm is a reminder that we inhabit a harsh cosmos where meaning is hard to find. But it doesn't ground any new objection to theism.

2.3.2 Is our Post-Catastrophe Universe Too Empty?

Post-Cataclysm Pessimist: My second explanatory argument against theism—the argument from scale—received comparatively little Pre-Cataclysm philosophical attention.[10] However, it reflects a common intuition that has captured our Post-Cataclysm imagination. As it is less familiar, I illustrate this argument via a contrasting pair of quotations from two Pre-Cataclysm atheist and Christian philosophers:

> Is the universe as it is revealed to us by modern science roughly the sort of universe which we would antecedently expect the God of traditional theism to create?... The short answer to this is 'No'. In almost every respect, the universe as it is revealed to us by modern science is hugely unlike the sort of universe which the traditional thesis would lead us to expect.[11]

> The sheer size of the universe is no reason to depreciate the significance of the evolution of mind in one tiny corner of one solar system in one galaxy among myriads. The quantitative dimensions of the physical base of the evolution of life, consciousness, and intelligence are totally irrelevant to the question of the significance of these qualitative developments.[12]

---

[10] For an overview of treatments of the argument, see Vainio, 'The Argument from Scale Revisited'. The most sustained defense is Everitt, *The Non-Existence of God*, pp. 213–226; cf. Mulgan, *Purpose in the Universe*, pp. 193–219. For an exploration of similar themes from a theological perspective, see Gustafson, *Ethics from a Theocentric Perspective*, especially volume one, pp. 88–99.

[11] Everitt, *The Non-Existence of God*, p. 216.

[12] Hebblethwaite, *In Defence of Christianity*, pp. 11–12.

Theist: Like the argument from evil, the scale argument alleges that our universe has some feature that is incompatible with divine creation. But what exactly *is* that objectionable feature?

Post-Cataclysm Pessimist: Everitt argues (i) that God would create a universe 'on a *human* scale';[13] (ii) that our universe is *not* human-sized; and therefore (iii) that there is no God. He contrasts two possible worlds. In *Genesis World*, human beings occupy a significant place at the centre of the physical universe. We emerge near the beginning, and stay till the end. In *Science World*, the universe has existed for billions of years and will continue for billions more. Human beings emerged only very recently and are unlikely to survive very long. There are billions of galaxies and many billions of stars. Our Sun is one small star in one non-descript galaxy. Life on Earth has existed for several billion years, and humans are a tiny fraction of all living things. And so on. *Genesis World* is human-sized, while *Science World* is not. God would create Genesis World, but we inhabit Science World. When we look at the size and scale of the universe, it is easy to conclude that human beings are insignificant.

Theist: I agree that the *intuition* is easy to grasp. But is the *argument* any good? More generally, do we have *any* reasonable expectations about the kind of physical universe that God would create? As your second quotation shows, Hebblethwaite objects that our only reasonable expectation is that God will create a suitable abode for rational beings like ourselves. We have no good reason to expect a universe of any size, either temporal or spatial. And besides, the Cataclysm tells us nothing *new* about the *size* of the physical universe.

Post-Cataclysm Pessimist: Size alone is not the real issue. If the Cataclysm truly supports the argument from scale, as I believe it does, then we must look elsewhere. I think the *real* atheist worry is that, *if* a God who cared about human beings had created such a vast universe, *then* humanity would have a much more prominent role *within* that universe.[14] If we are so special, why are there so few of us? Why is the universe so sparsely inhabited? If human beings are so central to God's plan, why aren't we everywhere? Surely God would create a universe teeming with life. *This* scale-based argument clearly *is* strengthened by the Cataclysm! We now *know* that future humans will not create a galaxy-spanning supercivilisation lasting billions of years. Our entire story is confined to one tiny fragment of space and time.

Theist: Your summary brings out two key questions. (1) Is this sparsely-populated-universe version of the argument from scale any good? (2) What difference does

---

[13] Everett, *The Non-Existence of God*, p. 215.
[14] Here I draw loosely on Everitt, *The Non-Existence of God*, p. 221.

the Cataclysm make? I assume that you—as a *Post-Cataclysm* pessimist—think the Cataclysm is decisive.

Post-Cataclysm Pessimist: Yes, I do. I think the Cataclysm deprives theists of their most plausible Pre-Cataclysm reply to this argument. First, let me set the scene a bit more. I distinguish three possible complaints about the inhabitants of our universe: *Quantity* (there are too few rational beings), *Variety* (this world lacks variety among rational beings), and *Quality* (this world lacks superior rational beings). Personally, I find the *Quality* complaint the most powerful. Humans are simply too puny to be the main characters in such a vast cosmic tale. We can *imagine* superior beings who would *truly* appreciate and comprehend this vast and complex universe. Once we recognise how good the universe could have been, we see how self-aggrandising it is for contemporary humans to expect to find *ourselves* as its most impressive inhabitants.

We can now see where the Cataclysm plays its decisive role. *Before the Cataclysm*, the obvious place to find an answer to this scale-based argument was *the human future*. Indeed, if humanity continued to develop, evolve, and spread through the universe, then all three possible scale-based complaints (Quantity, Variety, Quality) would be dissolved. We could then say that God *has* created a universe containing vast numbers of rational beings, in very great variety, and including many who are (or will be) superior to us. But those rational beings would all live *in the distant human future*.

This Pre-Cataclysm theist reply retains Leibniz's appealing optimism.[15] Leibniz infamously argued that, as God would create the best of all possible worlds, this world *is* the best. The argument from scale objects that we can imagine better worlds—and therefore this is not the best. Our present theist reply counters that, although human beings currently occupy only a tiny corner of the universe, this is still the best possible world, because it *will* contain vast numbers of future beings whose achievements, existence, or flourishing are genuinely cosmically significant. *The human future* provided a perfectly satisfactory reason for God to create *this* world. As the Cataclysm fatally undermines this best Pre-Cataclysm theist reply, it greatly strengthens the argument from scale.

Theist: Theists have three good replies to your argument: an ad hominem objection to atheist transhumanism; an appeal to extra-terrestrial life; and a rejection of Leibnizian optimism.

First, your argument presupposes that, before the Cataclysm, theists' best option was to join forces with *atheist transhumanists*, and locate God's purpose in

---

[15] Leibniz, *On the Ultimate Origination of Things*; cf. Adams, *Leibniz*, pp. 113–213. For contemporary discussion of Leibnizian optimism, see Adams, 'Must God Create the Best?'; Adams, *Finite and Infinite Goods*, especially pp. 77–82; cf. Wielenberg, 'A Morally Unsurpassable God Must Create the Best'; Rowe, *Can God Be Free?* I discuss optimism myself in Mulgan, *Purpose in the Universe*, pp. 201–210; 'Can the Best Possible World Contain Death?'

the distant human future.[16] But the Cataclysm undermines *atheist* transhumanism entirely. So your argument can't give atheists any comparative advantage over theists *in the search for meaning*.

Post-Cataclysm Pessimist: Of course, that is grist to my pessimist mill. Before the Cataclysm, transhumanism offered the best hope for both theists and *optimistic atheists*. Therefore, the Cataclysm is bad news for *all* optimists.

Escapist: I think transhumanism—whether theist or atheist—can meet this challenge. I agree that the Cataclysm certainly greatly reduces the range of possible transhumanist projects. However, two hundred years is a long time. Post-Cataclysm transhumanists insist that our descendants still have time to create superior superhumans before omega rays hit—and that we should make this our first ethical priority. And, as I will argue in our virtualism debate, we can give our own lives meaning by laying the foundations to enable later generations to inhabit a very different, vastly superior, and much more long-lasting *digital* utopia where even the most ambitious Pre-Cataclysm transhumanist fantasy can come true (Section 9.10).

I therefore reinterpret the dialectic around scale-based arguments. Theists must hope that transhumanist escapism succeeds—because only then can their faith in a benevolent God be vindicated. This is only the best possible world if transhumanist escapism succeeds. God would create the best possible world. Therefore, if God exists, then transhumanist escapism will succeed!

I note in passing that, if theists *need* transhumanism to rebut the argument from scale, then they cannot so easily rely on your *moral* argument from the previous section—because atheists now *do* have a plausible (non-supernatural) source of meaning of their own.

Presentist: I agree with the Post-Cataclysm pessimist that *theist* transhumanism is in trouble. But I don't think *atheists* need transhumanism at all. As I said in the previous section, whatever theists must believe, the rest of us *don't* need to believe that we inhabit a just cosmos or a best possible world. Present-focused projects are sufficient for human meaning, even if our human-sized canvas is too puny to justify divine creation. Therefore, if theists need transhumanism to succeed, then it is theists who should be worried by the Cataclysm, not atheists.

Theist: I agree that relying on transhumanism is a risky strategy—as it always has been. Fortunately, theists don't need transhumanism—because the Cataclysm leaves untouched two better Pre-Cataclysm theist replies to any scale-based argument. The first appeals to extra-terrestrial life.[17]

---

[16] On the philosophical significance of transhumanism, see Agar, *Humanity's End*; Hauskeller, *Better Humans*.

[17] On the fascinating history of debates about the existence of extraterrestrial life, and its relationship to theism, see Crowe, *The Extraterrestrial Life Debate 1750–1900*; and Dick, *Plurality of Worlds*. For an introduction to contemporary debates about the existence of extraterrestrials, see, e.g., Webb, *If*

68 PHILOSOPHY FOR AN ENDING WORLD

Post-Cataclysm Pessimist: I've always thought that theists rejected extra-terrestrial life. Don't you think humans are cosmically special?

Theist: I admit that many specific theist religious doctrines do have difficulty accommodating sentient and/or rational extra-terrestrials. To take one much-discussed example: insofar as Christianity is committed to the uniqueness of the Incarnation, it has long struggled with the possibility of non-human rational souls—a theme that runs through much Roman Catholic science fiction in particular.[18]

However, once we set aside particular doctrinal issues, and focus on larger theological questions, we see a different picture. For instance, Leibniz himself argued that a perfect cosmos must be maximally full of life.[19] We *should* expect God to create other rational beings on other worlds. After all, if the other planets are *not* home to rational beings, then what are they *for*? While the existence of extra-terrestrials may cause problems for the specific doctrines of some religions, theism per se can easily agree that God would fill the universe with life.

Post-Cataclysm Pessimist: Then why don't we see life *everywhere*?

Theist: The sheer size of the cosmos now *helps* theism. In such a vast universe, life could be *abundant* without being *ubiquitous*. Perhaps intelligent life is found in very many places, but never too close together. Perhaps God wants each tool-using, civilisation-building, intelligent species to grow to space-faring maturity without interference from (or interfering with) other intelligent species. We should therefore expect that we share the cosmos with countless rational aliens *who we were never going to meet* even without the Cataclysm.

Post-Cataclysm Pessimist: But we could never know that life was ubiquitous.

Theist: I disagree. On the contrary, if we discover *any* sign of life elsewhere, this would be compelling evidence that life *is* ubiquitous. At any point in time, we will only have searched a tiny fraction of the observable universe. If we discover that life has emerged twice in our tiny sample (once on Earth, and a second time somewhere else), then we can reasonably conclude that life has emerged many times. On the other side of the equation, we will only ever have explored a tiny fraction of the universe. Therefore, even if we never encounter other life, we can never have any real confidence that we are alone. The Cataclysm clearly exacerbates this asymmetry. In the brief time that humanity has left, the search for

---

the Universe Is Teeming with Aliens... Where Is Everybody? Seventy-Five Solutions to the Fermi Paradox and the Problem of Extraterrestrial Life. For a sceptical theist perspective, see Hebblethwaite, *In Defence of Christianity*, pp. 11–12. I discuss philosophical issues relating to extra-terrestrial life in Mulgan, *Purpose in the Universe*, pp. 214–219; and 'The Moral Significance of Extra-Terrestrial Life'.

[18] See, e.g., Roberts, *The History of Science Fiction*, pp. 163–166; 215–218; cf. Rutledge, 'Tempering the Cosmic Scope Problem in Christian Soteriology'.

[19] Crowe, *The Extraterrestrial Life Debate 1750–1900*, pp. 27–30.

extra-terrestrial life can only yield either a positive result or no result at all. In the meantime, I would suggest that, for theists, the Cataclysm actually *raises* the probability that we are not alone, because extra-terrestrial life is even more likely to be essential to God's plan.

Presentist: I'm glad *my* worldview doesn't oblige *me* to gamble on our imminent discovery of little green men!

Theist: Fortunately, neither does mine! The combination of optimalism and extra-terrestrial life is one route that theists could take. But Pre-Cataclysm theists had another, more philosophically robust option that is untouched by the Cataclysm. This is to abandon Leibnizian optimalism entirely—as many Pre-Cataclysm theists did. For instance, Robert Adams argued that God's moral perfection does not oblige God to create the best possible world.[20] God creates, not from a consequentialist desire to maximise value, but from gracious love for individual creatures. And *gracious* love is not proportional to the worth of the recipient, nor to her happiness. 'God could have chosen to create the best of all possible creatures... [But] there is nothing in God's nature or character which would require Him to act on the principle of choosing the best possible creatures to be the object of His creative powers.'[21]

Theists who emphasise divine graciousness are completely untroubled by the Cataclysm. God *could* have chosen to create either (a) superior rational beings; or (b) human beings whose history was not interrupted by the Cataclysm. In crude utilitarian terms, these possible creations would have been 'better'. But a loving gracious God might instead create (c) humans whose history *is* cut short by the Cataclysm. There is no reason for God to choose (a) or (b) over (c). Therefore, the discovery that this is what God *has* done does not threaten theism. The Cataclysm teaches us, not that there is no God, but that the God who created *this* universe is definitely not a consequentialist!

Post-Cataclysm Pessimist: Of course, Adams's argument was controversial before the Cataclysm.[22] Eric Wielenberg puts one objection very well: '[Adams's argument from grace] goes wrong when it moves from the claim that (1) God exhibits the virtue of grace and acts in a supererogatory fashion in actualising the less valuable world, to the claim that (2) God does not exhibit a lack of moral virtue in actualising the less valuable world. The latter claim does not follow from the former.'[23]

---

[20] Adams, 'Must God Create the Best?'; cf. Wielenberg, 'A Morally Unsurpassable God Must Create the Best'; Rowe, *Can God be Free?*; Adams, *Finite and Infinite Goods*, especially pp. 77–82; Mulgan, *Purpose in the Universe*, pp. 201–210.
[21] Adams, 'Must God Create the Best?' p. 324.
[22] Wielenberg, 'A Morally Unsurpassable God Must Create the Best'; Rowe, *Can God Be Free?*
[23] Wielenberg, 'A Morally Unsurpassable God Must Create the Best', p. 52.

Gracious love for individual creatures cannot be God's *only* motivation. God must also care about the excellence of states of affairs. Other things equal, a morally perfect being will aim to create the best possible world. If a gracious God *could* create the most excellent creatures—if grace itself gives God no positive reason to *prefer* less excellent creatures—then God *will* create the best possible world with the best possible creatures *if God has any preference for better possible worlds*.

Theist: This argument sounds too consequentialist to me. Why should theists agree that God values *states of affairs* (whatever those are)? Most theists are not consequentialists.[24] And pure consequentialism—where God's *only* motivation is to produce the best possible world—is clearly incompatible with divine grace.

Post-Cataclysm Pessimist: I agree that an appeal to *pure* consequentialism would beg the question against theism. But what about a *moderate* consequentialism where gracious love is one divine motivation among others? This view is consistent with theism. Surely it is excessive hubris to assume that God has *no* 'dispositions to pursue intrinsically good states of affairs'.[25] But if God has *any* such disposition, then God will prefer the best possible world.

Theist: I still deny that God's dispositions include any responses to utilitarian, consequentialism, aggregate values. From God's perspective, there is no sense in which a world containing more good lives is a better cosmos. I know that sounds incoherent to consequentialists—but it doesn't sound odd to non-consequentialist theists.

In any event, I do insist that the *Cataclysm* adds nothing to this debate. The Cataclysm is only relevant if theism agrees that God evaluates states of affairs in some aggregate way. But any theist who admits *that* has already lost—with or without the Cataclysm. There were arguments on both sides of this debate before the Cataclysm, and the underlying dispute remains. There are *still* arguments on both sides. I don't claim that my theist counter-argument is decisive. But my main point is that *the Cataclysm* makes no difference to the Pre-Cataclysm state of play. Theism's best reply to scale-based arguments was always to reject Leibnizian optimalism. And that reply remains untouched by the Cataclysm.

In addition, there is clear connection between this dispute and our earlier discussion of evil. Leibnizian optimism notoriously makes the problem of evil much harder for theists to solve—and many Pre-Cataclysm theists responded by denying that God creates the best possible world.[26] Of course that move was controversial—but if theists have already made it, then they need not be troubled by other troublesome implications of Leibnizian optimism. If the Cataclysm is

---

[24] Adams, *Finite and Infinite Goods*, especially pp. 77–82.
[25] Wielenberg, 'A Morally Unsurpassable God Must Create the Best', p. 46.
[26] See, especially, van Inwagen, *The Problem of Evil*.

not a new evil, then theists have no *new* reason to abandon Leibnizian optimism—but that doesn't mean we didn't already have decisive reasons to do so.

Post-Cataclysm Pessimist: I conclude instead that, precisely because debate over God's motivations is inconclusive, the fact that it does undermine *other* theist replies means that the Cataclysm *does* weaken theism's response to scale-based arguments overall.

2.3.3 Cosmology, Teleology, and Remarkableness

Post-Cataclysm Pessimist: As well as strengthening atheist arguments, the Cataclysm also weakens positive theist explanatory arguments. These arguments all posit God to explain some fact. They all rely on (often implicit) evaluative claims—and the Cataclysm threatens those claims.

I discuss three simple arguments: cosmological, specific design, and fine-tuning. A *cosmological* argument posits God to explain why there is something rather than nothing, why there is any physical universe at all.[27]

Theist: The Cataclysm is obviously irrelevant here. The argument's only empirical premise is the fact that something exists; and the Cataclysm has no impact on *that* claim!

Post-Cataclysm Pessimist: I disagree. I think it *is* reasonable to find cosmological arguments less persuasive now, because the Cataclysm reduces the credibility of the (implicit) *evaluative* premises such arguments require.

The most popular Pre-Cataclysm atheist reply to any cosmological argument is *brute fact*. Some things just happen to be true. There had to be either something or nothing. There is something. This fact has no further explanation. In the words of one physicist, 'Our universe is just one of those things that happen from time to time.'[28]

In turn, many Pre-Cataclysm *theist replies* to this brute fact objection explicitly introduce *evaluative* claims. For instance, Richard Swinburne argues that God's creation of a physical universe is a more palatable brute fact than the existence of an uncreated universe: 'It is extraordinary that there should exist anything at all. Surely the most natural state of affairs is simply nothing: no universe, no God, nothing. But there is something.'[29] Swinburne presumes that *some* facts can be

---

[27] My discussion of cosmological arguments draws heavily on Mulgan, *Purpose in the Universe*, chapter three, pp. 65–98. My own thinking about these arguments has been especially influenced by Nozick, *Philosophical Explanations*, pp. 115–164; Swinburne, *The Existence of God*, pp. 133–152; and the works of John Leslie: *Value and Existence*; *Universes*; *Infinite Minds*, pp. 155–188.

[28] Tyron, 'Is the Universe a Vacuum Fluctuation?' p. 244.

[29] Swinburne, *Is There a God?*, p. 48.

accepted without explanation, while others are 'too remarkable' to be brute facts. But that, in turn, presupposes some *objective criterion* of remarkableness.

I leave the dialectic here for the moment—because the role of evaluative claims is even clearer in our two *teleological* arguments:[30]

1. *Specific design argument*: This universe contains living things. This remarkable fact cries out for explanation. The best/only explanation is that this universe contains life because it was created by God. Therefore, God exists.
2. *Fine-tuning argument*: This universe is governed by physical laws. In a universe like this one, it is not remarkable that life emerged via natural evolution. But it *is* remarkable that there exists a universe where *that emergence itself* is not remarkable. In other words, it is remarkable that our universe is 'friendly-to-life'. The best/only explanation for *this* remarkable fact is that this universe is friendly-to-life because it was created by God. Therefore, God exists.

These arguments explicitly cite the remarkableness of what is to be explained—either the existence of life, or the purely natural emergence of life.

And *this* is where the Cataclysm comes in. It weakens all theist appeals to evaluative claims in two ways: deep and shallow. The deep way is that the Cataclysm itself *casts doubt on the very idea of objective values*. The shallower—more obvious—worry is that, even if we do admit objective values in general, we can still reject *particular* value claims. I begin with this shallower worry.

On any plausible theory of value, the Cataclysm greatly *reduces* the amount of value in the universe. Suppose—for the sake of the present argument—that human beings are the only rational beings in the cosmos. If so, then a universe containing the Cataclysm is much less valuable than a universe without any Cataclysm—because the latter *contains many more happy lives*. Indeed, our Cataclysm-containing universe is *astronomically* less valuable than an alternative Cataclysm-free universe where human civilisation covers the galaxy for billions of years. The Cataclysm thus greatly reduces the likelihood that this physical universe passes the *threshold of remarkability* necessary to reasonably reject brute fact. Therefore, the Cataclysm reduces the strength of any cosmological, specific design, or fine-tuning argument.

Theist: I agree that the Cataclysm reduces the total utilitarian value of this physical universe. But this is irrelevant to theist *explanatory* arguments. No cosmological,

---

[30] My discussion of teleological arguments draws heavily on Mulgan, *Purpose in the Universe*, chapter four, pp. 99–129. My own thinking about these arguments has been especially influenced by Collins, 'Evidence for Fine-Tuning'; Mellor, 'Too Many Universes'; Nagel, *Mind and Cosmos*; Leslie, *Immortality Defended*, pp. 77–86; Leslie, *Infinite Minds*, pp. 205–216.

specific design, or fine-tuning argument ever sought to explain the *amount* of value in the universe.

Post-Cataclysm Pessimist: So you deny that theists rely on evaluative claims?

Theist: Not at all. Every theist explanatory argument has some evaluative element. But *remarkableness* was never about quantity. There is no 'threshold of remarkableness' marked on some aggregative utilitarian scale—or on any other scale. As I argued earlier, God does not respond to total utilitarian values (Section 2.3.2). The intuitive sense of wonder that prompts theist explanatory arguments is simply not about the total value of states of affairs. It is remarkable that any fragile, contingent physical universe exists, when there could have been nothing all. And *this* universe is remarkable because it is complex, beautiful, orderly, and contains creatures whose lives can have meaning, value, or cosmic significance. Period. The Cataclysm does nothing to change *these* evaluative facts. The vast majority of logically possible worlds lack the *priceless* value of rational life. These worlds are valueless. The existence of a possible world that *does* contain this value is what cries out for explanation, irrespective of the number or distribution of valuable lives.

It is worth noting that, with the exception of the cosmological argument, theists' evaluative claims are almost never questioned by atheists. Cosmological arguments claim it is remarkable that something exists. Some people (both theists and atheists) do find *this* comparative evaluative claim problematic. Brute fact is a plausible alternative. But remarkableness is much more obvious when the explanandum is the existence of life or the existence of a universe where life can evolve naturally. In these cases, atheists very rarely dispute theism's evaluative claims. Brute fact has never been the preferred atheist reply to any teleological argument. Instead, atheists have sought alternative God-free *explanations*. Most obviously, evolution by natural selection promises a purely naturalistic explanation of the emergence of life—as well as life's diversity and adaptedness. We no longer need God to explain these remarkable facts. Similarly, most atheists counter fine-tuning arguments with *alternative (naturalistic) explanations*—such as those that cite some kind of *multiverse*.[31]

Post-Cataclysm Pessimist: I agree that, setting aside cosmological arguments, Pre-Cataclysm atheists did typically accept their opponents' evaluative claims. But I think they conceded too much too soon. We should push back against

---

[31] Evaluative claims enter the philosophical debate about Multiverse-based replies to the Fine-Tuning Argument for theism in a different way, as theists object that any *atheist* multiverse hypothesis is unconvincing without possible-world-transcending objective values to ground an objective ordering of possible worlds—which in turn is necessary to establish the competing probability claims of multiverse and divine creation (Mellor, 'Too Many Universes'; McGrew et al., 'Probabilities and the Fine-Tuning Argument: A Sceptical View'; Mulgan, *Purpose in the Universe*, chapter three, pp. 117–127). However, I have omitted these issues in the text, as they would take us too far afield.

theism's evaluative claims, rather than simply conceding them. Note how *extreme* those evaluative claims are! It is not enough to glibly say, 'Everyone agrees that the existence or emergence of life is "remarkable"'! Theists and atheists simply do not use that word in the same way. In a successful explanatory argument for theism, the explanandum must be remarkable according to values that are *possible-world-transcendent*. (It is not enough that this physical universe satisfies the subjective values of its own inhabitants, or that it measures up to a standard of value defined with reference to its own particular physical properties.) Of course, *once we have God*, we can ground these transcendent objective values either in God's nature or in God's creative decisions.[32] But if our transcendent objective values depend on God, then we obviously cannot use those values in an argument *for God's existence*. Atheists can—and should—simply reject the very idea of possible-world-transcending objective values.

Presentist: Are you suggesting that we, as atheists, should deny that either the existence of life or its emergence via evolution is remarkable?

Post-Cataclysm Pessimist: Yes and No. I agree that much about life and evolution astonishes us. It strikes us as remarkable. It cries out for explanation. But I don't think atheists must accept that life, the universe, or anything is remarkable *in any possible-world-transcending sense*. At that point, we can reasonably dig our heels in. The claim that there are possible world- (and physical-universe-)transcending objective values is too dubious—and it is simply hubris to claim that human beings have any reliable knowledge of such values.

Theism: I would reply that the burden of proof falls on the atheist. The emergence of life in our universe is obviously remarkable—and theism alone explains why it happened. If atheists cannot even understand the question, then so much the worse for atheism. Furthermore, I don't agree that theists cannot appeal to evaluative claims just because we ground our objective values in God. We have several distinct things to explain: the existence of this universe, the fact that it is remarkably valuable, the nature of objective value, and the fact that humans can know about objective value. Theism explains all of these things, while atheism explains none. If there is an explanatory circle here, it is not a vicious one.

In any event, these are all familiar Pre-Cataclysm debates. You claim that the Cataclysm *adds* something new. I still don't see that that is.

Post-Cataclysm Pessimist: The Cataclysm casts new doubt on theism's possible-world-transcending values. The mere *emergence* of something valuable is not a

---

[32] On the option of grounding objective values in God's *nature*, see Adams, *Finite and Infinite Goods*—especially chapters one and two. On the option of grounding objective values in God's *will*, see, e.g., Murphy, 'Theological Voluntarism'. A third alternative grounds values in God's *motivations* (see Zagzebski, *Divine Motivation Theory*); cf. Mulgan, *Purpose in the Universe*, pp. 52–59. (And, of course, lurking in the background are the notorious Euthyphro Dilemma and the medieval debates between voluntarists and intellectualists.)

plausible object of fine-tuning. Suppose you care about life. You might engineer a universe where life emerged. But you would hardly stop there. You would also ensure that life *flourishes*. Otherwise, why bother? This is why the Cataclysm is an *unprecedented evil*. Unlike other natural processes, the Cataclysm does not change, challenge, or influence the trajectory of terrestrial evolution. It cuts it short. An omniscient omnipotent creator *who valued life* would not do that. Therefore, the Cataclysm suggests that *God* doesn't think life is so valuable! But the idea that *some things* are possible-world-transcendingly valuable *but life is not* is absurd. What could be valuable if life isn't? Therefore, the Cataclysm undermines the very idea of possible-world-transcending values.

Theist: I think this takes us back to our earlier discussion about consequentialism—where I insisted that God is *not* a consequentialist.

Post-Cataclysm Pessimist: I would then say that theists cannot have it both ways. If God is completely non-consequentialist, then how can we make sense of the idea that God is responding to possible-world-transcending values at all?

Theist: I think theists can consistently claim that God chose to create this universe because it contains life—and because God values life—without conceding that God values states of affairs. So I don't agree that theism's meta-ethical picture is really threatened by the Cataclysm. On the contrary, I think that the Cataclysm *does* undermine any *naturalist* moral realism that identifies objective moral facts *with fact about the natural world*—leaving a stark choice between moral nihilism and a supernatural moral realism where objective moral facts lie beyond the physical universe.[33]

There are three basic approaches to meta-ethics: to locate values beyond the physical universe; to locate values within the physical universe; and to reject the very idea of value. Possible-world-transcendent values have two opponents: the moral nihilist who rejects all objective values and the non-transcendent moral realist who identifies objective values with features of this physical universe.

Post-Cataclysm Pessimist: If my argument supports moral nihilism, then that is fine by me! After all, moral nihilism and pessimism go well together.

Presentist: By contrast, I reject both moral nihilism and moral supernaturalism. I don't see how the Cataclym affects the obvious atheist alternative—the only values that we need (and the only values that make sense) are human-sized values located within the same physical universe as everything else. How? *That's* a puzzle I leave to meta-ethicists. Many meta-ethical positions lie between moral nihilism and your very demanding, metaphysically loaded, supernatural moral realism.

---

[33] For an overview of contemporary debates in meta-ethics, see Sayre-McCord, 'Metaethics'. I do not pretend to engage properly with those debates in the text, where I abbreviate a much longer discussion in Mulgan, *Purpose in the Universe*, chapter two, pp. 33–62.

What about non-cognitivism, quasi-realism, constructivism, moral naturalism, non-metaphysically loaded non-naturalism, and so on? Most Pre-Cataclysm meta-ethicists—especially those who were not already theists—would reject both of your extreme 'alternatives'.

Theist: I agree that *some* alternatives are untouched by the Cataclysm. But I still think the Cataclysm is relevant—because it creates difficulties for the naturalist position that is *closest* to possible-world-transcendent value. Once again, the Cataclysm is most problematic precisely for those secular optimists who want to stay as close as possible to the 'lost' worldview of theism. They reject God. But they want to retain objective values that transcend the practices of particular societies, and even the evolved nature of particular species. For instance, one prominent Pre-Cataclysm non-transcendent moral realist view is moral *naturalism*—where moral facts are tied to this universe because they are reducible to *natural facts* that may vary across possible physical universes, but remain constant within this universe.

Presentist: I still don't see the problem. How does the Cataclysm cast any doubt on moral naturalism?

Theist: There are two links between moral naturalist objective values and *the indefinite human future*. The first is methodological. If objective moral facts are *natural*, then they are presumably legitimate objects *of scientific inquiry*. Moral naturalists, who identify moral facts with natural facts, expect those identities to be discoverable by future moral inquiry—indeed, some even identify moral facts *with the natural facts that will be identified with them by future empirical inquiry*.[34] The realisation that the moral facts will never be discovered—and *could* never have been discovered in this universe—then threatens our empirical grip on what those facts are meant to be. When we imagine a world where future moral inquiry continues, we are (in fact) imagining a physical universe very different from this one.

A more direct link between present values and the indefinite future is that transhumanist moral naturalists base *their* objective values on the ideal transhumanist future utopia that retrospectively confers meaning on the whole human story (Section 2.3.2). Remove the very *possibility* of that future utopia, and this particular moral naturalist edifice collapses.

Presentist: Unsurprisingly, I remain unconvinced. Relying on the human future was never a smart move—no more in meta-ethics than anywhere else. Our everyday human-sized values rest on a more secure foundation. We know that pain is bad for creatures like us; that pleasure, desire-satisfaction, and achievement are

---

[34] cf. Boyd, 'How to Be a Moral Realist'; Jackson, *From Metaphysics to Ethics*; cf. Mulgan, *Purpose in the Universe*, p. 43; Mulgan, 'Utilitarianism for a Broken World'.

good for creatures like us; that cruelty is a bad way for us to treat one another; that compassion is virtuous; and so on. We know these things as surely as we know anything. Competing metaphysical stories about the ultimate nature of reality are irrelevant to everyday life—and to normative ethics. If I had to pick a meta-ethic, I might opt either for Parfit's non-metaphysical moral non-naturalism or for some non-realist, quasi-realist, or non-cognitivist option. These views are *very* different from one another. Yet *none* of them is affected by the Cataclysm at all.

Theist: Meta-ethics is a huge topic, and I agree that I have barely scratched the surface. As ever, I would be happy if we agreed that the Cataclysm makes no difference at all. I just wanted to point out that, if the Cataclysm has any impact, it is not obvious that it (only) supports the atheist side of the argument.

Presentist: Personally, I don't see any reason why values should be 'grounded' in anything!

Post-Cataclysm Pessimist: I think there is a deep divide here *among atheists*. I am drawn to pessimism in part because I agree that anti-realists just change the subject; and I don't find non-natural values plausible without God. *Sui generis*, free-standing, objective values raise too many questions. How do they fit into an otherwise purely natural worldview? How can human beings know about them? And so on. While the Cataclysm doesn't directly affect these perennial disagreements, it does raise the stakes. Now that we have fewer routes to meaning, it matters more than ever whether any of them actually works. Without the indefinite human future, we must now choose between the metaphysically un-grounded values of Presentism, the supernaturally grounded values of Theism, and the moral nihilism that leads back to pessimism.

Multigenerationalist: I think there is another alternative. I explore it in the next section.

2.4 Alternatives to Atheism and Theism

Multigenerationalist: In this section, I briefly explore alternatives to both theism and atheism. Atheism and benevolent theism are contraries rather than contradictories. They cannot both be true, but they might both be false. Several Pre-Cataclysm philosophers defended possible 'third ways'.[35] Dissatisfaction with extant theodicies motived some departures from the classical theist omni-God. If

---

[35] On alternative concepts of the divine, see Buckareff and Nagasawa, *Alternative Concepts of God: Essays on the Metaphysics of the Divine*; Diller and Kasher, *Models of God and Alternative Ultimate Realities*; Gasser and Kittle, *Personal and A-Personal Aspects of the Divine*. On the need for a more pluralist, less 'Western-centric' approach to philosophy of religion, see, e.g., Burley, *A Radical Pluralist Philosophy of Religion*; Harrison, *Eastern Philosophy of Religion*.

we are not persuaded that theists can reconcile God's omnipotence and benevolence with this world's evils, then we may weaken either divine omnipotence or divine benevolence. God either cannot prevent all evils, or does not want to. Other alternatives were motivated by engagement with non-Western religions, pre-theist Greek philosophy, and non-traditional pathways within Western philosophy. These include impersonal sources of cosmic purpose, Platonic Forms, eternal cycles of rebirth, nineteenth-century British and German Idealism, process theology, and many others.

In the interests of time, I focus on one alternative account: *ananthropocentric purposivism*.[36] The universe has a purpose, but human beings are completely irrelevant or incidental to that purpose. This non-human-centred purpose could come from a personal creator. But if a *personal* God is too anthropocentric, ananthropocentric purposivism can take other forms—modelled on axiarchism, Idealism, or Platonism.[37]

Ananthropocentric purposivism explains the existence and nature of the universe better than either of its rivals: materialist atheism and benevolent theism. It borrows the best theist arguments against atheism, and the best atheist arguments against theism. Atheism cannot explain the normativity of objective moral facts or the existence of a universe that is fine-tuned for the emergence of life; while traditional benevolent theism cannot explain the presence of evil, the scale of the physical universe, or the lack of more obvious evidence for God's existence.

I suspect that the Cataclysm is a problem, not for theism or purposivism per se, but only for the specific idea that our universe has a *human-centred purpose*. The Cataclysm opens our eyes to alternative cosmic purposes where humanity is not central and God creates in response to non-human-centred criteria of cosmic remarkableness.

I therefore have a different perspective on our present debate. The Cataclysm's primary impact on debates about evil is to reinforce the old lesson that God's purpose is not exhausted by, or even primarily concerned with, what happens to human beings in this life. Benevolent theists respond to the inadequacy of our earthly existence by positing a personal afterlife where God proportions happiness to desert. By contrast, ananthropocentric purposivists seek the divine purpose elsewhere in this universe without reference to human happiness.

Alternative cosmic purposes also decisively change the dialectical situation regarding scale-based argument and extra-terrestrial life. Suppose that, alongside

---

[36] I develop ananthropocentric purposivism in *Purpose in the Universe*; 'Alternatives to Benevolent Theism'; 'Can the Best Possible World Contain Death?'; 'Beyond Theism and Atheism'; and 'Could We Worship a Non-Human-Centred Impersonal Cosmic Purpose?' This debate draws freely on my earlier work. It is very brief and schematic, because I do not want to put too much weight on my own particular alternative. Instead, my goal is illustrate the need to explore all alternatives to traditional theism and atheism.

[37] On axiarchism, see Leslie, *Universes*; Mulgan, 'Beyond Theism and Atheism'.

several billion humans, the universe also contains billions of non-human rational beings who possess the very features that (according to *benevolent* theism) make humans valuable, only to a much higher degree. These aliens are smarter, wiser, more imaginative, more moral, more free, or whatever. If we believe in a benevolent God, then we must explain this state of affairs by insisting that *we* are part of God's reason to create. Ananthropocentric purposivism argues instead that we do not matter; that we are no part of God's reason to create; and that cosmic significance is found (only) in higher rational beings or in other features of the cosmos that are independent of rational life altogether.

The Cataclysm teaches us something sobering about our place in the universe. We are not destined to live among the stars, to colonise the Galaxy, or to reshape the visible universe in our image. The whole of human history is confined to a very small time period on one particular planet. We must then ask what this vast physical universe *is for*. Or more particularly, *who* is it for? For ananthropocentric purposivists, the Cataclysm reinforces the case for believing *that we are not alone*.

Ananthropocentric purposivism urges us to seek cosmic purpose, not in the *human* future, but in something beyond humanity altogether—whether in superior extra-terrestrial life or in features of the universe that transcend life altogether, such as beauty, order, complexity, or elegance.

Turning now to explanatory arguments for theism, I find myself sympathetic to both sides in our present debate. I agree with the Post-Cataclysm Pessimist's atheist critique that explanatory arguments for theism need evaluative premises. I also agree with the theist that the Cataclysm doesn't undermine the *plausibility* of evaluative premises in general. However, I would add that the Cataclysm *should* affect the *content* of our evaluative premises. The Cataclysm teaches us that the correct cosmic standard of remarkableness cannot include the welfare, history, or future trajectory of humanity. The remarkableness of our universe must instead involve the flourishing of extraterrestrials, the fact that the universe is governed by mathematically complex and beautiful laws, the fact that it contains life, or something else about this universe that is, at best, only incidentally related to us.

I reject the anthropomorphism that lies behind both benevolent theist arguments and atheist critiques. Our data is simply the fact that some events in our universe are both extremely unlikely and objectively remarkable. This points to a cosmic purpose. It is mere self-aggrandising caprice to infer that this cosmic purpose fits our own values or expectations. And the Cataclysm clearly teaches us that it does not!

Theist: I worry that, if we allow too great a gap between the purposes of the cosmic creator and our own values, then we lose our grip on our evaluative premises altogether. If humans don't matter, how can we be confident that anything does? More generally, I don't think any non-human cosmic purpose can hope to play *all* the same roles (both philosophical and non-philosophical) that a benevolent God can. An indifferent creator is no substitute for a personal God who cares deeply for each one of us. In particular, your non-human-centred cosmic purpose is no better-equipped to ground human meaningfulness *than atheism is*. What would we gain by supplementing the atheist's meaningless, materialist universe with a cosmic purpose to which *all human interests are irrelevant*?

Multigenerationalist: I agree that, like every other alternative position, ananthropocentric purposivism faces major challenges! But I think we can separate (a) the *values* at play in arguments from evil and scale and (b) the *remarkableness* underlying cosmological and teleological arguments. This separation opens a space for alternative accounts of divine purpose, where God responds to objective remarkableness but not to human-centred values. And this is where the Cataclysm bites. It increases the gap between human-centred value and objective remarkableness. This universe is not particularly valuable *from our point of view*. (It is certainly a long way from being the *best possible* universe from any human-centred perspective.) But it is still remarkable. Therefore, cosmic remarkableness cannot be about us. This is the real impact of the Cataclysm.

Indeed, I would go further. Reflection on the grim reality of imminent human extinction, and other unpalatable features of human life, raises the starker possibility that remarkability and value could come apart completely. At the extreme, a physical universe could be remarkable even if it contained (only) negative value. A universe where living creatures only ever experienced intense agony would be just as remarkable—just as hard to accept as a brute fact—as a blissful universe. Philosophical pessimism, even if it succeeds, does not undermine theist or purposivist explanatory arguments *per se*. It only undermines those specific arguments that seek to prove the existence of an omnipotent *benevolent* God.

Presentist: But now you really have left all human-sized values behind! If God doesn't even notice human suffering, why should we care about God's purposes?

Multigenerationalist: Fortunately, I don't think we need to go to this bleak extreme. Pre-Cataclysm ananthropocentric purposivist philosophers suggested several ways that we *could* build human meaning on a foundation of non-human-centred cosmic purpose.[38] I concede that relying on these tentative explorations demands its own leap of faith. This is not the familiar leap to *belief* that there *is* some non-human-centred cosmic purpose itself; but rather a leap to *confidence* that human projects built around that purpose can deliver genuine human meaning.

In my defense, however, this second kind of leap is ubiquitous. There is always *some* gap between is and ought; between metaphysics and ethics; between the recognition that the world is X and the resolution that the world should become Y;

---

[38] Mulgan, *Purpose in the Universe*, part three, especially chapter eleven.

between the recognition of cosmic values and their incorporation into our human lives. We must all leap across *some* gap. The benevolent theist's gap is so familiar, and seems so small, that we do not notice that we have leapt at all. The *atheist's* gap is the leap *to meaningfulness of any kind* in a purposeless dying universe. This gap is also invisible to us due to its familiarity. Ananthropocentric purposivism clearly requires a bigger leap than benevolent theism does. On the other hand, it requires a *smaller* leap than atheism. Building my life on non-human-centred cosmic values is less ambitious than creating values *ex nihilo* in the inherently meaningless universe of modern materialism.

I don't have a metaphysically compelling and existentially satisfying story about the cosmos and our place in it. No one does. This is why we need a multi-generational approach. We lack satisfactory accounts of cosmic purpose and human value. Every Pre-Cataclysm view is unsettled by the Cataclysm. The task of finding a new account is too large for one generation. We cannot finish the task of discovering the cosmic purpose, and connecting it to human values, by ourselves. We must cooperate with *future people*. Our *present* task is to equip future people to explore the possibility of cosmic purpose—following familiar theist and atheist arguments wherever they may lead. Our best hope—and theirs—is a multigenerational project that is (initially) open-minded about human values, ultimate reality, and cosmic purpose. I return to these ideas in my final lecture on Post-Cataclysm utopias. Before then, however, I have a lot of scene-setting to do.

Philosophy for an Ending World. Tim Mulgan, Oxford University Press. © Tim Mulgan 2024.
DOI: 10.1093/9780191946479.003.0002

3
Lecture One
Introducing Multigenerationalism

Multigenerationalist: In my lectures, I explore a new approach to Post-Cataclysm ethics, which I dub 'multigenerationalism'. Multigenerationalism claims that the present generation should devote themselves to initiating terminal intergenerational projects, especially those that aim to reorient current future-dependent traditions and practices in ways that enable those traditions and practices to still provide meaning even in the last generation.

Multigenerationalism is a thesis in *normative ethics*—a claim about what we ought to do. It is *related* to claims about meaningfulness, value, obligations, and reasons. But it is *distinct* from those other claims. Multigenerationalism is a claim about *what* we ought to do, not about *why* we ought to do it. Of course, any particular argument for multigenerationalism will present some particular reasons why we should do this. But multigenerationalism per se is not committed to any particular explanation.

Multigenerationalism raises several questions. What is a multigenerational project? What is multigenerational reorientation? Why should we consider devoting ourselves to multigenerational projects and reorientations?

I will organise my discussion of multigenerationalism around the following very basic argument:

1. *Conditional Premise*: If multigenerational projects are feasible, and if there are compelling reasons to pursue them, then we should pursue them.
2. *Desirability Premise*: There are compelling reasons to pursue multigenerational projects.
3. *Feasibility Premise*: Multigenerational projects are feasible.
4. *Conclusion*: Therefore, we should pursue multigenerational projects.

The argument is valid. I trust the Conditional Premise is uncontroversial. I address the Feasibility Premise in my fifth and sixth lectures. The present lecture outlines several distinct arguments for the Desirability Premise, based on meaningfulness, intergenerational obligation, rectification, and procreative permissibility. I then explore the procreative permissibility argument at length over my next three lectures.

It is useful to separate a number of different claims and promises that multigenerationalism makes. I first distinguish two claims:

1. *Basic Multigenerational Claim*: We (present people) should devote ourselves to initiating terminal intergenerational projects (which I dub 'multigenerational projects').
2. *Reorientation Claim*: We (present people) should devote ourselves to initiating a particular kind of multigenerational project that aims to reorient our current, inherited, future-dependent traditions and practices so that they remain fit for purpose even at humanity's end.

Reorientation projects are a special class of multigenerational projects. Any argument for the Reorientation Claim is thus also an argument for the Basic Multigenerational Claim. In principle, we could defend the Basic Multigenerational Claim without the Reorientation Claim. However, I will defend both. Unless otherwise specified, when I talk generally about argument 'for multigenerationalism', I have both these claims in mind.

Multigenerationalism also makes a number of promises. Three are especially important:

1. *The Meaningfulness Promise*: If we initiate multigenerational projects (and/or reorientation projects), then we can enjoy meaningful lives.
2. *The Last Generation Promise*: If we initiate multigenerational projects (and/or reorientation projects), then the last generation can enjoy meaningful lives.
3. *The Procreation Promise*: If we initiate multigenerational projects (and/or reorientation projects), then we can permissibly create new people—despite impending human extinction.

Each of these promises is mirrored by an ambitious claim about the superiority of multigenerational projects over their rivals:

1. *The Meaningfulness Claim*: We can enjoy meaningful lives *only if* we initiate multigenerational projects (and/or reorientation projects).
2. *The Last Generation Claim*: The last generation can enjoy meaningful lives *only if* we initiate multigenerational projects (and/or reorientation projects).
3. *The Procreation Claim*: We can permissibly create new people—despite impending human extinction—*only if* we initiate multigenerational projects (and/or reorientation projects).

I defend all these promises and claims. They obviously strengthen the case for the Basic Multigenerational Claim and the Reorientation Claim. If multigenerational projects are necessary for meaningful lives or procreative permissibility, then we do have compelling reasons to pursue them. However, multigenerationalism itself is not committed to all these controversial claims.

Here is a very brief overview of the arguments sketched in this lecture:

1. *Piecemeal arguments*: We should embrace this or that particular multigenerational project or reorientation because this will enhance our well-being and/or constitute an independently valuable achievement.
2. *The meaningfulness argument*: We should initiate multigenerational projects and reorientations because this is necessary for present and future people to enjoy meaningful lives.
3. *The interpersonal obligation argument*: We should initiate multigenerational projects and reorientations because we owe this to one another.
4. *The intergenerational obligation argument*: We should initiate multigenerational projects and reorientations because we owe this to future people.
5. *The rectification argument*: We should initiate multigenerational projects and reorientations because we owe this to past, present, and future people (and to non-human nature) as part of our duty to provide adequate rectification for past historical injustices.
6. *The procreative permissibility argument*: We should initiate multigenerational projects and reorientations because otherwise present people cannot permissibly create a new generation.

My lecture is organised as follows. In Section 3.1, I present a variety of examples of multigenerational projects and reorientations. In Section 3.2, I ask what makes a project multigenerational. In Section 3.3, I explain multigenerational reorientation. In Section 3.4, I briefly explore piecemeal arguments that defend multigenerationalism by defending some particular multigenerational project. In Section 3.5, I explore an ambitious argument for multigenerationalism based on meaningfulness. In Section 3.6, I ask whether we owe it to others to initiate multigenerational projects and reorientations. In Section 3.7, I explore connections between multigenerationalism and rectification for historical injustice. Finally, in Section 3.8, I briefly outline the procreative permissibility argument that I explore at length over my three procreative ethics lectures. I consider this the most powerful argument for multigenerationalism. The procreative permissibility argument claims: (1) that we cannot permissibly create new people unless we are confident that the last generation will enjoy comparable levels of opportunity, value, and meaning; and (2) that only multigenerationalism can justify this confidence. The argument concludes that present people must choose between multigenerationalism and anti-natalism.

3.1 Examples

In this section, I briefly illustrate the kinds of projects I have in mind when I talk about multigenerationalism and reorientation. Some projects are explored in depth in later lectures, others feature in our final debate on virtual futures, while others draw on our two earlier debates.

The Spatiotemporal Reorientation of Philosophy: I begin with our own tradition of philosophy. While many specific philosophical projects are entirely present-focused, philosophy *itself* is future-directed. Philosophers have always aimed both to bequeath a living tradition *to future philosophers*, and also (through their teaching) to ensure that there *are* future philosophers. The last philosophers cannot teach philosophy to a new generation. They can only teach their own contemporaries. Philosophical teaching must be radically reimagined.

This example may seem trivial. Philosophers have always taught their contemporaries. Intra-generational teaching is nothing new. However, the real challenge is to reorient philosophy *without any loss of intergenerational meaning*. This is necessary because philosophy faces stiff competition from other future-directed cultural and intellectual traditions that are attempting similar reorientations. We all seek new disciples in the present instead of the future. These competing reorientation projects cannot *all* succeed. When each tradition sought only a few *future* adherents, they could all co-exist. When everyone seeks to convert their own contemporaries, there won't be enough potential adherents to go around.

Inter-tradition competition drives multigenerational ambition. In isolation, traditions might accept incomplete reorientations that (only) partly replace lost future-dependent meaning. When everyone is doing so, modest reorientations cannot remain competitive. After two hundred years, only those traditions that imaginatively reorient themselves to minimise lost intergenerational meaning will survive. *Every* spatiotemporal reorientation requires future moral *transformation*.

Hartmann at Humanity's End: Eduard von Hartmann's original nineteenth-century philosophy combined pessimism about individual well-being with optimism about meaning (Section 1.7). Even if we cannot be happy, 'we can still find value...through striving for cultural achievement and moral improvement'.[1]

As I argued in our pessimism debate, we can adapt Hartmann's blend of pessimism and optimism to our own times—seeking meaning in collective activities that are not (only) devoted to the promotion of happiness. I agree with the Post-Cataclysm Pessimist that our existing concepts of culture, meaning, and progress do typically presuppose either (a) a focus on improving human well-being; or (b) an indefinite human future into which humanity can 'progress'. We cannot escape pessimism unless we radically rethink what we mean by progress. Multigenerationalist

---

[1] Beiser, *Weltschmerz*, p. 135.

followers of Hartmann do precisely that—seeking to find meaning in building future utopias *that are never designed to last*; or exploring religious and metaphysical re-interpretations that take seriously Hartmann's attempts to found a new religion to overcome both the spiritual poverty of materialist atheism and the out-of-date metaphysics and morality of traditional theism. This ambitious task must take several generations, but it may be our best hope for meaning in our fallen world. In my final lecture, I return to Hartmann-inspired attitudes to non-human nature when I discuss ecological utopias (Section 8.4), and to Hartmann-inspired religious themes when I discuss religious utopias (Section 8.5.2).

Redirecting Johnstonian Self-Concern: According to Mark Johnston, personal identity is constituted by a certain kind of concern for future personalities (Section 1.8). A *good person*, who feels *the very same concern* for *all* future personalities, is less affected by death than a selfish person.[2] In our First Debate, the Post-Cataclysm Pessimist insisted that any consolation Johnston could have offered *before the Cataclysm* is now lost. I replied that I find Johnston's consolation inspiring. *Our* present patterns of self-concern are both self-interested *and future-directed*. Johnston's good person redirects their self-concern impersonally into the future. They care equally about all (good) future personalities. It is very difficult psychological question whether human beings could be trained—en masse—to redirect their self-concern in this way. My alternative *multigenerational* question is whether human beings could instead be trained to redirect the *temporality* of their self-concern. Could I identify myself, not only with *future* good people, but also with all the good people who have lived *before*? If so, the last generation of good people might conquer death by caring as much about past human flourishing as about future flourishing. Can I live on in the 'ongoing rush of mankind' even *after* it has rushed past?

This reimagining of our patterns of self-concern is very ambitious. We could not do it *for ourselves*—and I doubt we can raise a new generation who saw the world (and themselves) in this way overnight. But perhaps it *could* be done over several generations. More generally, whether or not we embrace Johnston's controversial account of personal identity, one promising way to retain intergenerational connections *even in the last generation when no further future remains* is to replace concern for future people with concern for *past people* (and their *posthumous interests*). I explore this general theme in my discussions of rectification, posthumous interests, and utopias (Sections 3.6, 3.7, 6.3.2, 6.3.4, 9.5, and throughout Chapter Eight).

Rethinking Cosmic Purpose: I ended our religion debate by arguing that alternatives to both theism and atheism are better suited to our Post-Cataclysm world.

---

[2] Johnston, *Surviving Death*, p. 15.

If we move away from an insistence on *human-centred* cosmic purpose, then we may find a new worldview that is both (a) more credible than traditional benevolent omni-God theism; and (b) provides a firmer foundation for human values, hopes, and meaning than anything available in the cold, heartless universe of materialist atheism. Every extant alternative account of cosmic purpose and human meaningfulness is problematic—both philosophically and existentially. We cannot now identify a suitable replacement for theism and atheism. However, an open-ended, intergenerational search for the most appealing Post-Cataclysm worldview may be our best way to cooperate with future people in bringing the human story to a good end. I explore this possibility in my final lecture (Section 8.5.2).

Can We Give Non-Human Nature a Good End? The Cataclysm signals, not only the end of humanity, but the end of all life on Earth. All non-human terrestrial species now face imminent extinction. Pre-Cataclysm environmental philosophy placed considerable weight on long-term *intergenerational* properties such as sustainability, ecosystem equilibrium, population health, and species extinction.[3] How can ecosystems, populations, or species flourish when *every living thing* will become extinct within two centuries? Post-Cataclysm pessimists conclude that, after the Cataclysm, non-human nature cannot flourish. Therefore, another Pre-Cataclysm source of meaningful *human* projects disappears. We cannot escape despair by caring for the non-human world. By contrast, multigenerational ecologists seek new ways to rectify our unjust relations with the natural world by bringing non-human nature to a good end. I argue in my final lecture that present and future humans can find intergenerational meaning through a shared commitment to bring non-human nature to a satisfactory end (Section 8.4).

Reimagining Rectification for Historical Injustice: One motivation for a wide range of multigenerational projects is to rectify historical injustice—making amends (to both past people and their descendants) for wrongs inflicted by our predecessors (Section 3.7). I argue that rectification is now more significant than before the Cataclysm; that Post-Cataclysm rectification is more ambitious (because the removal of Pre-Cataclysm constraints opens up new utopian possibilities); and that, after the Cataclysm, rectification is one of our few ways to meaningfully connect with other generations. Rectification is thus one important motivation for all the Post-Cataclysm utopian projects that I explore in my final lecture.

Post-Cataclysm rectification demands future moral *transformation* of a kind that is only possible over several generations. In particular, if (a) rectification for past injustice demands a future just society—a future utopia; and if (b) the establishment of any future Post-Cataclysm utopia itself demands future moral

---

[3] For overviews of environmental philosophy, see Brennan and Lo, 'Environmental Ethics'; Brennan and Lo, *Understanding Environmental Philosophy*.

transformation; then (c) rectification in turn demands future moral transformation. Rectification must now be multigenerational.

Reimagining Liberal Egalitarianism: John Rawls's Pre-Cataclysm theory of justice focused primarily on relations within a particular generation.[4] His explicit discussion of the just savings problem is very brief. You might therefore think that Rawls translates easily to our Post-Cataclysm world. Sadly, things are not so simple. Rawls also devoted much attention to one *essentially intergenerational* property of any social order—namely, its ability to remain *stable* across generations. I argue in my final lecture that removing the need for intergenerational stability has a very destabilising effect on Rawls's overall theory of justice. Post-Cataclysm proponents of Rawls's liberal egalitarianism must reimagine his commitments to moderate redistribution, just savings, and religious pluralism, among many others. The result is an exciting, more ambitious, Post-Cataclysm, Post-Rawlsian utopian vision that I explore in my final lecture (Section 8.2).

Reimagining Libertarianism: In Robert Nozick's libertarianism, justice is all about individual property and self-ownership rights.[5] In my final lecture, I argue that several Pre-Cataclysm critiques of Nozick's libertarianism, considered in sequence, open up exciting new Post-Cataclysm libertarian possibilities (Section 8.3). Removing the need to recognise the rights of future people (and to predict their behaviour) makes possible a much more ambitious, final generation libertarian utopia.

Memorials for Humanity: Many religious traditions emphasise the importance of creating memorials for the dead. Multigenerationalists extend these existing practices to create memorials to humanity itself. Some construct monuments that might have endured if the Cataclysm had not intervened. However, their primary purpose is the creation of an intergenerational collaborative community itself. The fact that the resulting edifice will never be used, enjoyed, or witnessed by anyone is beside the point.[6] Other traditions create deliberately ephemeral memorials—vast mandalas made of grains of sand or points of light—whose whole point is that they disintegrate the moment they are finished. Every religious or cultural traditions has always recognised the transience of this world—and found ways to respond to that transience. Reimagining those responses for the end of the world itself is now a central focus of many peoples' lives.

Procreative Cooperation at Humanity's End: Many defenses of procreative permissibility emphasise the importance to potential parents of entering into parent–child relationships with their future children. A theme of my procreative

---

[4] Rawls, *A Theory of Justice*; Rawls, *Political Liberalism*.
[5] Nozick, *Anarchy, State, and Utopia*.
[6] For instance, Mike Parker Pearson has recently suggested that the primary motivation for the original construction of the Standing Stones at Stonehenge may have been the desire to build social cooperation between communities in different parts of the British Isles, not any desire to create an enduring site of ongoing religious activities (Parker Pearson, *Stonehenge*).

ethics lectures is that this way of defending procreative freedom is problematic after the Cataclysm. No one in the last generation can possibly have children of their own. How can the penultimate generation justify themselves to their own children by citing the importance of parent–child relationships *that those children themselves can never enjoy*? Post-Cataclysm anti-natalists reply that procreation can no longer be justified (Section 4.3.1). By contrast, multigenerationalists replace specific parent–child relationships with broader cooperative relationships between generations (Section 5.2.1). The last generation cannot have children of their own. But they can join with earlier generations in the profoundly meaningful project of working together to bring the human story to a good end. Like my new Johnston-inspired, temporally neutral, good person, these people aspire to live on in those who have gone before.

I hope these examples illustrate the range of multigenerational projects. The rest of my series of lectures provides some philosophical justification for the general approach.

3.2 What Is a Multigenerational Project?

A multigenerational project is one that spans several generations; only comes to fruition after the present generation are gone; and is explicitly designed to end—definitely within 200 years, and possibly sooner. These projects are future-directed (to start with), but not open-ended.

More formally, I define a *multigenerational project* as any project that meets the following two conditions:

1. *Intergenerational Condition*: The project requires the cooperation of at least three generations: a founding or initiating generation, one or more intermediate generations, and a last, final, or concluding generation.
2. *Terminal Condition*: The project has a definite end-point, as opposed to being open-ended. The number of generations may not be specified at the outset, but everyone involved in the project must know that it will conclude soon. In our Post-Cataclysm world, obviously, the maximum number of generations is 'however many you can fit into 200 years'.

There were many Pre-Cataclysm intergenerational projects. By contrast, it is harder to find clear Pre-Cataclysm examples of the terminal condition. Most Pre-Cataclysm intergenerational projects were open-ended. For instance, even if the construction of a building was a project of fixed duration, the use of the building was typically open-ended. However, it is easy to construct imaginary-yet-intelligible fixed duration projects—based on actual historical cases where the initial *construction* phase was arguably more important than any subsequent use.

A multigenerational project is a terminal intergenerational project. Projects can be multigenerational in many different ways, because they can be intergenerational in different ways, and terminal in different ways. I stipulate that a genuinely multigenerational project must be both genuinely intergenerational and genuinely terminal.

Some projects are intergenerational for contingent reasons, such as projects that would take too long for a single generation to complete. Other projects are essentially intergenerational, because their substantive aim is the creation of new generations.

I distinguish *genuinely* intergenerational projects from those that are only *incidentally* intergenerational. Any project that spans several generations is *intergenerational* in a loose sense. However, I use the term more narrowly. If some (timeless) goal is better promoted when more people participate, and if creating new people maximises future participants, then this goal is *actually* best pursued intergenerationally. However if, in theory, an equal number of *present* participants would be just as good, then the project is *not* genuinely intergenerational.

Other projects are *essentially temporally extended*, but still only *incidentally intergenerational*. The goal of terraforming the moon cannot be achieved in a single human lifetime—but only due to contingent facts about human longevity. In theory, a sufficiently long-lived human generation—or a workforce of durable robots—would do just as well. This project is therefore *not* intergenerational for my purposes.

A project is *genuinely intergenerational* only if it intrinsically requires the existence of future people. For instance, the following goal *could not* be pursued without future people: raising a *new* generation who suffer no ill-effects from living closer to humanity's end.

Projects can be *intergenerational* in different ways. They can also be *terminal* in different ways. Some projects are only accidentally multigenerational because, although they are genuinely intergenerational, they are only accidentally terminal. The project could have been open-ended before the Cataclysm, but it happens to be curtailed by the Cataclysm. By contrast, a genuinely *terminal* project is one that *requires* an ending—such as the project of creating a last generation who enjoy meaningful lives, or the project of giving the human story a good end.

In short, a genuine multigenerational project is one that is both essentially intergenerational and essentially terminal. It requires future people, but it also requires an end point.

Multigenerational projects can be either *active* or *passive*. Active projects need later generations who *endorse and continue* the project. A passive project, by contrast, could produce a last generation of contented non-human animals (Section 8.4), or people dwelling in a virtual world unaware that they are the last humans (Chapter Nine). Active projects require future people's voluntary cooperation *in the multigenerational project itself*; while passive projects only need their *existence* or *flourishing*.

Active multigenerational projects are riskier than passive ones, precisely *because* they rely on future peoples' voluntary cooperation. However, as I argue in later lectures, some procreative principles, especially Kantian ones, can only be satisfied by *active* multigenerational projects. If permissible procreation presupposes a *cooperative relationship* with future people, then only active multigenerationalism will do (Section 5.2.1).

The most interesting multigenerational projects last *more than two generations*. These include a founding generation, a last generation, *and one or more intermediate generations*. Whether our project is active or passive regarding the last generation, the cooperation of these intermediate generations is always essential.

Some goals can be pursued in either multigenerational or non-multigenerational ways. Suppose our goal is *that the last generation suffer no last generation burden*. We could pursue this project multigenerationally—working collaboratively over several generations toward the final creation of a new generation who suffer no burden. But we could instead re-train, re-educate, or otherwise re-engineer *the present generation*, so that *we* suffer no burden despite belonging to the last generation. This way of pursuing our goal is anti-multigenerational, because it abandons the possibility of creating any new people.

A central motivation for multigenerational*ism* is that, in many such cases, the multigenerational alternative is superior. Why should we think this? One short answer is that, as collective consequentialists and others have long argued, human nature and human values are more plastic for new generations than for existing ones. If a person's good depends, in part, on their present beliefs, desires, values, or projects, then, even if imminent human extinction *would* be bad *for us*, we can still hope to create new people for whom it would not be bad. (I return to this feature of collective consequentialism in my procreative lectures in Section 6.3.5). I return to the significance of attitudes and values many times throughout my lectures.

Multigenerationalism claims that some genuinely multigenerational projects are feasible, distinctive, and worth pursuing; and that we ought to devote ourselves to such projects.

3.3 What Is Multigenerational Reorientation?

The most ambitious multigenerational projects seek to reorient some future-dependent tradition—aiming to replace future-dependent, intergenerational meaning with something similar that remains available at humanity's end. One motivation for multigenerationalism is the worry that the traditions, practices, and values that we have inherited from past generations will *not* be fit for purpose at humanity's end. We can only pass them down at all if we simultaneously transform them so that they *will* be fit for purpose when the end comes.

A multigenerational *reorientation* is any multigenerational project whose goal is to reimagine, reorient, or reconfigure an existing open-ended, future-dependent tradition, culture, or practice. In principle, this reorientation *could* occur within a generation or two. However, the most interesting and ambitious reorientations are multigenerational ones. Indeed, once we realise what is required, I think the more difficult challenge is to demonstrate, not that we need *at least* two generations, but that the necessary reorientation is possible at all *within 200 years*!

Multigenerational reorientation is thus essentially intergenerational. It is also essentially terminal, because the whole point is to prepare future people to live well at humanity's end. Without the threat of imminent extinction, reorientation would make no sense.

More formally: a multigenerational reorientation is a multigenerational project that meets the following two conditions:

1. *Reorientation Condition*: The goal of the project is to reorient an existing open-ended future-dependent tradition.
2. *Replacement Condition*: The reoriented tradition will be able to play all the same roles in people's lives that the open-ended tradition played before the reorientation.

The replacement condition provides the point or purpose of reorientation. Crucially, the replacement condition covers all participants in the multigenerational project across all generations—the present people who initiate it; the last generation who bring the human story to a good end; and everyone in-between who carries the project on. Everyone involved in the project must benefit from the resulting reorientation of meaning. Otherwise, we cannot reasonably expect them to voluntarily cooperate.

Reorientation is always an *active* multigenerational project—because remaking a tradition over several generations must happen deliberately. Therefore, reorientation requires the voluntary cooperation of all generations. This is why the replacement condition is particularly important.

Reorientation therefore aims to *repurpose* an open-ended tradition. This was *possible*, in principle, before the Cataclysm. Pre-Cataclysm people could have voluntarily embraced early extinction, and then set about remaking their traditions accordingly. Unsurprisingly, this was not a popular activity. By contrast, reorientation comes into its own in our Post-Cataclysm world.

To defend multigenerational reorientation, I must say more about how it works, and why we should attempt it. I explore the *how* in my final two lectures on moral transformation and multigenerational utopias. In the rest of this lecture, I ask why we should even consider embarking on such ambitious projects.

All genuine multigenerational projects involve a risky leap into the unknown. Success depends on the voluntary cooperation of intermediate generations who could opt out at any time. Multigenerational reorientation is especially risky. If it fails, then our successors may be left without any coherent tradition at all. These risks are only worth taking if the potential payoffs are very significant. I will argue that multigenerational reorientation, in particular, *is* worth considering, because it is our only way to meet a number of urgent moral needs.

3.4 Piecemeal Arguments for Multigenerationalism

I will explore four kinds of argument for multigenerationalism: piecemeal, meaningfulness-based, interpersonal obligation, and procreative permissibility.

Piecemeal arguments for my Basic Multigenerational Claim and my Reorientation Claim take some particular multigenerational project and explore our reasons to initiate it. Multigenerational projects are valuable projects that make a distinctive (and perhaps irreplaceable) contribution to our lives. Insofar as people flourish by finding enjoyment and satisfaction by collectively pursing valuable goals, multigenerational projects are worth pursuing. In our Post-Cataclysm world, a successful multigenerational project is a source of satisfaction, enjoyment, and achievement—especially for people (like us) who are already accustomed to finding satisfaction and enjoyment in intergenerational projects and traditions. Pursuing such projects enhances people's well-being. Insofar as we should promote our own well-being—and that of others—we should therefore initiate multigenerational projects.

Multigenerational projects could also be worth pursuing even if they don't directly enhance anyone's well-being. Valuable achievements are good *in themselves*. It is often not irrational to sacrifice some of one's own well-being in order to contribute to independently valuable goals within one's own generation. If so, then it is surely also worthwhile to sacrifice present well-being in pursuit of independently valuable intergenerational goals.

Many people, especially those whose lives are already embedded in intergenerational projects and traditions, will find some piecemeal argument compelling. Many of us are already multigenerationalists. My subsequent lectures offer a series of piecemeal arguments recommending a range of different multigenerational endeavours.

However, while piecemeal arguments will convert many readers to multigenerationalism, they are not very satisfying philosophically. Piecemeal arguments seldom are. Philosophers always seek something more general. Opponents can always simply reply that, for *them*, multigenerational projects are too risky because other projects are sufficient. I therefore devote the rest of this lecture to three more ambitious, general arguments for multigenerationalism. These present multigenerational projects, and especially reorientations, as necessary for a meaningful life, as something we owe to others, as a corollary of our duties of rectification, and as a necessary precondition for permissible procreation.

3.5 An Intergenerational Meaningfulness Argument for Multigenerationalism

Meaningfulness arguments for multigenerationalism draw on our pessimism debate. In this section, I explore one particular argument, based on an intergenerational account of meaningfulness.

We could appeal to meaningfulness to defend either of my two main multigenerational claims. We could argue that we can only enjoy meaningful lives if we initiate some multigenerational projects, or that we can only enjoy meaningful lives if we initiate multigenerational reorientation in particular.

Arguments for reorientation are more ambitious, more philosophically interesting, and closer to the themes of our pessimism debate. I therefore begin with one such argument. We need to reorient our inherited, future-dependent traditions to enable both present and future people to enjoy meaningful lives.

I focus on one particularly ambitious meaningfulness-based argument. It claims that, in our Post-Cataclysm world, multigenerational reorientation is necessary to preserve *intergenerationally grounded* meaning. I first outline the argument (Section 3.5.1). I then recap some material from our pessimism debate (Section 3.5.2), explain what I mean by *intergenerationally grounded meaning*—contrast it with other accounts of meaningfulness (Section 3.5.3); and contrast multigenerationalism with other views explored in our pessimism debate (Sections 3.5.4 and 3.5.5). Finally, I discuss less ambitious meaningfulness-based arguments for multigenerationalism (Section 3.5.6).

3.5.1 What Is the Intergenerational Meaningfulness Argument?

In this section, I explore the following argument:

1. *First Premise: The Necessity of Intergenerational Meaning*: Every meaningful human life must contain some projects whose meaningfulness is *intergenerationally grounded* (i.e., some projects that are only meaningful for human beings because they connect us to other generations).
2. *Second Premise: Intergenerational Meaning Is Currently Future-Dependent*: Like our ancestors living before the Cataclysm, *we currently* ground intergenerational meaningfulness in the indefinite human future. Unless we reorient our current traditions, we cannot enjoy intergenerational meaningfulness—and neither can our descendants.

3. Therefore, *Pessimist Interim Conclusion*: Unless we reorient our current traditions, no one in our Post-Cataclysm world can enjoy a meaningful human life.
4. *Third Premise: Reorientation Is Feasible*: The future-dependent Pre-Cataclysm traditions that we have inherited *can* be reoriented to provide intergenerational meaning, and to give people meaningful lives, without an indefinite human future—even in the last generation when no human future remains. This reorientation has the following features:
   a. *Immediate Reorientation Is Not Feasible*: Unfortunately, this reorientation *cannot* occur overnight or in a single generation. Present people cannot reimagine intergenerational meaning on their own. In Scheffler's original, immediate extinction scenarios, pessimism is the only reasonable response.
   b. *Multigenerational Reorientation Is Feasible*: Fortunately, this reorientation *can* occur over several generations. Present and future people *together* can reimagine intergenerational meaning. In our Post-Cataclysm situation, pessimism is no longer the only reasonable response.
   c. *Reorientation Restores Intergenerational Meaning for Everyone*: If multigenerational reorientation succeeds, then the resulting reoriented tradition grounds intergenerational meaning *for all generations* who participate in that project—including the last generation who, by definition, cannot enjoy any future-dependent meaning at all.
5. *Fourth Premise: Normative Conditional*: If life would be meaningless without intergenerational meaning, and if we can (only) restore intergenerational meaning by initiating multigenerational reorientation, then we should do so.
6. Therefore, *Reorientation Claim*: We (present people) should devote ourselves to initiating a particular kind of multigenerational project that aims to reorient our current, inherited, future-dependent traditions and practices so that they remain fit for purpose even at humanity's end.

This argument is valid. I trust the Normative Conditional Premise is uncontroversial (other things equal). The rest of this section seeks to establish the other three premises. I argue that intergenerational meaning is essential for a meaningful human life, that our inherited traditions tie intergenerational meaning to the indefinite human future, and that multigenerational reorientation is feasible. The first two premises draw on our pessimism debate, while the main argument for the feasibility of multigenerational reorientation lies in future lectures.

3.5.2 Themes from Post-Cataclysm Pessimism

I begin by briefly recapping Scheffler's original Pre-Cataclysm arguments from our pessimism debate (Section 1.4). Scheffler himself talks about reasons. But I will freely translate his work into the vocabulary of meaningfulness.

Scheffler explored a *doomsday scenario* where the world will be destroyed thirty days after my death, and an *infertility scenario* where everyone on earth becomes infertile and the present generation know they will be the last. In these scenarios, humanity faces unavoidable immediate extinction.

Scheffler argues that, in his scenarios, two things are lost. More obviously, future-directed *projects* are no longer available. I cannot find meaning by laying the foundation stone for a structure that future people will build; or play a founding role in a long-term project to find a cure for cancer. Less obviously, although non-future-directed projects are still practically available, they are no longer as *meaningful* as they were before—because their meaning was grounded in some broader story about human traditions and values that we inherit from the past and pass down to the future. We can still listen to music, enjoy a beautiful sunset, and be compassionate to others. But these present-focused activities no longer make sense in all the ways that they used to.

In other words, Scheffler argues that many non-future-*directed* projects are nonetheless future-*dependent*. Without the human future, they lose their ability to make our lives meaningful.

Consider an analogy. I am a theist who suddenly loses my faith in God. I then suffer two losses. More obviously, God-directed projects are no longer available to me. If I no longer believe that God exists, then I cannot find meaning by worshipping God, seeking union with God, or contemplating God. Less obviously, while non-God-directed projects are still practically available to me, they are no longer meaningful in the ways they used to be—because their meaning *for me as a theist* was grounded in some broader story about my relationship to God. I can still care for others. But I can no longer understand this care as part of God's plan for my life, as an appropriate response to my recognition of God's image in others, as a way to imitate God's creative benevolence, or in any other God-dependent way.

In both cases—loss of the human future and loss of God—the more *philosophically* troubling loss is the broader loss of meaning, not the specific loss of particular projects. For Scheffler, future-dependent meaning is wider than future-directed projects. For theists, God-dependent meaning is wider than God-directed projects.

People react very differently to Scheffler's immediate extinction scenarios. Some people find them much more depressing than others. I believe this is because we endorse very different background theories about what makes human lives meaningful. In particular, immediate extinction is very troubling if you believe either of the following two claims:

1. The Necessity of Future-*Directed* Meaning: A meaningful life requires some future-directed projects—some projects whose substantive content depends on the existence of future people.
2. The Necessity of Future-*Dependent* Meaning: A meaningful life can be built entirely around present-focused projects whose substantive content does

not depend on the existence of future people. However, those present-focused projects are themselves only sufficiently meaningful if they are grounded in traditions whose meaningfulness *does* depend on a human future. Our projects are not future-directed, but they are future-dependent.

In Scheffler's scenarios, either of these two claims leads directly to last generation pessimism. Without either future-directed projects or future-dependent meaning, no one can enjoy a meaningful life. Similarly, *Post-Cataclysm* pessimists argue that, even the loss of the *indefinite* human future leads to pessimism—because any meaningful human life requires an open-ended human future.

I aim to meet this Scheffler-inspired Post-Cataclysm pessimism on its own terms. I agree with Scheffler that, *for us*, present meaning depends on future descendants who will continue our projects and traditions. If *we* were the last generation, then our lives would be meaningless. Intergenerational meaning *is* lost in Scheffler's doomsday and infertility scenarios—and there is no time to replace it.

However, I regard this loss of meaning as a *contingent feature of the way we have been raised or acculturated*—of the traditions we have inherited—rather than an *essential feature of the human condition*. We need an indefinite human future to give our projects meaning. But other people—including our own descendants—might not be so dependent. As people living at the *start* of a Post-Cataclysm world, we can initiate a future transformation so that *later generations* can find meaning without relying on (further) future people.

This argument for multigenerationalism will appeal most to those who are sympathetic to Post-Cataclysm pessimism, and especially to the Scheffler-inspired idea that the scope of intergenerational meaning is wider than it initially appears—because many present-focused projects and activities ultimately derive their meaningfulness from intergenerational traditions. The next challenge, to which I return in subsequent lectures, is to demonstrate that multigenerational reorientation is *possible*—and that the same kind of meaning can be delivered through intergenerational connections with past people and/or a finite number of future generations.

3.5.3 What Is the Intergenerational Meaning View?

My intergenerational meaningfulness argument argues (1) that a meaningful life requires projects whose meaningfulness is *intergenerationally grounded*; and (2) that, after the Cataclysm, we can only salvage this kind of meaningfulness if we initiate some multigenerational reorientation of our inherited future-dependent traditions.

We want to know that it means to say that the meaningfulness of a project is 'intergenerationally grounded'. I begin with a prior question: What do I mean by *'grounding'* in the first place? The basic idea is that the fact that some specific human experience, project, activity, state, relationship, or achievement is meaningful for some particular person is not a brute fact. We can always ask, *Why* is project P meaningful for agent A? Meaning is not a basic property of projects, states, experiences, and so on. If we ask what *makes* P meaningful for A, there must be *some* explanation.

I explore the idea of intergenerational grounding further by distinguishing it from other familiar Pre-Cataclysm attempts to ground the meaningfulness of P for A.

1. *First Alternative: Intrinsic Grounding: Meaningfulness does not depend on anything beyond the thing itself.* Meaning supervenes on the intrinsic properties of the project, state, or experience. For instance, a hedonist might say that, if we ask what makes pleasure meaningful (or why pleasure is meaningful, or what it is about pleasure that makes it meaningful), then the intrinsic features of pleasure provide a complete answer. Non-hedonist experientialists might appeal to features of the experience that go beyond pleasure and pain. The key point is that nothing outside the experience itself is necessary to *give* it meaning or *make* it meaningful.[7]
2. *Second Alternative: Individual Subjectivism: Meaningfulness depends entirely on A's attitude to P.* According to individual subjectivism about meaning, P is meaningful for A because A has this or that positive attitude towards P. Perhaps A has chosen P, or A desires P, or A enjoys P, or A values P, or whatever. There are many varieties of individual subjectivism. The differences between them do not matter for our present purposes. The key point is that nothing beyond A's individual attitude is necessary to make P meaningful for A.[8]

These two alternatives are very different from the intergenerational grounding view. They both deny that anything beyond A and P is necessary to make P meaningful for A. Meaningfulness therefore cannot depend (in any way) on future people.

3. *Third Alternative: Theist/Transcendent/Supernatural Grounding: Meaningfulness depends entirely on God.* The fact that P is meaningful for A is ultimately grounded in facts about God. These might be facts about God's nature, A's relation to God, God's attitude to P, God's plan for human beings, God's plan for A, and so on.[9]

---

[7] On hedonism, see Crisp, 'Hedonism Reconsidered'; Feldman, *Pleasure and the Good Life*; Moore, 'Hedonism'. On experientialism, see Kraut, *The Quality of Life*. On different approaches to meaning in life, see Metz, 'The Meaning of Life'; Wolf, *Meaning in Life and Why It Matters*.
[8] On subjectivism, see Heathwood, 'Subjective Theories of Well-Being'.
[9] On supernatural accounts of meaning in life, see Mawson, 'Recent Work on the Meaning of Life and Philosophy of Religion'; Mawson, *God and the Meaning of Life*; Metz, *Meaning in Life*, part two: 'Supernaturalist Theories of Meaning in Life', pp. 75–161; Metz, *God, Soul and the Meaning of Life*. On God as a transcendent standard of value, see Adams, *Finite and Infinite Goods*.

God-based meaning is a particular kind of *metaphysically transcendent* meaning, where the meaningfulness of P to A depends, ultimately, on something beyond the physical universe. Other transcendent or supernatural views ground meaning in facts about immortal souls, other divine or supernatural beings, impersonal forms, cosmic purposes, transcendent values, and so on. In my lectures, I largely set metaphysically transcendent meaning aside, to focus on non-supernatural responses to pessimism. I seek to meet atheist Post-Cataclysm pessimism on its own terms as much as possible. However, I do return to theism in my discussion of religious utopias in my final lecture (Section 8.5), and we revisit transcendent metaphysics in our virtualism debate (Section 9.6).

In our religion debate, the theist panellist identified different ways that meaning could be 'transcendent'. I am now talking about the strongest of those senses— where *transcendent meaning* requires something beyond the physical universe (and not just beyond the human present). *This* idea of transcendent meaning is clearly opposed to the very idea of intergenerational grounding. If we deny that *anything in the physical world* is either necessary or sufficient to ground meaning, then we obviously cannot ground meaning in intergenerational connections. However, it does not follow that theists must reject multigenerationalist claims *about normative ethics*. Theists distinguish between ultimate ground and proximate ground. For theists, the ultimate ground of all values, reasons, and meaningfulness is God. But theists can recognise intermediate or proximate sources of meaning. In particular, many theists admit that, even though atheists do not realise that all values ultimately depend on God, atheists can still appreciate values, respond to moral reasons, and live good lives. All values ultimately depend on God. But people who don't believe in God can still understand and appreciate those values without understanding their true (divine) nature.[10] For instance, a theist and a subjectivist might agree that P is meaningful for A *only if* A values P. They thus agree that P is meaningful for A *because* A values P. However, for the theist, the general ethical principle here (that A's valuing P is necessary for P's meaningfulness to A) must *itself* be made true (one way or another) by God.[11] I argue below that distinguishing between ultimate and proximate grounding enables theists who reject intergenerational accounts of meaning to endorse multigenerationalist substantive claims in normative ethics (Section 3.5.5).

4. *Fourth Alternative: Interpersonal Meaning: Meaningfulness depends, in part, on other present people.* Something about other present people is necessary to ground the fact that P is meaningful for A. For instance, perhaps P is meaningful for A only if A's peers, contemporaries, or society attach significance to P, value P, collectively pursue P, or simply believe that P is good for A.

---

[10] cf. Adams, *Finite and Infinite Goods*, chapter one; Mulgan, Purpose in this Universe, chapter two.
[11] A further difference is that theists are very unlikely to agree that A's valuing P is *sufficient* to make P meaningful for A (even if this is a *necessary* condition). Most theists would also insist that P must be *worth valuing*.

We are now getting closer to the intergenerational grounding view. The interpersonal meaning view acknowledges the need to ground meaningfulness in something that is both intersubjective and human (as opposed to individual subjectivism or intersubjective connections with God).

5. *Fifth Alternative: Past-dependent Meaning: Meaningfulness depends, in part, on past people.* Something about past people (i.e., those who are no longer alive) is necessary to ground the fact that P is meaningful for A. For instance, perhaps P is only meaningful for A if prior generations (possibly *as well as* present people) valued or pursued P. Meaning can only arise in the context of intergenerational traditions and commitments.

This gets us very close to the intergenerational meaning view, as meaningfulness is no longer grounded entirely in the human present.

6. *Sixth Alternative: Future-Dependent Meaning: Meaningfulness depends, in part, on future people.* Connections to future people are necessary to ground the fact that P is meaningful for A. This is the distinctive view of meaning inspired by Scheffler's remarks about reasons, traditions, and values. Without future people, present people cannot enjoy fully meaningful lives (Section 1.4).

This sixth alternative is the account of meaningfulness that best fits with Post-Cataclysm pessimism. The intergenerational grounding view takes this Scheffler-inspired future-dependent account of meaning as its starting point, and then replaces it via a multigenerational reorientation of our open-ended, future-dependent traditions. The intergenerational grounding view re-categorises Scheffler-inspired *future*-dependent meaning as one species of *intergenerational meaning*. All intergenerational meaning is grounded in traditions and values that spread across several generations. However, on this broader view, these traditions *don't necessarily have to extend indefinitely into the future*. The goal of multigenerational reorientation is then to replace Scheffler future-dependent meaningfulness with a something that (a) is not-future-dependent, but also (b) is recognisably an instance of the same broad kind of interpersonal, intergenerational meaning.

As for our original, Scheffler-inspired, future-dependent account of meaning, we can make more or less ambitious claims about our new broader category of *intergenerational meaning*. We could insist that *all* human meaningfulness must be grounded in some intergenerational tradition. Nothing is meaningful for us without some connection to other generations. Or we could claim only that *some* aspects of human meaningfulness are intergenerational in this way. The most interesting intermediate position says that, even if there are other sources of meaningfulness—even if not all meaning depends on human traditions—any truly meaningful life must contain some projects whose meaning is grounded in some intergenerational tradition. This is the approach I will defend. My intergenerational meaningfulness argument says that a surprisingly broad subset of our projects is meaningful to us in ways that depend on some intergenerational connection; that *any* human life that is meaningful overall must include *some* of those projects; and that multigenerational reorientation can retain *that intergenerational meaning* throughout our Post-Cataclysm world.

3.5.4 Multigenerationalism and its Rivals

I have just distinguished a range of views about what grounds meaningfulness in human lives. How do these views relate to the various positions represented in our pessimism debate? And how does multigenerationalism relate to those positions?

The non-multigenerational positions in our pessimism debate were perennial pessimism, Post-Cataclysm pessimism, presentism, and theism.

Pessimism, per se, says only that, whatever makes people's lives meaningful, our present lives are not meaningful. In principle, this is consistent with pretty much any story about what (if anything) would ground meaningful lives if there were any. However, *Post-Cataclysm* pessimism, which says that the Cataclysm has *made* our lives meaningless, is most plausibly combined with a Scheffler-inspired future-dependent account of meaning, where a meaningful life requires some projects whose meaning is grounded in the (indefinite) human future. My aim is to meet this kind of pessimism on its own terms.

I have already contrasted multigenerationalism with Post-Cataclysm pessimism. I agree with Post-Cataclysm pessimism both (a) that, like our ancestors living before the Cataclysm, *we currently* ground meaningfulness in the indefinite human future; and (b) that *everyone* needs some kind of intergenerational meaning. However, as an optimistic multigenerationalist, I also defend the following additional claims—drawn from the central premise in my intergenerational meaningfulness argument:

Third Premise: Reorientation Is Feasible: The future-dependent Pre-Cataclysm traditions that we have inherited *can* be reoriented to provide intergenerational meaning, and to give people meaningful lives, without an indefinite human future—even in the last generation when no human future remains. This reorientation has the following features:

a. *Immediate Reorientation Is Not Feasible*: Unfortunately, this reorientation *cannot* occur overnight or in a single generation. Present people cannot reimagine intergenerational meaning on their own. In Scheffler's original immediate extinction scenarios, pessimism is the only reasonable response.

b. *Multigenerational Reorientation Is Feasible*: Fortunately, this reorientation *can* occur over several generations. Present and future people *together* can reimagine intergenerational meaning. In our Post-Cataclysm situation, pessimism is no longer the only reasonable response.
c. *Reorientation Restores Intergenerational Meaning for Everyone*: If multigenerational reorientation succeeds, then the resulting reoriented tradition grounds intergenerational meaning *for all generations* who participate in that project—including the last generation who, by definition, cannot enjoy any future-dependent meaning at all.

Multigenerationalists and Post-Cataclysm pessimists agree that, without radical reorientation of our inherited traditions, human lives cannot be meaningful in our Post-Cataclysm world. They disagree about whether that radical reorientation is feasible.

The other two main characters in our first two debates were the Presentist and the Theist. According to *presentism*, present-focused projects are sufficient for a meaningful life *without any grounding in anything beyond the human present*. The most obvious present-focused projects are those based on individual pleasure, compassion for others, or self-contained (i.e., non-future-dependent) achievements. When we turn to what grounds the meaning of these present-focused projects, presentists have a wide range of options. A presentist could believe that nothing grounds meaning; that meaning is grounded in the intrinsic nature of pleasure, compassion, or achievement; or that it is grounded in the individual or collective attitudes of present people. Presentists' accounts of meaning can be intrinsic, individually subjective, or intersubjective—so long as they are not intergenerational. In my broad usage, Harry Frankfurt and Susan Wolf, in their original responses to Scheffler, despite their very different views about meaningfulness, both defend versions of presentism.[12] Presentists find life perfectly satisfactory *without* future-dependent intergenerational meaning. Present-focused projects are sufficient to avoid pessimism; it is always foolish to put *any* faith in the human future; and multigenerational projects are always unnecessarily risky. While people can still indulge in multigenerational projects if they want to, such projects are not essential for a meaningful life.

Contra presentism, my intergenerational meaningfulness argument insists that the meaningfulness of our present-focused projects cannot be grounded entirely in nothing, in their intrinsic properties, in our present attitudes, or in anything else within the human present. We need something that is either transcendent or intergenerational.

My intergenerational account of *meaning* thus goes far beyond claims about the meaningfulness of *intergenerational projects*. Many *other* projects are also

---

[12] Frankfurt, 'How the Afterlife Matters'; Wolf, 'The Significance of Doomsday'.

grounded in some intergenerational tradition. The primary goal of multigenerational reorientation is to enable our previously future-dependent traditions to ground the meaning of *other* (non-multigenerational) projects, even in the last generation. Imagine someone whose own projects are entirely present-focused. This person doesn't directly engage in multigenerational projects themselves. I argue that they still need it to be the case that *other people* do (successfully) pursue such projects. This is necessary for the first person's own present-focused projects *to continue to be fully meaningful after the Cataclysm*. This is one reason why, as I argue below, multigenerational reorientation is something that we owe to each other, and that present people owe to future people.

The beauty of the intergenerational meaningfulness argument is that opponents of multigenerationalism cannot simply point to a range of meaningful present-focused projects. They must *also* demonstrate that all our present-focused projects still make sense *without any connections to future people*.

3.5.5 Multigenerationalism and Theism

The relationship between multigenerationalism and theism is worth exploring. As I noted earlier, theists claim that the meaningfulness of all our projects is ultimately grounded in God. Contra pessimism, theists argue that we can enjoy meaningful lives—because God will ensure that a range of sufficiently meaningful projects is available. Contra secular optimism, theists argue that nothing in the mundane world is an adequate substitute for transcendent meaning. In particular, theists deny that the secular human future was ever an adequate replacement for God.

Contra theism, my intergenerational meaningfulness argument insists that meaningfulness need not be grounded in anything beyond the physical universe. Intergenerational grounding was sufficient before the Cataclysm—and it can still be sufficient even after the Cataclysm.

I said earlier that, while theism is opposed to any intergenerational account of *ultimate grounding*, it is not necessarily opposed to intergenerational *proximate* grounding. Similarly, theism is not necessarily opposed to multigenerationalism's distinctive substantive claims *in normative ethics*. For theists, a meaningful human life does not need any intergenerational ultimate grounding, because it needs no ultimate grounding in anything beyond God. But a meaningful life may still include multigenerational projects and/or multigenerational reorientation. And theists *could* even agree that, after the Cataclysm, meaningful human lives *demand* such projects and reorientations. God is the ultimate ground of all meaning. But theists can recognise different kinds of *non-ultimate meaning*, all ultimately grounded in God. Perhaps what immediately makes particular human projects or experiences meaningful is their intrinsic properties, our attitude to them, *or their connections to intergenerational traditions*. And, perhaps, without intergenerational connections, our lives cannot be meaningful—even for theists. If God has designed us to derive meaning from intergenerational traditions, then perhaps we all need some sources of meaning that are (proximately) grounded in those traditions. After the Cataclysm, we may *need* re-imagined intergenerational connections to ensure that we enjoy sufficient God-grounded meaning.

In our pessimism debate, the theist insisted that God makes our projects meaningful, and that God will ensure that we still have access to meaningful projects, despite the Cataclysm. But theists need not insist that all those meaningful projects are *God-directed*. Most theists believe that we should pursue *some* God-directed projects. We should worship, contemplate, encounter, imitate the divine. But theists can admit the desirability—and perhaps even the necessity—of also pursing non-God-directed projects. Our current store of sufficiently meaningful projects includes *initiating multigenerational reorientation*. Theists can agree with multigenerationalists that reorientation is necessary—because it is now our only way to realise vital goods whose goodness is ultimately grounded in God. This would be good news for multigenerationalists—as God's benevolence presumably ensures that, if reorientation is necessary, then it must at least be possible!

I conclude that, while theists must reject any intergenerational account of ultimate meaning, they can endorse multigenerationalism. Theism thus offers an alternative, meaningfulness-based way to defend multigenerationalism's normative claims.

3.5.6 Less Ambitious Arguments for Multigenerationalism

I have presented the most ambitious meaningfulness-based defense of multigenerationalism, based on an intergenerational account of meaning. This argument is very controversial, as it rests on one specific account of meaning in life. Fortunately, my overall case for multigenerationalism is not dependent on this particular argument. I can defend multigenerationalism in several other ways.

My intergenerational meaningfulness argument is ambitious and/or controversial in at least three ways. Most obviously, the argument insists that multigenerational projects are intimately related to meaningfulness in life—rather than arguing that such projects contribute to well-being, are valuable in themselves, or fall under other reasons or obligations. As I said earlier, many arguments for multigenerationalism eschew meaningfulness entirely. Multigenerationalism itself is a claim about our reasons and obligations—about what *we should do*—not about the meaning of our lives. We could still have many reasons to pursue multigenerational projects even if they provide no unique kind of meaning, even if there is no intergenerational meaning, and even if the very notion of 'meaning in life' is incoherent. Multigenerational projects are still worth pursuing, even at considerable cost or risk, for many other reasons.

Suppose, however, that we do wish to base our argument for multigenerationalism on claims about the meaningfulness of human lives. My intergenerational meaningfulness argument is still ambitious and controversial in two remaining ways. First, it argues, not only that intergenerational meaning is valuable, but also that it is *necessary* for a meaningful human life. Second, it argues that a meaningful life requires, not only multigenerational projects and reorientations, but also some specifically intergenerational *kind* of meaning.

There are thus two ways to make our meaningfulness-based defense of multigenerationalism less ambitious. First, we could argue that, while intergenerational meaning is not necessary for a meaningful life, it is nonetheless a distinctive kind of meaning whose loss cannot simply be compensated by additional pleasures or present-focused achievements. We still have strong meaningfulness-based reasons to initiate multigenerational reorientation, even if this is not essential to rebut Post-Cataclysm pessimism. Ideally, we want access to as many distinct *kinds* of meaningful activities as possible. And we certainly want future people to enjoy the widest possible range of meaningful *choices*. Therefore, we might have compelling reasons to pursue multigenerational reorientation, not because it is *necessary* for any meaningful life, but simply because it *enhances* the meaning of every life.

The intergenerational meaningfulness argument posits a special account of the ultimate grounding of meaning—intergenerational meaning. Yet multigenerationalism, as a position in *normative* ethics, is not committed to any particular story about what (if anything) *grounds* the meaningfulness of our projects. We could simply argue that multigenerational projects and reorientations are essential for a meaningful life according to standards of meaningfulness that are not intergenerational at all.

All multigenerational projects presume that intergenerational *cooperation* is important. But they can be completely agnostic about future-dependent or intergenerational accounts of what *grounds* meaning. A multigenerational project might simply be enjoyable, rewarding, or satisfying to its participants in ways that any plausible account of meaningfulness will accommodate. Our ultimate account of the meaningfulness of a multigenerational project might be ungrounded, intrinsic, subjective, theist, or entirely dependent on the attitudes of other present people. For instance, hedonists and theists both pursue intergenerational projects, but neither believes their meaning is grounded in anything intergenerational.

Many multigenerational projects do *not* presuppose an intergenerational account of *grounding*. Nor does multigenerational *reorientation*. Our reasons for repurposing an existing human tradition might be unrelated to any specific tradition-based account of the nature of meaningfulness itself. Indeed, our reasons for reorientation might have nothing to do with *meaningfulness* at all. Hedonists might reorient or repurpose a tradition that no longer delivers maximum pleasure. Theists might reorient an open-ended tradition of worship and contemplation so that it continues to make sense after the Cataclysm. But the ultimate reasons for this reorientation are grounded in God, not in the human tradition itself.

This concludes my discussion of arguments for multigenerationalism based primarily on meaningfulness. However, meaningfulness is also relevant to my next set of arguments for multigenerationalism—those based on intergenerational obligation. If multigenerational projects and/or reorientations are necessary for a meaningful life, and if we owe it to other people to make *their* lives meaningful, then an obligation to initiate multigenerational projects is a corollary of our duties to others.

This connection is important for several reasons. First, obligations to other people have a normative force that self-directed reasons often do not. I can chose not to make my own life meaningful. I can certainly ignore important particular sources of meaningfulness for myself and/or chose a less-than-maximally meaningful live. But I cannot so easily choose to ignore my obligations to enhance the meaningfulness of other people's lives. Second, while some individuals may find self-contained, present-focused projects entirely satisfactory, others do not. I may owe it to others to ensure that *they* can find their lives meaningful—even if I am personally happy with things as they are. Third, on many accounts of intergenerational justice, we should leave future people with the widest possible range of different meaningful options and different kinds of values.[13] If this is so, then we have compelling interpersonal reasons to initiate multigenerational projects even if these are not essential to a (minimally) meaningful life.

3.6 Do We Owe Multigenerationalism to Others?

The strongest argument for multigenerationalism is that multigenerational projects, and especially multigenerational reorientations, are *things that we owe to others*. Multigenerational reorientation is a public good. We collectively owe it to one another, and present people owe it to future people.

We can have obligations to one another (i.e., to other present people), to past people, and to future people. All three demand multigenerational reorientation. Insofar as present meaningfulness depends on multigenerational reorientation, launching multigenerational projects of reorientation is something we collectively owe to each other. Insofar as past people's *posthumous interests* depend on salvaging their investment in otherwise incoherent future-dependent traditions, the reorientation of those traditions is something we owe to our predecessors. Finally,

---

[13] I draw here loosely on Joseph Raz's suggestion that valuable freedom consists in a choice between *incommensurable* values (Raz, *The Morality of Freedom*, p. 322; Raz, 'Incommensurability and Agency'). See also Chang, *Incommensurability, Incomparability, and Practical Reason*; Griffin, *Well-Being*, pp. 75–92; Mulgan, *Future People*, pp. 104–111.

our obligations to future people include a duty to equip them to make sense of their own lives. Insofar as intergenerational meaning is important to human flourishing, we must enable future people (and especially the last generation) to enjoy some intergenerational meaning. We must initiate terminal intergenerational projects that *they* can cooperate with.

The general claim that we owe it to others to initiate multigenerational projects can be fleshed-out in many ways. I now explore two. We owe it to past, present, and future people to provide rectification for past injustice, and to ensure that the necessary conditions for procreative permissibility can be met throughout our Post-Cataclysm world. If multigenerational projects are necessary preconditions of these two specific obligations, then we must initiate such projects.

3.7 The Rectification Argument

In this section, I argue that we owe it to others to initiate multigenerational projects as part of our general duties of rectification.[14] I first distinguish several possible kinds of rectification:

1. *Contemporary Human Injustice*: If present people suffer injustice, then they are owed restoration or compensation. (If I steal your goat, I should return it. If I have eaten it, I should either replace it or give you money.)
2. *Particular Historical Human Injustice*: Injustice to *past people* is more puzzling. Who *now* owes what to whom? What possible present actions could rectify *this particular historical wrong*? Is rectification owed *to* (a) descendants of the original sufferers; (b) present people who still suffer as a direct consequence of the original historical injustice; or (c) continuing entities (family, tribe, nation, people) that still exist? On the other side of the equation: Is rectification owed *by* (a) descendants of the original wrongdoer; (b) present people who still benefit from the original historical injustice; or (c) continuing entities (family, tribe, nation, people) that still exist and were responsible for the original injustice? To complicate matters further, actual cases typically include all of the above.
3. *Universal Historical Human Injustice*: Human history is a tale of continual injustice. If a just history is a precondition for a just present, then no present holding, national territory, or other legal regime is remotely just. Instead of rectifying *particular* (comparatively recent) historical injustices,

---

[14] For philosophical debate on rectification in general, see, e.g., Murphy, *A Moral Theory of Political Reconciliation*; and Thompson, *Should Current Generations Make Reparations for Slavery?*

we might seek *global* rectification—a new beginning that resets all holdings. Rectification often leads to utopianism.
4. *Ecological Injustice*: Humans are not the only victims of human injustice. We also treat non-human nature unjustly. We must therefore rectify this injustice.

All these kinds of injustice could, in principle, generate a rectification-based argument for multigenerationalism. I focus here on historical human injustice—both particular and universal. However, I return to ecological injustice in my final lecture, when I discuss Post-Cataclysm ecological utopias (Section 8.4).

I believe that the Cataclysm transforms Pre-Cataclysm philosophical debates about rectification in several ways. Most obviously, rectification now cannot be *postponed*. If past wrongs are ever to be rectified, we must act now. Reasons to rectify injustice are now more urgent than before the Cataclysm. In addition, even if our reasons for rectification were unchanged, their *comparative* strength has increased, because the opportunity costs of rectification are now greatly reduced. Pre-Cataclysm rectification competed against long-term, future-directed investment. Post-Cataclysm rectification faces no such competition for resources.

By definition, historical injustice happened in the past. Most victims of historical injustice no longer exist. Insofar as rectification is owed to victims of injustice, the case for duties of rectification is obviously most compelling if we recognise *significant posthumous interests*. I argue in my procreative ethics lectures that, while such interests were very controversial before the Catastrophe, they are much less controversial now, especially in our present dialectical context. There are two main reasons for this. First, reflection on the loss of future-dependent meaning has persuaded many of us that posthumous interests *are* important (Sections 1.4 and 6.3.2). If there were no posthumous interests, then the prospect of imminent human extinction would not bother *us*. How can something that happens long after our deaths affect the value or meaning of our lives? Insofar as the prospect of imminent extinction *does* bother us, this suggests that we already (implicitly) believe in significant posthumous interests. Second, I argue later that multigenerationalists, in particular, should embrace posthumous interests—because connections to past people provide our most secure source of intergenerational meaning (Sections 6.3.2 and 6.3.4). I conclude that when we now approach the question of rectification, we are *already predisposed* to take past people's posthumous interests much more seriously than our Pre-Cataclysm predecessors did.

As well as being more significant, rectification can now become more ambitious. Our Post-Cataclysm world makes possible a more thoroughgoing rectification than ever before. We owe it to past generations to create a just *future* society. I argue at length in my final lecture on Post-Cataclysm utopias that the removal of Pre-Cataclysm constraints (especially the requirement that any utopia be *sustainable* into an indefinite future) opens up new utopian possibilities, especially in the last generation (Section 8.1).

After the Cataclysm, when we enjoy far fewer routes to intergenerational meaning, rectification is one of the few ways we can meaningfully connect ourselves to other generations (Section 6.3.2).

Of course, the loss of future-dependent reasons raises the *comparative* significance of *all* projects that emphasise connections to the past. If this were the main impact of the Cataclysm, then there would be nothing special about *rectification*. However, I think rectification is *distinctively* important. It provides an argument for multigenerationalism built on *non-tradition-based* past-directed reasons. Unlike the kinds of reasons highlighted by Scheffler—and incorporated into my earlier intergenerational meaningfulness argument for multigenerationalism— the demand for rectification bites *whatever our relationship to our own cultural traditions*. The *wrongness* of past injustice is not tradition-dependent. Therefore, the increased significance of rectification-based reasons provides a non-tradition-dependent reason why the present generation should initiate multigenerational projects. And those multigenerational projects may include reorientation. Perhaps we must reorient *our* traditional thinking *about justice* in order to deliver future rectification and/or construct a future just society. I say a lot more about the latter in my final lecture. The important point now is that our underlying reason to deliver rectification does *not* itself depend on any reasons that are internal to any inherited tradition.

Suppose we agree that rectification *is* now more important than it was before the Cataclysm. How does this give us an argument *for multigenerationalism*? In other words, Why would *rectification* need to be a *multigenerational* project?

Rectification is obviously *intergenerational*, in a minimal sense, simply because it naturally spreads across generations. Rectification takes time to implement and to come to fruition. Beneficiaries of rectification need time to truly enjoy what is returned, restored, or compensated. Rectification is thus *inevitably* intergenerational. I believe it is also *genuinely* intergenerational. Present individuals are often too damaged, disadvantaged, or elderly to benefit fully from any present rectification. Full rectification demands a new generation who enjoy the *full restoration* of what was lost *throughout their whole lives*. Furthermore, rectification is a two-way street. We also need a new generation *on the other side*—a generation of descendants of beneficiaries or perpetrators *who do not themselves enjoy any continuing unjust benefits from historical injustice*. Rectification should remove the guilt of historical injustice as well as its burdens.

More importantly, I also believe that rectification is intergenerational in a deeper sense. Full rectification often demands future moral *transformation* of a kind that is only possible over several generations. In particular, if (a) rectification for past injustice demands a future just society—a future utopia; and if (b) the establishment of any future Post-Cataclysm utopia itself demands future moral transformation; then (c) rectification in turn demands future moral transformation. I argue in my fifth and sixth lectures that, in our Post-Cataclysm world, any utopian project demands *a lot* of future moral transformation! Therefore, for us, rectification is essentially multigenerational.

I conclude that our urgent duty to rectify past injustices *does* generate a compelling argument for multigenerationalism. We must now initiate new multigenerational rectification projects, especially if we aim to create a future just society or do justice to non-human nature.

3.8 The Procreative Permissibility Argument

My final argument for multigenerationalism appeals to procreative permissibility. The relationship between multigenerationalism and procreative permissibility goes both ways. On the one hand, multigenerationalism obviously presupposes permissible procreation.

Any project that requires the participation (or existence) of future people presupposes the creation of new people. Permissible intergenerational projects demand *permissible* procreation. Multigenerationalism presupposes procreative permissibility. If multigenerational projects last *more than two* generations, then procreation must *remain* permissible for *all intermediate generations*. In particular, the *penultimate* generation must be permitted to create the *last human generation*.

The last generation are the acid test for Post-Cataclysm procreative permissibility. If they cannot enjoy fully meaningful lives, then the penultimate generation face a stark choice—accept meaninglessness for themselves or impose it on their own children. But then every earlier generation faces an analogous choice between embracing meaninglessness now and pushing it down the line. But surely we cannot make our own lives meaningful by imposing meaninglessness on others! I don't just mean that we *shouldn't* make our lives meaningful in this way. I mean that we cannot do so, because genuine meaningfulness cannot be built on other people's suffering.

This, of course, is Mark Johnston's Ponzi challenge to Scheffler. There is something odd about arguing *from* the premise that it is undesirable to belong to the last human generation *to* the conclusion that we ought to continue the human story. Human extinction cannot be avoided; it can only be *postponed*. We cannot *remove* the burden of last-generation-hood. We can only avoid that burden for ourselves *by passing it down the line to some unspecified future generation*. As we saw in our pessimism debate, Johnston likens this inter-generational buck-passing to continuing a Ponzi scheme (Section 1.4).

If we were the last generation, then our only task would be to strive to make our own lives meaningful. But we are not the last generation—or, at least, we might not be. There *could* be future generations. We must therefore also ask whether we can achieve something greater by collaborating with future people. But now we must justify ourselves *to those new generations*—especially the last humans who cannot possibly make their own lives meaningful by creating further new people.

The shift from Scheffler's imaginary immediate extinction scenarios to our actual Post-Cataclysm world of *imminent* extinction reintroduces procreative ethics and intergenerational equity. This significantly raises the stakes. Procreative permissibility is much harder to establish than meaningfulness. Anti-natalism is much harder to refute than pessimism. Suppose that, if we were the last generation, we could make our own lives meaningful to degree M. It simply doesn't follow that we can permissibly create new people who can (only) enjoy lives of meaning level M. No plausible standard of procreative permissibility allows you to create a child whose life is barely worth living or minimally meaningful.

In my procreative ethics lectures, I defend a range of constraints on permissible Post-Cataclysm procreation. In particular, I argue that, after the Cataclysm, procreation is only permissible when two demanding conditions are met. We can only create new people if we both (a) remove the harm of lost future-dependent meaning altogether; and also (b) ensure that the last generation are no worse-off than previous generations overall.

Multigenerationalism presupposes the permissible creation of future people. So it *must* meet all plausible constraints on permissible procreation. This sounds like a very serious problem for multigenerationalism. However, things are not so simple. Multigenerationalists are not alone. Everyone in our Post-Cataclysm world who wants to create new people must meet the same constraints. The demands of procreative permissibility apply to each of us, multigenerationalist or not. Furthermore, anyone who accepts that Scheffler-inspired, future-dependent meaning has *some* significance must also agree that, unless we do *something* radical, the last generation will *not* enjoy as much meaning as earlier generations. But then it follows that, unless we do something radical, no one can ever permissibly procreate!

By definition, the last generation enjoy no future-dependent intergenerational meaning. If we cannot offer them a replacement, then procreation is only permissible if intergenerational meaning *has no value*. But this would be a very ambitious claim about what makes human lives meaningful. If we reject it—if we think connections between generations are part of what makes life meaningful—then, without a radical transformation of lost future-dependent intergenerational meaning, procreation cannot be permissible *even if the last generation would enjoy meaningful lives overall*. Everyone in our Post-Cataclysm world who is not an anti-natalist must find *something* to replace future-dependent intergenerational meaning.

I said at the start of this section that the relationship between multigenerationalism and procreative permissibility goes both ways. We can now see why. Multigenerationalism makes a serious attempt to replace future-dependent meaning. The demanding requirements of Post-Cataclysm procreative permissibility *support* multigenerationalism. Only by initiating multigenerational projects can we reasonably hope to meet those demands—transforming the moral landscape so the last generation still enjoy as much intergenerational meaning as anyone else.

In principle, opponents of multigenerationalism could simply embrace anti-natalism. Both presentists and theists could insist that present people do not *need* any connection to future people. Our lives can still be meaningful even if we create no new people. Presentists and theists *could* embrace anti-natalism without sliding into pessimism. But very few actual presentists or theists would be happy with this reply. They reject anti-natalism alongside pessimism. It would be a serious blow for any non-pessimist to have to concede that, after the Cataclysm, present people cannot create any new people.

I develop this procreative permissibility argument at much greater length in my procreative ethics lectures. I argue that every plausible procreative permissibility principle favours multigenerationalism. But I also argue that some principles also constrain the range of permissible multigenerational projects.

I conclude that multigenerationalism is plausible. It is supported by a wide variety of arguments. We have several compelling reasons to initiate multigenerational projects if it is feasible to do so. In my fifth lecture, I argue that this is feasible. In the meantime, however, I explore Post-Cataclysm procreative ethics at length over three separate lectures. Understanding the constraints on permissible procreation both strengthens the case for multigenerationalism and tells us how it must be pursued.

Philosophy for an Ending World. Tim Mulgan, Oxford University Press. © Tim Mulgan 2024.
DOI: 10.1093/9780191946479.003.0003

4
Lecture Two
Introducing Procreative Ethics

Multigenerationalist: Procreative ethics asks what ethical principles, reasons, obligations, and constraints govern the creation of new human beings. In the next three lectures, I address the challenges of our Post-Cataclysm world—drawing on several Pre-Cataclysm procreative ethical theories. I consider two non-consequentialist accounts (Elizabeth Harman's child-focused theory of justified harm and Rivka Weinberg's Rawlsian contractualism) and two consequentialist accounts (Melinda Roberts's person-affecting consequentialism and Tim Mulgan's liberal collective consequentialism).[1]

My overarching goals are (a) to identify the conditions for permissible procreation in our Post-Cataclysm world; and (b) to determine whether those conditions can ever be met. I also explore the constraints on permissible *multigenerational projects*, thus setting the scene for my final two lectures on multigenerational transformation and Post-Cataclysm utopias.

An exploration of procreative ethics is vital to my case for multigenerationalism. But it is also of wider interest. We all want to know whether we can permissibly create new people who will live even closer to humanity's end. Therefore, as far as possible, I make my discussion accessible to all readers—whether or not they have any interest in multigenerationalism itself.

I seek to remain agnostic between competing accounts of procreative ethics—and especially between consequentialism and non-consequentialism. Multigenerationalism is not committed to either approach. My goal is to show that multigenerationalism is consistent with, and supported by, both traditions in procreative ethics. I also explore overlaps between the best Pre-Cataclysm versions of both consequentialism and non-consequentialism.

In Section 4.1, I explain where I intend to end up. I introduce a range of constraints on Post-Cataclysm procreative ethics, all of which I defend later. In Section 4.2, I outline the main themes of Pre-Cataclysm procreative ethics. In Section 4.3, I outline the main challenges that organised Pre-Cataclysm debates. In Sections 4.4 and 4.5, I briefly explore two prominent Pre-Cataclysm approaches

---

[1] See, e.g., Harman, 'Can We Harm and Benefit in Creating?'; Roberts, 'A New Way of Doing the Best We Can'; Weinberg, *The Risk of a Lifetime*; Mulgan, *Future People*; and other works cited over the next three chapters.

to procreative ethics—those of Elizabeth Harman and Melinda Roberts—and apply them to our Post-Cataclysm world.

4.1 Constraints on Post-Cataclysm Procreation

Every procreative principle posits some Procreative Permissibility Threshold which must be met if procreation is to be morally permitted. I will argue that initiating multigenerational projects is both *necessary* and *sufficient* to ensure that Procreative Permissibility Thresholds are met throughout our Post-Cataclysm world, and especially when the penultimate generation create the last generation. Multigenerationalism, and *only* multigenerationalism, guarantees Post-Cataclysm procreative permissibility.

If we are already committed to some particular procreative ethical theory, with its own specific Procreative Permissibility Threshold, then that makes our task easier. Our chosen Procreative Permissibility Threshold will then influence the design of our multigenerational projects, because it will constrain the range of possible futures we can permissibly create. My own aim, however, is much more ambitious. I hope to remain broadly *agnostic* about procreative ethics. This is not really a matter of choice. I think multigenerationalism must remain agnostic. I don't think we can reasonably hope to settle Pre-Cataclysm debates within procreative ethics *in any way that we could then build into any multigenerational project that we initiate*. In particular, if our multigenerational project relies on the *voluntary cooperation* of future (intermediate) generations, then we can only build in assumptions about procreative permissibility *that we can reasonably expect all future people to endorse*. Otherwise, we run the risk that some intermediate generation, endorsing a different account of procreative ethics, will refuse to create further generations—thus causing our multigenerational project to collapse uncompleted. The only way to avoid this fate is to ensure that all future people will find procreation (at least) permissible—no matter what their theory of procreative ethics.

I therefore seek multigenerational projects that satisfy *all* plausible constraints on procreative permissibility that future people, raised within those projects, might endorse. These constraints will include the following:

- *Zero Constraint*: Procreation is permissible only if life in the next generation is (on the whole) worth living and meaningful. (This is endorsed by virtually all Pre-Cataclysm theories.)
- *Sufficiency Constraint*: Procreation is permissible only if life in the next generation is (on the whole) good enough. (This is also endorsed by virtually all Pre-Cataclysm theories.)

- *No Unjustified Harms Constraint*: Procreation is permissible only if life in the next generation contains no unjustified harms. (This constraint emerges from Harman's theory in Section 4.4.1.)
- *Intergenerational Meaning Constraint*: Life in the next generation contains (on the whole) sufficient intergenerational meaning. (This constraint is necessary to rebut Post-Cataclysm pessimism.)
- *Intergenerational Cooperation Constraint*: People in the next generation can engage in cooperative relationships with members of the present generation. (This constraint emerges from Weinberg's theory in Section 5.2.1)
- *Same Person Comparative Constraints*: My future child's life compares favourably with other lives that they could possibly have lived—where favourable comparison may involve overall superiority and/or the absence of avoidable harms. Procreation is then permissible only if my child could not have lived a better life and/or the harms they suffer were unavoidable *for them*. (Most Pre-Cataclysm theories endorse some Same Person Comparisons. I discuss them especially in relation to Roberts's theory in Section 4.5, as Roberts's theory employs *only* Same Person Comparisons).
- *Different Person Comparative Constraints*: My future child's life compares favourably with other lives that *someone else* could possibly have lived *instead*—where favourable comparison may involve overall superiority and/or the absence of avoidable harms. Procreation is then permissible only if *no child of mine* could have lived a better life and/or avoided the harms that my actual child suffers. (Many Pre-Cataclysm theories endorse some Different Person Comparative Constraints in addition to Same Person ones. I discuss them especially in relation to Harman's theory in Section 4.4 and Weinberg's theory in Section 5.2.)
- *Rational Risk Constraint*: The *ex ante* risks that I impose on my child, by creating them, are risks that it would be rational for me to choose myself in exchange for permission to procreate in this situation. (Variations of this constraint stipulate instead that it must be *not irrational* for me to take that risk and/or that I actually *would* take it.) These constraints emerge from Weinberg's theory in Section 5.2.2.
- *No Intergenerational Decline Constraint*: Procreation is permissible only if life in the next generation is (on the whole) no worse than life in the present generation.
- *No Avoidable Intergenerational Decline Constraint*: Procreation is permissible only if life in the next generation is (on the whole) no worse than life in the present generation—if this could have been avoided. (Unlike the previous constraint, this one *could* permit *unavoidable* intergenerational decline.)

- *No Post-Cataclysm Decline Constraint*: Procreation is permissible only if life in the next generation is (on the whole) no worse than life in earlier generations in our Post-Cataclysm world.
- *No Post-Cataclysm Avoidable Decline Constraint*: Procreation is permissible only if life in the next generation is (on the whole) no worse than life in earlier generations in our Post-Cataclysm world—if this could have been avoided. (Unlike the previous constraint, this one *could* permit *unavoidable* Post-Cataclysm decline.)

The last four constraints are the most ambitious. To meet them, we must completely reverse the loss of future-dependent intergenerational meaning—at least whenever it is *possible* to do so. I argued in my introductory lecture that multigenerationalism *does* strive to meet these ambitious constraints. I argue throughout the next three lectures that *if* multigenerationalism *can* meet these constraints, then rival approaches must do so also. In particular, if multigenerational reorientation would enable us to avoid intergenerational decline, and if we endorse any of my four No Decline Constraints, then procreation *without multigenerational reorientation* will be impermissible.

4.2 Themes in Pre-Cataclysm Procreative Ethics

Despite their differences, the four theories I have selected all represent a broad consensus within Pre-Cataclysm procreative ethics. In particular, they share three central commitments:

1. *Procreative Freedom*: People are morally free to decide when, whether, with whom, and how often they will create new people.

However, this freedom is not unconstrained:

2. *The Zero Constraint*: It is only permissible to procreate if one's future child's life will be worth living (above the 'zero level').

Virtually all Pre-Cataclysm procreative ethicists regard the Zero Constraint as a *necessary* condition for permissible procreation. But few regard it as *sufficient*. Most posit *additional* necessary conditions: it is permissible to procreate only if one's future child's life will be *good enough*. We then naturally ask whether life can still be good enough in our Post-Cataclysm world.

3. *The Autonomy of Procreative Ethics*: Procreative ethics is independent of broader ethical, political, and public policy debates about population

policy, sustainability, or extinction-avoidance. Philosophers can thus discover procreative ethical principles without considering those broader questions; and individual agents can apply those principles—and make actual procreative decisions—without addressing them.

While the autonomy of procreative ethics is seldom articulated, I believe it underlies many Pre-Cataclysm debates. This theoretical autonomy naturally supports a *substantive* commitment to procreative freedom. But the two are distinct. For instance, as we'll soon see, anti-natalists often defend autonomous procreative principles that forbid procreation (Section 4.3.1).

One aspect of the autonomy of procreative ethics is that Pre-Cataclysm non-consequentialist procreative ethics, in particular, restricts the kinds of reasons we consider. Borrowing a distinction from Rivka Weinberg, we can distinguish two main types of procreative ethic:[2]

- *Child-focused* theories insist that *only good things in the future child's own life* can justify procreative freedom.
- *Parent-focused* theories *balance* the interests of possible future children and those of prospective parents—sometimes allowing parental interests to tip the balance.

Every procreative ethic recognises *some* child-focused reasons—such as the Zero Constraint. The question is whether we should *also* recognise competing *parent-focused* reasons. I will explore both child-focused and parent-focused accounts, both consequentialist and non-consequentialist.

Many *possible* theories fall outside this simple dichotomy. We can imagine principles that are neither child-focused nor parent-focused—based on impersonal values or on third-party interests. (Should I procreate to maximise well-being, or to give my parents a grandchild, or my city future citizens?) Weinberg's dichotomy reflects Pre-Cataclysm *procreative liberalism*, which concentrates on child-focused and parent-focused reasons, setting aside impersonal values and third-party interests. As we'll see, this narrow focus is clearer for non-consequentialist theories than for consequentialism. I will ask later on whether it continues to make sense in our Post-Cataclysm world—or whether wider issues must now impinge on procreative decisions (see, e.g., Sections 5.2.1 and 6.3).

---

[2] cf. Weinberg, 'Procreative Justice', p. 405. Weinberg distinguishes child-focused theories from what we might call 'pure' parent-focused theories—which only take account of parent-focused reasons and ignore child-focused reasons. Weinberg then presents her own contractualist account as a third (superior) alternative that balances the two sets of reasons. However, as pure parent-focused accounts are rare, I repurpose her distinction to differentiate the two main approaches in Pre-Cataclysm procreative ethics.

If we only consider child-focused and parent-focused reasons, we still face two important questions. (1) What additional child-focused constraints should supplement our Zero Constraint? (2) How do we balance child-focused and parent-focused reasons?

We can categorise additional child-focused constraints along three dimensions:

1. *Global vs particular*: *Global constraints* set a minimum threshold for the future child's *lifetime well-being*. (The most permissive global constraint is the Zero Constraint.) By contrast, *particular constraints* cite specific rights or interests that must be fulfilled, or specific harms to be avoided, independent of overall well-being. For instance, procreation might be impermissible if one's child will be enslaved—no matter how well-off they are.
2. *Wellbeing vs Meaning*: The phrases 'life worth living' and 'good enough life' are both ambiguous between well-being and meaningfulness. Like well-being standards, meaning standards can be either global or particular. We might insist that any future child's life is meaningful overall, or that it contains *this or that particular kind of meaning*. We can also set higher thresholds. We might insist that the future child's life be *meaningful enough*, not just barely meaningful. *Our* principal Post-Cataclysm question, of course, is whether the loss of *future-dependent meaning* renders procreation impermissible.
3. *Non-Comparative vs Comparative*: The Zero Constraint uses a non-comparative standard ('above zero'). *Comparative* constraints instead compare the future child's life to *other* (actual or possible) lives—such as (i) other possible lives for *this child*; (ii) the lives of *other possible future children* we might have created instead; (iii) lives in the same generation in the same society; or (iv) 'typical' human lives. Comparative constraints are invoked to explain why (in modern societies) it is wrong to create a child who is illiterate, enslaved, or deaf, but not one who is mortal and cannot breathe underwater.

One important division *within* comparative constraints is whether we compare the possible future child's life with (a) other lives *that the same child might have lived*; or (b) the lives of *other possible future children* who would have existed if we had acted differently. This brings us to a central puzzle in Pre-Cataclysm future ethics: Derek Parfit's *Non-Identity Problem*.[3] Parfit argues that non-consequentialist theories are designed for *Same People Choices* where our actions only affect people who will exist anyway. Therefore, they cope poorly with *Different People Choices* where our actions determine who will ever exist.[4] Unfortunately, Parfit continues, Different People Choices are more frequent than we realise.

---

[3] Parfit, *Reasons and Persons*, pp. 351–379.   [4] Parfit, *Reasons and Persons*, p. 356.

Some Different People Choices are personal. In Parfit's classic example, a fourteen-year-old girl has a child.[5] While her child enjoys a worthwhile life, any child she bore later in life would have enjoyed a much better life. We naturally conclude that this mother has *harmed* her child, who is worse-off *than they might otherwise have been*. But this is a mistake. If the mother had waited ten years, she would have had *a different child*. Her *actual child* would never have existed. Given mundane facts about human reproduction, and 'uncontroversial' facts about personal identity across possible worlds, the same child could not actually have been born ten years later.[6]

Other Different People Choices are collective. In Parfit's classic example, we bury nuclear waste where there is a significant earthquake risk in the distant future.[7] Many centuries later, an earthquake releases radiation, killing thousands of people. Intuitively, our choice is wrong because we harm those who die. But suppose our initial choice influences migration patterns over several generations. (We build an unsafe nuclear-waste-processing facility somewhere uninhabited—people move there from many places, and have children with people they would not otherwise have met.) Any particular individual killed by the future catastrophe would never have existed at all if we had chosen differently. (Their parents would never have met—or they would never have existed themselves.) Our choice thus harms no one. But then how can it be *wrong*?

Parfit's non-identity problem targets *person-affecting theories* which insist that actions are only wrong if some particular person is worse-off than they would otherwise have been. As we'll see, many Pre-Cataclysm non-consequentialists deny that *their* theories *are* person-affecting *in Parfit's sense* (Sections 4.4.1, 4.5.1, and 5.1).

Alongside Parfit's original distinction between Same People and Different People Choices, I would add a third alternative: *Extra People Choices*, where the salient alternatives are (a) to create a future child; and (b) to create no one. Extra People Choices raises particular ethical challenges. Many theories find it easier to justify procreation when the salient alternative is to create no one rather than to create someone else (Sections 4.4.1, 4.5.1, and 5.2.7).

The case for additional standards to supplement the Zero Constraint is compelling in Same People Choices. You should have given *this very child* a better life! The analogous complaint is much harder to motivate in Different People Choices, and especially in Extra People Choices. How can *this child* (whose life is worth living) complain that you should instead have given a better life to a *different* child, or that you should have created no one at all?

---

[5] Parfit, *Reasons and Persons*, p. 358.
[6] Parfit, *Reasons and Persons*, pp. 351–355.
[7] Parfit, *Reasons and Persons*, p. 371.

My question is: How should Pre-Cataclysm procreative ethical theories adapt to our Post-Cataclysm world? In particular, if life is either less worthwhile now, or less meaningful, is procreation still permissible?

I begin by borrowing two lessons from our pessimism debate. First, I focus on the loss of *future-dependent meaning* (Sections 1.4 and 3.5). This loss potentially cuts both ways. On the one hand, the fact that one's *future child's life* lacks future-dependent meaning is a reason *not* to procreate. This loss of meaning weighs *against* procreative freedom. On the other hand, if one's *own* life lacks other kinds of future-dependent meaning, then creating a child of one's own might offer a rare opportunity to bring meaning into one's own life. This loss of meaning may provide both a *reason* to procreate and a *justification* for procreative freedom.

Second, as we did in our pessimism debate, I will often focus on the plight of the last generation (Section 1.2). I therefore explore procreative freedom *in the penultimate generation*. Is it permissible to create someone who will live at humanity's end? Is it permissible to create people who cannot possibly procreate themselves? This last question matters because many justifications for procreative freedom cite the importance *to potential parents* of the ability to (permissibly) have children of their own. Such justifications are obviously problematic in the penultimate generation, when everyone knows that *no* future child can procreate in their turn. Emphasising the importance of procreation thus highlights the burden that penultimate parents impose on their own children.

4.3 Challenges in Pre-Cataclysm Procreative Ethics

In this section, I briefly outline four challenges that structured Pre-Cataclysm debates in procreative ethics: the anti-natalist challenge, the pro-natalist challenge, the act consequentialist challenge, and the procreative asymmetry.

4.3.1 The Anti-Natalist Challenge

The Cataclysm's most obvious impact on procreative ethics is to lend addition support to *anti-natalism*. Anti-natalism says that no one should ever have children. Procreation is always prohibited.

Anti-natalism is obviously related to pessimism. *Pessimism* says that life is bad. *Anti-natalism* says we should not create new people. If we accept the Zero Constraint, then well-being-based pessimism implies anti-natalism. If one's future child cannot enjoy a worthwhile life, then procreation is never permissible. Similarly, under a minimal *meaningfulness* standard for permissible procreation, meaning-based pessimism implies anti-natalism.

Most Pre-Cataclysm pessimists were anti-natalists. But not all anti-natalists were pessimists. Anti-natalism does not *require* pessimism. Procreation might still be impermissible, even if one's future child enjoys a worthwhile or meaningful life, because either (a) their lifetime well-being or meaningfulness would fall below some higher minimum threshold; or (b) they would be deprived of some specific essential good thing; or (c) procreation is disrespectful (perhaps because no one consents to being born).[8]

If any argument for pessimism succeeds, then there is almost certainly a compelling argument for anti-natalism. Recall the distinction between *Post-Cataclysm* pessimism and *last generation* pessimism—introduced in Section 1.2. If Post-Cataclysm pessimism is correct, then we should endorse Post-Cataclysm anti-natalism. If life has *become* too bad, then procreation has become impermissible. Suppose instead that we endorse last generation pessimism, but we reject Post-Cataclysm pessimism. Life is too bad in the last generation, but not earlier in our Post-Cataclysm world. Last generation pessimism implies *penultimate* anti-natalism. The 'penultimate' generation cannot permissibly procreate—they must *become* the last generation. This suggests a Ponzi-style argument for *Post-Cataclysm* anti-natalism, where each generation, in its turn, is forbidden to create new people. We ourselves must become the last generation (Section 1.5).

I think most procreative liberals will agree that, *if* pessimism were correct, *then* anti-natalism would be compelling. Procreative ethics is much more interesting when pessimism fails. I also want to avoid overlap with our pessimism debate. Therefore, I will stipulate both (a) that procreation *was* (sometimes) permissible before the Cataclysm; and (b) that life in our Post-Cataclysm world can be both meaningful and worth living, even in the last generation. We then ask whether procreation is still permissible.

I realise these assumptions are controversial—and I will often revisit them. But, for the moment, let's be optimistic!

If the Zero Constraint exhausts our procreative ethic—if procreation is always permissible whenever one's future child's life is worth living—then anti-natalism stands or falls with (well-being-based) pessimism. But if we add *stronger* procreative constraints—if procreation is sometimes impermissible even when one's future child's life would be worth living—then some anti-natalist argument might succeed even if the analogous pessimist argument fails. Although the Zero Constraint is satisfied, some *stronger* constraint cannot be met—either in the penultimate generation or throughout our Post-Cataclysm world.

Anti-natalism is a serious challenge in our Post-Cataclysm world. Any procreative principle that forbids procreation in condition C will demand immediate extinction if every potential parent always faces C. And most Pre-Cataclysm

---

[8] On disrespectful procreation, see Shiffrin, 'Wrongful Life, Procreative Responsibility, and the Significance of Harm', and the discussion of Weinberg in Section 5.2.

philosophers agreed that procreation is *sometimes* forbidden. Therefore, if humanity's situation worsens, Pre-Cataclysm liberal principles might *now* support anti-natalism.

If their principles do forbid procreation, procreative liberals can either abandon the principle in question, reinterpret it so that it does not prohibit procreation, or bite the bullet and accept that procreation *is* now universally prohibited. While extinction avoidance lurked in the background before the Cataclysm, it moves centre stage for us. As we'll see, different procreative ethicists respond very differently to this challenge (Sections 4.4.2, 4.5.2, 5.2.1, and 6.3.3).

4.3.2 The Pro-Natalist Challenge

Anti-natalism challenges procreative freedom from one direction. But the Cataclysm could also strengthen arguments for *pro-natalism*. Pro-natalism says that procreation is (often) obligatory. Here, I use 'pro-natalism' as a term of art, to complement 'anti-natalism'. In ordinary usage, 'pro-natal' suggests, not an *obligation* to have children, but rather a presumption in favour of procreation. Weaker pro-natalist views were very common before the Cataclysm. And, while few Pre-Cataclysm philosophers explicitly defended procreative obligations, the literature contains implicit pro-natalist strands, especially in relation to *extinction avoidance*.

Procreative liberals hope that people's actual exercise of their procreative freedom (including the freedom to *not* procreate) will not lead to either human extinction or over-population.[9] This hope is based on empirical assumptions that may no longer be plausible (if they ever were). If procreative freedom will *not*, as a matter of fact, guarantee a sustainable future population, then pro-natalists argue that our underlying obligation to ensure a sustainable future trumps individual procreative freedom.

Procreative freedom occupies an uneasy middle road between prohibition and obligation. Any unfamiliar future raises two opposite threats. On the one hand, if the lives of the next generation are too undesirable, then it is not permissible to create new people at all. Selfish or optimistic people may then exercise their procreative freedom to create *too many* new people. In this case, procreative freedom should instead give way to anti-natalism. On the other hand, if circumstances decline but procreation is still desirable, then too many people will refuse to have children *because* their children's lives might be less wonderful than their own—even though those children would enjoy good lives. If people are free to choose, then the next generation may be *too small*. In this case, we can only *guarantee* a large-enough next generation if people feel obliged *to* have children.

[9] Mulgan, *Future People*, pp. 179–185.

In our Post-Cataclysm world, three main factors *strengthen* pro-natalism. First, if things are worse now, but procreation still remains desirable all things considered, then procreative obligations may be especially necessary, because too few people will want to procreate. Second, confident predictions about how future people will exercise *their* procreative freedom are especially unreliable when circumstances are rapidly changing, as they are throughout our Post-Cataclysm world. We may *hope* that procreative freedom will secure an optimal future population. But can we rely on this hope? Third, multigenerationalism generates a new pro-natalist argument. Suppose our pessimism debate—together with my earlier lecture—has persuaded you that our only viable alternatives are pessimism and multigenerationalism. (In other words, you reject presentism, supernaturalism, and other non-multigenerationalist optimist views.) Present people cannot flourish *unless there are future people* (Section 1.4). Present people then owe it *to one another* to create future people. They also owe this *to past generations*. We owe it to our predecessors to continue (or, in the last generation, to complete) the multigenerational project(s) that give meaning to all our lives (Section 3.6).

In the previous lecture, I presented a procreative permissibility argument for multigenerationalism (Section 3.8). The present argument goes in the opposite direction—from the feasibility of multigenerational projects to a procreative *obligation*. Of course, this argument only goes through if multigenerational projects *are* feasible. I return to *that* question in my fifth lecture.

4.3.3 Consequentialist Procreative Ethics: Beyond Act Consequentialism

A third challenge to procreative liberalism comes from act consequentialism. Act consequentialism rejects both procreative freedom and the autonomy of procreative ethics. It rejects procreative freedom, simply because it rejects *all* moral freedom. Everyone should always maximise the good. The utilitarian principle covers *all* human choices. Potential parents should have a child if (and *only* if) this act best maximises total future well-being.

Act consequentialism has many advantages in procreative ethics. As a *consequentialist* ethic, act consequentialism is untroubled by non-identity. It treats Same and Different People Choices identically—embracing Parfit's 'no difference view'.[10] What matters is how happy future people are, not which people are happy. Discovering that we face a Different People Choice makes no moral difference. Act consequentialism is equally untroubled by non-pessimist anti-natalism. Procreation is prima facie unproblematic whenever one's future child would enjoy a worthwhile life.

---

[10] Parfit, *Reasons and Persons*, p. 367.

However, act consequentialism faces its own problems. All consequentialists have difficulties with Different *Number* Choices, where our decision affects how many people ever exist. Consequentialists seek what Parfit dubs 'Theory X'—a complete ranking of the comparative values of possible outcomes involving different numbers of people.[11] Parfit argues that Theory X has not been found, and that all plausible candidates have very intuitively unappealing consequences.[12] (I return to aggregation, in relation to collective consequentialism, in Section 6.1.)

More broadly, most philosophers simply find act consequentialism too demanding and alienating, especially in procreative ethics.[13] Far from supporting individual procreation, act consequentialism probably forbids it, due to opportunity costs. Affluent agents should donate their resources to charity rather than using them to raise their own children. Act consequentialism paradoxically favours *individual* anti-natalism, even though it wants most people to procreate!

More fundamentally, whatever act consequentialism *actually* demands, it leaves *no room* for *procreative freedom*, simply because it rejects all moral freedom. Act consequentialism *demands* whatever maximises the good. No actual person has ever not found act consequentialism too extreme. No one has ever tried to live an act consequentialist life. Therefore, when I turn to consequentialism in my third procreative ethics lecture, I will focus on less demanding theories that seek to incorporate procreative freedom within a moderate liberal consequentialism. We return to extreme act consequentialism at the end of our final debate, in the context of digital escapism (Section 9.10).

4.3.4 The Procreative Asymmetry

Another tension that runs through Pre-Cataclysm procreative ethics is the much-discussed *procreative asymmetry*, which contrasts two intuitively compelling claims:[14]

- *Negative*: It is always wrong to knowingly create a person whose life will be not worth living; and
- *Positive*: There is no obligation to create a person whose life would be well worth living.

---

[11] Parfit, *Reasons and Persons*, p. 390.   [12] Parfit, *Reasons and Persons*, pp. 416–417.
[13] I defend this rejection of act consequentialism at length in Mulgan, *The Demands of Consequentialism*; Mulgan, *Future People*; and Mulgan, *Utilitarianism*.
[14] On the Asymmetry, see, e.g., McMahan, 'Causing People to Exist and Saving People's Lives'; Roberts, 'The Asymmetry: A Solution'; and Chappell, 'Rethinking the Asymmetry'.

Procreative ethics must either accommodate or reject this apparent asymmetry. This proves surprisingly difficult.

The procreative asymmetry challenges consequentialists and non-consequentialists in very different ways. Consequentialism easily explains the Negative side; but it struggles with the Positive. We should not create bad lives. But if we only consider the overall result, then *failing to add* a good life is (equally) wrong. By contrast, while non-consequentialists can easily recognise various asymmetries between creating a bad life and failing to create a good life, they struggle to reconcile procreative *asymmetry* with procreative *freedom*. If we endorse both the Positive and Negative claims, then the *risk* of a bad life suggests a simple argument for anti-natalism. If (a) it is so wrong to create a child whose life is not worth living; and if (b) there is no strong reason *to* create a child whose life is worth living; and if (c) there is always *some* risk that one's child's life will be not worth living; then (d) how can procreation ever be justified?

Consequentialists and non-consequentialists similarly disagree about *voluntary* human extinction. Consequentialists cannot easily accept voluntary immediate extinction, unless life in the next generation would be below zero; while *non*-consequentialist principles often permit voluntary immediate human extinction: if everyone choses not to procreate, then no one does anything *morally* wrong.

This non-consequentialist acceptance of voluntary extinction may seem implausible. But we should note that non-consequentialism can *permit* voluntary immediate extinction without *welcoming* it. Permissions and obligations do not exhaust our moral *reasons*. As Scheffler emphasised, present people have many reasons to *hope* that there will be future people. Even if those reasons do not give anyone an *obligation* to procreate, they do give many present people strong reasons which make it virtually inevitable (in ordinary times) that most people *will* procreate and that they will also support public policies to enable and encourage others to procreate. Given actual human motivations, these actions and policies almost certainly prevent immediate voluntary extinction in (Pre-Cataclysm) ordinary times. Human morality, and especially procreative ethics, is tailored to the realities of *human* life. If we insist on judging ethical principles by results, then we should look at actual (expected) results among human beings, not logically possible results among creatures very different from us. Procreative freedom only actually leads to voluntary extinction in extraordinary times—and perhaps *in those times* it is not objectionable.

In the remaining two sections of my first procreative ethics lecture, I briefly explore two theories: one non-consequentialist and one consequentialist. As both theories favour procreative freedom, they must address both anti-natalist and pro-natalist challenges.

4.4 Harman's Child-Focused Person-Affecting Procreative Ethic

Elizabeth Harman illustrates both the strengths and limitations of child-focused procreative ethics. Her account will introduce some central themes in non-consequentialist procreative ethics and multigenerationalism—which I return to in my second procreative ethics lecture. I first set out Harman's account (Section 4.4.1), and then apply it to our Post-Cataclysm world (Section 4.4.2). In Sections 4.4.3 and 4.4.4, I argue that multigenerationalism supports Harman's approach, but also constrains it.

4.4.1 Harman's Original Account

Harman offers four desiderata for a solution to the Non-Identity Problem:[15]

1. Explain *why* agents do something *wrong* in cases like Parfit's fourteen-year-old girl.
2. Vindicate our intuition that these actions are wrong *because they harm the relevant future people*.
3. Explain why there is *reasonable disagreement* about 'hard cases' where is it unclear whether or not procreation is permitted.
4. Only allow benefits to the child to *justify* procreation. (In Weinberg's terminology, Harman seeks a *child-focused* solution.)

Harman asks when *harms* parents inflict on their future children are justified by *benefits* they confer. Harman's first *necessary* condition is:

Outweighing Condition: Procreation is only justified if benefit *outweighs* harm. (The child is better-off with both benefit and harm than with neither.)

This condition is *not* sufficient. *Ex hypothesi*, in Parfit's classic non-identity cases, benefits outweigh harms. Harman respects—and hopes to *explain*—two common intuitions: (a) that these acts are nonetheless *wrong*, and (b) that they are wrong *because* they harm the person who is created, even though (c) that person has a life worth living and (d) they would otherwise never exist.

The Zero Constraint therefore does not exhaust Harman's procreative ethic. Harman adds a second necessary condition:

Eligibility Condition: Procreation can only be justified if the benefit is *eligible to justify* the harm.

---

[15] Harman, 'Can We Harm and Benefit in Creating?' and 'Harming as Causing Harm'.

A benefit is *eligible* if benefit and harm are *inseparable*. This is straightforward in Same People Choices. If I could benefit you *without harming you*, then benefits I confer cannot justify harms I inflict. Harman's distinctive claim concerns *Different* People Choices. Even if I cannot benefit *you* without harming you, benefits are still ineligible if I could instead have benefited *someone else* without harming *anyone*. Suppose I have a child who is deaf. If I could instead have had a (different) child who enjoyed the same benefits *and was not deaf*, then those benefits are *not eligible* to justify the harm of deafness.

For Harman, procreation is often justified in *Extra* People Choices when it would not be justified in the analogous *Different* People Choice. In a Different People Choice, benefits are only eligible if the harm is *unavoidable*. By contrast, in an Extra People Choice, the salient alternative is to create no one. Therefore, the agent *cannot* similarly benefit someone else. All benefits are eligible, because no harm is 'avoidable' in the relevant sense.

Harman's two necessary conditions—Outweighing and Eligibility—are still not jointly sufficient for justification. Not every *eligible* benefit *actually* justifies harm. We must exercise *judgement* about particular cases. At both end of the scale, judgement is relatively easy. At one end, we have *clearly unjustified harms*: 'Some harms are so bad that nothing can justify them, such as the harm of living a year in total agony.'[16] A century of bliss might *outweigh* a year of agony. And some benefits are *eligible* to justify this harm in particular cases. But no possible benefit could *actually justify* the year of agony.

At the other extreme, we have *clearly justified harms*. Harman defends procreative liberty. Ordinary procreation is justified. 'Other harms are not so bad that nothing can justify them, such as the harms in an ordinary life.'[17] Although every human life contains harms, ordinary human harms are justified by the benefits of an ordinary human life.

If procreation is justified in some cases and not others, then there must be some *threshold*—such that harms below the threshold *can* be justified, while harms above it *cannot*. There are *hard cases* because 'people implicitly place the threshold...in different places.'[18] Is it permissible for a woman to conceive if she knows that any child she conceives will be deaf? Is it permissible for an enslaved couple in the American South in 1800 to conceive if their child will also be enslaved? People disagree whether lifelong deafness or enslavement can be justified *in these cases*. While deafness and slavery both significantly diminish a child's quality of life, both harms can be outweighed. Deaf children and enslaved children can enjoy lives worth living. And if I know that *any* child of mine will be deaf or enslaved, then the good things in my child's life are *eligible* to justify the

---

[16] Harman, 'Harming as Causing Harm', p. 144.
[17] Harman, 'Harming as Causing Harm', p. 144.
[18] Harman, 'Harming as Causing Harm', p. 144.

harm. These *Extra* People Choices are hard cases because it is not clear whether these harms *are* actually justified.

Harman's view is thus *not* the simple person-affecting view that Parfit attacks—where every outweighing benefit is eligible, and every eligible benefit justifies. For Parfit's person-affecting theorist, it is sufficient, in any Different People Choice or Extra People Choice, to give your future child a worthwhile life. For Harman, by contrast, this is not sufficient. Not all outweighing benefits are eligible, and not all eligible benefits actually justify.

Harman evaluates the imposition of harm. Failure to confer a benefit is not necessarily a harm. I am not harmed just because my mother did not marry a wealthy aristocrat—even if her children would have been better-off if she had. The absence of a possible good is not always itself a harm. For Harman, harm is *species-relative*: 'an action harms someone if it causes the person to be in a bad state...[and] bad states are those states that are worse in some way than the normal healthy state for a member of one's species'.[19] Some apparent 'harms' are not harms at all. My inability to fly is not a harm. Therefore, imposing this 'harm' does not need to be justified. Even if my parents could have enabled me to fly, I cannot complain. (And I certainly cannot complain that they could instead have created someone else who could fly.) Normal healthy humans can hear. They cannot fly. My parents need not justify my inability to fly. But if I cannot *hear*, then this *is* a harm that must be justified.

4.4.2 Harman at Humanity's End

In Harman's terminology, our central procreative ethics question is: Do the harms of (normal) life *in our Post-Cataclysm world* render procreation unjusitifiable, or can we confer benefits on the last humans that both outweigh *and justify* those harms?

Whenever we consider any Post-Cataclysm-specific harm, we must ask four questions: Is this a *harm*? Is it *outweighed*? Are the relevant benefits *eligible*? Finally, do those benefits actually *justify*?

I will consider three possible harms facing people in the last generation: inability to have children of one's own, absence of any future people, and the loss of 'ordinary' benefits and/or greater incidence of 'ordinary' harms.

I begin with the fact that no one in the last generation can have children. This is clearly a harm. If we reject last generation pessimism, then benefits enjoyed by the last generation *do* (normally) outweigh this harm. The last humans can enjoy worthwhile lives. Eligibility is also unproblematic, because the relevant harm is

---

[19] Harman, 'Harming as Causing Harm', p. 139; cf. Harman, 'Can We Harm and Benefit in Creating?'

unavoidable. The penultimate generation can only create members of the last generation—who by definition cannot have children. This is an *Extra* People Choice, not a *Different* People Choice. (By contrast, for Harman, infertility is definitely *not* justified if it is avoidable. Suppose a six-month delay in conception would produce a fertile child instead of an infertile one. In this case, no possible benefit is eligible to justify the harm.)

Having satisfied both the outweighing condition and the eligibility condition, we must now use our ethical judgement. Do the benefits of ordinary life at humanity's end justify the harm of infertility? Consider Harman's own examples: Is infertility more like (a) a year of agony (*easy case*: procreation is impermissible); or (b) the harms of ordinary Pre-Cataclysm life (*easy case*: procreation is permissible); or (c) being deaf or enslaved (*hard case*: reasonable disagreement whether procreation is permissible)?

Infertility is nothing new. Every potential parent faces *some* risk that their future child will be unable to have children. If ordinary Pre-Cataclysm procreation was nonetheless permissible, then the ordinary background *risk* of infertility is not an unjustifiable harm for Harman.

By contrast, *certain* infertility is arguably (at least) a Pre-Cataclysm *hard* case. People will reasonably disagree whether or not infertility is worse than deafness. For what it is worth, my own judgement is that, if life in the last generation is *otherwise* good enough, then penultimate procreation can be justified, despite the harm of certain infertility. However, anti-natalists will obvious disagree. They disagree with procreative liberals (such as Harman) about hard cases—just as pessimists disagree with optimists whether certain lives are worth living in the first place. And such disputes about ethical judgement are very difficult to adjudicate.

A second harm suffered by everyone in the last generation is that infertility is not only certain, but also *universal*. Everyone else also cannot have children. Pre-Cataclysm infertile people had other ways to care for some members of the next generation. The last generation enjoy no such substitutes. Therefore, they suffer a new harm—the removal of all future people. Is this new harm sufficient to render procreation impermissible?

Universality cuts both ways. In the last generation, childlessness brings no stigma, envy, intragenerational disadvantage, or social exclusion. (Analogously, if everyone else is deaf, then any harm associated with social exclusion within a hearing-majority society disappears.) Last generation social life will *not* be built around parent–child activities. This is one respect in which the actual net harm of infertility is *reduced*. We must therefore now judge whether the removal of social exclusion balances the loss of *other* future-directed alternatives. Is universal infertility, on balance, better or worse than being infertile in a world of fertile people? This is another bedrock clash of intuitions that is very difficult to adjudicate.

Is there any way to break these intuitive deadlocks? Suppose we agree that, on balance, certain infertility remains a hard case. According to Harman, Pre-Cataclysm hard cases were comparatively rare. Most people could avoid wrongful procreation by 'playing it safe': procreate if your case is easy, refrain if it is hard. (When in doubt, don't create!) If *all* procreation is now a hard case, then universal safety leads to anti-natalism—and immediate extinction!

This highlights one distinctive feature of Harman's non-consequentialism. Harman rejects any justification based on impersonal good or parental desire. If benefits to the child cannot justify, then nothing can. If the imposition of certain infertility cannot be justified, then penultimate procreation is impermissible.

Harman has no objection, in principle, to voluntary immediate extinction. So this possibility is not really an objection to her theory. If procreation is a (universal) hard case, then all penultimate procreation is *morally risky*. Perhaps it *would* be best, in this tragic situation, if everyone refrained from procreation. Unlike consequentialists, non-consequentialists are not obsessed with extinction-avoidance at all costs.

Furthermore, Harman has philosophical resources to ameliorate the harshness of any ban on penultimate procreation. She argues that some *impermissible* procreation is nonetheless *excusable*.[20] Whether or not it is justified, the slave parents' decision to have a child who is a slave is almost certainly excused. Similarly, even if procreation is *forbidden* in the penultimate generation, it might be excused by a desire to avoid immediate extinction. Procreation is especially easy to excuse in a genuinely hard case, where we disagree whether or not it really *is* forbidden in the first place.

A more general possible harm facing the last generation occurs if life is generally less good in the last generation—either because 'ordinary' benefits are reduced or because 'ordinary' harms have increased. Life at humanity's end may be bleak and dangerous. Even if they reject last generation pessimism, most people would agree that—unless we do something radical soon—life will be worse at humanity's end.

The threat of declining quality of life has three implications on Harman's view. First, if the last generation enjoy fewer benefits, then those benefits are less likely to be sufficient to *justify* harms such as certain infertility or the loss of future people. Second, an increased risk of life's 'ordinary' harms is itself a new harm that must be justified. If the risk is too great, the balance may tip against procreative permissibility. Third, if the next generation would be much worse-off, then widespread *acceptance* of Harman's principles is more likely to lead to voluntary immediate extinction, even if procreation is technically permitted. Harman asks when parents are justified in procreating, on the assumption that procreation is

---

[20] Harman, 'Harming as Causing Harm', p. 145; cf. Harman, 'Can We Harm and Benefit in Creating?'

something they want to do. She does not address reasons to procreate, let alone procreative obligations. The fact that my child would be (unavoidably) worse-off may not affect justifiability, but it could reduce people's desire to procreate. (And, of course, if most other people will not procreate, then it becomes even harder to provide my child with the benefits of 'ordinary' human life.)

4.4.3 How Multigenerationalism Supports Harman

How does multigenerationalism affect Harman's view? In this section, I argue that multigenerationalism supports non-consequentialist procreative freedom better than presentism can. (A reminder: in our earlier debates, the 'Presentist' claims that present-focused projects are sufficient for a meaningful life without any grounding in, or connection to, future people.)

Most presentists acknowledge that losing future-directed projects is a genuine harm. They then seek eligible benefits that outweigh and justify this harm. This brings us back to bedrock clashes of judgement: we must ask whether *this* eligible benefit actually justifies *that* harm.

Multigenerationalism is more ambitious. We seek to remove the need for justification altogether by removing the relevant harm. The real harm facing the last generation is not infertility—nor even the loss of future people—but rather the loss of future-dependent *meaning*. Infertility is merely *one* way to lose future-dependent meaning, because parent–child relationships are one way to enjoy this kind of meaning. Instead of adding new instances of quite different kinds of meaningful activity, or additional compensating pleasures, multigenerationalism removes the harm altogether—by providing a new instance of *the same type of meaning*. We take an existing Pre-Cataclysm future-dependent tradition and (gradually) reorient it toward the present and the past. If this reorientation succeeds, then the last generation's future-dependent projects will be reoriented in ways that make sense without any future people. Their inability to have children is thus no harm *at all*. This is analogous to providing deaf people with *another way to hear*, rather than offering some other compensation to people who remain unable to hear.

According to multigenerationalism, the real Post-Cataclysm harm is the loss of *intergenerational* meaning—the broader kind of meaning that (before the Catalcysm) was most often embodied in future-directed projects. Multigenerational projects now deliver *the same* meaning. The last generation cannot enjoy *future-dependent* intergenerational meaning. But they can find non-future-dependent intergenerational meaning by bringing the human story to a good end (Section 3.5).

If multigenerationalism succeeds, then it justifies procreation even in the penultimate generation. Therefore, if procreation was permissible under Harman's approach before the Cataclysm, then it remains permissible today *when it is conducted in a multigenerational way*.

4.4.4 How Multigenerationalism Constrains Procreative Freedom

Multigenerationalism is a double-edged sword for procreative liberals. It promises to safeguard procreation freedom. But if it succeeds, it also threatens to undermine many parents' freedom to raise their own children *within their own cultural traditions*.

Recall that, for Harman, *avoidable* harms *cannot* be justified. If multigenerationalists *can* raise children without the harm of lost future-dependent meaning, then this harm is avoidable *for every potential parent*. Parents who reject multigenerationalism themselves could allow their children to be raised by multigenerationalists instead. But then parents who *can* give their children up to multigenerational communities *must* do so. Once the harm-free alternative is on the table, *no one* can permissibly procreate within an unreconstructed future-dependent tradition.

We can imagine a range of increasing baroque alternatives. Multigenerationalists might either (a) offer to adopt the non-multigenerationalist couple's child at birth (Same People Choice), or (b) ask them to forego procreation to support the creation of a *different* child living in a purely present-or-past-directed community (Different People Choice), or even (c) ask them to sponsor an additional 'uplifted' dolphin, octopus, or chimpanzee who does not suffer any loss of future-dependent meaning (Different Creature Choice).

As a multigenerationalist, I am happy to bite this bullet. The real harm here is not living in a Post-Cataclysm world per se, but rather *living in a Post-Cataclysm world within a future-dependent tradition-based community*. The former is inevitable, but it is not really a harm. The latter is a genuine harm, but it is avoidable.

In practice, I doubt that anyone will actually be obliged to give up their child. Potential parents can instead join the new non-future-dependent multigenerational community *themselves*, and raise their own child within it. If this option *is* realistic, then we *should* criticise any parent who doesn't take it. It is wrong to inflict the *avoidable* harm of future-dependent loss. Consider the analogy with deafness. If your child will be deaf, and if some other (equally desirable) country has successfully reduced the harm suffered by deaf children, and if you refuse to emigrate to that country, then you do (impermissibly) impose an *avoidable* harm on your own child.

Indeed, I think that Harman must go further. Even if emigration would delay conception, and you therefore face a Different People Choice, procreation is still impermissible, because, even though you could not avoid any harm for your actual child, you could emigrate *to give some other possible child a harm-free life*.

These issues will become very important in later lectures (Sections 5.2.5 and 6.3). To explore them further, I introduce a simple thought experiment.

Future-Lover's Choice: Future-lover is a potential parent who worries that, because their cultural tradition relies heavily on future-dependent meaning and presupposes an indefinite human future, their future children cannot enjoy a meaningful flourishing life in our Post-Cataclysm world. However, Future-lover very much wants to have children.

First, suppose Future-lover inhabits a closed society, where *every* available tradition presupposes an indefinite human future. Future-lover's child faces the *almost certain* loss of future-dependent meaning. This is a very significant harm. However, it is unavoidable (in Harman's sense), and the child's life will be worth living overall. Harman's outweighing condition and her eligibility condition are both met. Perhaps procreation can still be justified.

But now suppose instead that Future-lover inhabits a *pluralist* social world, where some traditions rely on future-dependent meaning *while others do not*. If Future-lover could rearrange their life around some alternative tradition, then they could offer their child an extinction-proofed life.

As we saw earlier, the shift from closed future-dependent society to pluralist social world cuts both ways for Future-lover. On the plus side, if Future-lover is willing to embrace a non-future-dependent tradition, then Future-lover can entirely avoid the harm that threatens their child. Procreation within a non-future-dependent tradition is unproblematically permissible. (Or, at least, it is as permissible now as it ever was.) Where there is no harm, there is nothing to justify. On the negative side, because the relevant harm is now avoidable, Future-lover *must* avoid it. Future-lover can *only* permissibly procreate within a non-future-dependent tradition—no matter how disruptive or unpleasant this is for Future-lover themselves.

In short, while it is now *more likely* that Future-lover can permissibly procreate; it is also *much less likely* that Future-lover can permissibly procreate *and raise their child within their own existing (future-dependent) tradition*.

Is it unreasonable to require Future-lover to abandon either (a) their cultural tradition; or (b) their parental aspirations? I don't think so. Future-lover only faces this difficult choice because their current tradition is no longer fit for purpose *relative to available alternatives*. Without an indefinite human future to ground its values, Future-lover's future-dependent tradition cannot offer their child a fully meaningful life. Reasonable pluralism does *not* defend traditions that are no longer conducive to human flourishing!

Consider another analogy. *God-lover's* current religion grounds all meaning in a personal relationship to God. When everyone shares the same religion, God-lover is confident their child will enjoy a personal divine connection. But in a pluralist society, God-lover cannot be confident that their child, growing up among a bewildering array of competing worldviews, will even believe in

God—let alone experience any personal divine connection. Raising a child who cannot find meaning without God now imposes a significant risk of harm. And this harm is avoidable (in Harman's sense) if alternative accounts of meaning are available, within God-lover's society, that are *not* dependent on God. God-lover must choose between (a) teaching their child a more open-ended secular conception of meaning; or (b) refraining from procreation altogether.

Adopting a completely new tradition—and trying to raise one's child within that new tradition—is very risky. Fortunately, multigenerationalism offers a safer alternative. The best option—for both parents and children—is to *reorient* the original future-dependent (or God-dependent) tradition, reinterpreting its future-dependent (or God-dependent) values in non-future-dependent (or non-God-dependent) ways—rather than replacing them with something entirely new. God-lover need not abandon their religion. Like progressive theists over the centuries, they might instead *reorient* their tradition so that meaning is no longer available only to believers—even though all meaning is *ultimately* grounded in God.[21] (As I argued in my first lecture, this gap between ultimate and proximate access to God-grounded values also allows theism to support multigenerationalism's normative claims, see Section 3.5.5.)

In our Post-Cataclysm world, under Harman's principles, procreative permission is most plausible if multigenerationalists can *reorient* future-dependent traditions, enabling both potential parents and future children to flourish within the same tradition even at humanity's end. And perhaps this is *only* way to defeat the anti-natalist challenge!

4.4.5 Harman and Constraints on Procreative Permissibility

In Section 4.1, I outlined several possible constraints on Post-Cataclysm procreative ethics. Which of these might Harman endorse?

Harman will endorse the Zero Constraint and Sufficiency Constraint: you cannot procreate if your child's life is not worth living, nor if their life is not good enough overall. Harman also endorses the No Unjustified Harms Constraint, which captures her claim that some harms cannot possibly be justified.

My Intergenerational Meaning and Intergenerational Cooperation Constraints both involve *specific harms*—loss of future-dependent meaning and loss of intergenerational cooperation. Harman's attitude to these constraints depends on whether these harms are avoidable and significant. Both harms do seem significant. If they are *avoidable*—if some other method of procreation and/or child-rearing would eliminate them—then procreation is definitely impermissible if they are not avoided. If multigenerational projects are feasible, then they are the

---

[21] cf. Adams, *Finite and Infinite Goods*, chapter one; Mulgan, *Purpose in the Universe*, chapter two.

only permissible option. Any significant harm we can avoid by initiating multigenerational projects is, by definition, avoidable. Therefore, according to Harman, it must be avoided.

If the harms of lost future-dependent meaning and/or lost intergenerational cooperation are not avoidable—if multigenerational projects are not a viable alternative—then we may have a hard case, in Harman's sense, where people reasonably disagree whether or not Post-Cataclysm procreation is ever permissible.

Harman's distinctive move is to consider Different Person Comparisons alongside Same Person Comparisons. If you could avoid some harm by creating a different person, then you cannot procreate in the way that you want to. Harman will thus endorse both Same Person and Different Person Comparative Constraints where the salient notion of 'favourable comparison' includes the absence of *any avoidable harms*. On the other hand, Harman does not endorse comparative constraints that insist I provide my future child with their best possible life—let alone the best possible life I could have given to any future child.

Recall my final four constraints:

- *No Intergenerational Decline Constraint*: Procreation is permissible only if life in the next generation is (on the whole) no worse than life in the present generation.
- *No Avoidable Intergenerational Decline Constraint*: Procreation is permissible only if life in the next generation is (on the whole) no worse than life in the present generation—if this could have been avoided. (Recall that, unlike the previous constraint, this one *could* permit *unavoidable* intergenerational decline.)
- *No Post-Cataclysm Decline Constraint*: Procreation is permissible only if life in the next generation is (on the whole) no worse than life in earlier generations in our Post-Cataclysm world.
- *No Post-Cataclysm Avoidable Decline Constraint*: Procreation is permissible only if life in the next generation is (on the whole) no worse than life in earlier generations in our Post-Cataclysm world—if this could have been avoided. (Recall that, unlike the previous constraint, this one *could* permit *unavoidable* Post-Cataclysm decline.)

Harman does not reject decline per se. There is no general obligation to leave your children as well-off as yourself, nor to confer all the benefits that people enjoyed in earlier Post-Cataclysm generations. However, *avoidable and significant* intergenerational *harm* is impermissible. Once again, these constraints will kick in if ambitious multigenerational projects promise to avoid the relevant intergenerational decline altogether—and if that decline involves significant harms.

We must remember that, for Harman, justification depends solely on harms and benefits to one's child. Costs to parents can only ever *excuse*. They never *justify*. If we baulk at this blanket dismissal of parent-focused justifications, then we must move beyond Harman's exclusively child-focused procreative ethics. This paves the way for my second non-consequentialist theory—Rivka Weinberg's contractualism—which seeks to balance child-focused and parent-focused reasons. First, however, I finish this lecture by introducing my first consequentialist theory.

4.5 Roberts's Person-Affecting Consequentialism

Melinda Roberts defends a *person-affecting consequentialism* that focuses on maximising the happiness of each individual.[22] I first explain Roberts's theory (Section 4.5.1), and then apply it to our Post-Cataclysm world (Section 4.5.2). Finally, I evaluate Roberts's theory in light of my list of constraints on procreative permissibility from Section 4.1 (Section 4.5.3). I conclude that Roberts supports one of multigenerationalism's key claims—that, if we *can* repair the loss of intergenerational meaning, then we *harm* future people if we fail to do so.

4.5.1 Roberts's Original Account

Roberts offers a simple *necessary* condition for wrongness:

Roberts's Harm Constraint: An action can be wrong *only if* it harms someone.

Roberts's account of harm is very different from Harman's; and it yields a very different procreative ethic, especially in Different People Choices. Roberts's account of harm is counterfactual and whole-life. A person is harmed by an action if and only if they are *worse-off than they could otherwise have been*.

Counterfactual harm is *very* inclusive. I harm someone whenever I choose not to improve their life. If I don't give all my money to some billionaire, then I harm that person. Therefore, every moment of my life, I am harming virtually everyone else. And whenever I don't maximise my own well-being, I harm *myself*. In Same People Choices, harm is ubiquitous; we cannot avoid harming *someone* or other; and therefore other necessary conditions for wrongness come to the fore.

---

[22] Roberts, 'A New Way of Doing the Best We Can'; Roberts, 'Can It Ever Be Better Never to Have Existed at All?'; Roberts, 'The Non-Identity Fallacy'; Roberts, 'The Asymmetry: A Solution'; Roberts, *Modal Ethics*.

However, in a genuine *Different* People Choice, things are very different. If I could not have given *that person* a better life, then I have not harmed them—and therefore my action *cannot* be wrong. Suppose my child's disability is *essentially* linked to their genetic identity. Even if I could have created a *different* healthy child instead, I have not harmed my *actual child*. Therefore, my action cannot be wrong.

In genuine Different People Choices, Roberts bites the bullet; denies that the future person has been harmed; and concludes that there is no wrongdoing. If we give every future person *their best possible life*, then we do nothing wrong. Roberts thus rejects Parfit's *No Difference View* (Section 4.3.3).[23] She treats Same People and Different People Choices *very* differently.

Roberts offers a necessary condition for wrongness, not a set of sufficient conditions. In Same People Choices, where harm is ubiquitous, this necessary conditions does little work. Everything turns on how we *aggregate* different harms to different people. In Different People Choices, however, it is crucial.

For Harman, the most significant difference is between *Extra* People Choices and *Different* People Choices (Section 4.4.1). For Roberts, it is between *Different* People Choices (whether Extra People or not) and *Same* People Choices. Roberts and Harman disagree quite strongly about Extra People Choices. Roberts is both more permissive than Harman, and less permissive. This reflects the underlying difference between counterfactual-whole-life harm and specific-interest-based harm.

On the one hand, Roberts is more permissive than Harman in Extra People Choices because, so long as I give my child their best possible life, I do nothing wrong, no matter how bad that life is.

This may seem too permissive. If Roberts's harm condition permitted the creation of lives containing nothing but agony whenever this was *that person's* best possible life, then it would be clearly unacceptable. Fortunately, Roberts has a simple reply. We should supplement the harm condition as follows:

Zero Interpretation: If I create a person whose life is not worth living, then I harm that person, even if the only salient alternative for that person is nonexistence.

We could treat this as an *interpretation* of counterfactual harm. (Someone whose life is not worth living is worse-off than if they did not exist.) Alternatively, we could treat it as a non-comparative *supplement* to counterfactual harm. (An act can then be wrong *either* if it harms someone *or* if it gives someone a life

---

[23] Parfit, *Reasons and Persons*, p. 367.

below zero.)²⁴ Either way, it is charitable to incorporate the Zero Interpretation into our person-affecting consequentialism.

The Zero *Interpretation* does not automatically entail the Zero *Constraint*. It merely allows the fact that my child's life is not worth living to count as a harm. This harm must then be weighed against harms to other people.

This may still seem too permissive. Would Roberts permit Kavka's notorious couple to create a child to sell into slavery to raise money to buy a luxury yacht—so long as their enslaved child's life is worth living overall?²⁵ Once again, Roberts has a simple reply. Kavka's yacht-buying parents *do* harm their child. The Harm Constraint *is* violated in *Won't Do Better* cases where the agent *could* give the very same child a better life but is *unwilling* to do so. Kavka's yacht-buyers could give their child a non-enslaved life. Therefore, they harm their child if they do not do so.

Roberts offers an analogy.²⁶ I shoot you in the leg. You complain that I have harmed you. I reply, 'Not so! I was so angry that, if I hadn't shot you in the leg, then I would have shot you in the head. You would have been *worse-off* if I had done otherwise. Therefore, I have not harmed you.' This excuse is not convincing. I *could*—and should—have refrained from shooting you at all.

The only cases where Roberts's harm constraint is *not* violated are *Can't Do Better* cases—where the agent could not possibly give this particular future person a better life. For Roberts, these are the only *genuine* Extra (or Different) People Choices. Harm is impossible in such cases, and therefore procreation cannot be wrong. But Can't Do Better cases are also extremely rare. Roberts argues that most classic 'non-identity cases' are really *Same* People Choices (Won't Do Better not Can't Do Better): Kavka's yacht-buyers *could* provide their actual child with a much better life; and in Parfit's risky policy and depletion cases, present policy-makers *could* follow some alternative policy that provides *the same future people* with a higher *ex ante* expected quality of life.²⁷

Roberts's account is also less permissive than it appears in a second respect. Even in an Extra People Choice, counterfactual harm is only absent if my future child enjoys *their best possible life*. Suppose any child of mine will have condition X. The fact that my actual child has condition X is therefore not itself a counterfactual harm. But this does not mean I have avoided counterfactual harm altogether. Far from it. Indeed, counterfactual harm is impossible to avoid. If I create someone, then there will inevitably be times when I fail to do what is best

---

²⁴ The debate whether the zero interpretation is an interpretation of, or a supplement to, Roberts's account of counterfactual harm is fascinating (cf. Roberts, 'The Asymmetry: A Solution', pp. 338–343; Roberts, *Modal Ethics*). But it is tangential to the arguments in the text, and so I set it aside here.
²⁵ Kavka, 'The Paradox of Future Individuals'.   ²⁶ Roberts, 'The Non-Identity Fallacy', p. 271.
²⁷ Parfit's Risky Policy actually belongs to a third category—Can't *Expect* Better. These cases are the primary focus of Roberts, 'The Non-Identity Fallacy'. Can't Expect Better cases are very interesting, but I set them aside here.

for them. Therefore, I will harm them. The only way to avoid harming your child is not to create them.

Is this a fatal blow for Roberts's person-affecting consequentialism? I don't think so. For Roberts, the presence of counterfactual harm is merely necessary for wrongdoing; it is not sufficient. Roberts does insist that these harms are *morally relevant*. They should at least be *counted*. By contrast, for Harman, some counterfactual harms do not count at all. Even if there is nothing on the other side—even if I have no reason not to do so—I do nothing wrong if I gratuitously refuse to provide a small benefit to my own child. In this case, Harman is more permissive than Roberts, not less permissive.

I think this difference between Harman and Roberts reflects a *distinguishing intuition* that divides consequentialists and non-consequentialists.[28] Consequentialists regard *any* failure to provide a benefit as a (counterfactual) harm that must be justified. Non-consequentialists reply that some failures to provide a good, even to one's own child, require no justification.

Whatever their disagreements about Extra People Choices, Roberts and Harman disagree *much more* strongly about Different People Choices. For Roberts, a Different People Choice is morally on a par with an Extra People Choice. What I could have done *for some other possible child* is morally irrelevant. By contrast, for Harman, Different People Choices are radically different from Extra People Choices. In an Extra People Choice, harm *can* be justified by benefits. In a Different People Choice, harm is never justified, because it is always avoidable. Roberts and Harman thus disagree twice. They offer different accounts of what harm *is*; and different accounts of when harm counts as *avoidable*.

This is another distinguishing intuition. However, ironically, this time Roberts is on the traditionally non-consequentialist side. She favours (in Parfit's terms) *narrow* person-affecting benevolence rather than *wide*.[29] Once again, we may reach intuitive bedrock. If we think the presence of Different People options is salient, then we will side with Harman. If not, we will side with Roberts. And, as I illustrate in my next lecture, just to complicate things even more, Weinberg offers a third account of the relationship between Different and Extra People Choices (Section 5.2.7).

In one sense, Roberts's Harm Condition always favours non-procreation over procreation. I cannot harm P if P never exists. By contrast, if I do create P, then I *will* harm P. It is virtually impossible to give any possible person their best possible life. Therefore, P's interests count *against* procreation.

---

[28] I introduce the notion of a *distinguishing* intuition that distinguishes competing theories—as opposed to a *decisive* intuition that decided between them—in Mulgan, *Future People*, pp. 2–4 (cf. Mulgan, *Purpose in the Universe*, p. 10).

[29] Parfit, *Reasons and Persons*, pp. 395–397.

However, Roberts's Harm Condition is not absolutely opposed to procreation. It certainly does not *prohibit* all harmful procreation. While the existence of counterfactual harm is always necessary for wrongdoing, it is seldom sufficient. Harm to my future child must be balanced against harms to others, including myself. Other people may be harmed if I do *not* create P. Indeed, given Roberts's broad counterfactual account of harm, there is almost certainly *someone* who would be better-off if I created P. In particular, if *I* would be better-off with a child, then *not* creating P would harm me.

Of course, the ubiquity of counterfactual harm cuts both ways. Even if I did (*per impossibile*) give P their best possible life, creating P would almost certainly harm *someone else*. There is bound to be someone who would be better-off if I either (a) created Q instead of P; or (b) created no one. For instance, I could give *you* all the resources that I would have devoted to raising P. If I raise P instead, then I harm you!

A child-focused application of Roberts's harm condition would only consider harm to the future child. This would count strongly against procreation. A parent-focused application would balance harms to the child against harms to the parent. If non-procreation is better for the potential parent, then it emerges as clearly the harm-free option. (There is no *obligation* to procreate.) If non-procreation harms the potential parent, then we need other ethical principles to fairly distribute harms between parent and child. (Both contractualists and collective consequentialists offer such principles, as I demonstrate in my next two lectures.)

However, person-affecting *consequentialism* does not limit itself to child-focused and parent-focused reasons. All harms count equally. We must also consider harms to third parties. What we do *not* count is the interests of (merely) possible future people who never exist. Procreation can be permissible if non-procreation would harm people *who actually exist*. But the loss of happier possible people who never exist does not enter our calculations. Non-existent people suffer no harm. This is the main difference between person-affecting consequentialism and impersonal consequentialism—which does count the lost well-being of possible future people who never actually exist. The two theories thus evaluate the threat of immediate extinction very differently.

4.5.2 Roberts in a Post-Cataclysm World

To apply person-affecting consequentialism in our Post-Cataclysm world, I ask three questions. (1) What does Robert say about immediate extinction? (2) What does she say about Post-Cataclysm Extra People Choices? And (3) how might she respond to multigenerationalist attempts to transform Extra People Choices into Different People Choices?

In principle, Roberts is not opposed to voluntary immediate extinction. If everyone opted not to procreate, and if this harmed no present person, then it could not be wrong. However, it doesn't follow that Roberts would favour voluntary immediate extinction *in practice*. If there could have been future people, then opting for *voluntary* immediate extinction may harm past or present people whose flourishing is dependent on future people. Suppose the penultimate generation opt for non-procreation, and thereby make *themselves* the last generation. Other things equal, this *is* a counterfactual harm. They have harmed *themselves* (and one another)—because they *could* have been members of a generation that wasn't the last. Roberts therefore *can* object to immediate extinction.

On the other hand, when immediate extinction is *unavoidable*, it is not a (counterfactual) harm. Unavoidable bad things are not counterfactual harms. In particular, membership of the last generation is not a *counterfactual* harm for those who live just before omega rays hit, as no one in *that* generation could have lived earlier. Therefore, Roberts can *permit* procreation in the penultimate generation—as such procreation does not involve any distinctive new harm. Similarly, even in our own Post-Cataclysm generation, the fact that our future children cannot enjoy an *indefinite* human future is also not a counterfactual harm—as *those children* could never have inhabited any world that *did* enjoy such a future.

There is one important exception. According to our Zero Interpretation, procreation *is* harmful if one's future child's life falls below the zero level. If life is generally worse at humanity's end, then it is more likely (in any given case) that one's future child's life *will* fall below the zero level. Furthermore, if the general principles balancing competing harms to different people give priority to harms suffered by those who are worse-off, then procreation is harder to justify when future children are worse-off than their parents. If there is intergenerational decline as humanity approaches its end, then it will become harder to justify procreation. On the other hand, of course, if membership of the last generation itself pushes life below the zero level, then each generation faces a harsh choice between inflicting that harm on itself, or pushing it down the line to fall on some later generation. Much depends, of course, on exactly how we balance different harms facing different people.

I conclude that, in a declining world, procreation becomes much harder to justify under person-affecting consequentialist principles. However, procreation may still continue to be justifiable all things considered, even in the last generation.

Roberts has another very significant lesson to teach us—one that supports multigenerationalism's strong claims about our obligations to future people. Roberts cautions against conflating what I *could* do with what I *would* do. We cannot gerrymander an avoidable bad outcome for the last human generation, and then pretend that we could not have done better *for those individuals*. Almost all actual cases, and especially most large-scale collective decisions, are not genuine non-identity cases. They are cases of *Won't* Do Better rather than *Can't* Do Better.

Multigenerationalists argue that we can—and should—initiate ambitious multigenerational reorientation projects that would, if successful, make life as good as possible at humanity's end. Under Roberts's Harm Condition, what matters is whether we *could* institute such a project—not whether we *would* even consider doing so. Our lack of moral imagination or will-power is not an excuse. Kavka's parents couldn't imagine life without a yacht—but that doesn't justify or excuse them! Sometimes a lack of imaginativeness is itself morally culpable—especially when many other people live perfectly satisfactory yacht-less lives.

Roberts would therefore support the search for multigenerational alternatives. And once those alternatives are on the table, failure to pursue them constitutes a morally relevant harm to future people. Only if all multigenerational options are genuinely *impossible*—as opposed to merely difficult, risky, counter-intuitive, or unappealing—can we honestly engage in business-as-usual unambitious procreation without inflicting counterfactual harm on our descendants.

4.5.3 Roberts and Constraints on Permissible Procreation

How does Roberts's person-affecting consequentialism relate to my list of constraints on Post-Cataclysm procreative permissibility from Section 4.1? It is hard to draw many definite conclusions here, as Roberts focuses on identifying (counterfactual) harms rather than assessing overall permissibility. If we incorporate the Zero Interpretation, then our person-affecting consequentialism will probably endorse the Zero Constraint—or at least recognise that the creation of a life below zero is a very serious harm.

The distinctive feature of Roberts's theory is that it rejects *all* Different Person Comparative Constraints. Comparative Constraints must be Same Person. However, Roberts also reminds us that Same Person Comparisons are much more common than the Pre-Cataclysm literature suggests. Very few actual choices are *genuinely* Different Person ones. Roberts will identify the loss of future-dependent meaning and/or intergenerational cooperation as genuine harms—*if they could have been avoided for that person*. Similarly, while intergenerational decline doesn't necessarily imply counterfactual harm, it does suggest the presence of some significant avoidable counterfactual harms. If some particular good is available to some people and not others, or if some bad thing happens to some people and not others, then we must ask whether things could have gone better *for the person who is worse-off*. If they could, then we do have a counterfactual harm. If intergenerational decline is avoidable, then it *is* a counterfactual harm. Once again, if multigenerationalism is feasible, then it may be compulsory. At the very least, we can only reject multigenerational projects if we have strong harm-based reasons on the other side.

Roberts offers a challenging account of procreative ethics in Different People Choices and Extra People Choices. She forces us to ask whether (and if so why) procreation really *is* problematic in such cases. However, Roberts also emphasises the rarity of *genuine* Different People Choices. Counterfactual harm is ubiquitous—for both present people and future people. And when such harm is present, everything turns on how we balance competing harms inflicted on different people. In my next two lectures, I explore two very different ways to do this.

5
Lecture Three
Weinberg's Contractualist Procreative Ethic

Multigenerationalist: In my previous lecture, I explored two specific procreative principles—those of Harman and Roberts. In the next two lectures, I explore two broader theories of procreative ethics—one contractualist and the other consequentialist. As I said at the start of my previous lecture, I seek to remain agnostic between consequentialism and non-consequentialism. Multigenerationalism is not committed to either approach. My goal is to show that multigenerationalism is consistent with, and supported by, both traditions in procreative ethics. I also explore overlaps between the best Pre-Cataclysm versions of both consequentialism and non-consequentialism.

Consequentialism balances person-affecting reasons within the impersonal aggregate good. By contrast, Rivka Weinberg's contractualist procreative ethic balances child-focused and parent-focused reasons directly. Her procreative ethic is all about balancing the *risks* borne by future children against their parents' legitimate interest in procreation. While Weinberg does appeal to intuitions, she also justifies her procreative principles within a broader ethical theory.

I will first briefly present Weinberg's original theory (Section 5.1), before testing it against our Post-Cataclysm world (Section 5.2). I then compare Weinberg's theory to my list of constraints on procreative permissibility from my previous lecture (Section 5.3). Weinberg's theory introduces several new constraints on permissible procreation, especially relating to intergenerational cooperation, risk, and different person comparisons.

5.1 Weinberg's Original Theory

Weinberg's procreative ethic is non-consequentialist, Kantian, Rawlsian, and contractualist:

> Contractualism views morality as a mutually respectful way of interacting with other people who are worthy of respect as ends in themselves. It presumes acknowledgement of the intrinsic moral worth of other people and the motivation to treat them with appropriate respect.[1]

---

[1] Weinberg, *The Risk of a Lifetime*, p. 154.

Crucially, contra both consequentialism and Parfit's simple person-affecting views, Weinberg insists that people can reasonably object to *disrespectful* treatment, even if it does not leave them counterfactually worse-off regarding well-being.[2] A future child who is glad to be alive can still object that their creation was *disrespectful*.

5.1.1 Weinberg's Ambivalence

Weinberg is ambivalent about procreation. Her *hazmat* model of parental responsibility treats procreation as an optional personal project that imposes risks of significant harm on others: 'our gametes...are a form of hazardous material... because they can join with the gametes of others and grow into extremely needy innocent persons with full moral status.'[3]

Furthermore, contra Harman, Weinberg insists that benefits to one's future child can *never* justify procreation. Procreation is not a *gift* bestowed on children, nor can we create *for the sake of the child themselves*. 'No one has an interest in being born because all interests are contingent upon existence. Instead of an interest in existence itself, future people have an interest in an excellent or utopian existence (which is hard if not impossible to fulfil).'[4]

Weinberg thus endorses a strong procreative asymmetry. The risk that your future child might have a life not worth living is a very strong reason *not* to create them. But the good things that their life will (almost certainly) contain provide *no reason at all* to create them. And there is always some risk of a life not worth living. Therefore, procreation can never be justified *by reference to the 'benefits' conferred on the created person*.

Weinberg sums up the dilemma as follows: 'If life is a risk, it is not altogether clear that it is a worthwhile risk to take or impose. Not only are there many ways for life to turn out really badly, there is also the matter of how wildly and incredibly uncertain life is. Adults who have been screened for all screenable genetic diseases may still give birth to a severely deformed, ill, disabled, suffering person; adults well-placed to care for a child can drop dead any time, lose their jobs, blow up their heretofore stable relationships; prosperous, productive societies can degenerate into civil war, anarchy, tyranny, and depression; anyone can get what we might call a great start in life and come to a horrific end (and middle). Is it prudent to place a bet with stakes so high and outcomes almost unfathomably uncertain? Is it permissible?'[5]

She makes the same point even more trenchantly earlier:

It's mind blowing, really. Here we are, in our strange and vast universe, living with many unknowns, uncertainties, and difficulties, and what do we do? We

---

[2] Weinberg, *The Risk of a Lifetime*, p. 116. [3] Weinberg, *The Risk of a Lifetime*, p. 60.
[4] Weinberg, *The Risk of a Lifetime*, p. 45.   [5] Weinberg, *The Risk of a Lifetime*, p. 21.

decide to create a creature like ourselves, a sentient, conscious *person*, with full moral status and future largely unknown except for the fact that the person will be helpless and dependent for a very long time. How odd of us. Who do we think we are, anyway? Where do we get off? When we procreate, what are we doing and why are we doing it?[6]

You might thus expect Weinberg to be an anti-natalist. But she is not. She believes that procreation is *often* justified. Indeed, as a political liberal, Weinberg endorses a *presumption* of procreative liberty. How does Weinberg reconcile her procreative liberalism with her acknowledgement of the dangers of procreation?

Three factors enable Weinberg to support procreative freedom. First, Weinberg rejects *objective* pessimism. Against Benatar's pessimist anti-natalism, Weinberg denies that we can know that life is objectively bad.[7] There is no privileged epistemic position from which we could issue such a declaration. As there is no objective privileged viewpoint, we can only rely on people's subjective reports— *and most people seem to enjoy life*.[8] If most people found life bad overall, then procreation would be very difficult to justify.[9] But as most people find life pretty good, a ban on procreation is very hard to justify. Second, as a liberal, Weinberg defers to individual people's own evaluations of life and their attitudes to risk. (I return to attitudes to risk in Sections 5.1.4 and 5.2.2.) Third, contra Harman, Weinberg denies that a satisfactory justification for procreation must cite *only* the interests of the child. Instead, Weinberg's procreative ethic *balances* the interests of the child *against those of their potential parent(s)*.

Weinberg's ambivalence extends to her own evaluation of life. Subjectively, she shares Benatar's gloomy verdict on humanity's fate. But she recognises that this evaluation is statistically unusual: 'I myself am partial to this exceptional view—I feel victimised to have been brought into existence, and I feel guilty for having brought my own children into existence, but I realise that this is a very uncommon way to see the world.'[10]

Procreation remains a very risky and hazardous activity. Weinberg's rejection of objective standards to measure life's overall goodness cuts both ways. We cannot know that life is objectively bad. But we also cannot know that life is objectively good. And we *do* know that, while most people think life is good, some people find it very bad. We also know that some actual lives *are* objectively very bad.

Weinberg argues that procreation can *only* be justified, if at all, by citing its significance *to the procreating agent*. More specifically, *only* the desire to

---

[6] Weinberg, *The Risk of a Lifetime*, p. 15.
[7] Benatar, *Better Never to Have Been*; Weinberg, *The Risk of a Lifetime*, pp. 122–130.
[8] Weinberg, *The Risk of a Lifetime*, pp. 127–128. [9] Weinberg, *The Risk of a Lifetime*, p. 130.
[10] Weinberg, *The Risk of a Lifetime*, chapter one, footnote 22.

participate in the unique parent–child relationship can justify procreation—and procreation is then justified only when it is consistent with the value of that relationship. (Having a child to sell into slavery to raise money to buy a yacht is never permissible!)

5.1.2 Weinberg's Procreative Principles

Weinberg defends two procreative principles:

1. *The Motivation Restriction*: 'Procreation must be motivated by the desire and intention to raise, love, and nurture one's child once it is born.'[11]
2. *The Balance Principle*: 'Procreation is permissible only when the risk you impose as a procreator on your children would not be irrational for you to accept as a condition of your own birth... in exchange for the permission to procreate under these risk conditions.'[12]

Weinberg defends these principles on intuitive, comparative, and contractualist grounds: they are independently plausible; they fit our intuitions better than any competing principles; and they would be chosen in a hypothetical 'procreative original position'.[13]

In Weinberg's procreative original position, parties choose *principles of procreative justice*. This is modelled, of course, on Rawls's original position.[14] Weinberg endorses Rawls's emphasis on self-respect: 'basic self-respect... is fundamental and crucial. It is certainly not worth risking for the very dubious privilege of being permitted to procreate in ways inconsistent with respecting one's child for her own sake.'[15]

However, Weinberg departs from Rawls in three key ways.[16] First, instead of complete principles of justice, Weinberg's parties only choose moral principle(s) to govern procreation.[17] Second, for Weinberg, procreative justice is *all* about balancing risks. Therefore, unlike Rawls's notorious combination of ignorance of probabilities and a maximin decision-procedure, Weinberg imagines parties who (i) know about probabilities and risks; and (ii) seek to maximise their ability to flourish.[18] Otherwise, the procreative original position could never justify some

---

[11] Weinberg, *The Risk of a Lifetime*, p. 153.
[12] Weinberg, *The Risk of a Lifetime*, p. 153.
[13] Weinberg, *The Risk of a Lifetime*, p. 153.
[14] Rawls, *A Theory of Justice*.
[15] Weinberg, *The Risk of a Lifetime*, p. 178.
[16] Other departures from Rawls are omitted, as they are not directly relevant here (cf. Weinberg, *The Risk of a Lifetime*, pp. 158–176).
[17] Weinberg, *The Risk of a Lifetime*, p. 159.
[18] In 'Procreative Justice', Weinberg argues that the appropriate decision-procedure is Maximising Capability (MaxC), rather than either Rawls's MaxiMin procedure or the utilitarian's Maximising Average Utility procedure (Weinberg, 'Procreative Justice', pp. 413–414).

procreative risks but not others: '*All* procreative acts risk grave harms, it's the *probability* of the risk that varies.'[19] Finally, while Rawls stumbles over the non-identity problem, Weinberg stipulates that her parties know that they will exist, and also that they will, in turn, occupy the roles of both child *and prospective parent*.[20] As a *child*, each party wants the best possible set of procreative goods and the most favourable environment. But as a *potential parent*, they also want to be permitted to enjoy parent–child relationships.

I focus on exploring Weinberg's two principles (Sections 5.1.3 and 5.1.4), and *then* applying them to our Post-Cataclysm world (Section 5.2). I also explore connections between Weinberg's principles and multigenerationalism (Section 5.2.5), and take a step back and ask whether her underlying contractualist framework still delivers the same principles in our Post-Cataclysm world (Section 5.2.6).

5.1.3 Weinberg's Motivation Restriction

Weinberg's Kantianism forbids procreation that fails to *respect* one's possible future child. Seana Shiffrin's Pre-Cataclysm *liberal anti-natalism* argued that procreation is always impermissible because it imposes 'pure benefits' on people without their consent.[21] Weinberg disagrees. She argues that (i) because children cannot consent, paternalism *is* appropriate; and (ii) the imposition of risk in exchange for pure benefit is often morally unproblematic when paternalism is appropriate.[22]

Procreation is not automatically disrespectful. But it is problematic. You cannot create a child (primarily) as a means to (any) end. You must treat them as an end-in-themselves. But your future child doesn't *yet* exist—and you can't create someone *for their own good*. So how can you respect them as an end while creating them?

Weinberg's solution, embodied in her Motivation Restriction, is that procreation is not disrespectful if you create a child *for the sake of enjoying a valuable relationship with them*. The Motivation Restriction rules out egregious (often imaginary) cases where parents privilege their own (comparatively trivial) interests over those of their possible future children, such as Kavka's parents who have a child to sell into slavery to buy a yacht. Here, the desire to enjoy a parent–child relationship is entirely absent.

Weinberg also systematically rejects other, less disreputable, procreative motivations. A consequentialist desire to improve the world is neither an explanatory

---

[19] Weinberg, 'Procreative Justice', p. 411.
[20] Weinberg, 'Procreative Justice', p. 410. On Rawls on the non-identity problem, see Mulgan, *Future People*, pp. 43–44.
[21] Shiffrin, 'Wrongful Life, Procreative Responsibility, and the Significance of Harm'.
[22] Weinberg, *The Risk of a Lifetime*, pp. 136–138.

motivation for procreation, nor a reasonable justification. This is not why real people actually have children, nor would it be a good reason: 'As a way of adding value to the world, it is a risky and high-handed way.... There are other ways to add value to the world that don't involve these risks.'[23] Desires to create future people, to maximise expected future well-being, or to enable humanity to conquer the galaxy are also *not* sufficient. Procreation is also impermissible in imaginary cases where we magically bring fully formed rational adults into existence without any nurturing parent–child relationship—as no *other* possible project can justify exposing someone to the inevitable risks of human existence.[24] Nor can potential parents procreate *in order to secure the survival of their (oppressed) community*. This motivation 'treat[s] the child as a mere means for the good of the group rather than as a separate self, entitled to respect as an end in herself'.[25]

However, Weinberg's Motivation Restriction does not *prohibit* other motivations altogether. All our actions have many motivations, and human procreative motivation is especially complex. Other motivations can be present. The parent-child motivation need not be exclusive. But it must be *prominent*.[26] At a minimum, the parent-child motivation must be *present*, and it must be strong enough that it would *prevent* you from procreating in a disrespectful way. But this might not be your *only* motivation. You might *also* want to give your parents grandchildren, or continue your traditions, or avoid immediate extinction.

Weinberg's Motivation Restriction says that the parent-child motivation is necessary for permissible procreation, and that it must be prominent. But Weinberg does *not* require the parent-child motivation to be *sufficient* on its own *to result in procreation*. Suppose my desire to establish a parent–child relationship would not be enough *without my desire to continue my tradition*. So long as the parent-child motivation is prominent, and I would not have procreated without it, I may still respect my future child even though this other motivation tips the balance in favour of procreation.

5.1.4 Weinberg's Balance Principle

Weinberg's Balance Principle transforms an interpersonal comparison into an intrapersonal choice. We balance the actual expected risk to the future child against the parent's interest in procreation. I ask whether I would take *that risk* in exchange for the freedom to procreate whenever my future child faces that risk.

---

[23] Weinberg, *The Risk of a Lifetime*, pp. 22–23.
[24] Weinberg, *The Risk of a Lifetime*, pp. 140–142.
[25] Weinberg, *The Risk of a Lifetime*, p. 229.
[26] Elsewhere, Weinberg claims explicitly that 'procreation [must] be at least partially, yet still prominently, motivated by' the relevant parental desire (Weinberg, 'Procreative Justice', p. 421).

Weinberg's treatment of risk is *very permissive*. Procreation is permissible if the relevant risk is *not irrational*. It need not be rationally required—or even rationally superior. And a risk is only *irrational* if 'everyone has decisive reasons to avoid [it]'.[27]

Weinberg's emphasis on *irrationality* is significant, because any less permissive approach to risk almost certainly leads to anti-natalism. Consider two examples. (1) We could ask whether it is rational to decline the risk. But this is *almost always* rational, especially if you don't want to procreate yourself. (How valuable is a freedom you will never exercise?) (2) Suppose instead that Weinberg followed Scanlon's contractualism, and asked whether the risk is one that no one can reasonably reject.[28] As no one needs to exist, your possible future children surely *could* reasonably reject any risk that lead to their (less than perfect) existence.

Weinberg's permissive treatment of risk is thus essential to her defense of procreative permissibility. Fortunately, she has a principled justification for it. Recall that, as a political liberal, Weinberg endorses a *presumption* of procreative liberty: 'Where different rational approaches to risk occur, we err on the side of liberty and permit procreation.'[29] Also, we should note that Weinberg's theory is not quite so permissive *overall*. The Balance Principle is constrained by the Motivation Restriction. Any potential parent applying the Balance Principle must care deeply about the interests of their future child. Suppose I am risk-averse. While I believe the risk represented by the Balance Principle is not *irrational*, I also know that I would not take that risk myself. The Balance Principle (on its own) permits me to procreate. But if I have the right motivations, then I will not impose a risk on my own child that I would not *actually* take myself. Properly motivated potential parents typically opt not to procreate if the Balance Principle risk is one they wouldn't take themselves. Conversely, the willingness to *impose on others* a risk that one would not take oneself is strong evidence that one lacks the necessary procreative motivation.

I find Weinberg's theory easier to apply if we add an explicit *Sincerity Requirement*, which permits procreation only when the potential parent *would willingly accept* the risk they impose on their children in exchange for the permission to procreate under these risk conditions. This Sincerity Requirement is probably entailed by the conjunction of the Motivation Restriction and the Balance Principle. But it is helpful to state it explicitly. Of course, in many cases, the parent cannot *actually* share the risk they impose on their child—what matters is whether they *would* be willing to.

Weinberg argues that, in 'ordinary' (affluent, Pre-Cataclysm) cases, the Balance Principle can be satisfied: 'Since most informed, competent adults seem to regard

---

[27] Weinberg, *The Risk of a Lifetime*, p. 176.
[28] Scanlon, *What We Owe to Each Other*. Weinberg explicitly rejects Scanlon's contractualism in favour of Rawls's (Weinberg, *The Risk of a Lifetime*, p. 158).
[29] Weinberg, *The Risk of a Lifetime*, p. 184.

life as a reasonable risk...procreation does not appear to be always morally problematic.'[30] It is not irrational to accept the risks of ordinary life in exchange for freedom to procreate in ordinary cases.

As with the evaluation of life itself, Weinberg insists that there is no privileged objectively correct attitude to risk. We can only defer to people's actual judgements. And those judgements favour procreative freedom.

If procreation is ordinarily permissible, then it is also clearly permissible for minor disabilities. It is *not* irrational to accept a 100 per cent 'risk' of colour-blindness in exchange for permission to procreate if you know your child will be colour-blind. If procreation is ordinarily permitted, then colour-blindness cannot tip the balance. By contrast, the Balance Principle clearly prohibits procreation for the most serious inherited conditions. It *is* irrational to accept a 10 per cent chance of developing schizophrenia in exchange for permission to procreate if your child faces that same risk.[31]

Weinberg offers a more realistic way to capture the comparison underlying the Balance Principle in the last case: Would it be irrational to undergo a fertility treatment that had the side-effect of causing schizophrenia in 10 per cent of the recipients? She argues that schizophrenia is so awful that this risk clearly *is* irrational. Therefore, if one's child faces a 10 per cent risk of schizophrenia, then procreation is impermissible.[32]

My future child's misfortunes might be due to disease, disability, or social injustice. It is often hard to disentangle these causes. (Is it bad to be born deaf because one cannot hear, or because one suffers discrimination in a hearing-majority society?) For Weinberg, causation is largely irrelevant: 'The child is disadvantaged by being black in an apartheid society and deaf in a hearing society. How much of this burden is natural and how much is social does not matter much to the child and her ability to live a life of human flourishing.'[33] The Balance Principle covers social disadvantage as much as inherited disability.

Weinberg considers social disadvantage caused by poverty, race-based oppression, and gender-based oppression. Parent and child often share social disadvantage. Your children are slaves because you are a slave, poor because you are poor, and so on. The relevant 'risk' is therefore 100 per cent (or 50 per cent for gender-based oppression).[34]

Weinberg argues that the Balance Principle does forbid procreation in very oppressive situations, such as the much-discussed case of American race-based

---

[30] Weinberg, *The Risk of a Lifetime*, p. 146.
[31] This is the probability that arises if one parent is schizophrenic themselves (Weinberg, *The Risk of a Lifetime*, p. 217).
[32] Weinberg, *The Risk of a Lifetime*, chapter six, footnote 23.
[33] Weinberg, *The Risk of a Lifetime*, p. 205.
[34] Nor does the 50 per cent chance that one's child will be born male in a very sexist society offer much consolation: 'it is not good for men to participate in sexist oppression either as it distorts their relationships, depriving them of true companionship and intimacy with the women in their lives' (Weinberg, *The Risk of a Lifetime*, chapter six, footnote 38).

slavery or the plight of women living under the Taliban regime or in Saudi Arabia.[35] However, she adds a number of important caveats: (i) in tragic circumstances, we can hardly blame people for continuing to procreate; (ii) women in oppressive regimes typically enjoy very low levels of procreative autonomy (so it is misleading to describe these women as 'choosing' to have children); and (iii) refusing to procreate might endanger the women's own life or health.

Disadvantage is also a two-way street. It is bad to be born into oppression. But if you are already oppressed, then a prohibition on procreation may be especially harmful—because procreation provides an oppressed person with a rare opportunity to experience human flourishing. (I return to this point in Sections 5.2.2, 5.2.4, and 5.2.7.)

Weinberg sharply distinguishes between *absolute* and *relative* poverty. It *is* irrational to accept a significant risk of abject poverty for the permission to procreate when one's children will be at risk of abject poverty. But it is *not* irrational to risk 'being poor relative to one society yet still have one's basic needs met at a basic level in exchange for the freedom to procreate'.[36] Absolute poverty prohibits absolutely; relative poverty does not.

The Balance Principle balances the risk to the child *against parental interests*. In most cases of oppression or social disadvantage, the relevant interest is procreation per se. Enslaved parents cannot have a child who is not a slave. In other cases, however, the relevant parental interest is narrower—not procreation per se, but procreation in such-and-such ways. The significance of *this* interest depends on the availability of alternatives. Weinberg contrasts two cases:[37]

- *Students*: Couple A want to have a baby *now*. If they wait until they complete their college education, they are far more likely to offer their child a middle-class life. (This was in the Pre-Cataclysm United States—a notoriously unequal society where non-middle-class life was pretty bleak.)
- *Home Health Aides*: Couple B know that, while their child's basic needs will likely be met, their child will not be middle class, no matter how long they wait—because they work in jobs that will never pay middle-class wages.

Couple A face a Different People Choice, while Couple B's choice is *Extra People*. While the risk to the child is the same (a non-middle-class life), the cost to the parents of avoiding that risk is very different. Weinberg argues that it *is* irrational to risk giving up being middle-class in the United States for 'the freedom to be sloppy about birth control for two years'.[38] By contrast, it is not irrational to risk a life of lesser flourishing 'for the freedom to procreate under circumstances where

---

[35] Weinberg, *The Risk of a Lifetime*, p. 231.   [36] Weinberg, *The Risk of a Lifetime*, p. 227.
[37] Weinberg, *The Risk of a Lifetime*, pp. 182–184.
[38] Weinberg, *The Risk of a Lifetime*, p. 182.

having no children at all is the only other choice."[39] Similarly, if a temporary medical condition would give your child a slight disability, then you must wait six months rather than having a child *now*. But the same risk of disability may be permissible if it is faced by *any child you ever have*.

Like Harman, though for different reasons, Weinberg thus permits procreation more frequently in Extra People Choices than in Different People Choices (Section 4.4.1).

In harder cases, the parental interest falls between (a) procreating at all; and (b) procreating now. Other salient alternatives might include: adopting someone else's biological child rather than procreating yourself; choosing a different procreative partner (to avoid some specific inherited genetic condition or social disadvantage); using artificial reproductive technology (which might be invasive or expensive); delaying procreation to emigrate to a place where your child would fare better, and so on. The Balance Principle always asks whether this particular parental interest justifies that particular risk.

5.2 Weinberg after the Cataclysm

To apply Weinberg's procreative principles in our Post-Cataclysm world, I first ask what Weinberg would say about voluntary immediate extinction, and whether multigenerationalist motivations could supplement Weinberg's parent-child motivation (Section 5.2.1). I then consider several related objections to Weinberg's view. These object that it either forbids procreation altogether (Sections 5.2.2 and 5.2.3) or collapses into incoherence (Section 5.2.4). This last objection leads to questions about the relationship between Weinberg's contractualism and multigenerationalism (Section 5.2.5) and about Weinberg's underlying Rawlsian contractualist framework (5.2.6). Finally, in Section 5.2.7, I return to the contrast between Different People Choices and Extra People Choices, asking whether Weinberg can meet familiar challenges from anti-natalists and multigenerationalists.

5.2.1 Weinberg, Extinction, and Motivation

As a non-consequentialist, Weinberg is not *morally* opposed to voluntary immediate extinction. Non-procreation is always permissible. Voluntary extinction need not violate any principle of procreative ethics. Furthermore, Weinberg clearly acknowledges *possible* scenarios where procreation would be *universally*

---

[39] Weinberg, *The Risk of a Lifetime*, pp. 182–183.

prohibited. If *all* future children faced a 10 per cent risk of schizophrenia, then *no one* could permissibly procreate. Finally, like the consequentialist desire to improve the world, or the narrower desire to continue one's own traditions, the desire to avoid immediate extinction is not a *sufficient* motivation for procreation. All these goals are simply too distant from the child's own life. They treat the child as a means rather than an end. Extinction-avoidance can be present as a subsidiary motivation, but it cannot *replace* the desire for a parent–child relationship.

As with Harman, I focus on penultimate procreation. Can the penultimate generation permissibly create a new generation who cannot procreate themselves? I address three questions. (1) Will enough people in the penultimate generation want to procreate if they are motivated by the respectful desire to form a parent–child relationship? (2) Could the desire to avoid extinction supplement or support other parental motivations? (3) Can multigenerational desires themselves satisfy Weinberg's Motivation Restriction instead of the 'ordinary' desire for a parent–child relationship?

If the Balance Principle is satisfied—if the risk is not irrational—then procreation is respectful so long as the desire for a parent–child relationship is prominent. The actual distribution of parental (and other) motivations within the population is then an empirical, sociological question. It is hard to speculate in advance. If life in the last generation is no worse than before, then parental motivations are likely to remain constant in the penultimate generation. Followers of Scheffler may worry that, in actual fact, parent–child relationships are so deeply embedded in future-dependent cultural traditions that they will *not* be as strong without connections to the further future. But others will reply that the removal of other routes to future-dependent meaning *increases* the significance of the parent–child relationship, because it now offers a rare future-dependent opportunity to flourish.

As ever, multigenerationalism is more ambitious. I will argue that suitable multigenerational projects remove all worries specific to the last generation. There is no last generation burden, because the last generation are equal co-participants in a project that gives meaning to everyone's lives. And there is nothing disrespectful about creating new equal co-participants.

Indeed, depending on the details of the most credible multigenerational projects, multigenerational motivations could even become an essential replacement for Weinberg's original parent-child motivation. For instance, in our final debate, I explore the possibility that the best (or only) hope for intergenerational meaning in the last generation is a *virtual ending* where the last generation are raised entirely within a virtual environment without any direct interaction with the penultimate generation who remain in the world outside the machine (Sections 9.5 and 9.7). In this scenario, no one in the penultimate generation can be motivated by Weinberg's parent–child relationship. But they might be motivated by a respectful desire to create new co-participants in the project of bringing humanity to a fitting (albeit virtual) end.

This raises the general question of how multigenerational motivations might fit into Weinberg's Kantian framework. Could they ever *replace* Weinberg's original parent–child relationship as an acceptable motivation for procreation? I will argue that they can.

I think the essence of a Kantian approach is that any justifying motivation must meet two general conditions:

1. *The respect for the child test.* One must respect one's possible future child, treating them as an end in themselves and not a mere means.
2. *The parental interest test.* One's motivation must link to some significant parental interest.

Weinberg lists obvious non-contenders: material gain; consequentialist value promotion; the desire to preserve one's community; and the desire to maximise one's future child's well-being. But I would argue that the desire to create co-participants who will sustain or complete a multigenerational community whose 'goal' is the flourishing of all its members through their joint participation in multigenerational projects is *no less respectful* than the desire to enjoy a parent–child relationship. Both of these motivations value the other person as an end-in-themselves *once they exist*. And, as Weinberg herself insists, in neither case is one really concerned for the person one creates *before they exist*. If the parent-child motivation can still be respectful *enough*, then why *can't* the multigenerational motivation be equally respectful?

One might worry that selecting a child *as a co-participant in your project* forecloses that child's *open future*. But the same worry already arises for ordinary parent–child relationships. Every parent–child relationship is imposed on the child. (No one chooses their parents. Indeed, no one chooses to have parents at all.) Weinberg is therefore already committed to the view that an unchosen relationship need not be oppressive—*if* it allows the future child to grow beyond their parents. A suitably open-ended multigenerational project could do the same.

Of course, this requirement of open-endedness will also *constrain the scope* of permissible multigenerational projects. Only *active* multigenerational projects based on mutual cooperation across generations will pass the test. I explore this constraint in my fifth lecture—where I explain in more detail what I mean by an 'active' multigenerational project (Section 7.1). Insofar as Weinberg's Motivation Restriction demands that every child enjoy an open future, it also implies that all acceptable multigenerational projects must involve voluntary cooperation between all participants across all generations—whether or not we allow multigenerational motivations to replace ordinary parental motivations. You cannot respect your child if you choose their life (and their projects) for them.

Open-endedness also raises the opposite worry that the future child will abandon the multigenerational project altogether, depriving all previous generations of intergenerational meaning. Once again, however, the analogous risk is ubiquitous. Any parent–child relationship carries the same risk. It too can be betrayed, destroyed, or undermined by the future child. Both parent–child relationships and multigenerational projects are leaps of faith. If one respects the person one creates, then the meaningfulness of one's own present projects is always at the mercy of that person's future free agency.

I conclude that collective analogues of Weinberg's individual parent-child motivation might satisfy the Motivation Restriction. At least, multigenerationalism is better-placed here than impersonal consequentialist or extinction-avoidance motivations—because it treats the child as an active co-participant, and therefore as an end-in-themselves.

We cannot use the last human generation—or any other generation—merely as a means to our own ends. But treating them entirely as independent ends is not sufficient either, as Weinberg's example of creating happy adult human beings *ex nihilo* makes clear. The fact that their lives will be worth living overall is not sufficient justification. *Only* our relationship with them, *and what we will do together*, can justify creating them. The desire to embark, together with future generations, on some suitable joint project is essential.

We could go further. A life where your *only* cooperative intergenerational relationship involves your own parents is, arguably, not a flourishing human life. Multigenerationalists might insist that you only respect your child if, in *addition* to desiring to enter into a parent–child relationship with them, you *also* desire to join with them in many other cooperative intergenerational projects. My additional multigenerational motivations are thus compulsory additions to Weinberg's Motivation Restriction, and not merely optional replacements.

5.2.2 A Riskier World

Our Post-Cataclysm world is riskier and less certain that Pre-Cataclysm affluent society. And life will probably become *even more unpredictable* as humanity approaches its end. Future children thus face greater risks of perennial harms caused by social disruption and lost future-dependent meaning. In Scheffler's cautionary tales, and in many other dystopian visions of humanity's end, immediate human extinction leads to a collapse of civilised norms, putting all future people at very high risk of enduring lives not worth living. While these bad things are perennial human risks, their *likelihood* and *severity* are greater than before. At the very least, future risks of harm are now much harder to calculate. Even if life is not necessarily worse overall in our Post-Cataclysm world, it is *riskier*.

Greater uncertainty raises the likelihood that the Balance Principle *prohibits all procreation*. Even if ordinary Pre-Cataclysm procreation was permissible, it may now be irrational to accept *our* ordinary Post-Cataclysm background risk.

The Balance Principle is therefore more prohibitive, and the case for anti-natalism is stronger.

Contractualists such as Weinberg have two main replies to this challenge. First, if Post-Cataclysm life *is* more limited than Pre-Cataclysm life, then procreation is more important for *potential parents*, as it offers a rare (perhaps unique) opportunity for future-dependent flourishing. Like poverty, disadvantage, or oppression, the loss of future-dependent meaning cuts both ways. It raises the risk to future children, but increases the parent's need to take that risk (Section 5.1.4).

Second, *uncertainty* itself also cuts both ways, especially for Weinberg. Life in the last generation *might* be much worse than before the Cataclysm. But it could also be much better. Future people *could* find sufficient meaning at humanity's end; social cohesion *might* increase rather than decreasing; and the removal of all Pre-Cataclysm concerns about sustainability *could* produce a post-scarcity paradise. When the potential pay-off is so high, is it really *irrational* to take the risk? Perhaps, on the contrary, greater uncertainty means that a *wider* range of attitudes to risk are now rationally permissible.

Unfortunately, this second reply puts a great deal of weight on Weinberg's (very) permissive treatment of risk. Intuitively, procreation should be *less* permissible in a riskier world, not more permissible! This raises the deeper question whether Weinberg's underlying presumption of liberty—which is the main justification for her permissive attitude to risk—is still appropriate for us. That presumption, which is built into Weinberg's contractualist foundations, flows from the values current in her own liberal society. Weinberg implicitly assumes the existence of an ongoing liberal society organised around those values. But that is precisely what is now at issue. Weinberg takes the existence of a next generation for granted. We cannot. Anti-natalists favour a presumption against procreation. Multigenerationalists might favour a presumption in favour of a procreative *obligation*—because we *must* initiate multigenerational transformations. Act consequentialists favour a *conditional obligation*, where we should all procreate if this maximises the good. Any of these alternative attitudes to risk would radically transform the Balance Principle. If we seek a neutral approach, then perhaps we *should* be risk-averse and agree with the anti-natalist claim that procreation is less permissible in a riskier world, because the likelihood that one's future child will be unable to flourish is greater.

My own solution is to sidestep this debate, by reducing the risk of social collapse (and other harms) to Pre-Cataclysm levels. If multigenerationalism delivers on this promise, then Weinberg's Balance Principle remains as permissive as before. Indeed, the most ambitious multigenerationalism aims to *reduce* the risk to bring it *below* Pre-Cataclysm levels—leading to a more stable society in the last generation than in any previous generation. (I return to *that* utopian aspiration in my final lecture.)

5.2.3 A Deteriorating World

A distinct threat to procreative permission is that our Post-Cataclysm world is *deteriorating*. If imminent extinction threatens social cohesion, then that risk will *increase over time*. Each generation imposes a *higher* risk on their future children than their parents imposed on them. This contrasts with Weinberg's Pre-Cataclysm cases of oppression, poverty, or injustice where future children face the same risks as their parents. Post-Cataclysm social disruption is thus closer to Weinberg's inherited disability cases, where potential parents impose risks that they do *not* face themselves.

Deterioration is not an insuperable barrier for Weinberg. Procreation is not automatically prohibited just because the future child is worse-off, or because they face a greater risk of (greater) harm than the parent. I can permissibly create a colour-blind child even if I am not colour-blind, and even though colour-blindness does (slightly) reduce my child's opportunity to flourish, as well as increasing various background risks (my child is slightly more likely to be killed running a traffic light, for instance). What matters is (a) whether I *would* accept colour-blindness as the price of procreative liberty (Sincerity Requirement); and (b) whether this acceptance is *not irrational* (Balance Principle). The fact that I do not (because I cannot) actually face that risk is irrelevant.

Of course, the threats facing the last generation are not as trivial as colour-blindness. The loss of all future-dependent meaning could be devastating, at least for some people. It is perhaps hyperbolic to equate living in the last generation with schizophrenia. But the risk of a meaningless life seems at least as great here as in other quite serious cases of disability, oppression, or social disadvantage.

We should also remember that the Balance Principle is not sufficient. The *Sincerity Requirement* and the *Motivation Restriction* must also both be met. Will potential parents actually want to create children who are (inevitably) worse-off? Could they honestly tell themselves—and tell their future children—that they would willingly have swapped places with them? Even if sincere permissible procreation is not impossible in the penultimate generation, it will be much less common.

As ever, I offer a simple reply to all these worries: our Post-Cataclysm world is not deteriorating *in the ways that matter*! Consider an analogy. I have a genetic condition that will prevent any child of mine from having children. However, I also know that predictable future improvements will give my childless child a *better* life than I can hope to enjoy (with or without children). In this case, I can reasonably want to create this child *for the sake of entering into a parent–child relationship with them*. This is not irrational, disrespectful, or insincere. Similarly, creating a childless child as a co-participant in a mutually fulfilling multigenerational project is also not disrespectful.

Unfortunately, reflection on infertility also reveals a potentially fatal contradiction at the heart of Weinberg's project, which I must resolve (Section 5.2.4) before I proceed to other issues (Sections 5.2.5, 5.2.6, and 5.2.7).

5.2.4 Infertility and Incoherence

Weinberg's Balance Principle seems to collapse into incoherence in the penultimate generation. Weinberg can accommodate risks of infertility.[40] It is (arguably) not irrational to accept a 10 per cent risk of infertility in exchange for permission to procreate if my child faces that same risk. After all, no risk of infertility is worse than a ban on procreation. But no one in the last human generation can have children. The salient 'risk' for penultimate procreation is thus *known certain infertility*. But how can Weinberg accommodate that 'risk'? How can I imagine accepting the certainty of not having children in exchange for permission to *procreate*? That doesn't even make sense. Alternatively, if the question *does* make sense, then the risk is obviously irrational, and procreation is prohibited. If procreation is universally prohibited in the *penultimate* human generation, then (by familiar Ponzi reasoning) it is presumably prohibited throughout our Post-Cataclysm world (Section 1.5). Weinberg's Balance Principle either leads nowhere, or it leads to anti-natalism.

This is a serious challenge. But I believe it can be met. I agree that, when infertility is certain, the original Balance Principle cannot be applied. The relevant intrapersonal risk is literally unimaginable. You cannot simultaneously (a) accept a 100 per cent chance that you will be unable to have children; and (b) contemplate procreation. However, we need to go back a step. Weinberg's principle is merely a convenient Rawlsian device to transform an interpersonal comparison into an intrapersonal choice. What really *matters* is the underlying interpersonal comparison. And that *does* still make sense. Is unavoidable infertility worse for your child than lost procreative freedom is for you? Can your interest in procreation justify the burden you impose on them? To answer that question directly, we must compare the two burdens.

The obvious problem for Weinberg is that the two burdens appear identical. Both involve the inability to procreate. But surely procreation is disrespectful when you impose a burden you are not willing to bear yourself? Can I respect my future child if I impose on them exactly what I seek to avoid for myself by creating them?

Contractualists need to distinguish the two burdens. One option is to argue that losing the *moral freedom* to procreate is worse than *unavoidable* infertility.

---

[40] cf. Weinberg, *The Risk of a Lifetime*, chapter six, footnote 15.

But anti-natalists will reply that, on the contrary, virtuously refraining from dubious procreation would give your life a meaningfulness that your future child's would lack!

An alternative way to differentiate the two burdens is that, if most people in the penultimate generation procreate, then one risks social exclusion if one does not; whereas no one in the last generation is deprived or excluded *relative to other members of their own generation*. Unfortunately, as we saw earlier, universality cuts both ways (Sections 5.1.4 and 5.2.2). If others have children while I do not, then I have non-procreative ways to contribute to the human future; whereas people in the last generation have no future-directed options at all.

Contractualists could persevere. For Weinberg, a difference that cuts both ways is better than no difference at all. The Balance Principle asks whether a risk (or exchange) is irrational. It is irrational to prefer X to X. It is not irrational to prefer X+Y to X+Z, even if people reasonably disagree whether Y is better or worse than Z. If I reasonably believe that my future child will be better-off—if I think my future child's childlessness would be less harmful than my own—then perhaps procreation is permissible. We must recall, as ever, that Weinberg's Motivation Restriction and our Sincerity Requirement together ensure that potential parents are sincerely and prominently motivated by the parent–child relationship. Therefore, they will at least try to apply the Balance Principle honestly.

5.2.5 Weinberg and Multigenerationalism

Where does this leave us? There are several ways that Weinberg might meet the challenge of defending procreative freedom in a declining world. That challenge is not impossible. However, I do think that it *is* very difficult for Weinberg to justify penultimate procreation *if life is worse in the last generation*. Weinberg is *more* vulnerable here than Harman, who doesn't *compare* the two generations' interests, but merely looks at the harms and benefits to the last generation in isolation (Section 4.4.2). Weinberg is also more vulnerable than Roberts, who doesn't regard universal unavoidable bad things as harms at all (Section 4.5.2).

And *this* is where multigenerationalism comes into its own. If multigenerationalism succeeds, then people in the last generation can *contribute to the culmination of humanity's story*. The most ambitious multigenerational projects promise the last generation something even *more* meaningful than any future-dependent Pre-Cataclysm alternative, or anything available to earlier Post-Cataclysm generations such as our own. The risk of procreation is worth it—because the last generation are *better-off* rather than worse-off. Of course, this particular multigenerational claim is *very* ambitious. But even if we don't go that far, all multigenerationalists hope to leave the last generation at least *no worse-off* than their predecessors. And satisfying *that* requirement may well be essential for

Post-Cataclysm procreative permissibility—at least under Weinberg's Balance Principle and our new Sincerity Requirement.

5.2.6 Rethinking Rawlsian Contractualism

The last generation's inability to procreate creates a paradox, not merely for Weinberg's particular Balance Principle, but also for her underlying Rawlsian framework. Rawlsian intergenerational justice notoriously has difficulties with the *first* generation.[41] If things are always improving, then any positive rate of intergenerational savings requires the worst-off (first) generation to make unreciprocated sacrifices to benefit better-off (later) generations. But how could this be justified *to* the first generation? What could motivate them to comply with any such savings principle? (This is especially bad for Rawls himself, because his maximin decision-procedure—which elsewhere forms the basis of his theory of justice—privileges the interests of the worst-off.)

In practice, contractualists usually meet this challenge by ignoring it. They simply pretend that there is no first generation. We consider intergenerational justice *from within an ongoing society*. The present generation always has both predecessors and successors. (Consider Rawls's framing question: What saving principle would you choose *on the assumption that previous generations have also followed it*?)[42]

Unfortunately, *our* parallel problem cannot be so easily imagined away. Our problematic generation is not the first but the last. And there *will* be a last generation, even if there was never a first! How can earlier generations' procreative freedom be justified *to a generation who can never exercise that freedom*? Weinberg needs her parties to occupy, in turn, the roles of both child and potential parent. But the *last generation* can never be parents.

If our contractualist framework presupposes an ongoing society, must it simply remain silent in the last generation? Have we moved beyond the realm of procreative justice? If so, we confront a familiar, Ponzi-inspired slippery slope. What can we now say to the *penultimate* generation, or the generation before that, or ... ?

The obvious Rawlsian solution is a veil of ignorance. What if you didn't know when *in the Post-Cataclysm world* you will live? You know that you live during the last two hundred years of humanity, but not how close to the end. Parties who *know* they will live in the last generation have no reason to accept *any* penultimate procreative freedom. But perhaps rational parties *will* accept some *risk* of

---

[41] For Rawls on intergenerational justice, see Rawls, *A Theory of Justice*, pp. 284–293; Rawls, *Political Liberalism*, pp. 273–274; Rawls, *Justice as Fairness: A Restatement*, pp. 159–160; Rawls, *The Law of Peoples*, p. 107. For further discussion, see Gosseries, 'What Do We Owe the Next Generation(s)?'; Brandstedt, 'The Just Savings Principle'.

[42] Rawls, *Political Liberalism*, pp. 273–274.

belonging to that generation—in exchange for the freedom to procreate *if (as is more probable) they end up living in an earlier (Post-Cataclysm) generation*.

We must recall that Weinberg replaces Rawls's maximin with a less risk-averse *maximisation of expected capabilities*. Her parties *trade off* risk and reward, rather than minimising risk. So the fact that the last generation are worse-off does not automatically give their interests absolute priority, as it would for Rawls.

The obvious worry, for contractualists, is that Weinberg's maximising-expected-capabilities is unfair to the last generation. We don't want to allow *all* earlier generations to gang up on the last—shifting the last generation burden onto those who cannot shift it further themselves. Rawlsian contractualism should not collapse into a utilitarian tyranny of the majority!

One obvious solution is to grant the last generation a veto on principles that avoidably leave them worse-off than other generations. To model intergenerational justice in our Post-Cataclysm world, I therefore suggest we supplement Weinberg's procreative original position as follows. We *first* imagine parties living early in our Post-Cataclysm world, and ask what principles they would chose. We then *add* a new restriction to protect the last generation. Procreation is now permissible if and only if *two* conditions are met:

1. *Post-Cataclysm Balance Principle*: It is not irrational to accept the risk of living in a Post-Cataclysm world in exchange for permission to procreate if you are not in the last generation; and also
2. *Last Generation No Regret Restriction*: Suppose you know in advance that you will live in a Post-Cataclysm world. You select principles of procreative justice to govern your society. You *then* discover that you belong to the last human generation. Your chosen principles of procreative justice satisfy the No Regret Restriction if and only you are not disappointed. Or, if we retain Weinberg's permissive attitude to risk, the No Regret Restriction is satisfied if and only if it would not be irrational to not find this discovery disappointing all things considered.

Crucially, it must be not irrational to maintain both attitudes *simultaneously*. You *first* accept the risk of living in a Post-Cataclysm world in exchange for permission to procreate *in earlier generations*; but *then* you are not disappointed to find yourself living instead in the last generation where procreation is impossible.

This is a demanding balance to maintain, as the two requirements are in tension. The Post-Cataclysm Balance Principle trades on the significance of procreation to potential parents; while the Last Generation No Regret Restriction assumes that the last generation can be *fully compensated* for their inability to procreate.

I have presented my No Regret Restriction as a requirement of *procreative* justice. But we could instead read it as a general requirement of justice in a liberal

Rawlsian society. The No Regret Restriction must then be interpreted alongside other general Rawlsian principles of justice that govern liberty, equal opportunity, and so on.

This new Weinberg-inspired Rawlsian theory permits procreation only if the last generation *fare no worse than earlier generations*. It thus supports antinatalism if there *is* any unavoidable last generation burden—if the last generation must be worse-off all things considered.

Is this *too restrictive*, especially when some last generation burden is *unavoidable*? I am not sure. I agree that we don't want all previous generations to impose horrendous burdens on the last generation. But should one generation have an absolute veto just because they are (unavoidably) very slightly worse-off? Does my No Regrets Restriction abandon what is most valuable about Weinberg's initial departures from Rawls's original contractualism?

If we seek a more moderate contractualist position, then we could replace self-interested disappointment with *reasonable resentment*. And we could then add another Sincerity Requirement, where procreation is only permissible, before the last generation, if you sincerely believe that you would not have resented belonging instead to the last generation. You *would* feel reasonable resentment if, finding yourself in the last generation, you suffered some relatively easily avoidable burden. But if the burden is light, and your life is otherwise pretty good, and the cost to previous generations of improving your lot was prohibitive, then, while you would be *disappointed* that you didn't live earlier (and perhaps also disappointed that your forebears were not altruistic saints), you would not *resent* those forebears—either for leaving you worse-off than they might have done, or for creating you at all.

This may all sound a bit circular. Can't we now get any degree of procreative permissibility out of our procreative original position simply by building it in? Perhaps. But this kind of circularity is a feature of the Rawlsian reflective equilibrium enterprise, not a defect. If there is reasonable disagreement about procreative permissibility, there will be reasonable disagreement about any No Regret Restriction. But we may still learn valuable lessons about the former by exploring the latter. The procreative original position cannot resolve our disagreements, but it can bring them into the open.

We learn two lessons here. First, if multigenerational projects are not feasible, then it is quite difficult (but not impossible) to justify procreation. Second, however, if multigenerational projects *are* feasible and we reject them, then we impose *avoidable* last generation burdens—and *then* procreation is *extremely* difficult to justify. The last generation would reasonably resent *that*! Multigenerationalism must be pursued if it is feasible. And even if very ambitious multigenerational projects are not feasible, we may still be obliged to pursue the most ambitious projects that *are* feasible.

5.2.7 Extra vs Different People Choices

As we saw earlier, like Harman's harm-based theory, Weinberg's Balance Principle is more permissive in Extra People Choices (where the salient alternative is *not procreating at all*) than in Different People Choices (where the salient alternative is *procreating later or in a different way*).

Prima facie, this is good news for procreative liberals. Post-Cataclysm-specific harms generate *Extra* People Choices. If I live in the penultimate generation, then *any* child of mine belongs to the last generation. Therefore, creating a member of the last generation is not a Different People Choice, but instead an Extra People Choice.

However, as we saw earlier, multigenerationalists insist that many *actual* Post-Cataclysm-specific harms are *avoidable*, because less harmful alternatives *are* available. In particular, multigenerationalists urge us to delay procreation until we have immersed ourselves in new non-future-dependent traditions that will still deliver intergenerational meaning in the last generation. The choice between reorienting a tradition and retaining a future-dependent tradition is *Different* People, not Extra People. There *are* less harmful alternatives. Therefore, procreation *outside of those alternatives* is much harder to justify under the Balance Principle—because the relevant parental interest is much less significant.

Recall Future-lover, the potential parent whose tradition presupposes an indefinite human future (Section 4.4.4). Future-lover satisfies the Motivation Restriction. Can they also satisfy the Balance Principle? Do they have viable alternatives to raising their child within their own future-dependent tradition? If so, are they obliged to choose those alternatives if they want to procreate at all?

First consider an Extra People Choice, where Future-lover has no non-future-dependent procreative alternatives. Any child of Future-lover faces a *significant* risk of a meaningless life. This risk must be balanced against Future-lover's interest in *being able to procreate at all*. Perhaps Future-lover *is* permitted to procreate, despite the risks. This might be a hard case for Weinberg's Balance Principle, as it was for Harman. (Though, of course, Weinberg and Harman have very different notions of what counts as a *hard* case, as Weinberg also weighs the cost to the potential parent while Harman does not.)

But now consider instead a pluralistic *Different* People Choice, where Future-lover *could* offer their child a non-future-dependent life—either (a) by reorienting their original tradition; (b) by adopting a different tradition themselves; or (c) by allowing others to raise their child in a non-future-dependent way. What is *now* at stake for Future-lover is not (a) the freedom to have a child; but rather (b) the freedom *to have a child and raise them in one's current tradition*. The latter freedom is not trivial, but it is not as significant as procreative freedom per se.

As I argued earlier in relation to Harman (Section 4.4.4), the availability of a non-future-dependent alternative cuts both ways. On the one hand, it is now *more likely* that Future-lover can permissibly procreate, because it is now more likely that they can give their future child a good life. On the other hand, it is now *less likely* that Future-lover can permissibly create a child *and raise them within their own existing (future-dependent) tradition.*

For Harman, no avoidable harm is ever justified. The availability of non-future-dependent alternatives automatically renders future-dependent procreation impermissible—no matter how important this lost option is to Future-lover. For Weinberg, things are less clear. The relevant risk must still be *balanced* against Future-lover's interest in raising their own child within their own tradition. Therefore, this multigenerationalist argument is *less* powerful against Weinberg than it was against Harman.

In addition, the *scope* of this particular multigenerationalist argument is narrower for Weinberg than for Harman. Weinberg's *Motivation Restriction* rules out many non-future-dependent 'alternatives' altogether. Even if adoption would be best for my future child, I cannot permissibly create someone with the intention of giving them up for adoption, as this clearly violates the Motivation Restriction. I don't respect any child I create with this aim. The availability of *this kind* of alternative is irrelevant to Weinberg's Balance Principle. (Wilder fantasies where I forego procreation to contribute funds to projects to 'uplift' super-intelligent-but-not-future-dependent chimpanzees, dolphins, or octopi are presumably even more suspect.)

Multigenerationalists can sidestep this particular objection, *if* we accept my earlier argument that some suitable multigenerational projects can *replace* the parent–child relationship *for the purposes of Weinberg's Motivation Restriction* (Section 5.2.1). On this amended Weinberg-inspired view, I can still respect my future child even if I don't raise them—so long as I create them in order that we can be co-participants in some mutually meaningful multigenerational endeavour. Conversely, I suggested in Section 5.2.1 that, rather than treating other modes of intergenerational cooperation as a potential *replacement* for Weinberg's original parent-child motivation, we might instead regard them as an *additional* motivational requirement that all procreation must satisfy. Procreation is then *only* permissible if I desire to join with my child in other cooperative intergenerational projects. In the same spirit, we might now also include a requirement that I participate in multigenerational projects myself. Am I still cooperating with my child if I am *not* myself involved in the multigenerational project that makes it possible for that child to enjoy a fully meaningful life? Do I respect my future child if I leave the burden of reorientation to others?

Of course, my amendment to Weinberg's theory will be very controversial. A less controversial multigenerationalist position would concede, for the sake of argument, that people are *sometimes* justified in raising children within their own future-dependent traditions, even if those very children would have been better-off in a radically different society. But multigenerationalists will still insist that, if I *can* preserve my parent–child relationship *without* exposing my future child to the risk of lost future-dependent meaning, then I *must* do so—even if this is less desirable for me overall. If I can *reorient* my existing tradition rather than abandoning it, then I disrespect my future child if I did not at least *try* to do so. And this conclusion seems perfectly reasonable. After all, I have no *valuable* interest in raising my child in a way that unnecessarily deprives them of intergenerational meaning.

As with Harman, procreative permission is thus most plausible if multigenerationalists can *reorient* future-dependent traditions, enabling both potential parents and future children to flourish within the same tradition even at humanity's end. This reinforces my earlier arguments for multigenerationalism. Procreative permissibility is difficult to defend if the last generation are worse-off—and especially if we could have reoriented our existing traditions to make them better-off (or, at least, less badly-off).

5.3 Weinberg and Constraints on Permissible Procreation

How does Weinberg's theory compare to my initial list of constraints in Section 4.1 in the previous lecture?

Weinberg will endorse my Zero and Sufficiency Constraints. It would be disrespectful to create a child whose life was not worth living, or insufficiently good overall.

Weinberg will endorse my Intergenerational Meaning Constraint if, but only if, (a) the loss of intergenerational meaning is significant in itself, and (b) the risk of suffering that loss is not one that I would be (not irrationally) willing to bear myself. If I can honestly say that I *would* take that risk, then it may be permissible to give one's future child a life without intergenerational meaning. In practice, this is only likely to happen (if it *ever* happens), when the alternative is not to create anyone at all. It is hard to imagine choosing to create a life without intergenerational meaning *instead of a life containing such meaning*. If the loss of intergenerational meaning is avoidable, then surely I do not respect my future child if I fail to avoid it.

Weinberg's original theory explicitly contains a limited Intergenerational Cooperation Constraint. Every child must enjoy a worthwhile parent–child relationship. If we amend Weinberg's theory to recognise other permissible motivations, then procreation may be permissible without a worthwhile parent–child relationship—but only if some other kind of *equally meaningful* intergenerational cooperation is available. Alternatively, as I suggested earlier, we might instead *strengthen* Weinberg's theory by insisting that broader intergenerational cooperation is always necessary *in addition to* a worthwhile parent–child relationship.

Weinberg would then impose a full Intergenerational Cooperation Constraint (Section 5.2.1).

Weinberg makes both Same Person and Different Person Comparisons. If I could have given any child of mine a much better life—or a life without this particular harm—then my procreation is disrespectful. However, Weinberg does not insist that you give your child their best possible life—nor that you remove all avoidable harms. The whole point of the *Balance Principle* is that, sometimes, the interests of the potential parent *do* trump the interests of the future child. We therefore cannot derive any specific Same Person or Different Person Comparative Constraints from Weinberg's principles.

Weinberg will endorse my Rational Risk Constraint, as it is modelled on her Balance Principle. Weinberg will also endorse a variant of my Harman-inspired No Unjustifed Harms Constraint. For Weinberg, however, an *unjustified* harm is one where (a) the potential parent would not actually take the relevant risk (thus failing our new Sincerity Requirement); and/or (b) it would be irrational to take that risk (thus failing the Balance Principle).

Recall my final four constraints:

- *No Intergenerational Decline Constraint*: Procreation is permissible only if life in the next generation is (on the whole) no worse than life in the present generation.
- *No Avoidable Intergenerational Decline Constraint*: Procreation is permissible only if life in the next generation is (on the whole) no worse than life in the present generation—if this could have been avoided. (Recall that, unlike the previous constraint, this one *could* permit *unavoidable* intergenerational decline.)
- *No Post-Cataclysm Decline Constraint*: Procreation is permissible only if life in the next generation is (on the whole) no worse than life in earlier generations in our Post-Cataclysm world.
- *No Post-Cataclysm Avoidable Decline Constraint*: Procreation is permissible only if life in the next generation is (on the whole) no worse than life in earlier generations in our Post-Cataclysm world—if this could have been avoided. (Recall that, unlike the previous constraint, this one *could* permit *unavoidable* Post-Cataclysm decline.)

Weinberg's original theory will not explicitly endorse these intergenerational constraints. Procreation can be permissible if things are (unavoidably) getting worse—or if the cost to present people (i.e., potential parents) of avoiding decline is too high. However, if some available option would leave future people no worse-off, then Weinberg's theory will probably insist on this *unless the cost is prohibitively high*. If feasible multigenerational projects are available, then they may be compulsory—even if this is not ideal for the present generation. Furthermore, if we add a No Regret Restriction to Weinberg's original Rawlsian contractualism, as I suggested in Section 5.2.6, then we *can* derive much stronger constraints. Once the No Regret Restriction is in place, we cannot leave future people worse-off that present people, and the penultimate generation cannot leave the last generation worse-off than themselves. Procreation is then permissible only if multigenerationalism is feasible—leaving a choice between multigenerationalism and anti-natalism.

This concludes my exploration of Weinberg's Rawlsian contractualist procreative ethic. While it provides many useful resources, it also faces significant challenges, especially from anti-natalists and multigenerationalists. In my next lecture, I ask whether consequentialism fares any better.

6
Lecture Four
Collective Consequentialist Procreative Ethics

Multigenerationalist: In this lecture, I explore consequentialist procreative ethics. As I said at the start of my first procreative ethics lecture, I seek to remain agnostic between consequentialism and non-consequentialism. Multigenerationalism is not committed to either approach. My goal is to show that multigenerationalism is consistent with, and supported by, both traditions in procreative ethics. I also explore overlaps between the best Pre-Cataclysm versions of both consequentialism and non-consequentialism.

A full exploration of consequentialist procreative ethics is beyond the scope of my lectures. Instead, I have selected one strand of Pre-Cataclysm consequentialist thinking about procreative ethics, developed by Brad Hooker and Tim Mulgan. I will ask how it adapts to our Post-Cataclysm world.[1] I begin by explaining the broader motivations for *collective* consequentialism.

6.1 Pre-Cataclysm Collective Consequentialism

Collective consequentialism (CC) seeks to combine the best features of consequentialism and non-consequentialism. It combines consequentialism's theoretical appeal with non-consequentialism's intuitive plausibility, building moderate liberal principles on a foundation of impartial impersonal value.

Consequentialists build morality on the *promotion* of value. Unlike person-affecting theorists, impersonal consequentialists seek to promote value by bringing about valuable outcomes. In particular, unlike Harman, Roberts, and Weinberg, CC recognises a general reason to promote the good. Other things

---

[1] The classic presentation is Hooker, *Ideal Code, Real World*. See also, Hooker, 'Review of Mulgan, T., *The Demands of Consequentialism*'; Hooker, 'Rule-Consequentialism, Incoherence, Fairness'; Hooker, 'Acts or rules? The Fine Tuning of Utilitarianism'; Hooker, 'The Role(s) of Rules in Consequentialist Ethics'; Hooker, 'Rule Consequentialism'; Mulgan, *The Demands of Consequentialism*, pp. 53–103; Mulgan, *Future People*, pp. 130–160; Mulgan, 'Rule Consequentialism and Non-Identity'; Mulgan, 'Utilitarianism for a Broken World'; Mulgan, 'How Should Utilitarians Think about the Future?'; Mulgan, *Utilitarianism*; Mulgan, 'From Brad to Worse: Rule Consequentialism and Undesirable Futures'. In the text, I omit several nuances in both Hooker's view and my departures from it, which are not relevant to the discussion here.

equal, we should improve the world. CC endorses the positive side of the procreative asymmetry. We have a strong reason to create new happy people.

However, CC also recognises the appeal of non-consequentialist principles, and rejects act consequentialism as too demanding and implausible (Section 4.3.3). CC promises a moderate consequentialism that can criticise both common-sense morality and existing moral practice, while avoiding the extreme alienation of individual act consequentialism.

CC thus combines two contrasting moral ideals: consequentialism and liberal moderation.

1. *Consequentialism*. CC selects the moral outlook that best promotes human well-being into the far distant future. CC embraces a defining commitment of the utilitarian tradition: *temporal impartiality*. We cannot discount future well-being *just because it occurs in the future*.[2]

Temporally impartial consequentialism is notoriously demanding. If we give equal weight to all generations, then present people must make great sacrifices to benefit future people. This *demandingness* objection motivates CC's second distinctive feature:

2. *Liberal Moderation*. CC promises a moderate liberal *alternative* to act consequentialism.[3] CC recognises a broad sphere of personal moral freedom where agents are free to *not* maximally promote the good. CC's ideal moral outlook includes person-affecting principles, non-Consequentialist distinctions like doing and allowing, priority to actual people over future people, and limits on moral or social coercion.

The trick, obviously, is to combine impartial consequentialism with liberal moderation. I return to that challenge shortly. But first I explore the collective moral perspective.

Act consequentialism says that the right act in any situation is the individual act that produces the best consequences. CC combines three departures from act consequentialism: alternative foci of evaluation; indirect evaluation; and collective evaluation.[4] CC evaluates both moral outlooks and actions; it evaluates particular acts in terms of ideal moral outlooks; and it adopts a collective moral perspective. CC sees morality as a collective enterprise. Its fundamental questions are: 'What if *we* did that?' and 'How should *we* live?'

---

[2] cf. Cowen and Parfit, 'Against the Social Discount Rate'; Mulgan, *Utilitarianism*, section 2.1.
[3] Hooker, *Ideal Code, Real World*; Mulgan, *The Demands of Consequentialism*, chapter three; Mulgan, *Future People*, chapters five and six.
[4] Mulgan, *Utilitarianism*, section 2.

Whatever its general merits, this collective perspective was ideally suited to Pre-Cataclysm *intergenerational* ethics, where the most pressing dilemmas were large-scale, long-term, collective action problems.[5] It retains its appeal in our Post-Cataclysm world, where the construction of meaningful moral projects *in the face of imminent human extinction* requires collective deliberation, imagination, and cooperation.

Collective consequentialism has two interlocking motivations. From a theoretical perspective, CC appeals if we believe that morality is a collective project—a task given to us collectively, not to each of us individually. Therefore, we ask what we together can do to best promote the good. Furthermore, CC appeals if we are also persuaded that individual consequentialism is *not* the correct answer *to this collective question*. What we should do together is *not* the sum of what each of us should do individually (taking others' behaviour as given). We can do more good together than any of us could do on their own. In other words, the (collectively) ideal moral outlook is not exhausted by the act consequentialist reason to promote the good. (I argue later in this section that this allows CC to reply to the notorious 'collapse' objection.)

If we combine the collective moral perspective with temporal impartiality, then it is natural to adopt an *intergenerational* collective perspective. We *could* ask what *our generation*, on its own, should do. But why not ask instead what humanity as a whole—spread across all generations—should do? If we think morality is a collective project, then why *not* imagine an intergenerational collective? We seek—not the best moral outlook for our generation—but rather the best moral outlook (or series of outlooks, or framework for developing an outlook, or...) for the rest of human history. CC thus supports multigenerationalism. And, in turn, multigenerationalism supports CC. This mutual support is a theme of my exploration of CC.

CC begins with Brad Hooker's rule-consequentialism, where an action is permissible if someone who had internalised the ideal code would feel morally free to perform that act—and the ideal code is the set of rules whose internalisation by (nearly) everyone in the next generation would produce the best consequences.[6]

CC is a two-stage theory. We first directly evaluate the *ideal moral code*—the code whose widespread internalisation in a new generation would best promote the good. We then assess acts *indirectly*: the right act is the act that would be performed by someone who had internalised that code.

CC is often called 'rule consequentialism'. But *rule* consequentialism is misnamed. Talk of 'rules' and 'codes' is distracting and potentially misleading. I prefer to speak instead of moral *outlooks*.[7] This leaves open whether CC's ideal is a

---

[5] Mulgan, 'Consequentialism as an Intergenerational Ethics'.
[6] Hooker, *Ideal Code, Real World*, p. 32.
[7] Mulgan, 'How Should Utilitarians Think about the Future?'; Mulgan, *Utilitarianism*, section 2.

code of rules, a set of dispositions, a package of virtues, a set of priorities, a general moral outlook, or (as seems most likely) some combination of these. We do not ask what behaviour is required by such-and-such set of rules. We ask instead how someone with the ideal moral outlook would respond in a given situation. As Hooker notes, an act is then *permissible*, not if this imaginary person *would* do it, but if they *would feel morally free* to do it.[8]

Pre-Cataclysm proponents of CC offered two distinct justifications: intuitive and theoretical. CC's most prominent intuitive defender is Hooker. He argues that CC delivers a moderate moral theory that is consistent with (and helps to explain) our considered moral judgements: 'the best argument for rule consequentialism is that it does a better job than its rivals of matching and tying together our moral convictions.'[9] Theoretical justifications cite general moral ideals: consequentialism, collectivism, and explanation. If morality is a *collective* enterprise that aims to make the world *better*, then collective consequentialism is the natural approach. And, as Hooker argues, CC is superior to a mere *list* of common-sense rules because, as well as *matching* our considered moral judgements, it explains *why* those rules are correct.

Both justifications exemplify a *reflective equilibrium* methodology.[10] We seek to unify our considered moral judgements about (a) the structure and purpose of morality; (b) particular moral rules, principles, and values; and (c) specific cases (whether actual or hypothetical). The more we emphasise abstract judgements—the more theoretical our case for CC—the more room CC has to depart from existing common-sense morality and/or actual moral practice.

One notorious objection is that CC 'collapses' into act consequentialism.[11] Act consequentialists argue that the 'ideal' moral outlook simply applies act consequentialism in every situation. CC is then just a cumbersome restatement of act consequentialism.

If CC coincides with act consequentialism, then CC can claim no comparative advantage. CC must differentiate itself. Following Hooker, CC emphasises the costs of getting any very demanding, alienating, or complicated outlook actually *internalised by* (or *taught to*) a new generation *of human beings*.[12] Moral outlooks that are *too* demanding, impersonal, or alien could not be effectively internalised by human beings or handed down the generations. As Hooker points out, these are not one-off costs borne only by the first generation—they are borne in turn by *every* generation who must internalise a very demanding outlook.

---

[8] Hooker, *Ideal Code, Real World*, p. 177.   [9] Hooker, *Ideal Code, Real World*, p. 101.
[10] Hooker, *Ideal Code, Real World*, pp. 9–16; Mulgan, 'Utilitarianism for a Broken World'.
[11] Hooker, *Ideal Code, Real World*, pp. 93–99.
[12] 'Internalised by' is Hooker's formulation (Hooker, *Ideal Code, Real World*, pp. 75–80); while 'taught to' is mine (Mulgan, *Future People*, chapter six; Mulgan, 'Utilitarianism for a Broken World'; Mulgan, 'How Should Utilitarians Think about the Future?'; Mulgan, *Utilitarianism*).

Human nature is not infinitely plastic. Any plausible moral outlook that promotes value when taught to, and internalised by, a population of real human beings will include many familiar moral dispositions and distinctions such as honesty, generosity, promise-keeping, courage, murder-aversion, and so on. People who internalise the ideal outlook will not walk callously past children drowning in ponds, take pleasure in the sufferings of others, or reject the basic goods of human life. Act consequentialism is too demanding to be taught to human beings; and its calculations are too complicated to be implemented by them. Things do not go best overall if everyone constantly tries to maximise the good! And they won't go well if we try to teach them to.

While CC objects to the *excessive* and *alienating* demands of act consequentialism, it remains a distinctively *consequentialist* ethic. Morality is ultimately all about promoting valuable outcomes. Morality *can* be very demanding, especially in an unequal world. CC's ideal moral outlook is likely to demand much more than either moral common sense or actual moral practice. In particular, the reason to promote the good is still very important. For act consequentialists, the reason to promote the good exhausts morality. To avoid collapse, CC must deny this. But the ideal moral outlook still *includes* a strong prima facie reason to promote the good. If you have internalised that outlook, you will regard the fact that an action would make things better (relative to other available alternatives) as a very good reason to perform it.

CC deploys a similar argument to defend a distinctively *intergenerational* moral perspective. Just as human nature limits the complexity of the ideal moral outlook that can be internalised by (or taught to) any given generation, it also limits the flexibility of morality from one generation to the next. Single-generation consequentialists (analogous to individual act consequentialists) would defend an 'ideal' moral outlook that changes abruptly from one generation to the next. Children would internalise and apply radically different rules from their parents. CC rejects this model. Even if such radical dislocation were desirable in theory, it simply won't work in practice. Intergenerational ethical change has a high cost. Other things equal, things go *much* better if each generation learns its moral outlook by *observing* and *imitating* its parents. Gradual evolution trumps radical change.

CC prefers a single outlook that *evolves* from one generation to another, where the same general moral tendencies, principles, and values can be extended from the Pre-Cataclysm world to the Post-Cataclysm world, and then from earlier to later generations after the Cataclysm, and finally from the penultimate generation to the last generation. This is why multigenerationalism and CC are mutually supporting. Insofar as multigenerationalism succeeds, it provides a coherent intergenerational moral outlook that evolves over time, just as CC wants. And, in its turn, CC provides additional reasons for believing that multigenerationalism *will* succeed.

CC favours an evolving moral outlook for another reason. CC connects *present obligations* to *future ethics*.[13] We determine our present ethical standards by asking what moral outlook it would be best for everyone to internalise *in the next generation*. And we select that outlook, in part, because of its impact *on the further future*. The optimal (future) moral outlook determines present rightness. This is not an arbitrary or ad hoc manoeuvre—or a device to gerrymander a moral outlook to fit our actual intuitions. It also has a principled justification. CC embraces temporal impartiality. The welfare of future people matters as much as our own. Therefore, we cannot reasonably insist on privileges and permissions that our descendants cannot enjoy. If they face harsh choices at humanity's end, then we must face those harsh choices too.

CC sharply distinguishes its *foundational values* (used to evaluate competing moral outlooks) from its *internal* values (the values of someone who has internalised the ideal outlook). For instance, CC is foundationally impartial—everyone's well-being counts for one, and no one counts for more than one. But *foundational* impartiality does not entail *internal* impartiality. Indeed, the two come apart. The outlook that best promotes impartial value will not instruct people to always act or think impartially. This is how CC defeats the collapse objection. Things go best—*from an impartial perspective*—if everyone gives priority to their own interests, values, and relationships.

Distinguishing internal values from foundational values enables CC to finesse many other controversial questions in consequentialist ethics, in two different ways. Sometimes, as with impartiality, CC *separates* internal values from foundational values: a foundational commitment to impartiality sits alongside internal partiality. This enables CC to retain the theoretical appeal of consequentialist impartiality while avoiding its most counter-intuitive results. CC allows moral agents to privilege their own moral point of view, without losing sight of the fundamental moral equality of all human interests.

CC separates internal values from foundational values in several other contexts. For instance, *maximisers* insist that the right act is the one with the greatest (expected) value; while *satisficers* say it is sufficient to pick any act whose (expected) results are good enough.[14] CC combines foundational maximising with internal satisficing. The moral outlook that maximises value won't always demand a maximising approach to life.

CC also separates internal values from foundational values to sidestep the intractable debates about aggregation and axiology that dominated Pre-Cataclysm consequentialist future ethics. The Pre-Cataclysm aggregation literature's 'organising problem' is Parfit's Repugnant Conclusion.[15] The simplest consequentialist

---

[13] Mulgan, 'Utilitarianism for a Broken World'.
[14] On satisficing consequentialism, see Mulgan, *The Demands of Consequentialism*, chapter five.
[15] Parfit, *Reasons and Persons*, p. 381–390.

account of aggregation is *Totalism*, where the best outcome has greatest *total wellbeing*. Totalism implies that world A where ten billion people flourish is *worse* than world Z where a vast population endure lives barely worth living. Parfit argues that this conclusion is 'intrinsically repugnant';[16] and that alternatives to Totalism that avoid the Repugnant Conclusion yield even more counter-intuitive results.

Aggregation debates remain unresolved. Some hope to find Parfit's Theory X. Popular alternatives to totalism include averagism, lexical views, diminishing marginal value views, prioritarianism, egalitarianism, and many more.[17] Others reply that Theory X cannot exist, because no possible theory can satisfy a set of intuitively compelling constraints.[18] Some defend Totalism for its theoretical simplicity, while downplaying its counter-intuitiveness.[19] Others seek to remain *agnostic*, arguing that we can derive consequentialist principles to guide our future ethics without identifying Parfit's Theory X.

Pre-Cataclysm CC offers two main responses to Parfit's repugnant conclusion. The first uses a strategy of *separation* to *simultaneously* agree with both totalism and commonsense. World Z is *better* than world A. But there is no *obligation* to transform an existing A-world into a Z-world. CC can thus combine totalist foundational values with a non-totalist moral outlook.[20] For instance, Mulgan argues that future people who have internalised the moral code whose widespread internalisation would *maximise total happiness* across all future generations will set a *lexical threshold* below which they will not allow their own lives, the lives of their contemporaries, *or the lives of their descendants* to fall.[21] Mulgan's lexical thresholds embody the central liberal consequentialist idea that everyone enjoys greater security—and hence higher well-being—if each enjoys a privileged moral sphere where their interests are secure against the incursions of the consequentialist reason to promote the good. In practice, therefore, lexical moral outlooks trump outlooks that encourage widespread trade-offs between the welfare of different individuals. (I return to the relationship between lexicality and procreative ethics in Section 6.2.)

Alongside separation, the distinction between foundational values and internal values also grounds a second popular CC technique: *agnosticism*. The simplest

---

[16] Parfit, *Reasons and Persons*, p. 388.
[17] For overviews of the vast recent literature on aggregation, see Arrhenius et al., 'The Repugnant Conclusion'; Arrhenius et al., *The Oxford Handbook of Population Ethics*; Greaves, 'Population Axiology'; Mulgan, *Utilitarianism*, especially sections 3 and 4.1. The classic distinction between total view, average view, lexical views, and diminishing marginal value views is from Parfit, *Reasons and Persons*, pp. 391–441. On prioritarianism and egalitarianism, see Parfit, 'Equality and Priority'; Holtug, *Persons, Interests, and Justice*.
[18] Arrhenius, 'The Paradoxes of Future Generations and Normative Theory'.
[19] Broome, *Weighing Lives*.
[20] Mulgan, *Future People*, chapter three; Mulgan, 'Two Parfit Puzzles'.
[21] Mulgan, *Future People*, p. 144.

consequentialism embraces welfarism, hedonism, and totalism. The best outcome contains the greatest total human happiness, measured exclusively in terms of pleasure and pain. Other consequentialists consider non-welfarist, non-human, or distributive features of outcomes; recognise non-hedonist elements of human well-being; and explore alternative theories of aggregation such as averagism or lexical views. Agnostic CC stands aloof from all these debates. In one sense, this is obvious. CC could be combined with any credible story about the value of outcomes. Particular interpretations of CC could be hedonist, preference-based, or objectivist; totalist, averagist, or egalitarian; and so on. But CC can also be more ambitiously agnostic.[22] It can claim that a *single CC theory* could remain agnostic between competing accounts of value, because those competing accounts yield the same ideal moral outlook in practice. In particular, Pre-Cataclysm CC was often *agnostic about particular controversies relating to the nature of well-being*. We can identify the ideal outlook without settling perennial debates about what makes human lives worth living, because the same flexible, moderate, liberal outlook will promote future well-being *whatever well-being turns out to be*. For instance, hedonists, preference theorists, perfectionists, and objective list theorists all agree that, in practice, people's lives go best if they feel morally free to pursue their own goals, and have the resources and opportunities to do so.

One promising Pre-Cataclysm response was that, in response to the ongoing debate about Parfit's Repugnant Conclusion, CC should seek to remain *agnostic about aggregation*. In theory, totalism and averagism yield very different orderings of possible futures. In practice, however, they largely point in the same direction. Both total human well-being and average human well-being are best-promoted by a flourishing and sustainable future population; and sustainability rules out the opposite extremes favoured by competing theories—neither totalism's vast population of barely worth living lives nor averagism's tiny population of extraordinarily happy people would be sustainable.

Unfortunately, I argue below that consequentialist agnosticism about both well-being and aggregation is under threat after the Cataclysm. Indeed, I argue that CC *must* now abandon agnosticism—and that doing so strengthens its support for multigenerationalism (Section 6.3.4).

6.2 Pre-Cataclysm CC Procreative Ethics

CC's procreative ethic is also consequentialist, moderate, and liberal. CC seeks a middle path between (a) asymmetric non-consequentialism that recognises *no* reason to create new happy people; and (b) the extreme act consequentialist rejection of any procreative asymmetry. CC's ideal moral outlook can include

---

[22] cf. Mulgan, *Future People*, chapter six; Mulgan, 'Ethics for Possible Futures'.

person-affecting principles, non-consequentialist distinctions like doing and allowing, priority to actual people over future people, and a rejection of procreative coercion. People who have internalised that ideal outlook will not feel obliged to create the happiest children they possibly can—let alone the possible children whose existence would maximise *other people's happiness*.[23]

For instance, Mulgan argues that CC accommodates the following intuitively plausible principles:[24]

1. *Zero Constraint*: It is wrong to create a child whose life is not worth living.
2. *Gratuitous Sub-Optimality*. It is wrong to gratuitously create a child whose life is much worse than it could have been.[25]
3. *Liberty*: People should enjoy broad moral, practical, political, social, and legal freedom to choose when, with whom, in what way, and how often they procreate. This includes a permission not to have children, even if one could (at comparatively little cost to oneself) create people whose lives were extremely worth living.[26]

The conjunction of Zero Constraint, Gratuitous Sub-Optimality, and Liberty ensures that CC respects a *moderate* procreative asymmetry. While CC does recognise *some* reason to create new people whose lives will be very good, this reason is *weaker* than our reason not to create a life *not* worth living.[27]

4. *Moderate Obligations*: Parents' obligations to their children are much stronger than their obligations to strangers, close friends, or other relatives. But parents also enjoy broad moral freedom to raise their children as they see fit, and there is no overriding obligation to maximise the quality of one's child's life.
5. *Liberal Population Policy*: There is no exact 'optimal' population size, and the population can be kept within desirable upper and lower bounds by social policy incentives and nudges rather than by legal, social, or moral coercion.

These are all claims about CC's *internal values*. CC's *foundational values* may recognise a precise 'optimal' possible population. But human beings would not best-promote those foundational values by aiming at that theoretical optimum.

Act consequentialism rejects the autonomy of procreative ethics. Procreate ethics is just another application of the universal consequentialist principle

---

[23] Mulgan, *Future People*, pp. 172–173.
[24] This list of principles condenses a much longer discussion in Mulgan, *Future People*, chapter six.
[25] Mulgan, *Future People*, p. 5.   [26] Mulgan, *Future People*, pp. 134–135.
[27] cf. Chappell, 'Rethinking the Asymmetry'.

(Section 4.3.3). By contrast, Mulgan (implicitly) argues that CC does respect the following autonomy constraint:[28]

6. *Autonomy of Procreative Liberty*: Procreative liberty is not, in practice, limited by the *Disaster Avoidance Motivation*.

This claim requires some explanation. Hooker adds the *Disaster Avoidance Motivation* to ensure that the ideal code does not lead to disaster in our (non-ideal) real world. This motivation tells us to follow the rest of the ideal outlook except when this would lead to disaster, in which case we should do whatever is necessary to avoid disaster.[29] Mulgan's autonomy claim thus says that any emergency measures demanded by the ideal moral outlook do *not* include obligations (a) to have children, (b) to not have children, or (c) to treat one's children in otherwise unacceptable ways. Procreative and parental liberty are not subordinated to disaster prevention.

CC's case for procreative freedom and the autonomy of procreative ethics has two main inspirations. The first is Hooker's observation that CC's central question is not 'What if everyone did that?' but rather 'What if everyone *felt free* to do that?' As Hooker himself explains, 'Suppose my nephew tells me he refuses to have children. If everyone refuses to have children, the human species will die out. This would be a disastrous consequence. But it is irrelevant to the morality of my nephew's decision. What is relevant is that everyone's feeling free not to have children will not lead to the extinction of the species. Plenty of people who do not feel obligated to have children nevertheless *want* to—and, if free to do so, will. Thus, there is no need for a moral obligation to have children.'[30]

CC's second inspiration is familiar liberal consequentialist arguments going back to J. S. Mill.[31] Freedom is significantly better for the present generation than any alternative. Each successive generation, in its turn, enjoys freedom's benefits. Therefore, procreative freedom can only *fail* to maximise well-being if some alternative would produce much greater total well-being for some later generation. But this alternative scenario is extremely unlikely. We can *describe* imaginary illiberal policies which would, if perfectly implemented, produce consequences superior to the haphazard results of procreative liberty. But such illiberal outlooks could never be successfully internalised by—or taught to—a new generation of human moral agents.

CC does *not* claim that moral outlooks with procreative freedom always do a great job of promoting future well-being. CC *does* claim that liberal outlooks

---

[28] Mulgan, *Future People*, chapter six.   [29] cf. Hooker, *Ideal Code, Real World*, pp. 98–99.
[30] Hooker, *Ideal Code, Real World*, p. 177.
[31] The classic text is Mill, *On Liberty*. See also Sen, *Development as Freedom*; Mulgan *Future People*, chapter six.

reliably do a *better* job than any feasible, internalisable, teachable illiberal alternative.

This CC case for procreative freedom leaves many hostages to empirical fortune. Any consequentialist evaluation of competing moral outlooks depends on how people *would actually exercise their moral freedom*. And the more moral freedom people have, the harder it becomes to *predict* what they will actually *do*. And, as ever, even if CC's empirical claims were discoverable and/or plausible before the Cataclysm, they may be much harder to defend now. I return to these difficulties in Section 6.3.4, and in my later discussion of Post-Cataclysm libertarianism, because libertarians need especially ambitious predictions about the future exercise of freedom (Section 8.3.3).

Mulgan's CC procreative ethic incorporates the *lexical* internal values I sketched earlier (Section 6.1). Once our ideal moral outlook contains some lexical values, then any lexical threshold that applies to contemporaries will also apply to procreation. Parents who want their *existing* children to enjoy lives above the threshold will *not* feel free to gratuitously create a child living below that level.

Mulgan concludes that, once we factor in risk and uncertainty, CC endorses the following:

> *The Flexible Lexical Rule.* Reproduce if and only if you want to, so long as you are *reasonably sure* that your child will enjoy a life *above the lexical level*, and *very sure* that the risk of your child falling *below the zero level* is *very small*.[32]

This rule is very vague. Much depends on how we interpret the italicised phrases: *reasonably sure, above the lexical level, very sure, below the lexical level, very small*. However, as Hooker argues, vagueness is often a strength of CC, rather than a weakness. As Hooker says, 'Rule Consequentialists are as aware as anyone that figuring out whether a rule applies can require not merely attention to detail, but also sensitivity, imagination, interpretation, and judgement.'[33] The need for sensitive judgement only increases when we consider the impact of our ideal moral outlook on people living at humanity's end.

Because it recognises a generic reason to promote the good, even the most liberal CC is more demanding in many ways than non-consequentialist theories. In particular, CC will require us to provide the next generation (and the last generation) with their best possible lives *unless the cost to us is especially prohibitive*. And, like Harman and Weinberg, CC extends its comparisons from Same Person cases to Different Person cases. As we'll see, this threatens to make CC very demanding after the Cataclysm, as it is now very difficult to justify failing to create the optimal last generation (Section 6.3.4).

[32] Mulgan, *Future People*, p. 174.   [33] Hooker, *Ideal Code, Real World*, p. 88.

6.3 Collective Consequentialism after the Cataclysm

Our Post-Cataclysm world challenges CC in several ways. I simplify my discussion by focussing primarily on the relationship between the penultimate and last generations. My first challenge, in Section 6.3.1, is whether CC even makes *sense* for the last generation. (How can *they* ask what moral outlook they should teach to the next generation?) This may seem irrelevant, as the last generation surely don't need any *procreative* ethic. However, as CC is meant to cover the whole of moral life, it should apply even at humanity's end. We must ask what CC *says* to the last generation. Only then can we step back to ask how CC deals with penultimate procreation, and whether CC really does mutually support multigenerationalism.

I will argue that CC *can* apply to the last generation, but only if we re-imagine it (Sections 6.3.1 and 6.3.2), as we did for Weinberg's contractualism. I also argue that CC can offer plausible advice to the penultimate generation from a distinctively moderate consequentialist perspective (Sections 6.3.3 and 6.3.4). I end my series of procreative ethics lectures by explaining the mutual support between CC and multigenerationalism, which sets the scene for my next two lectures on moral transformation and multigenerational utopias (Sections 6.3.5).

6.3.1 Incoherence Revisited

CC presupposes future generations. Hooker asks what would happen if this or that code were internalised by a *new* generation.[34] Mulgan asks what moral outlook we should teach to the *next* generation.[35] In the last generation, neither question makes sense. CC thus seems to collapse into incoherence.

As with the parallel challenge to Weinberg (Section 5.2.4), CC can sidestep this objection. Asking what we should teach the next generation, or what a new generation could internalise, are useful devices to imagine away any costs involved in *changing* existing entrenched moral beliefs and attitudes, and therefore ensure that we don't over-privilege the status quo. (If we ask what *we* could best internalise now, then our ideal outlook will be too conservative!) However, we can achieve the same distance from our existing ethical outlook by asking questions based on *some hypothetical present or past* rather than on some possible future. *Past*: What moral code *should* our parents have taught us? *Present*: If we *could* step outside our own current moral outlook, what outlook should we adopt? If conditions don't change across generations, then all three questions (past, present, future)

---

[34] Hooker, *Ideal Code, Real World*, pp. 75–80.
[35] Mulgan, *Future People*, chapter six; Mulgan, 'Utilitarianism for a Broken World'; Mulgan, 'How Should Utilitarians Think about the Future?'; Mulgan, *Utilitarianism*.

converge. In rapidly changing circumstances, they may diverge. In the last generation, while future-directed questions are incoherent, past- or present-directed questions still make sense. For *consequentialists*, what ultimately matters is the result. We should ask whatever questions it is *most useful* for us to ask.

Unfortunately, there is a deeper incoherence challenge. In our Post-Cataclysm world, circumstances change rapidly from one generation to the next. The moral outlook we should teach the next generation is not the outlook we should follow *now*. And the moral outlook that maximises well-being in the last generation *must* differ radically from all previous outlooks, because it contains no procreative ethics or other future-directed elements at all. This raises the worry that CC's advice will fluctuate wildly from one generation to the next.

Such a fluctuation would raise two acute problems for CC. First, if different CC questions give very different answers, then it really matters *which* question CC asks. But the choice of question seems arbitrary. Second, if CC's ideal moral outlook changes radically from one generation to the next, then there can be no ongoing CC *society*. All versions of CC presume a stable society where parents hand their moral outlook down to their children. But this collapses if we suddenly expect present people to teach their own children a radically new morality.

CC has two possible ways to meet this challenge: modest conservatism and ambitious multigenerationalism. If different CC questions give different answers—if the outlook we should teach is not the outlook our parents should have taught—then CC can remain agnostic, acknowledge a genuine plurality of morally reasonably options, concentrate on areas where the different questions agree, or defer to commonsense morality. For instance, Hooker's 'wary rule-consequentialism' only recommends departures from common-sense morality when we are confident that some particular moral outlook would do better.[36] When such confidence is missing, we fall back on the tried-and-true rules of current moral practice. Another resource for conservative CC is Pre-Cataclysm *global* consequentialism, which combined competing direct evaluations of acts, motives, rules, and outlooks.[37] When different consequentialist questions come apart, global consequentialism offers no single answer. We must exercise our own judgement to decide what to do.

While this modesty is commendable, it is clearly in tension with CC's claim to offer *distinctive practical advice*. Personally, I therefore favour a different response. My more ambitious, more flexible interpretation of CC denies that changing *times* require a *new* moral outlook. CC seeks a flexible outlook that will not change radically across generations, because it is suitable to a range of possible futures. The outlook we inherit, the outlook we should follow, and the outlook we

---

[36] Hooker, *Ideal Code, Real World*, pp. 114–117.
[37] cf. Pettit and Smith, 'Global Consequentialism'; Driver, 'Global Utilitarianism'.

should bequeath are all the same. This intergenerational flexibility is one cornerstone in CC's case *for multigenerationalism*, to which I return in Section 6.3.5.

6.3.2 What Does CC Say to the Last Generation?

Procreative ethics does not apply directly to the last generation. However, because CC is a complete moral theory, it must say something to that generation. If CC seeks a flexible moral outlook that remains constant (or at least similar) across generations, even up to the end, then we must ask what CC says to the last humans.

There is good reason to hope that the last generation's ideal moral outlook is not *too* different from our own. After all, Pre-Cataclysm CC concentrated on relations between contemporaries. Therefore, most Pre-Cataclysm CC conclusions will hold true without any future people, even at humanity's end. Indeed, the last generation should find CC *easier* to apply, as the removal of *all* future people means the last generation face only Same People Choices. We might even hope that all the complications introduced by Parfit's Non-Identity Problem will now disappear!

Unfortunately, things are not quite so simple. In the last generation, CC faces a new challenge—or at least a new variation on an old theme.

Any CC theory considers two sets of sentient beings: agents and patients. Agents act together to promote the well-being of patients. Agents, of course, are themselves patients—sentient beings whose well-being matters. But not all patients are agents. The demandingness objection to CC is especially troubling when *few agents* can make great sacrifices to promote the well-being of *many patients*. If all patients are also agents, then any sacrifice imposed on all agents also falls on all patients. Therefore, average individual cost to agents cannot exceed average individual benefit to patients. But when agents are few and patients are many, average costs for agents may greatly exceed average benefits to patients. CC may then make very great demands.

The Pre-Cataclysm literature explored two main Few Agents/Many Patients problems:[38]

1. *Few Rich, Many Poor*: A few rich people must each make a great sacrifice to maximise total well-being by raising a very large number of poor people out of abject poverty. (We might call this 'the tyranny of the poor'.)

---

[38] I introduce this 'wrong facts objection' in Mulgan, 'Rule Consequentialism and Famine'; cf. Hooker, 'Rule-Consequentialism, Incoherence, Fairness'; and Mulgan, *The Demands of Consequentialism*, section 3.6, pp. 90–98. Another class of Few Agents/Many Patients cases involves *non-human* patients. I return to that issue in my discussion of Post-Cataclysm ecological utopias in Section 8.4.

2. *Few Present People, Many Future People*: A few present people must each make a great sacrifice to maximise total well-being by improving the lives of a very large number of future people. (We might call this 'the tyranny of the future'.)

Few Agents/Many Patients cases can generate two distinct objections to CC:

1. *Hypothetical Comparative Objection*: By comparing different possible scenarios containing different numbers of agents and/or patients, we see that CC's demands are too dependent on morally irrelevant empirical factors. (Should my individual obligations increase tenfold just because I am one of ten million rich people in the world rather than a hundred million—or just because the number of poor people is ten billion rather than 'only' one billion?)
2. *Actual Absolute Objection*: Whatever it says about purely hypothetical cases, CC makes unreasonable demands in *this actual* Few Agent/Many Patient case.

Hypothetical Few Agents/Many Patients cases generate hypothetical comparative objections. Even if CC's actual demands are reasonable, CC is unacceptable if it *would* make unreasonable demands if things were different in ways that should not matter (or, at least, should not matter *so much*).

In principle, CC can sidestep *this* complaint by denying that implausible implications in purely hypothetical situations are a decisive blow to an otherwise plausible moral theory. After all, the history of moral philosophy clearly shows that *every* moral theory is tripped up by *some* ingenious thought experiment or other!

Unfortunately, this kind of denial is problematic for two reasons. First, many moral philosophers will insist that an acceptable theory must give correct verdicts in (plausible) hypothetical cases as well as actual ones. Second, the most pressing Post-Cataclysm Few Agents/Many Patients cases are *actual* ones. CC therefore now confronts the actual absolute objection, which is much harder to sidestep than the hypothetical comparative objection.

Our new Post-Cataclysm case is as follows:

Few Present People, Many Past People: A few present people must each make a great sacrifice to maximise total well-being by improving the lives of a very large number of *past* people by fulfilling those past people's *posthumous* interests. (I dub this '*the Tyranny of the Past*'.)

This tyranny of the past mirrors the more familiar tyranny of the future, where the interests of many future people trump the interests of few present people. The tyranny of the past threatens both CC's agnosticism regarding well-being and CC's liberal moderation (Sections 6.1 and 6.2).

As we saw in our pessimism debate, the existence and significance of posthumous harms or benefits is a perennial site of philosophical controversy (Section 1.1). Can events after a person's death affect how well that person's life went? If so, can posthumous interests compete with, and perhaps outweigh, living interests?[39] (See also Sections 3.6, 3.7, 6.3.4, 9.5.)

Pre-Cataclysm CC largely ignored posthumous interests.[40] I think there are two plausible explanations for this omission. First, many consquentialists simply rejected posthumous interests. For instance, hedonists find the very idea of posthumous harm incoherent. If you no longer exist, then nothing can be good or bad for you. A second explanation is that Pre-Cataclysm CC operated with an implicit assumption that, even if they exist, posthumous interests are either (a) swamped by, or (b) aligned with, the broad interests of present people and future people. If we do what is best for present and future people, then we will also maximise the morally important posthumous interests of past people, if they have any. Posthumous interests would thus provide another striking example of Pre-Cataclysm CC's agnosticism regarding controversial questions of value.

Unfortunately, this comfortable agnosticism breaks down in the last generation. Without any future people, present people are vastly outnumbered by past people. And all the posthumous interests of all past people now converge on the present generation. Present people's interests may thus be insufficient to trump posthumous interests. If present people could do something to increase the well-being or meaningfulness of past lives, then posthumous interests threaten to overwhelm *all* present interests. CC makes the last generation the slaves, not of the future, but of the past.

The tyranny of the past generates two distinct objections. First, if there *are* significant posthumous interests, then CC is unreasonably demanding in the last generation. Second, if the demands of CC depend so much on *whether or not there are* posthumous interests, then CC can no longer remain agnostic. The first objection supports the second. If significant posthumous interests would impose significant *new* demands, then CC cannot remain agnostic.

This is *not* just another familiar example of the demandingness of consequentialism. It is a more serious threat to CC, because the tyranny of the past undermines the most prominent Pre-Cataclysm response to the demandingness objection, especially in relation to Few Agents/Many Patients cases. This CC response, in effect, denies that there *are* any *actual* Few Agents/Many Patients

---

[39] On posthumous harm, see Luper, 'Death'—section 6 'Posthumous Harm'; Luper, 'Retroactive Harms and Wrongs'; Boonin, *Dead Wrong*; Keller, 'Posthumous Harm'; Kraut, *The Quality of Life*, pp. 139–144.

[40] I am not aware of any significant discussion of posthumous interests in collective consequentialism.

cases. As Hooker insists, the same ideal moral outlook must be internalised *by everyone*—including very poor present people and all future people.[41] All patients must always bear the burdens that fall on agents. A very demanding ethic would have to be internalised by everyone in every succeeding generation. We can imagine a world with comparatively few rich people or comparatively many future people. But we cannot imagine a world with *comparatively* few agents—where agents are vastly out-numbered by patients. All ordinary humans are both patients *and agents*.

CC thus concedes that a moral outlook that is only internalised once could be *very* demanding. But because, as Hooker argues, the costs of teaching a demanding morality recur again in every subsequent generation, no moral outlook is only internalised once. All patients are also agents in their turn.

Hooker's reply was controversial before the Cataclysm. We can set *that* controversy aside. Whatever its merits in relation to rich and poor or present and future, the identification of patients and agents is a non-starter in relation to the past. The tyranny *of the past* objection to CC is immune to Hooker's ingenious solution. The last generation cannot cite the future costs of passing on their moral outlook to a new generation. Past people benefit from the present internalisation of this demanding outlook, but they do not pay the costs of internalisation themselves. Past patients *are no longer agents*. Therefore, patients do now outnumber agents.

I conclude that CC can no longer remain agnostic regarding posthumous interests. CC must decide whether or not posthumous interests are, in principle, sufficiently significant to trump present (pre-mortem) interests. The tyranny of the past demonstrates that, if posthumous interests *can* trump pre-mortem interests, then they *will* do so in the last generation.

Fortunately, I don't think the need to abandon agnosticism is a bad thing—either for CC or for multigenerationalism. I argue below that CC *should* abandon agnosticism more broadly—and embrace its own distinctive foundational values (Section 6.3.4), and that doing so strengthens the relation of mutual support between CC and multigenerationalism.

Once it abandons agnosticism regarding posthumous interests, CC has three options. First, CC can bite the bullet. CC is very demanding in the last generation, because past posthumous interests trump present interests. This reply is unattractive. It deprives CC of its main advantage over act consequentialism; it threatens to lead to last generation pessimism (if morality is too demanding, then *no one* in the last generation can enjoy a life that is both flourishing and morally permissible); and it makes it very difficult for CC to justify procreation in the penultimate generation—or in any earlier generation in our Post-Cataclysm world.

[41] Hooker, *Ideal Code, Real World*, pp. 173–174.

Second, CC can simply reject posthumous interests. Indeed, perhaps the tyranny of the past is a *reductio ad absurdum* of the very idea of posthumous interests! If this is where posthumous interests lead, then we *should* reject them. More modestly, CC might insist that, even if they exist, posthumous interests are necessarily always *lexically inferior* to present interests. No set of posthumous interests ever trumps the present interests of an entire generation.

While this solution is tempting, it is very hard for *me*, as a multigenerationalist, to reject significant posthumous interests. Post-Cataclysm pessimists often appeal to posthumous interests to explain why life is bad at humanity's end (Section 1.1). In particular, posthumous interests are the obvious way to ground Scheffler-inspired pessimism (Section 1.4). Multigenerationalism seeks to meet such pessimism on its own terms—conceding that the loss of future-dependent meaning is a very significant blow. But future-dependent meaning only matters (in itself) if there are significant posthumous interests. Abandoning posthumous interests would leave CC unable to mutually support multigenerationalism; as well as depriving CC of much of its distinctiveness. While hedonist, totalist, presentist act consequentialism reduces morality to the maximisation of future pleasures, multigenerationalist CC concedes the significance of future-dependent meaning *and then tries to restore what has been lost.*

Why does the significance of future-dependent meaning depend on posthumous interests? Suppose there are no posthumous interests. Nothing that happens after your death can directly affect either your well-being or the meaningfulness of your life. Future-dependent meaning thus cannot depend on facts about our *actual* connections to future people—because those facts clearly *do* depend on what happens after your death. The only kind of 'future-dependent' meaning that is available is meaning derived entirely from *your present beliefs about future people*—where you get the same meaning whether those beliefs are true or false. Intuitively, this purely subjective future-dependent meaning is not sufficient—and it is certainly not what philosophers who emphasise future-dependent meaning (such as Scheffler) have in mind (Section 1.4). A universal false belief in an indefinite human future is not a substitute for an *actual* human future.

Multigenerationalists must avoid extreme demands without abandoning posthumous interests. I must therefore embrace CC's final option, and deny that there is *unavoidable conflict* between past and present interests. The best possible outcome *could not* involve sacrificing present (pre-mortem) interests in favour of past (posthumous) interests. The tyranny of the past is not an *actual* tyranny.

I think the most promising way forward here is to claim that past people's *valuable* posthumous interests always depend upon the flourishing of those they leave behind. The creation of a miserable last generation cannot benefit earlier generations *in morally important ways*. While this might be *possible* on some crude hedonist or preference theories, it is impossible if well-being depends on idealised preferences and/or objective goods. Posthumous 'interests' fulfilled by miserable descendants are *not* morally significant!

This is not an eccentric account of posthumous interests. The very idea of posthumous interests relies on some broader category of *unfelt harm*—where people can be harmed by events or actions that never affect their experiences.[42] If we recognise unfelt harms, then we presumably endorse either some desire-satisfaction-based account of well-being or something like an objective list theory. For instance, I might be harmed after death because my desires are posthumously thwarted or because my achievements are undermined. Many ideal desire-satisfaction theories, and most objective list theories, will agree that my well-being is only enhanced by worthwhile desires and achievements.

This also explains why even totalist CC can never, in practice, seek a last generation whose lives fall below the zero level, because this would *not* maximise total well-being. Past people's posthumous interests are not irrelevant. They can influence present decisions; and there can be some tension between what is best for us and what is best for them. But morally valuable posthumous interests can only ever require us to *compromise* present interests, not to sacrifice them altogether. If I try to improve my life by creating a miserable slave who will memorialise me after my death, then I necessarily fail—because such tyranny cannot truly promote my own valuable posthumous interests. In many everyday cases, I *can* promote my interests by sacrificing other people. (If I save myself by pushing you in front of the bus instead of me, then I am better-off.) But *valuable posthumous interests* can only be promoted by enabling future people to flourish.

While it is ambitious and controversial, I believe this is the only plausible solution that is consistent with multigenerationalism. The interests of past and present people coincide because what is best *for all generations* is to work together on the best multigenerational project. Once again, it therefore turns out that, despite appearances, there are no actual Few Agents/Many Patients cases. The tyranny of the past remains merely hypothetical.

This argument presupposes multigenerationalism. CC will be extremely demanding if multigenerationalism is *not* feasible. But if multigenerationalism *is* feasible, then the tyranny of the past disappears, and CC can retain its moderate credentials.

6.3.3 Can CC Avoid Immediate Extinction?

I now take a step back, and ask whether CC can deliver a plausible procreative ethic in the penultimate generation. CC faces two opposite objections: that it is too restrictive (this section) and that it is too demanding (Section 6.3.4).

The first objection is that, whenever the next generation would be worse-off than their parents, Pre-Cataclysm CC must prohibit all procreation—and

---

[42] On unfelt harms and desire-based theories, see Boonin, *Dead Wrong*, especially chapters two and three, to whom I owe the term 'unfelt harm' (Boonin, *Dead Wrong*, p. 14).

therefore it cannot avoid immediate extinction. Therefore, if there is *any* last generation burden, then CC prohibits penultimate procreation; requires the penultimate generation to become the last generation; and therefore (by familiar Ponzi-style iteration) CC prohibits all Post-Cataclysm procreation.

Recall Mulgan's Flexible Lexical Rule (Section 6.2):

> *The Flexible Lexical Rule.* Reproduce if and only if you want to, so long as you are *reasonably sure* that your child will enjoy a life *above the lexical level*, and *very sure* that the risk of your child falling *below the zero level* is *very small*.[43]

Anyone in the penultimate generation who applies *this* rule will be unwilling to procreate if the last generation fall below the *current* lexical level. But the current lexical level is presumably set as high as possible, in order to maximise well-being overall. Therefore, if there is *any* last-generation burden, then penultimate procreation is forbidden.

CC can reasonably question the last step in this argument. Although CC's foundational values might be maximising, its ideal moral outlook is not. CC will never set the current lexical level so high that even the slightest deterioration in quality of life would plunge people below that level. That would create an overly demanding moral outlook, and a very anxious society, which would *not* best-promote human flourishing. Things do not go best if everyone lives in constant fear of slipping below the current lexical level. Therefore, unwillingness to procreate if one's child would fall below the current lexical level doesn't automatically translate into unwillingness to procreate *whenever* the next generation would be worse-off.

Unfortunately, this reply is not sufficient. *Significant* intergenerational decline *would* take the next generation below the current lexical level. At the very least, it would greatly increase the likelihood that any particular potential parent's future child would fall below that level. The strategy of distinguishing between (a) declining well-being; and (b) increased risk of falling below the current lexical level cannot save CC on its own. CC needs a more robust response. In general, CC has three possible strategies in any deteriorating (or changing) situation: inflexibility, disaster avoidance, and relativism:

1. *Inflexibility*: We retain our existing affluent Pre-Cataclysm procreative principles. If I cannot be confident that my future child would live above the lexical level I set for myself, then I should not procreate. If everyone thinks like this, then humanity becomes immediately extinct.

---

[43] Mulgan, *Future People*, p. 174.

While inflexibility is not crazy, it is not a very appealing option *for consequentialists*. If the next generation would enjoy good lives, then consequentialists surely must encourage procreation. If we retain the central consequentialist idea that morality strives to make the world better, then we must choose between our remaining two options. The next alternative is:

> 2. *Disaster Avoidance*: Hooker's disaster avoidance motivation trumps procreative freedom. If procreative freedom would yield an unsustainable future population, then procreation becomes either (a) obligatory (if the population would otherwise be too small); or (b) forbidden (if it would otherwise be too large).

No individual decision is 'disastrous' in this sense. One person's non-procreation could never usher in immediate extinction. However, we must remember that CC is a *collective* ethic (Section 6.1). What matters is what happens if we *all* behave (or think) in a certain way. And if we all reason the same way, then *our collective refusal* to have children *will* lead to immediate extinction. If future lives would have been (on average) worth living, then, from a consequentialist perspective, immediate extinction *is* a disaster. To avoid *this* disaster, we must each waive our procreative freedom *if we know that not enough others will exercise their procreative freedom in the 'right' way*.

The third CC strategy is as follows:

> 3. *Relativism*: We build changing social circumstances explicitly into our ideal moral outlook. Procreation is permitted whenever one's future child lives above a *context-dependent lexical level*.

I prefer Relativism to Disaster Avoidance. Pre-Cataclysm CC teaches us that, as a general response to changing future circumstances, Relativism is superior to Disaster Avoidance.[44] Relativism is easier to comply with, psychologically healthier, and more likely to produce a well-adjusted morally motivated future population. For instance, Mulgan argues that people living in a post-catastrophe world should see their lives, not as *unacceptable-but-required-for-the-survival-of-humanity*, but rather as *worthwhile-in-their-situation*. Future well-being is not maximised if we raise a new generation who see their world as a catastrophic emergency where the 'normal' moral rules do not apply.

Relativism enables CC to avoid immediate extinction, in any changing or even deteriorating situation—so long as the next generation enjoy lives that are worth living. It also enables CC's ideal moral outlook to evolve across generations rather

---

[44] Mulgan, *Future People*, pp. 181–185, 315–318; Mulgan, 'Utilitarianism for a Broken World'.

than being replaced every time circumstances change. I conclude that the Relativist strategy does enable CC to permit procreation and avoid immediate extinction.

6.3.4 Does CC Demand Too Much Procreation?

Unfortunately, if Relativism does enable CC to avoid immediate extinction, it then opens CC to the opposite objection that it countenances (or even demands) *too much* procreation.

One underlying question, of course, is how much procreation is 'too much'. Consequentialists *should* set a lower threshold for procreative permissibility than non-consequentialists. Adding an extra good life increases impersonal value, which always provides consequentialists with a strong prima facie reason to favour procreation. Even if CC recognises *some* procreative asymmetry, it must also recognise a pervasive and powerful reason to promote the (impersonal) good. In the everyday sense, where 'pro-natalism' just means that one *favours* procreation, CC is definitely more pro-natalist than non-consquentialism. And CC may also be pro-natalist in my stronger sense—it may generate obligations to procreate. CC will permit, recommend, and perhaps even demand procreation in some cases where non-consequentialism would not.

The objection now is that CC goes too far. CC's foundational values regard early extinction as a bad thing *whenever future lives would have been (even marginally) worth living*. CC will thus favour procreation when it ought to prohibit it. In its pursuit of the optimal outcome, CC must also replace procreative freedom with pro-natalist obligation. And this shift from recommendation to obligation is most likely to happen when people are otherwise reluctant to procreate, which is precisely when procreation is most morally questionable.

To focus our discussion, let's start with the starkest case. Suppose CC's foundational values are welfarist, totalist, maximising, and expectational. We rank outcomes by *total well-being*, and we then select the moral outlook that *maximises expected* total well-being. What will that ideal moral outlook say to the penultimate generation? Non-consequentialists will now raise several related objections:

1. CC seeks to maximise the *size* of the last generation. The lack of any further future removes all sustainability-based constraints on the pursuit of total well-being. Therefore, Parfit's repugnant conclusion threatens to push CC toward a large population of barely worth living lives.
2. CC will favour procreation whenever the last generation enjoy lives above the zero level. Therefore, in many possible scenarios, CC *requires* procreation when all plausible non-consequentialist principles *forbid* it.

3. To maximise total (impersonal) value, CC may even demand the creation of future lives that are *not worth living*. Consequentialism notoriously sacrifices some people for the greater good. What if the best human history includes a last generation whose lives are (on average) below zero? The penultimate generation's interests, together with the posthumous interests of past people, may trump even the basic needs of the last generation.
4. If CC maximises *expected* value, then CC may be dominated by very improbable outcomes of very high value.[45] This is especially troubling in our Post-Cataclysm world. If there is *any* chance of escaping imminent extinction, then the potential payoff (in total well-being) is so enormous that any present cost is worth paying, no matter how minimal the likelihood of success. CC's 'ideal' moral outlook will breed an obsession with vanishingly unlikely projects to restore the indefinite human future (cf. Section 9.10).

CC has five general responses to this suite of non-consequentialist objections. I will first list all five responses, and then evaluate them:

1. *Bite the Bullet*. CC says what it should. If an obligation to create a vast last generation, or to risk everything on some vanishingly unlikely way to extend humanity's story, *is* the best way to maximise expected total well-being, then that is what present people *should* do. Counter-intuitiveness is not an objection. An 'incredulous stare' is not an argument.[46]
2. *A Distinctive Position*. While CC's demands seem extreme to non-consequentialists, CC is nonetheless a respectable, distinctively consequentialist, option—one credible theory among a plurality of other reasonable views in the very contested and under-theorised realm of procreative ethics. CC is therefore at least worth of further exploration. There are very few truly decisive intuitions in this area, and CC's counter-intuitiveness is thus (at least) not fatal.

These first two replies concede that CC *does* make very extreme demands. The other three replies all deny this:

3. *Denial without Changing Foundational Values*: CC does not make this particular demand, because this is *not* the best way to maximise expected total well-being. This is not the best possible outcome, even by totalist lights; or that is not the way to maximise expected value.

---

[45] cf. Mulgan, *Utilitarianism*, section 4.6; Kaczmarek, 'How Much Is Rule-Consequentialism Really Willing to Give Up to Save the Future of Humanity?'

[46] The phrase 'incredulous stare' is from David Lewis, describing a common reaction to his modal realism. See, e.g., Lewis, *On the Plurality of Worlds*, p. 133.

4. *New Foundational Values*: CC replaces welfarism, totalism, and/or maximising expected value with other foundational values and/or responses to value. CC then argues that the ideal moral outlook that best responds to these new foundational values is *not* too demanding.
5. *Feasibility not Optimality*: CC's ideal moral outlook aims, not at the best *possible* outcome, but at the best *achievable* outcome, which may be very different. This reply, which draws on familiar CC attempts to avoid the collapse into act consequentialism, is essential to CC's defense of procreative *freedom*.

CC's strongest overall response combines these five replies, especially the last two forms of denial.

In rapidly changing times, CC must bite *some* bullets. After all, reflective equilibrium is a constantly moving target. The moral outlook that CC now recommends may not match Pre-Cataclysm optimistic affluent moral judgements. What matters is whether it matches the judgements we *now* hold—after we have thought through the harsh realities of life at humanity's end.[47] CC will now accept some results that would have seemed very counter-intuitive before the Cataclysm.

However, CC cannot bite *all* bullets. Such hard-headed embracing of counter-intuitiveness is the path taken by *act* consequentialism. It will not appeal to those who seek in CC a moderate liberal *alternative* to act consequentialist extremes.

I believe CC should present itself as a distinctive philosophical voice—not as the definitive ethical truth. One side of CC's distinctiveness is that CC is *more willing* than *non-consequentialism* to recognise a positive reason to promote *future* human flourishing by creating new people. But the other side is that CC rejects act consequentialism—both in its responses to value, and in its values themselves.

Denial without changing foundational values is plausible for the most extreme objections. For instance, as I argued earlier, adding a last generation below zero would never actually improve total well-being (Section 6.3.2). And totalism will only recommend adding a whole generation whose lives are barely worth living *in very rare circumstances*. CC does not *prefer* lives that are barely worth living. CC only recommends the creation of such lives *if the salient alternative is to create no lives at all*. If we can create *happier* future people, then we clearly should do so. When intergenerational decline is *avoidable*, CC invariably seeks to avoid it. The present generation should instead adopt a lower lexical threshold for themselves—making present sacrifices to improve things for future people. Even if our totalist foundational values give no explicit weight to distribution, the pervasiveness of diminishing marginal returns suggests that a more equal distribution of resources—both within and between generations—is much more likely to maximise total future well-being.

[47] cf. Mulgan, 'Utilitarianism for a Broken World'.

However, I also believe that CC's Pre-Cataclysm foundational values are unlikely to be sufficient. Even the most modest totalist CC still leaves too many hostages to fortune. Maximising expected total well-being will *sometimes* lead to counter-intuitive demands. Therefore, the best CC response must also deploy our two stronger denials. I return to feasibility in Section 6.3.5. The rest of this section explores possible departures from maximising expected total well-being. As I have already argued, I believe that CC should abandon agnosticism about both well-being and aggregation (Section 6.3.2). Our views about what *is* valuable cannot be completely independent of our response to value. CC defends a particular story about how we should respond to value. Therefore, CC should unashamedly defend its own (non-totalist) foundational values. If our moral task is collective and intergenerational, then our foundational values should also be collective and intergenerational.

This is a vital step in my CC defense of multigenerationalism. So I will reiterate it. CC has already abandoned agnosticism about well-being. Within individual lives, connections between people—and especially connections between past, present, and future people—have intrinsic as well as instrumental value. My life goes better if I join with others—and other generations—in some larger task, tradition, or project that transcends all our individual lives and lifetimes. CC thus has principled reason to embrace posthumous interests, along with some non-hedonist account of human well-being that recognises the objective value of intergenerational connections (Section 6.3.2).

CC should also abandon agnosticism about aggregation. Such agnosticism is no longer tenable. The removal of constraints based on future sustainability allows totalism and averagism to diverge sharply in their practical recommendations in the penultimate generation. Even when totalism and averagism agree *that* there should be more people, they disagree sharply about how *many* people we should add. CC must choose sides. I then argue that, for several reasons, CC should abandon totalism. In particular, CC must reject the *combination* of hedonism, totalism, and expected-value-maximisation which generates so many absurd demands.

Here is a thought experiment to distinguish CC from its harder-nosed act consequentialist brethren. Suppose the penultimate generation face a stark choice between a vast population of barely sentient non-human animals, or a much smaller population of flourishing human beings. Which outcome is better? Hedonist totalists prefer the former—freed from sustainability constraints, non-human well-being can easily exceed possible human well-being. If *we* prefer the latter—if we think it would still be *better* to create humans—then we are not hedonist totalists.

So far, so obvious. My controversial claim is that anyone sympathetic to CC *will* prefer the smaller population of flourishing humans. I can offer no decisive argument from CC to non-hedonist or non-totalist values. The connection is indirect and suggestive. Insofar as we find CC an intuitively and theoretically appealing *response* to value, we are likely to find these alternative accounts of well-being and aggregation appealing as well.

CC can deliver a preference for the smaller flourishing human population in many ways. I have already argued that we must abandon hedonism *to the extent of accepting posthumous interests* (Section 6.3.2). It is natural for CC to go further, embracing an objective account of well-being where flourishing human lives are lexically superior to even the best non-human lives. This would bring CC's foundational values closer to its internal values—something that is prima facie always desirable, at least in terms of the theoretical virtue of simplicity.

Of course, there are many alternatives to totalism: averagism, lexical views, diminishing marginal value views, prioritarian, egalitarian, and many more. I cannot explore them all here. One natural departure, given CC's collective intergenerational moral perspective, is to acknowledge the intrinsic significance of distribution and fairness. This would also return CC to its Pre-Cataclysm roots. Partly driven by worries about a utilitarian tyranny of the majority, Hooker favours a *non-utilitarian* CC that recognises both well-being *and distributive fairness*.[48] CC should embrace *and extend* Hooker's original concern for fairness. The value of human history depends on distribution as well as total well-being. In particular, distribution *between* generations matters. It matters *in itself* that the human story ends well, and that the last generation is *not* worse-off than its predecessors. If CC seeks a fair distribution of well-being and opportunity across generations, then it rejects moral outlooks that permit one generation to benefit at the expense of another—even if this would maximise total well-being. This reinforces CC's reluctance to allow earlier generations to sacrifice the last generation; and it supports CC's search for multigenerational win-win alternatives. If CC seeks the best way for humanity to end, then it will not add a worse-off last generation. If you asked why we should add these miserable people, and I replied that this produces the best possible human history, then you would not be convinced!

Once CC abandons totalism, maximising expected *value* is much less likely to yield the same obsession with extinction-risk-minimisation-at-all-costs. However, CC could also explicitly abandon the expected-value-maximisation approach, especially for very small probabilities, where that approach delivers obviously very irrational results. As the Presentist speaker argued in our pessimism debate, no sane individual has ever even tried to follow it (Section 1.3). Why should CC retain it? CC rejects act consequentialism's other counter-intuitive extremes. Why not also reject its obsession with maximising expected value? (We return to this issue in relation to digital futures in our final debate—see Section 9.10.)

---

[48] Hooker, *Ideal Code, Real World*, pp. 43–66.

CC has many non-hedonist options, many non-totalist options, and many non-expectation-maximising options. Departures in one area may reinforce departures in another, or remove the need for them. A full discussion would defend a complete set of departures, or at least some complicated disjunction of them. I cannot hope to provide that full discussion here. My goal in this section has merely been to demonstrate the range of resources that are available to CC if we are willing to depart from extreme act consequentialism.

6.3.5 Feasibility and the Limits of CC

CC's final response to the objection that it is unreasonably demanding is to deny that the best *possible* future is the best *feasible* one. We could not teach a whole (penultimate) generation of human beings to raise children whose lives were predictably not worth living. People would simply refuse to procreate. Any attempt to inculcate this outlook would lead instead to widespread failures of moral compliance.

More generally, any moral outlook that obliges people to procreate when they don't want to is prima facie inferior to otherwise similar outlooks that respect procreative freedom. The easiest obligations to internalise are *prohibitions* on sub-optimal procreation such as the Zero Constraint or the Flexible Lexical Rule. Few people would want to procreate in these situations anyway, and prohibition reinforces other desirable general features of the ideal moral outlook such as harm prevention and respect for persons. By contrast, an *obligation* to procreate is much more problematic, especially when one is reluctant to procreate *because of one's concern for one's possible future child*.

A moral obligation that goes against most people's actual values is not easily or efficiently internalised. A new generation will only be created if most people believe that it should be created. If there is widespread support for creating a new generation, then public policy can be used to incentivise parents. However, such measures work best (and perhaps can only work at all) when they seek, not to create a desire to have children, nor to get people to procreate without desiring to, but only to remove *practical barriers* (economic, work-place, lifestyle, other caring responsibilities, and so on) that prevent potential parents from having as many children as they already 'ideally' would like to have.[49]

Our ideal moral outlook is not programmed into automata, bred into non-rational animals, or trained into unthinking slaves. It is taught to, internalised by, and believed by a generation of thoughtful, imaginative, free-thinking human beings. They will naturally ask why they should, for instance, create a new

---

[49] I owe this point to a conversation with Fiona Woollard during a workshop at the University of Southampton in September 2018.

generation whose lives are less happy than their own. They will criticise their own moral outlook *from the inside*. If someone asks why our moral outlook includes reasons to assist strangers, then we can give a variety of straightforward answers, most of which do not appeal directly to foundational values, and therefore do not conflict with the outlook's other internal values. Things are different when it comes to creating the next generation. No credible, *internalisable* moral outlook can ask people to act against the best interests of their own children without citing values that are widely shared within that outlook itself.

Of course, as I argued earlier, when intergenerational decline is genuinely *unavoidable*, then CC may need to bite the bullet (Section 6.3.3). Decline is regrettable, but there is no obligation to leave one's descendants better-off than oneself *if one cannot do so*. In this case, people who have internalised the ideal outlook may (reluctantly) leave their children worse-off than themselves, so long as those children's lives are well worth living.

However, as we learnt from Roberts, many actual examples of intergenerational decline are *not* really unavoidable (Section 4.5.2). We must avoid the temptation to conflate Can't Do Better with *Won't* Do Better! Before we condemn our descendants to a lesser life, CC urges us to exhaust every option that might give the next generation better lives. We cannot reject multigenerationalism until we are sure that it cannot succeed.

Taking feasibility seriously thus brings CC closer to Weinberg (Section 5.2). In practice, human parents will not create happy children unless they want to create them, desire to enter into parent–child relationships (or other cooperative respectful relationships) with them, and are confident their children will not fall below *their own* lexical level (at least where this is possible). Given our actual human nature, it will be very difficult for CC to actually *deliver* widespread procreation at humanity's end if life is unavoidably getting worse. CC's ideal moral outlook may *permit* procreation—but it is another question whether a population who have internalised that outlook will actually *want* to procreate.

CC thus offers a new argument for multigenerationalism. A successful multigenerational project both (a) binds present people to future people so that the former will only desire to create *flourishing* people; and (b) offers future people the hope of a better life than present people (or at least one that is *not clearly worse*). CC selects, not the logically best outcome, but the best achievable outcome. And multigenerationalism is the best way to promote well-being collectively across generations. An ideal code that implements worthwhile multigenerational projects offers the best feasible remaining history of humanity.

A theme of Pre-Cataclysm CC was that the diverse challenges of different possible futures demand a flexible moral outlook that enables future generations to develop, exercise, and follow their moral imaginativeness.[50] I take up the

---

[50] Mulgan, 'How Should Utilitarians Think about the Future?'; Mulgan, 'Moral Imaginativeness, Moral Creativity and Possible Futures'.

challenge of finding and bequeathing such an outlook in my final two lectures. In my next lecture, I argue that moral imaginativeness is central to any plausible defense of multigenerationalism in our Post-Cataclysm world (Section 7.2).

The tight connection between parental desire and child welfare reinforces my earlier conclusion that CC seeks a single moral outlook that evolves over time (Section 6.3.3). One generation must pass on its moral outlook to the next, rather than trying to inculcate something entirely new. This does not entitle CC to assume that a suitable flexible moral outlook is available. But it does mean that CC, like any other defense of Post-Cataclysm procreative permissibility, is in serious trouble if it is not.

We live early in a Post-Cataclysm world. CC asks *us* several questions: What moral outlook should we have been taught? What moral outlook should we follow? What moral outlook should we teach to the next generation? What moral outlook should we bequeath to later generations? What moral outlook would work best throughout our Post-Cataclysm world? What moral outlook would work best at humanity's end? CC is most plausible, and most helpful, when these disparate questions all have the same answer. CC works best if multigenerationalism is true. CC in its turn supports multigenerationalism. CC and multigenerationalism are mutually reinforcing.

6.4 CC and Constraints on Permissible Procreation

How does CC measure against my list of constraints on permissible procreation in my first procreative ethics lecture (Section 4.1)? Like our other theories, CC endorses the Zero Constraint and Sufficiency Constraint. It is very hard to imagine realistic cases where CC permits the deliberate creation of lives below zero, or lives that are not good enough. Insofar as Intergenerational Meaning and Cooperation are important components of flourishing human lives, CC forbids procreation without these things *if they are available.* It is very hard to imagine that anyone who had internalised an ideal moral outlook would want to create a child whose life lacked these important goods. Similarly, it is hard to imagine such a person imposing a risk on their child that they would be unwilling to bear themselves. CC thus also endorses my Weinberg-inspired Rational Risk Constraint.

In principle, consequentialists do not recognise unjustifiable particular harms. Any harm can, in principle, be outweighed and justified. In this respect, CC is less demanding than Harman or Weinberg. On the other hand, CC is more demanding than any non-consequentialist approach because its Different Person Comparisons demand, prima facie, the creation of the best possible lives—not just the avoidance of particular harms.

CC doesn't automatically endorse my four intergenerational No Decline Constraints. Procreation *could*, in principle, be permissible when decline is either unavoidable or prohibitively costly. However, CC will almost certainly only permit intergenerational decline (if at all) when there is no feasible alternative. Like Roberts, CC is also very reluctant to admit that decline *is* unavoidable. At the very least, all possible alternatives must be explored before we accept any intergenerational decline. As I noted in my previous lecture, if it incorporates any No Regrets Requirement, then Weinberg's contractualism does endorse stronger intergenerational decline constraints (Section 5.3). The same is true for CC. If we prohibit procreation when the next generation would be (even unavoidably) worse-off, then procreation is only permissible when multigenerational reorientation succeeds.

This concludes my exploration of procreative ethics. Along the way, I have uncovered several desiderata that an acceptable and feasible multigenerational project must meet. My next task is to demonstrate that these desiderata can be met.

7
Lecture Five
Moral Progress, Transformation, and Imaginativeness

Multigenerationalist: In this lecture, I defend the Feasibility Premise in the basic argument for multigenerationalism that I introduced at the start of my first lecture. In other words: I argue that multigenerational projects are feasible—even the most ambitious projects that aim to reorient future-dependent traditions to provide a new kind of intergenerational meaning even in the last generation.

There are two ways to defend the Feasibility Premise: piecemeal and wholesale. A piecemeal defense would proceed by establishing the feasibility of particular multigenerational projects. My final lecture on Post-Cataclysm utopias offers this kind of defense. I defend both the desirability and the feasibility of distinctive new multigenerational utopian projects. I also offered piecemeal defenses throughout my procreative ethics lectures, when I argued that multigenerational projects are necessary to render Post-Cataclysm procreation permissible under particular procreative principles (Sections 4.4.4, 4.5.2, 5.2.5, 6.3.4, and 6.3.5).

In the present lecture, by contrast, I defend the ambitious claims about moral progress, moral imaginativeness, and moral transformation that underpin *all* ambitious multigenerational projects. This lecture is obvious vital to my overall defense of multigenerationalism. But I hope it also interests anyone who cares about the future—whether or not they find multigenerationalism plausible. In particular, anyone who wants to permissibly create future people in our Post-Cataclysm world needs some faith in future moral progress—because otherwise we cannot reasonably be confident that future people will flourish at humanity's end.

In our pessimism debate, we encountered Ponzi arguments insisting that we cannot permissibly pass the burden of belonging to the last generation on to later generations. Multigenerationalism seeks to defuse these Ponzi worries by (somehow) *reducing* the last generation burden as that burden is passed down the generations (Sections 1.5 and 6.3.3). A necessary condition for any *permissible* multigenerational project is therefore that things go better for later generations, and especially for the last generation, *than they would have gone for us if we had ended the human story now*. We must equip future people to cope with immediate human extinction better than we could ourselves.

Multigenerationalism thus needs future moral progress. That sounds straightforward. Unfortunately, 'moral progress' covers many different phenomena, and multigenerationalism needs one very specific (and very controversial) kind of progress. In Sections 7.1 and 7.2, I outline the claims about moral transformation and moral imaginativeness that multigenerationalism needs. In Section 7.3, I defend those claims against attacks from progressive and conservative opponents.

I argued in my procreative ethics lectures that, after the Cataclysm, everyone who is not an anti-natalist—everyone who wants to permissibly create new people who will live closer to humanity's end—must launch *some* multigenerational project to provide future people with something to replace lost future-dependent intergenerational meaning. In other words, everyone who rejects anti-natalism must now embrace multigenerationalism. Therefore, the stakes are higher than they initially appear. The feasibility of multigenerational projects is not an optional commitment. It is something everyone needs. Accordingly, the standard of proof required to establish feasibility is lowered. If everyone needs future moral transformation, then it is sufficient to establish that it is reasonable to hope for such transformation. I need not prove that future moral transformation is easy or inevitable.

7.1 Moral Transformation

We can distinguish (at least) five broad kinds of morally relevant progress.[1]

1. *Bare improvement*: Future people enjoy better lives for reasons independent of human agency. For instance, random temperature fluctuations kill off parasites spreading deadly infectious diseases.
2. *Human improvement*: Future people enjoy better lives due to morally neutral human agency. For instance, new scientific discoveries protect against infectious disease.
3. *Social improvement*: Future people enjoy better lives because *social* institutions better promote human flourishing—either by design or as an unintended by-product.
4. *Moral improvement*: Future people are morally better, measured against *existing moral standards*. They comply better with moral norms; have stronger moral motivations; and display superior moral reasoning.
5. *Moral transformation*: Future people have better *moral standards*.

---

[1] My discussion of moral progress draws especially on Buchanan and Powell, *The Evolution of Moral Progress*; Sauer et al., 'Moral Progress: Recent Developments'. Other important philosophical discussions include: Kitcher, *The Ethical Project*; Macklin, *Against Relativity*; Moody-Adams, 'The Idea of Moral Progress'; Shermer, *The Moral Arc*; and Singer, *The Expanding Circle*. I have discussed moral imaginativeness and moral progress in Mulgan, 'Moral Imaginativeness, Moral Creativity and Possible Futures'.

These categories overlap. It is hard to distinguish between bare improvement, human improvement, social improvement, and moral improvement. (Does an increase in public funding for science, education, or health care reflect a *moral* improvement or just greater rational self-interest?) The most controversial category is the last. We usually measure moral progress *against our existing values*. We measure and compare societies' performance over time in terms of well-being, freedom, education, democracy, or tolerance. More radical moral progress—where the standards themselves improve—is less familiar. But it is possible. And *this* is what the most ambitious multigenerational projects *need*.

Multigenerationalists recommend moral *transformation*, not moral re-invention *ex nihilo*. We cannot replace our existing moral standards with something entirely new. We must build on our existing, inherited, evolved moral traditions. Moral transformation is thus continuous with other kinds of moral progress, which can also often involve reimagining existing standards to cover new situations.

In one sense of 'improvement', moral *transformation* does not necessarily involve any moral *improvement* at all. I don't need to claim that future people will be closer to some timeless moral truth. It is sufficient, for my purposes, if moral transformation delivers future moral outlooks that better reflect our (timeless?) values *in very different human circumstances*. The values that future people will need to bring the human story to a suitable end are not necessarily *superior* to the Pre-Cataclysm values of people who thought they were facing an indefinite human future. But they will be *different* values, and future people must exercise their moral imaginativeness to discover them.

Moral transformation thus need not involve moral improvement in any strongly objective sense. (Multigenerationalists, per se, are not automatically committed to the idea that we are constantly improving relative to some independent scale of goodness.) On the other hand, there are two other senses in which every successful moral transformation must constitute an 'improvement'. First, moral transformation promises future people values, outlooks, and worldviews that are better suited to their situation than our own present morality would be. We might call this *temporal improvement*. Second, moral transformation also promises *counterfactual* improvement—it offers future people better values than they *would otherwise* have had.

Temporal improvement and counterfactual improvement are not identical. Indeed, as we'll soon see, multigenerationalism's progressive opponents defend one without the other (Section 7.3). They agree that future people will need different values from our present ones—but they deny that we need moral *transformation* to get there. Progressivists argue that the necessary temporal improvement will be delivered by ordinary (non-transformative) moral progress. Multigenerationalists reply that the values that future people would inherit *without* moral transformation would not be sufficient—even if they would be superior to our present values.

Moral transformation is very important to my overall defense of multigenerationalism. I will now illustrate it with two brief historical examples. Recall, from our pessimism debate, Plenty Coups' re-imagining of traditional Crow values—designed for a world dominated by tribal warfare—to fit a new world where traditional warfare is mere pointless criminality (Section 1.6). Plenty Coups sought, not merely a variation on a familiar theme (such as a new way of being courageous in battle), but something entirely new: a way to be courageous in a world without war. This demanded moral *transformation*, because traditional Crow ethics had no vocabulary or concepts to deal with this unprecedented and unforeseen challenge, and it was not obvious how to proceed. Indeed, it was not clear to Plenty Coups' contemporaries whether it was possible to go forward *at all*.

A second historical example is the extension of our circle of moral concern to include animals, plants, eco-systems, and perhaps even inanimate nature.[2] Any extension of moral concern *beyond humanity* requires moral transformation because it is not clear how, in what ways, or indeed *whether* our circle of concern should be extended.[3] Even if we agree that we *should* bring non-human nature into our ethical thinking, we must then decide *how* we should do so. Similar difficulties surround possible extensions of moral concern to encompass virtual, digital, or artificial entities whose sentience, autonomy, and rationality are in doubt.[4] We cannot simply assume that moral expansion is always a good thing, as opposed to a morally misguided 'fetishism' that mistakenly attributes agency to nonconscious material objects.[5]

All multigenerationalists posit some moral transformation at some time. How else could we reorient our present future-dependent meaning to deliver non-future-dependent intergenerational meaning for some future generation? But different multigenerational projects locate this transformation in different places. Is the burden of moral transformation borne primarily by the founding generation, by intermediate generations, or by the last generation? There are four main alternatives:

1. *Initial transformation*: The most passive multigenerationalism puts all moral transformation upfront. Founders exercise moral imaginativeness, inaugurate a new ethical paradigm, and set it in motion; intermediate

---

[2] For overviews of environmental philosophy, see Brennan and Lo, 'Environmental Ethics'; Brennan and Lo, *Understanding Environmental Philosophy*. Within philosophy, prominent landmarks included Leopold's *A Sand County Almanac*, Singer's *Animal Liberation*, Jonas's *The Imperative of Responsibility*, and Taylor's *Respect for Nature*.

[3] Ebenreck, 'Opening Pandora's Box'; King, 'Narrative, Imagination, and the Search for Intelligibility in Environmental Ethics'; Brady, 'Adam Smith's "Sympathetic Imagination" and the Aesthetic Appreciation of Environment'.

[4] cf. Mulgan, 'Ethics for Possible Futures'; Mulgan, 'How Should Utilitarians Think about the Future'.

[5] Buchanan and Powell, *The Evolution of Moral Progress*, p. 63.

generations merely follow the founders' plan; and the last generation enjoy its fruits. Many traditional philosophical utopias take this founder-first, imaginativeness-up-front approach.
2. *Ongoing transformation*: Moral transformation itself is now a multigenerational task. The founding generation initiate an ongoing ethical reinvention whose future development they themselves cannot imagine.
3. *Accelerating transformation*: Moral transformation now shifts further into the future. Founders only lay the very basic groundwork for *future* moral imaginativeness. They create a next generation with greater moral imaginativeness, who in turn create later generations of even greater moral imaginativeness. The result is an accelerating ethical reinvention that culminates in the last generation.
4. *Ultimate transformation*: True moral transformation exists only at the end. Founding and intermediate generations *all* merely lay the groundwork for an explosion of moral imaginativeness in the last generation.

Different multigenerational projects thus make different claims about present and future moral transformation. The appeal of initial transformation is obvious, as founders naturally want to control the ethical future. But the contrasting appeal of ongoing, accelerating, or ultimate transformation is equally clear. If we are confident that we can produce new generations whose moral sensitivity and moral imaginativeness are significantly greater than our own—whose judgements about value and well-being are more finely nuanced—then why *not* delegate the difficult business of designing utopia and pursuing moral transformation *to them*? Instead of teaching the next generation what to do, we encourage them to first develop their moral imaginativeness and then to do whatever *they* judge to be most valuable.

Unfortunately, each approach also has clear drawbacks. Initial transformation requires enormous faith in *our present generation*. Even in stable times, it is impossible to predict the future of human values. Is it simply hubris to expect to predict (let alone *dictate*) *how* our descendants will construct meaningful lives? How can we be confident *that* they *will* construct meaningful lives? How can we gamble *their* welfare, or meaning, or sanity? This would be as absurd as setting our own present constitutional priorities in stone to bind all our descendants.

On the other side, alternatives to initial transformation (whether ongoing, accelerating, or ultimate) exacerbate the fragility of any active multigenerational project. What if intermediate generations don't cooperate? And what about *moral risks* of coercion or manipulation? Can we both (a) ensure that the last generation will play their part; while also (b) avoiding questionable manipulation of their attitudes, desires, motivations, or values? If we leave future people free to choose *how* to continue our traditions, might they choose *not* to continue them at all? *Active* multigenerationalists accept this risk—and then seek to mitigate it by binding generations together in a common collaborative endeavour. But is that realistic?

These questions are especially important because, as I argued in my procreative ethics lectures, Post-Cataclysm procreative permissibility may *demand* active multigenerational projects. We can only permissibly create future people if we leave them free to decide whether they will cooperate with our projects *or not* (Sections 4.4.3, 5.2.1, and 6.3.5). In particular, if we endorse anything like Weinberg's Motivation Restriction (or the additions to that restriction that I defended in Section 5.2.1), then we must treat future people as partners in our multigenerational endeavours—because otherwise we risk failing to respect those future people as ends-in-themselves. *Everyone* in our Post-Cataclysm world must pursue active, cooperative, intergenerational projects. Faith in future moral transformation is not a peculiar commitment of multigenerationalists. It is something we *all* need.

7.2 Moral Imaginativeness

Active multigenerationalism relies on *future* moral transformation. It therefore assumes that future people are better equipped than ourselves to reimagine the traditions, practices, and values we bequeath.[6] Is that plausible? Can we reasonably believe in *moral progress* driven by *moral imaginativeness*? Or does any non-initial multigenerationalism—any project that doesn't rely entirely on the moral imaginativeness of present founders—place too much faith in *future* moral imaginativeness?

Before I defend my faith in future moral imaginativeness, I should first explain what I *mean*. What *is* moral imaginativeness?

The Pre-Cataclysm philosophical literature on creativity and imaginativeness offers many competing definitions and distinctions—especially across different sub-disciplines of philosophy. Aestheticians writing about artistic creativity seldom engaged directly with moral philosophers discussing moral imagination.[7]

I first distinguish between *imaginativeness* and *imagination*.[8] Imagination is the ability to visualise, picture, or entertain an object, scenario, or state of affairs; while imaginativeness is the ability to recognise or invent new possibilities. Imagination can be exercised very *unimaginatively*; while a person can be

---

[6] This section draws freely on Mulgan, 'Moral Imaginativeness, Moral Creativity and Possible Futures'.

[7] Contrast, e.g., Boden, *The Creative Mind*; Gaut, 'The Philosophy of Creativity'; Paul and Kaufman, 'Introducing *The Philosophy of Creativity*'; with, e.g., Hargrave, 'Moral Imagination, Collective Action, and the Achievement of Moral Outcomes'; Johnson, *Moral Imagination*; Kekes, *The Enlargement of Life*; Martin, 'Moral Creativity'.

[8] Gaut, 'Creativity and Imagination'; Gaut, 'The Philosophy of Creativity'; Grant, 'The Value of Imaginativeness'; Stokes, 'The Role of Imagination in Creativity'.

imaginative without using their 'imagination', insofar as the latter term suggests both visualisation (or something like it) and premeditation. If we need a definition, I offer the following: X is imaginative if and only if X is new, surprising, and valuable.[9]

Multigenerationalism needs imaginativeness not imagination. We must imagine the future imaginatively. Multigenerationalists accuse their opponents of lacking imaginativeness. Pessimism, anti-natalism, presentism, and complacent optimism all rely on *unimaginative* future imaginings, where the future merely continues the past.

I next distinguish, somewhat artificially, between 'imaginativeness' and 'creativity'.[10] The *morally imaginative* person envisages new ethical possibilities, while the *morally creative* person puts them into practice. My use of these terms does not track ordinary usage. But the distinction is important; and no pair of terms fully captures actual usage.

Plenty Coups displayed both moral imaginativeness and moral creativity. He imagined a future for his people; he did so imaginatively, as it was not obvious how to adapt Crow values into their new future; and he took others with him—transforming his private imagining into a shared public moral experiment in living. The same is true of imaginative and creative environmental activists—both before and after the Cataclysm.

Originality is central to both imaginativeness and creativity. Boden helpfully distinguishes two kinds of originality: historical and psychological.[11] Something is h-original if it is new *to human beings*. No one has ever done it before. What is p-original is only 'original' *for that person*. They discover it themselves, rather than copying it from others.

Analytically, p-originality is more basic. The first time for anyone is also the first time *for that person*. This is pedagogically important. To promote future moral *h-originality*, we must first promote widespread *p-originality*. The best way to introduce new moral ideas into human history is to raise individuals who invent new moral ideas for themselves.

---

[9] My definition of 'imaginative' is adapted from Margaret Boden's influential definition of creativity (Boden, *The Creative Mind*, p. 1). While Boden's definition is controversial, it will suffice for our purposes. (For other definitions, see: Kronfeldner, 'Creativity Naturalized', p. 578; Gaut, 'The Philosophy of Creativity', p. 1040; Grant, 'The Value of Imaginativeness', p. 277; Kieran, 'Creativity as a Virtue of Character', p. 127.) Paul and Kaufman note that: 'There is an emerging consensus that a product must meet two conditions in order to be creative. It must be *new*, of course, but since novelty can be worthless (as in a meaningless string of letters), it must also be *of value*' (Paul and Kaufman, 'Introducing *The Philosophy of Creativity*', p. 6) My 'imaginativeness' also has affinities with Baehr's 'intellectual creativity' (Baehr, 'Intellectual Creativity').

[10] Some philosophers use 'imaginative' and 'creative' as synonyms, while others draw various distinctions between them (Paul and Kaufman, 'Introducing *The Philosophy of Creativity*', p. 10; Audi, 'Creativity, Imagination, and Intellectual Virtue').

[11] See, e.g., Boden, 'Creativity and AI: A Contradiction in Terms?' p. 228.

Philosophical discussion of moral imaginativeness typically addresses moral p-originality. But multigenerationalism needs *moral h-originality*. Plenty Coups' reimagining of Crow ethics was not just original *to him*. It was not a familiar step in individual moral development within his culture—the whole point of Plenty Coups' dilemma is that Crow warriors were only equipped to exercise courage in 'business-as-usual' situations. Similarly, early proponents of animal rights and eco-centrism went far beyond what their culture expected from a child learning to apply the Golden Rule! They deliberately extended familiar moral idioms in radical new ways.

While h-originality transcends existing cultural norms, it cannot occur in a vacuum. Moral creativity *re*-images, extends, adapts, modifies, or *re*-applies familiar moral concepts, values, rules, principles, or idioms. Plenty Coups' challenge, as he saw it, was to remain true to his ethical heritage, not simply to replace it with something entirely alien. (Replacing one's traditional identity with one based entirely on Western values is not historically original. Many people have done *that* before.)

Similarly, multigenerationalists seek to *transform* future-dependent traditions and values—not to replace them with something new. Indeed, this *conservatism* is key to multigenerationalism's appeal. If we sought something entirely new, then why *not* focus entirely on the present? I highlighted multigenerationalism's conservative streak several times in my procreative ethics lectures (Sections 4.4.3, 5.2.1, 6.3.4, and 6.3.5). In particular, I argued that multigenerationalism mutually supports collective consequentialism, which departs from act consequentialism by favouring existing, tried-and-tested moral outlooks and recognising the importance of connections between past, present, and future people (Sections 6.3.4 and 6.3.5). I also argued earlier that, if we instead embrace a contractualist procreative ethic such as Weinberg's, that we can only justify procreation in the context of relationships and projects that unite present and future people—a condition that obviously presupposes *some* overlap in moral outlook across generations (Sections 5.2.1, 5.2.5, and 5.2.7).

Despite stereotypes of individual genius, *moral* imaginativeness and creativity are highly collective, in several ways.[12] First, individual moral imaginativeness builds on our inherited collective store of moral concepts. Second, individual moral thought requires *interpersonal* justification and debate to articulate, develop, and defend new *moral* concepts.[13] No one could formulate an original *ethical* idea in isolation. Third, individual creators cannot reliably judge their own creations' *lasting value*. We need others to help us distinguish between valuable imaginativeness and self-indulgent whimsy. Fourth, as J. S. Mill taught us, all

---

[12] cf. Hargrave, 'Moral Imagination, Collective Action, and the Achievement of Moral Outcomes'; Werhane, *Moral Imagination and Management Decision Making*.

[13] Darwall, *The Second-Person Standpoint*; Mulgan, 'Answering to Future People'.

individual imaginativeness only flourishes against a sympathetic social background—otherwise it remains theoretical and satirical rather than constructive and practical.[14] Finally, even if moral *imaginativeness* could be solitary, moral *creativity* cannot. Experiments in living must be *lived*, not merely fantasised. Every ethical experiment is inherently collective. Moral innovations only work once they are widely adopted. *I* can *imagine* a moral revolution; but only *we* can introduce a new social norm.

I argued in my procreative ethics lectures that multigenerationalism mutually supports exactly this kind of collective moral perspective—especially when multigenerationalism is combined with either contractualism or collective consequentialism (Sections 5.2.5, 5.2.7, 6.3.4, and 6.3.5). The collective dimension of moral creativity thus complements multigenerationalism's other philosophical commitments.

Moral reformers first exercise their moral imaginativeness when they recognise the *need* for moral imaginativeness itself. The presuppositions of one's current worldview are seldom obvious. We naturally treat both our current moral standards, and the social environment in which they evolved, as universal. The more pervasive and enduring a presupposition, the harder it is either to appreciate its significance or to imagine its absence. Plenty Coups' first insight was to recognise that the Crow moral worldview rested on contingent foundations *that were about to disappear*. Similarly, before we begin to imagine our own moral revolutions, we must first recognise that our inherited Pre-Cataclysm ethics *has* contingent presuppositions, and then also recognise that those foundations are under threat.

Initial multigenerationalism seeks to side-step *future* moral creativity by front-loading all moral imaginativeness. Founders design future ethics to meet all foreseeable challenges. But this will not work. The future is inherently unpredictable. Different possible futures raise different imaginative challenges. We cannot prepare future people for every possible future. Therefore, we can only bequeath moral imaginativeness—and hope that our descendants exercise it well in whatever possible futures(s) they inhabit.[15]

Of course, Pre-Cataclysm thinkers faced (or thought they faced) an indefinite series of possible futures. Our time horizon is shorter. But the difficulties of predicting the ethical future are, if anything, greater now than before the Cataclysm—because we can only guess how future people will behave at humanity's end. Crucially, what the future is like depends on what people do, which in turn depends on what they feel permitted (or obliged) to do. We cannot develop an ethic *for the future* without predicting *the future of ethics*. But to predict the future of ethics we must predict future *moral creativity*. And *that* requires unprecedented *present* moral imaginativeness.

---

[14] Mill, *On Liberty*.   [15] cf. Mulgan, 'How Should Utilitarians Think about the Future?'

This suggests a stark dilemma for multigenerationalism: the only *predictable* human futures are undesirable futures where *no one* can exercise historically original moral imaginativeness—futures where nothing new ever happens and people cannot meet new challenges. *Active* multigenerational projects cannot operate in such futures—and therefore procreation is not permissible. We cannot respect our descendants as equal cooperative partners if we bequeath *that* kind of future! On the other hand, once we accept that later generations must exercise *their own* historically original moral imaginativeness, surely every multigenerational project is a leap of faith into an unknowable future.

I reply that, while this situation is challenging, it is not a genuine *dilemma*. It is merely a fact of human life. In the face of the collapse of future-dependent meaning, we must turn to multigenerational projects. And those multigenerational projects must be (a) active and (b) at least ongoing (if not accelerating or ultimate). We must put our faith in future moral imaginativeness. We simply have no alternative.

7.3 Opponents: Progressive and Conservative

Unsurprisingly, opponents of multigenerationalism disagree. Some deny the *need* for future moral transformation. Presentists and theists argue that we already possess a sufficient range of worthwhile options. Other opponents deny the *feasibility* of future moral transformation. Post-Cataclysm Pessimists object that life is meaningless in our Post-Cataclysm world, and especially in the last generation; and that multigenerationalism cannot change this; while Post-Cataclysm anti-natalists object that procreation is prohibited after the Cataclysm, and especially in the penultimate generation; that multigenerationalism cannot change this; and therefore that multigenerational projects are impermissible.

The best reply to all these familiar objections is to develop distinctive and feasible multigenerational projects. Multigenerationalism promises an optimistic alternative for those who reject pessimism and anti-natalism, find present-focused actions insufficient, and seek non-supernatural sources of meaning. I attempt to meet this challenge head-on in my final lecture, by sketching ambitious new Post-Cataclysm utopian projects.

Multigenerationalism's *new* opponents question its ambitious attempts to transform future-dependent meaning into non-future-dependent intergenerational meaning. These opponents object that this radical moral transformation is either unnecessary or impossible.

Pessimists, anti-natalists, presentists, and theists can all borrow these new complaints—and then use them to explain *why* multigenerationalists cannot make life meaningful, cannot secure procreative permissibility, and cannot adequately replace present-focused or divinely grounded meaning. However, multigenerationalism's opponents need not embrace any particular pessimist, anti-natalist, presentist, or theist agenda. While many progressivists or conservatives do endorse particular pessimist, anti-natalist, presentist, or theist views, the division between progressivists and conservatives itself cuts across these earlier categories.

Both progressivists and conservatives deny the *feasibility* of projects based on moral transformation. Therefore, both reject my Feasibility Premise. Progressivists and conservatives also, in different ways, reject the Desirability Premise in the basic argument for multigenerationalism that I introduced at the start of my first lecture. In particular, they both deny that ambitious multigenerational reorientation is necessary—and therefore they insist that it is not worth the risk. My focus in this lecture is feasibility.

Progressive opponents object that future moral progress is inevitable; that it requires no radical moral transformation; and therefore that risky multigenerational experiments are unnecessary. If we can continue our present business-as-usual, then future people will be better-off than present people, even at humanity's end. There is no problem for multigenerationalism to solve. Ordinary moral progress is enough. Predictable improvements over the next two centuries suffice to ensure that *even the last generation* will enjoy sufficiently rewarding present-focused activities.

Progressivists argue that moral *progress* is possible. But they deny that moral *transformation* is either possible or necessary. Real moral progress is more mundane. It consists in improvements to living conditions and infrastructure; better social organisation; and the gradual expansion of our circle of moral concern. Progressivists can cite evolutionary constraints. Our inherited evolved morality can become more inclusive, less competitive, and less brutal. But it cannot be radically transformed.

This progressivist critique of multigenerationalism objects that, whether or not other kinds of moral progress are possible, it is *not* possible to reorient future-dependent meaning in the radical ways that multigenerationalists want. We can only reasonably hope to replace future-dependent meaning with, for instance, greater present-focused enjoyments or transcendent God-grounded activities. The important divide is therefore between progressivists who see moral progress primarily (or exclusively) as a matter of *expansion*: greater empathy; more consistent reasoning; increasing inclusivity to bring previously excluded groups within our circle of moral concern (women, other tribes, other nations, other species); and multigenerationalists who insist on more radical transformation.

Progressivists defend *some* moral progress while rejecting moral transformation. By contrast, *conservatives* reject all future moral progress, including moral transformation. Different conservatives offer different critiques. Some appeal to history or 'common-sense' to demonstrate that moral revolutions never succeed. More systematically, *evolutionary* conservatives argue that, if morality is a product of past human evolution, then radical moral transformation is impossible.[16] Different Post-Cataclysm evolutionary conservatives then flesh-out these evolutionary constraints in different ways. Some argue that morality's evolutionary function is tied to future survival and reproduction; and therefore that morality will inevitably collapse in the last generation. Other Post-Cataclysm conservatives argue that morality's evolutionary origin ties it to future-dependent meaning; and therefore future-dependent meaning is irreplaceable. Still others argue that, because morality *evolved*, future moral change could only occur over evolutionary timescales; and therefore morality cannot be transformed in a mere two centuries.

Post-Cataclysm evolutionary conservatives draw on Pre-Cataclysm arguments that 'evolved human nature is a serious obstacle to moral progress, especially in inclusivist form'.[17] Human morality 'is essentially an intragroup affair';[18] it cannot become significantly more inclusive; and therefore any future attempt to make us more inclusive (or less tribal) is doomed to fail. Multigenerationalism is just one casualty among many.

To counter all these objections—both progressive and conservative—multigenerationalists must show that moral transformation is possible in principle and feasible in practice; that moral progress more generally is possible but not inevitable; and that 'mundane' moral progress (without moral transformation) is insufficient.

We begin with the evolutionary conservative critique of all moral progress. Buchanan and Powell turn that critique on its head. Contemporary human morality already *is* 'strikingly more inclusive than one would expect if selectionist explanations were the whole story, or even most of it'.[19] If evolutionary conservativism rules out significant increases in inclusivity, then evolutionary conservativism is simply false. In particular, Buchanan and Powell argue that evolutionary conservatives cannot accommodate *any* non-strategic extension of moral concern to include non-human animals, future generations, or people with disabilities.[20] Indeed, this familiar kind of moral progress is a stumbling block for *any* functionalist, evolutionary, or strategic account of moral progress. If morality were merely a bargain for collective advantage, then these extensions would be unthinkable. And yet they are not merely thinkable, but actual.

---

[16] For a representative defense of evolutionary conservatism, see Arnhart, *Darwinian Conservatism*; cf. Buchanan and Powell, *The Evolution of Moral Progress*, especially chapter four.
[17] Buchanan and Powell, *The Evolution of Moral Progress*, p. 116.
[18] Buchanan and Powell, *The Evolution of Moral Progress*, p. 132.
[19] Buchanan and Powell, *The Evolution of Moral Progress*, p. 153.
[20] Buchanan and Powell, *The Evolution of Moral Progress*, p. 183.

Multigenerationalists are not directly concerned with moral *inclusivity*. I draw a more general lesson from Buchanan and Powell's critique of evolutionary conservativism. Contemporary morality has many features that cannot be explained as evolutionary adaptations.[21] Even if morality *began* as an adaptation to promote in-group cohesion, it is no longer constrained by that original role. Therefore, the fact that a human capacity for moral transformation *also* cannot be explained as an evolutionary adaptation is not sufficient to demonstrate that future moral transformation is impossible. Indeed, like Buchanan and Powell, multigenerationalism turns the evolutionary conservative critique on its head. If contemporary morality *already* exhibits the results of *past* radical moral transformations, and if moral transformation cannot be explained as an evolutionary adaptation, then this is another strike against evolutionary conservatism.

I draw on Buchanan and Powell because their accounts of moral improvement and moral progress are comparatively broad. This breadth enables me to deflect one obvious progressive objection. Progressivists will object that, even when it goes beyond bare improvement or social improvement, *real* moral progress is just a matter of increasing compliance with (already recognised) moral norms.[22] Past moral progress was all about expanding our circle of moral concern. The kind of radical moral transformation that multigenerationalism needs is therefore both unprecedented and unnecessary.

In reply, I draw on Buchanan and Powell's much broader account of moral progress. Crucially, they recognise 'better moral concepts',[23] 'better understandings of the virtues',[24] improved understanding of 'the nature of morality',[25] and 'better understandings of justice'[26] alongside better compliance and increased inclusivity. Actual historical moral progress displays considerable variety. In particular, the *reorientation* of existing values and traditions in previously unimaginable ways is *not unprecedented*. Indeed, it arguably constitutes the most impressive and important kind of *actual* moral progress—as illustrated by my two core examples of Plenty Coups and Pre-Cataclysm environmental philosophy. Plenty Coups needed moral *transformation*, because traditional Crow ethics had reached an impasse where it was not clear how to go on at all. And, as I argued earlier, while environmental ethics often looks like a simple exercise in greater inclusivity, it too demands moral transformation—because it is not clear *how* we *should* extend our circle of moral concern.

In short, moral transformation has already occurred. If moral transformation is real, then it cannot be impossible!

---

[21] Buchanan and Powell, *The Evolution of Moral Progress*, p. 80.
[22] cf. Shermer, *The Moral Arc*; Singer, *The Expanding Circle*.
[23] Buchanan and Powell, *The Evolution of Moral Progress*, p. 54.
[24] Buchanan and Powell, *The Evolution of Moral Progress*, p. 54.
[25] Buchanan and Powell, *The Evolution of Moral Progress*, p. 57.
[26] Buchanan and Powell, *The Evolution of Moral Progress*, p. 59.

Progressivists will *now* object that multigenerationalism is still an unnecessary risk, because future moral improvement is inevitable *without it*. If future people will be better-off whatever we do, then why gamble on moral transformation?

I reply that *no* kind of future moral improvement is *inevitable*. On the contrary, future moral *regression* is an ever-present threat. Moral progress is neither inevitable nor irreversible. Anecdotally, human history see-saws between moral improvement and moral decline. Evolutionarily, Buchanan and Powell argue that, while our *adaptively plastic* evolved moral psychology supports greater inclusivity in some situations, it supports *greater exclusivity in others*. Very roughly, while greater exclusivity is maladaptive in non-threatening times because it 'reduce[s] the chances of mutually beneficial interactions with neighboring groups',[27] it is adaptive in threatening environments. Our ancestors thus evolved the ability to become more inclusive *but only in less threatening environments*. This evolutionary adaptability means that past moral progress is reversible: 'Inclusivist gains can be eroded if these harsh conditions reappear or if significant numbers of people come to believe that they exist.'[28]

Nor is the threat of moral decline behind us. The Cataclysm introduces a *new* threat to future moral improvement—a new route to future moral decline. If our morality remains future-dependent, then the loss of future-dependent meaning could erode future people's faith in morality itself, or in the social institutions that promote and preserve it.

On the other hand, we should not despair! While future moral decline is possible, it is not inevitable. We can do things that make future moral decline much less likely. Buchanan and Powell focus on threats posed by a *lack (or perceived lack) of resources*—arguing that the best way to prevent future moral decline is a wealthy, open, equal society. By contrast, our new threat is a loss of *meaningfulness*. Our Post-Cataclysm world is bad only because people *think* it is bad. If we *can* develop and bequeath ways to make sense of life at humanity's end, then the last humans can enjoy a very good future with comparatively very *few* threats to moral progress.

At this point, *conservatives* will object that, even if future moral transformation is *possible*, it is *not desirable to pursue it*—because doing so is too risky. It is much safer to stick with our existing tried-and-tested ethical traditions. This is a direct attack on my Feasibility Premise. Multigenerational reorientation is too risky for present people to reasonably consider embarking on it.

I agree that moral imaginativeness is always a double-edged sword. There are costs, risks, and dangers in departing from (or even questioning) time-honoured traditions and values. Conservatives have a point. But the central motivation for

---

[27] Buchanan and Powell, *The Evolution of Moral Progress*, p. 189.
[28] Buchanan and Powell, *The Evolution of Moral Progress*, p. 188.

multigenerationalism is the realisation that *ethical business-as-usual won't do*. Moral imaginativeness is worth the risk—because we really don't have any alternative.

Suppose we agree that future moral transformation would be desirable. Why think we can make it work? Is it something we can *aim at*? Can we *enhance* future people's moral imaginativeness? Can we reliably make them *more* imaginative than ourselves?

I believe that we can reasonably be cautiously optimistic here. While there is little direct evidence on the teachability of *moral* imaginativeness—and especially moral *h-originality*[29]—multigenerationalists *can* draw on several adjacent bodies of evidence. First, there is a substantial empirical and philosophical literature on the teachability of imagination, imaginativeness, and creativity in general.[30] While moral imaginativeness is not identical to non-moral imaginativeness, the two are closely related. Any increase in future non-moral imaginativeness will (other things equal) enhance future moral imaginativeness. Second, there is considerable evidence that there are reliable ways to encourage empathy, sympathy, and 'mindreading' (the ability to imagine things from others' points of view).[31] We clearly *can* promote these general capacities, which are further building-blocks for greater ethical competence more broadly. If nothing else, future people who are better moral reasoners will at least *target* their moral imaginativeness more reliably.

Finally, multigenerationalists can appeal to the empirical literature on moral progress in general. This is relevant in two ways. First, greater moral progress is prima facie likely to indirectly promote greater moral transformation. For instance, a more inclusive society enables more people to develop moral (and non-moral) imaginativeness to a higher degree. Second, insofar as past moral progress relied on moral imaginativeness, we can reasonably *infer* that conditions favouring the former also favour the latter.

The empirical evidence about past moral progress is reassuring, even if it is not very surprising. Moral progress is enhanced by liberal open societies; individual security; affluence; and social equality. Conversely, illiberal, closed, insecure, poor, or unequal circumstances fuel in-group/out-group animosity—undermining moral progress by encouraging people to be *less* inclusive in drawing their circle of moral concern, and *less* generous to anyone outside that circle.[32]

Further evidence is needed. We don't know exactly how to best promote future moral imaginativeness. But that is grist to the mill of *non-initial* multigenerationalists—especially those who favour an accelerating or ultimate

---

[29] At least, I have found little that is directly relevant.
[30] Gaut, 'Educating for Creativity'; Audi, 'Creativity, Imagination, and Intellectual Virtue'.
[31] Gaut, 'Educating for Creativity'; Audi, 'Creativity, Imagination, and Intellectual Virtue'.
[32] Buchanan and Powell, *The Evolution of Moral Progress*, chapter six.

approach. We must rely on the moral imaginativeness of later generations—trusting that they will imagine ways to further increase moral imaginativeness itself. And the existing evidence does, at least, suggest that it is not unreasonable to hope that intermediate generations can raise a last generation whose moral imaginativeness significantly exceeds our own.

I conclude that the Feasibility Premise is defensible. Present people can reasonably institute multigenerational reorientation projects, secure in the confidence that their reliance on future moral transformation is not hopelessly optimistic. I argued in my previous lectures that, if it is feasible, the *desirability* of multigenerational reorientation means that it is worth the risk. Indeed, I have argued that multigenerational reorientation is not only desirable but *essential*. Everyone in our Post-Cataclysm world who wants to permissibly create new people must hope that future moral transformation will make life as meaningful as ever at humanity's end. We *all* already rely on multigenerational reorientation. In my final lecture, I ask what society this reorientation might produce.

8
Lecture Six
Post-Cataclysm Utopias

Multigenerationalist: In my final lecture, I explore the most ambitious multigenerational projects of all—those that seek to construct a Post-Cataclysm utopia that makes sense even at humanity's end. Utopian projects are interesting in their own right; and the Cataclysm radically alters utopian thinking. In addition, multigenerational utopian projects form the backdrop against which present and future people will pursue other, more localised, intergenerational projects and reorientations.

The Cataclysm stimulates utopian thinking. Pre-Cataclysm utopians worried about intergenerational scarcity, sustainability, and husbanding resources for the distant future. By contrast, the last human generation *could* inhabit a post-scarcity paradise of unparalleled affluence, leisure time, and equality. Post-Cataclysm utopias can be more ambitious *because* they are not built to last. Utopianism also has a new urgency. We cannot defer utopia to the far distant future. We must realise it now. Furthermore, embarking on the multigenerational project of building a utopia at humanity's end may offer *present people* our best chance at a truly meaningful, worthwhile life.

I first outline the general types of Post-Cataclysm utopianism (Section 8.1), and then explore four prominent examples. I noted in my fifth lecture that multigenerationalism's reliance on future moral transformation ties it to open liberal societies where moral imaginativeness can flourish. I also argued in my procreative ethics lectures that multigenerationalists should embrace free intergenerational cooperation and procreative freedom. It is therefore no surprise that I draw my first two exemplars from two competing Pre-Cataclysm liberal philosophers: John Rawls (Section 8.2) and Robert Nozick (Section 8.3). My final two utopias go beyond a narrow preoccupation with secular human flourishing, as I explore ecological utopias (Section 8.4) and religious utopias (Section 8.5). The latter sets the scene for our collective exploration of virtual utopias in our next debate.

8.1 A Typology of Post-Cataclysm Utopias

Pre-Cataclysm philosophy offers many competing utopian visions. And any given Pre-Cataclysm utopia has many different *Post-Cataclysm* interpretations. Our options are very numerous. To impose some order on our explorations, I first sketch a taxonomy of Post-Cataclysm utopias based on three interrelated distinctions:

1. *Immediate or natal.* Do we design utopia for ourselves or for future people? Can you enter utopia as an adult, or must you be born into it? Many classic utopias are implicitly *natal*. A visitor from another society (e.g., the author's own) struggles to recognise utopia's true value. (This conveniently prompts the visitor to return home and write a book called *Utopia*.)
2. *Enduring or terminal.* Ideally, would our utopia endure indefinitely or not? Is it tailored to Pre-Cataclysm conditions or to our Post-Cataclysm world? Most utopias only work very imperfectly in the world they were *not* designed for. But there is an important asymmetry. Someone living in a world without any Cataclysm *could* deliberately establish a utopia that has a definite end-point—and some Pre-Cataclysm utopias *were* designed to end. By contrast, enduring utopias are no longer possible at all. Our Post-Cataclysm utopia must end (and soon). Our utopias must be terminal.
3. *Finite or final.* Post-Cataclysm terminal utopias come in two varieties. Finite utopias last several generations; while final utopias last only one generation.

It is easy to confuse *final* utopianism and *natal* utopianism. *Natal* utopians say that only those who are born into utopia can truly appreciate it. By contrast, *final* utopians say that there is no procreation within utopia. Natal utopias can be enduring, finite, or final; while final utopias can be either immediate or natal. If we then combine the two—if we favour a final natal utopia—then the first generation born into utopia must be the last.

I have just suggested that *the same* utopia could be both final and natal. This may seem impossible. How can anyone be born into a world without procreation? Here is why this *is* possible. If procreation is morally incompatible with the requirements of a perfect society, then there is no procreation *within utopia*. Utopia is final. However, suppose that all current adults, who were raised in traditions that presuppose future generations, cannot flourish in this child-less utopia. The creation of a true utopia then demands a *new* generation who neither need to procreate themselves, nor would contemplate it. This new utopia will thus be both natal and final.

This illustrates a general tension that plagues many utopian visions. To establish any natal utopia, we must do (sub-optimal) things that might be forbidden, and perhaps even unthinkable, within the future perfect society itself. The end (utopia) is justified by means that its own inhabitants could not contemplate.

Pursuing an enduring utopia in a Post-Cataclysm world is a recipe for disappointment. The most distinctive Post-Cataclysm utopias are therefore either finite or final. Post-Cataclysm utopian thinkers see the Cataclym, not as an unmitigated disaster, but rather as an opportunity for greater utopian ambition.

I will therefore consider four distinct kinds of Post-Cataclysm utopia: immediate final, natal final, immediate finite, and natal finite. However, I set the first option aside. An *immediate final* utopia is the antithesis of a multigenerational project. It is instead a community of *currently existing adults who never reproduce*. Shaker religious communities offer a real-life example. Anti-natalists favour this utopia. If procreation is *impermissible*, then there must be no more future people. Anti-natalism is a credible Post-Cataclysm view. Indeed, I argued in my procreative ethics lectures that anti-natalism is the only credible alternative to multigenerationalism! However, as I am currently exploring the resources and commitments *of Post-Cataclysm multigenerationalism*, I will focus on non-anti-natalist alternatives. If none of these succeeds, then we must abandon multigenerationalism—along with procreation—and fall back on anti-natal utopias.

Multigenerational utopians have only three Post-Cataclysm options: natal final, natal finite, and immediate finite. I begin with natal final utopias. This utopia is not *itself* multigenerational. Our utopian society lasts only a single generation. However, a natal final utopia could be the *object* of a multigenerational project where several earlier generations cooperate to lay the foundations for a last generation utopia that brings humanity's story to a fitting end.

This raises three immediate questions: Why choose a *natal* utopia? Why choose a *final* utopia? Why would the project of establishing this utopia be *multigenerational*? (In other words, why not create our final natal utopia *in the next generation*?)

There are two main arguments for *natal* utopia: distributive and formative. If utopia justly distributes goods and opportunities across a person's whole life, then utopians must be born into it. If we wanted to place existing people in a utopia, then we would first have to *undo existing inequalities*. But this may be impossible—given the burdens those existing inequalities have already placed on the worst-off. Furthermore, what makes utopia a perfect society, in large part, is the character and values of its inhabitants. People raised *within* utopia will be better-suited to utopian life than people who have already internalised a non-utopian moral outlook. This formative argument is especially strong in the last generation, because they need an unprecedented moral outlook to face their unprecedented situation. All Post-Cataclysm utopians must address the fate of the last generation. We must justify our utopian experiment to those who will live at its end. *Final natal* utopians meet this challenge head on.

Suppose we agree that our utopia should be natal. The next question is why we should expect is to also be *final*. The perennial case for *final* (natal) utopia—as opposed to a finite intergenerational natal utopia—is inspired by the difficulty of imagining *any* coherent *intergenerational* utopia. Opponents often criticised

Pre-Cataclysm utopian thinking for its inability to cope with human procreation or the indefinite future. Indeed, Pre-Cataclysm political philosophy often simply ignored the reality of human procreation, childhood, and child-rearing—leading to 'utopias' that would collapse into incoherence after a single generation. Okin's critique of Nozick, discussed in Section 8.3.2, is a classic example. Similarly, many intergenerational Pre-Cataclysm liberal regimes struggled to make sense of *inheritance*—caught between present people's right to control their resources and future people's right to equal opportunities.

Pre-Cataclysm anti-utopians concluded that, if a just society must endure indefinitely, and if no just society *can* endure indefinitely, then our utopian dreams are unrealistic. Final utopians draw the opposite conclusion. If true utopian principles cannot accommodate the creation and nurturing of a new generation, then the true utopia can only last a single generation. *Our* multigenerational utopian *project* is then, not to create an impossible intergenerational utopia, but rather to lay the foundations for the future realisation of a vision of perfect justice that can only exist within the last generation. A last generation who are freed from the burden of creating or caring for any new people could aspire to a more perfectly just society than anything previously conceivable.

Suppose we agree that our utopia should be natal and final. Why is our utopian *project* multigenerational? The obvious objection is that any delay introduces unnecessary risks. We should instead create this final utopia *now*. Why not raise a next generation who will be the last? Why take the risk of relying on *intermediate* generations who might drop the ball?

There are several reasons why multigenerational utopian projects are preferable. Some considerations are mundane. The longer we delay our natal final utopia, the better its infrastructure, resources, technology, and so on. This motivates us to pursue an incidentally multigenerational project (Section 3.2). The motivation for *genuinely* multigenerational projects is that the future natal utopia must itself be morally transformative. Our *final utopians* will only find life meaningful if they are equipped with unprecedented moral imaginativeness (Section 7.2). And we ourselves are not yet equipped to provide this. Our project is genuinely multigenerational because we need the imaginative cooperation of intermediate generations to create the springboard for the final generation's moral transformation.

I distinguish three basic kinds of natal final utopia. The simplest is a *hedonist present-focused* utopia, where sentient beings (whether human or not) enjoy maximum pleasure. Our pre-utopian project is then only incidentally multigenerational, for technological or resource reasons. (One significant kind of hedonist utopia involves non-human sentient animals. I return to that possibility in Section 8.4.) A second natal final utopia is *imaginative-but-self-contained*. The last generation use moral imaginativeness to generate a suitable replacement for lost future-dependent intergenerational meaning, but without reference to past generations. While their utopia is the culmination of our multigenerational project, this connection does not matter *to them*. They don't need *intergenerational* meaning at all. My third final natal utopia is *imaginative-and-past-directed*. Utopians derive non-future-dependent intergenerational meaning from the realisation that they are bringing *our* multigenerational project to a satisfactory conclusion. This third alternative is the most challenging of all, as it seeks to replace future-dependent intergenerational meaning with a new kind of intergenerational meaning (cf. Sections 3.5 and 6.3.2). However, if procreative permissibility always demands *cooperation* with future people, then this may be the only kind of utopian project that is permissible—because only then can the penultimate generation create a last generation inhabiting a final natal utopia (cf. Sections 5.2.1, 5.2.5, and 5.2.7). Once again, we see the impact of procreative ethics on the design of our multigenerational projects!

While final natal utopia is the most distinctive Post-Cataclysm option, it is not the only one. Multigenerationalists could also embrace *finite utopias*: either immediate or natal. Every finite utopia lasts several generations. It is thus minimally multigenerational. If our finite utopia is natal rather than immediate, then we must again distinguish between (a) the future utopia itself; and (b) *our present pre-utopian project*. In theory, the latter need not be multigenerational. We could create a finite (natal) utopia that begins in the next generation and then endures for several generations. But the previous argument for multigenerational pre-utopian projects still holds. Insofar as we want utopians to exercise moral imaginativeness in ways that we cannot yet predict, we need the imaginative cooperation of *intermediate* (pre-utopian) generations. Of course, if our utopia is *finite*, rather than final, then we cannot delay too long. We must inaugurate it before the last generation.

Our finite utopia *itself* can be transformational in any of the senses that I outlined in my previous lecture: initial, ongoing, accelerating, or ultimate (Section 7.1). Intermediate generations, and the last generation, can be entirely passive, with all imaginativeness exercised by the founding generation; or imaginativeness can be spread evenly throughout utopia's generations; or it can increase towards the end; or it can even be entirely concentrated in the last generation. Again, if procreative permissibility demands intergenerational cooperation, then our utopia must itself constitute an *active* multigenerational project. We then have two multigenerational projects—one laying the foundations for the other.

If either our *utopia* or our *pre-utopian project* is genuinely multigenerational—and especially if it involves ongoing, accelerating, or ultimate moral transformation—then we can (at best) only sketch its basic principles.

Multigenerationalists' third option is an *immediate* final utopia that collapses the distinction between utopia and pre-utopian project. The present generation inaugurates an ongoing utopia, which can then be multigenerational in any of the familiar ways. This is the least radical option, as it is closest to Pre-Cataclysm utopianism. Our utopia itself contains as many generations as we can fit into two centuries. But this utopia will still be *essentially terminal*—it must be designed to come to a good end.

I close my series of lectures by briefly exploring four different Post-Cataclysm utopias: Rawlsian liberal egalitarianism, Nozickian libertarianism, ecological utopias, and religious utopias.

How do these four examples fit into my taxonomy of possible utopias? I argue below that both Rawls's liberal egalitarianism and Nozick's libertarianism are most interesting and distinctive, after the Cataclysm, when interpreted as final natal utopias—where earlier generations strive to create a one-generation just society that the last generation are born into (Sections 8.2 and 8.3). Ecological utopias focus on respecting or promoting non-human flourishing. If our goal is only to give non-human nature its best possible end, then ecological utopias can be only incidentally multigenerational. However, I also discuss genuinely multigenerational ecological utopias where humanity strives to live justly alongside non-human nature (Section 8.4). Finally, my religious utopias involve ambitiously multigenerational projects that are designed to enable future people to reimagine our inherited religious traditions in radical new ways (Section 8.5).

8.2 Rawlsian Utopias

John Rawls's Pre-Cataclysm theory of justice focused primarily on relations within a particular generation.[1] His explicit discussion of the just savings problem is very brief.[2] You might therefore think that Rawls translates easily to our Post-Cataclysm world. Sadly, things are not so simple. Rawls also devoted much attention to the problem of *stability*.[3] Stability is an *essentially intergenerational* property of a social order—namely, its ability to survive across several generations. Removing the need for intergenerational stability could have a very destabilising effect on Rawls's overall theory of justice.

---

[1] Rawls, *A Theory of Justice*; Rawls, *Political Liberalism*. This section draws on Mulgan, *Future People*, pp. 39–50 and Mulgan, *Ethics for a Broken World*, pp. 160–196. For overviews of the vast literature on Rawls, see Freeman, *Rawls*; Wenar, 'John Rawls'. For Rawls's original accounts of intergenerational justice, see Rawls, *A Theory of Justice*, pp. 284–293. For Rawls's later views on intergenerational justice, see Rawls, *Political Liberalism*, pp. 273–274; Rawls, *Justice as Fairness: A Restatement*, pp. 159–160; Rawls, *The Law of Peoples*, p. 107. For further discussion on Rawls and intergenerational justice, see Gosseries, 'What Do We Owe the Next Generation(s)?'; Brandstedt, 'The Just Savings Principle'.

[2] Rawls, *A Theory of Justice*, pp. 284–293.

[3] Rawls, *A Theory of Justice*, chapter eight, 'The Sense of Justice', pp. 397–459; Rawls, *Political Liberalism*, pp. 140–144. On Rawls's evolving views about stability, see, e.g., Hill, 'Stability, a Sense of Justice, and Self-Respect'; and Freeman, *Rawls*, chapter six (Freeman devotes one chapter to stability, out of seven substantive chapters covering all aspects of Rawls's theory).

More generally, Rawls's overall theory of justice delivers four intergenerational desiderata:

1. *Just Savings Principle*: Each generation should leave the next generation better-off regarding wealth and infrastructure.
2. *No Decline Principle*: Each generation should leave the next generation no worse-off regarding wealth and infrastructure.
3. *Preservation of Favourable Conditions*: Each generation should ensure that the next generation can establish a just society where basic needs are met and basic liberties are respected.
4. *Stability*: Each generation should ensure the next generation enjoy a stable liberal society where people grow up with a sense of justice and the psychological bases of self-respect.

The Pre-Cataclysm literature on Rawls is vast and overwhelming. I cannot hope to recap it here, nor to explore all the implications of imminent human extinction. I address only a small range of controversies within Post-Cataclysm Rawlsianism: Are Rawlsian principles of justice now more redistributive (Section 8.2.1)? Why would Rawlsians be multigenerationalists (Section 8.2.2)? Does behaviour in the Rawlsian utopia go beyond what justice demands (Section 8.2.3)? (In my later discussion of Post-Cataclysm *religious* utopias, I also ask whether the best Post-Cataclysm Rawlsian utopia is more or less pluralistic than Rawls's original—Section 8.5.1.)

Lurking in the background, throughout, is a new anti-natalist challenge—that Pre-Cataclysm Rawlsian constraints on just continuation cannot be met, especially in the last generation, and therefore that the only possible 'Rawlsian utopia' is both immediate and final. We cannot justly continue our liberal society, and so we must bring it to an end as best we can *in the present generation*. For instance, if self-respect requires procreative permissibility and/or actual connections to future generations, then self-respect is impossible in the last generation—and therefore no possible institutions can deliver the minimal requirements of justice to that generation.

If the last generation cannot enjoy self-respect, and if we can only create new people who will enjoy self-respect, then we must make ourselves the last generation. Of course, we would thus deprive ourselves of self-respect—so we cannot construct a just Rawlsian society. Our immediate final Rawlsian 'utopia' will thus be very second best!

The central challenge for non-anti-natalist Post-Cataclysm Rawlsians is therefore to show that self-respect, in particular, *is* available to the last generation.

The most distinctively *new* Post-Cataclysm Rawlsian view is *Natal Final Rawlsianism*. It is my main focus here—although I do consider other

Post-Cataclysm Rawlsian utopias briefly in Section 8.2.4. I concentrate on the last generation, because their situation raises the most significant new challenges. There are two ways to justify this focus. Some Post-Cataclysm Rawlsians would argue that justice *only* applies in the last generation; while others believe that, while justice does come into play earlier, the really hard problem for Post-Cataclysm Rawlsian justice is to determine the principles of justice for humanity's end.

To explore justice in the last generation, Natal Final Rawlsians posit a one-shot single-generation original position to answer the following question: What principles of justice would you choose to govern your society *if you knew you belonged to the last generation*?

This *final original position* differs from Rawls's original original position in two principal ways.[4] First, removing the need for *intergenerational* stability allows our parties to choose more radical distributive principles. Second, to ensure that both intergenerational meaning and self-respect are available, the parties must find *additional* stability-enhancing resources *within* the last generation. I consider this second challenge in my broader discussion of religious utopias in Section 8.5.1. I explore the first challenge in Section 8.2.1. I then ask how Post-Cataclysm Rawlsians should think about earlier generations in our Post-Cataclysm world—including our own generation (Sections 8.2.2, 8.2.3, 8.2.4).

I discussed Rawlsian contractualism in my third lecture on Weinberg's procreative ethics (Chapter Five). Weinberg focuses exclusively on principles of procreative justice. My current final original position covers all principles of justice. Rawls himself doesn't address procreative justice. He regards procreative *decisions* as individual moral choices rather than matters of public policy. In a Rawlsian liberal society, potential parents decide for themselves whether or not to have children. They apply their own moral codes—and conceptions of the good—rather than the principles of liberal justice. However, we can ask how people living *within* our final natal utopia will think about those individual decisions, which public policy programmes they will support, and whether or not they will seek to *encourage* procreation in their society.

8.2.1 Redistributive Justice in the Last Generation

I begin with the potential for radical redistribution. Rawls rejects *demanding* principles (especially utilitarian distributive principles) because they are incompatible with the empirical principles governing human moral psychological

[4] Rawls, *A Theory of Justice*, pp. 17–22.

development.⁵ No one could raise a new generation who internalised such demanding principles. (I considered a similar argument for moderate rule consequentialism in my third procreative ethics lecture—Section 6.3.5.)

Some utilitarian critics will object that this Rawlsian argument for moderation collapses in the last generation. The removal of the need to safeguard intergenerational stability thus enables the parties in a *final* original position to choose much more radical *intragenerational* redistribution.

However, I think we must not over-estimate the potential for radical redistribution within Rawls's framework. Even in a *natal* final utopia, the last generation *themselves* must still be raised somehow—and there are limits on how altruistic humans can become. This is Rawls's main point against full-blown utilitarianism, and it remains intact. The basic principles of human psychological development still constrain demandingness for Rawls—just as I argued earlier that they do for collective consequentialism (Section 6.3.5).

In addition, Rawls has other objections to utilitarianism—related in particular to the separateness of persons—that are not directly related to intergenerational stability.⁶ If our final original position preserves Rawls's maximin decision-procedure—and thereby ensures that the parties select principles that respect the separateness of persons—then the parties will definitely *not* choose consequentialist principles that sacrifice some people for the greater good. The final original position won't deliver act consequentialism!

Post-Cataclysm Rawlsians and their act consequentialist critics derive very different principles from their final original positions. I think the truth lies somewhere in-between. While it will not deliver anything like act consequentialism, our new final original position will deliver more demanding redistributive principles than Rawls's original original position did. People in the last generation don't view themselves as 'heads of families' choosing on behalf of their descendants.⁷ They don't worry about investing for their children and grandchildren. This removes one very powerful motivation to acquire and retain resources—and therefore one very significant constraint on people's *actual* willingness to endorse redistributive principles. The separateness of persons is not only about self-interest—it also covers the natural human desire to do what is best *for one's nearest and dearest*. In a natal final utopia, where future-dependent intergenerational meaning is reoriented toward the present, and concern for one's own descendants is replaced by concern for one's contemporaries, any freedom to favour one's nearest and dearest is transformed from a powerful constraint on intra-generational

---

⁵ Rawls, *A Theory of Justice*, pp. 437–439. On the relationship between Rawls's theory of justice and utilitarianism, see Scheffler, 'Rawls and Utilitarianism'.

⁶ Rawls, *A Theory of Justice*, pp. 23–24.

⁷ Rawls, *A Theory of Justice*, p. 111. Rawls later rejected this 'heads of families' account of intergenerational justice—Rawls, *Political Liberalism*, pp. 273–274.

redistribution into a powerful direct motivation for more intra-generational redistribution.

I also have another, more indirect, argument for greater intra-generational redistribution. Many Pre-Cataclysm philosophers drew parallels between collective consequentialism and contractualism. The classic example was Parfit's argument that the best form of contractualism coincides—in its selection of moral principles—with the best form of collective consequentialism.[8] Insofar as Parfit's coincidence argument succeeds, it suggests that, if collective consequentialism becomes more demanding in the last generation, then so does Rawlsian contractualism. (I argued earlier that collective consequentialism *does* become more demanding in the last generation—Section 6.3.2. Therefore, we should expect Rawlsian contractualism to also increase its demands.)

Finally, even if the parties to the final original position choose the same principles of justice as in Rawls's original, the behaviour of citizens in the Rawlsian natal final utopia may still be much more other-regarding—for reasons that I explore in Section 8.2.3.

I conclude that, while falling short of act consequentialism, our new Rawlsian utopia *will* be more redistributive than Rawls's original.

8.2.2 Why Is Post-Cataclysm Rawlsianism Multigenerational?

My next question is: If our Rawlsian ideal society is final and natal, why should our utopian project be multigenerational?

Natal Finite Rawlsians have two main reasons to delay the founding of utopia. The first is mundane. Later generations may be better placed to imagine and build a better society within the same liberal framework. For Rawlsian liberals constructing a theory of justice, and for the parties to the original position within that theory, the selection of principles of justice is not an end-in-itself. The parties seek *primary goods*. Primary goods do include self-respect, which is partly dependent on how one is treated within society. But many other primary goods are more mundane: 'liberty and opportunity, income and wealth'.[9] A wealthier, more sophisticated, more technologically advanced society offers better opportunities to acquire primary goods than a poorer *equally just* society. Therefore, from a Rawlsian perspective, the former is superior. If our goal is a *future* Rawlsian utopia, then why not aim for the most affluent one possible?

The second reason to delay utopia is more philosophical. Later generations may be able to imagine superior principles of justice. Our Rawlsian final natal utopia is then the endpoint of a genuinely *multigenerational* project. Of course, in

---

[8] Parfit, *On What Matters*, volume one, pp. 244–253.   [9] Rawls, *A Theory of Justice*, p. 303.

that case, we (the founding generation) can only guess at the ultimate principles of justice that will govern that utopia.

Once we locate utopia in the future, we must ask how Rawlsians should think about our current *pre-utopian* phase. If justice applies only in our future natal utopia, then can we speak of pre-utopian *justice* at all?

Rawls himself admits that his own liberal democratic principles of justice apply only to a certain kind of society under specific historical conditions.[10] He imagines that justice is *now* possible in the present. *Earlier* generations could not establish a just society as we now understand justice. They lacked the 'favourable conditions' that make justice possible for us. But our very enjoyment of those favourable conditions today depends on their past *striving toward justice*.

The existence of these precursor (pre-justice) societies naturally raises an unsettling thought for Post-Cataclysm Rawlsians. Was it Pre-Cataclysm arrogance for Rawls's contemporaries to assume that the consummation of this process was *their present society* rather than *someone else's future society*? Perhaps, instead of thinking of ourselves as building a just society now, we should think of *ourselves* as *precursors*. We cannot enjoy true justice ourselves. We can only lay the foundations for future justice.

While this is a natural way to frame our own thinking about justice, I'm not sure it is helpful. Indeed, I'm not sure it is possible for us to really think like this. Can any human generation really think of itself as *only* (or primarily) a precursor to future justice? Can we truly believe that *real* justice lies only in the future? Or does every generation need its own (presently applicable) concept of justice, tied to its own 'circumstances of justice'?

I think the idea that justice lies *only* in the future is *too* unsettling. I suggest instead a broader notion of justice that covers both the future natal utopia *and our present-pre-utopian multigenerational project*. We must address the challenges facing the last generation. But a complete theory of justice also cannot ignore earlier generations. In particular, we need intergenerational principles to govern our present multigenerational utopian project. We might imagine an *intergenerational original position*, whose parties know that they live in some earlier generation in a Post-Cataclysm world (but not which generation). These parties have two distinct projects. They need (a) principles to govern their own pre-utopian society; and (b) principles to ensure that their multigenerational project treats *all* generations fairly—including the last generation who inhabit the final natal utopia at which that project aims.

One obvious worry is that, if our multigenerational pre-utopian project involves moral transformation, then we cannot imagine our own final natal utopia—or its principles of justice—in any detail. We cannot imagine the goal of

---

[10] Rawls, *A Theory of Justice*, pp. 109–112; Rawls, *The Law of Peoples*, part two: 'The Second Part of Ideal Theory'.

the very project we are initiating! Our intergenerational original position will only deliver very general principles that are too vague to guide *us now*. I address this challenge in the next section.

8.2.3 Fleshing Out the Rawlsian Utopia

We want to know more about what life is actually like in our Rawlsian utopia. Two features of Rawls's original theory may help here. First, Rawls's own intergenerational original position (introduced in *Political Liberalism*) only governs the principles of just intergenerational savings.[11] Each generation chooses its own principles of contemporary justice, establishes its own institutions, and creates its own just society. But then we place representatives of each generation in a new single-purpose original position where they select (only) a just rate of savings for all generations to follow. This suggests that, in theory, we could derive our just savings principle without knowing every detail about every generation's liberal society. Similarly, generations who cooperate in a single multigenerational project (aimed at establishing a final natal utopia) need not agree on every detail about justice *within* their successive pre-utopian societies.

The anti-natalist objects that justice permits no multigenerational projects at all, because procreation is no longer permissible. How does our intergenerational original position meet this challenge? Parties will prefer multigenerational pre-utopian projects to an immediate final utopia *only if all generations benefit from the former*. As any intergenerational investment requires earlier generations to forego resources they could have enjoyed, initiating (or continuing) a multigenerational project can only meet this test if it delivers *something extra* to every generation—including both the last *and the first*. It must be worth everyone's while to keep the ball rolling from one generation to the next.

The first generation is crucial. Traditional Rawlsian intergenerational justice faces a puzzle regarding the first generation. (Why should the first generation, who cannot benefit from any saving by earlier generations, agree to a non-zero rate of intergenerational saving?) As I noted in my procreative ethics lectures, actual Rawlsians sidestep that puzzle by acting as if there were no first generation (Section 5.2.6). Unfortunately, Post-Cataclysm Rawlsians cannot sidestep that puzzle so easily. While we are not the first generation in our society, we *are* the first generation *who face a Post-Cataclysm world*. Our intergenerational question is whether we should launch a new multigenerational project. To do so, we must be confident that our present generation will benefit from this new endeavour. Otherwise, it is irrational for us to embark on it. But how can we have this

---

[11] Rawls, *Political Liberalism*, pp. 273–274.

confidence? Why should we benefit later generations at the expense of our own worse-off contemporaries?

The obvious solution, as ever, lies in intergenerational meaning. A key lesson of my procreative ethics lectures was that procreation is permissible, and launching multigenerational projects is permissible, only if *all* generations derive compensating intergenerational meaning for their efforts—or they gain some other, fully compensating source of meaningfulness, well-being, or valuable achievement.

Another important point here is that Rawls's principles of justice are not a complete description of the resulting just society. Indeed we might say that Rawls's just society is not itself a *utopia* at all. It is merely a framework within which *individuals* (and communities) construct their own utopias—based around their own worldviews and conceptions of the good. (This metaphor of the liberal meta-utopia is drawn from Nozick's libertarianism—Section 8.3.5.)

Rawls's principles of justice underdetermine what life is actually like in the resulting society in two ways: strength and scope. The question of strength applies especially to principles of *distributive* justice. Rawls's principles themselves impose comparatively weak requirements. (At least, they are weak compared to demanding utilitarian alternatives!) They capture only what individuals can *demand* from their institutions, and what they *owe* to one another *as a matter of justice*. Similarly, the just savings principle captures what each generation can *demand* from its predecessors, and what it *owes* to its successors *as a matter of justice*. However, when it comes to either (a) the redistribution of wealth within a generation, or (b) investment for the sake of future generations, the principles of justice *permit* individuals to go much further. Individuals are free to do more to help their contemporaries—and generations can save more for their descendants—than justice strictly requires. For instance, wealthy individuals can donate to charities which redistribute wealth much more than Rawls's Difference Principle demands.

This important gap between the demands of justice and the behaviour of individuals helps my defense of Rawlsian multigenerationalism in the following way. The goal of our pre-utopian multigenerational project is the establishment of future justice. But perhaps, for *present* individuals, this project is not only (and perhaps not primarily) about meeting the requirements of intergenerational justice (in Rawlsian terms). It is instead an optional commitment that goes far beyond what justice *now* requires. Indeed, insofar as our pre-utopian project offers a rare source of non-supernatural intergenerational meaning to each succeeding generation, we would expect that many people will voluntarily contribute beyond what justice demands. Therefore, as a whole, each generation invests more than its intergenerational obligations require.

Rawlsian citizens can go beyond the requirements of justice *in their pursuit of justice*. They are permitted to care more about justice (especially future justice) than they are obliged to. But everyone also cares about many other things. The principles of justice are limited, not just in strength, but in scope. Most human activity within a Rawlsian just society consists of citizens pursuing non-justice-related goals within the framework of the principles of justice.

The multigenerational pre-utopian project of laying the foundations for a future final natal utopia—the project of ensuring future justice—is very important for some people. But it is unlikely to be the most significant project in most individuals' lives. People will pursue many other non-justice-based projects—and those other projects will also themselves be *multigenerational*. Rawlsian citizens will exercise moral imaginativeness within their separate traditions. After all, if the future natal Rawlsian utopia is itself a liberal society where people pursue diverse conceptions of the good, then those specific conceptions themselves must be inherited from previous generations who have exercised their own moral imaginativeness *to bequeath traditions that make sense at humanity's end*.

Therefore, multigenerationalism applies both to the construction of our Rawlsian utopia, and to life within it. Present people should initiate a range of multigenerational projects—both justice-based and non-justice-based.

8.2.4 Beyond Natal Final Utopia

I have presented my Rawslian utopia as a multigenerational project culminating in a single-generation final natal utopia. This presumes a sharp divide between utopia and pre-utopia. Post-Cataclysm Rawlsians could reduce that divide (imagining a multigenerational pre-utopian project leading to an intergenerational *finite* utopia) or obliterate it altogether (imagining an immediate finite utopia whose principles of justice begin now). However, these options are less radical, and therefore less philosophically interesting. This is why I will not explore them in the same detail.

The choice between the three possible non-anti-natalist Rawlsian options (final natal utopia, finite natal utopia, and immediate finite utopia) depends on two factors: (i) whether we think the same principles of justice apply to all remaining generations in our Post-Cataclysm world; and (ii) whether, if not, we think the most significant dividing line falls between the last generation and all previous generations, or somewhere earlier.

Immediate finite utopians unite the present generation, intermediate generations, and the last generation into a single finite original position whose parties (a) *do know* that they inhabit a Post-Cataclysm world; but also (b) *do not know* how close to the end they live. They might find themselves inhabiting the present generation, or the last generation, or any generation in between. These parties seek principles of justice that are fair *to all generations*. All generations belong to a single evolving utopian society, and therefore all share common principles of justice—and not merely a very thin common just *savings* principle.

If we are concerned to safeguard the interests of the last generation, then we might add a No Regrets Restriction to this finite original position to ensure that the last generation is no worse-off than its predecessors, as I did for Weinberg's procreative original position in my second procreative ethics lecture (Section 5.2.6).

On the other hand, if we care about the *first* generation, we could also add a No Regrets Restriction, No Disappointment Restriction, or No Reasonable Resentment Restriction for them as well. Our multigenerational project would then be permissible only if the first generation would not *regret* choosing it behind an intergenerational veil of ignorance, would not be *disappointed* not to live later, or would not *reasonably resent* the decisions of other generations.

I introduced this distinction between regret, disappointment, and resentment in my discussion of Weinberg's contractualism in my second procreative ethics lecture (Section 5.2.6). Parties to an original position can regret their own decisions. (Why did I choose those principles of justice?) Anyone in a Rawlsian liberal society can be disappointed—either by their situation or by the impact of the principles of justice on them. (I don't regret choosing those principles—but I am disappointed that I have ended up on the wrong side of them.) If things are improving, everyone is disappointed to find themselves in the first generation. If things are declining, everyone is disappointed *not* to find themselves in the first generation.

In my discussion of Weinberg, I argued that reasonable resentment is a better test than either regret or disappointment. Once the veil is removed, will those who find themselves in the first (or last) generation reasonably resent either (a) the choice of principles of intergenerational justice; or (b) the behaviour of other generations; or (c) (in the *last* generation) the decision of earlier generations to create them?

It may seem that the very idea of reasonable resentment makes no sense for the first generation. They cannot resent the behaviour of other generations—because no one has yet done anything. However, I think reasonable resentment is a useful idiom to use when we discuss whether the first generation reject a particular scheme of intergenerational cooperation. If the first generation feel that, under the actual scheme of intergenerational cooperation that operates in their liberal society, they are being exploited by later generations—that sacrifices are demanded of them that will not be demanded of later generations—then they may resent this. Therefore, they will refuse to enter into that scheme of intergenerational cooperation in the first place—and no further people will be created. If we add a No Reasonable Resentment Restriction to our original position, then we seek a scheme of intergenerational cooperation that does not exploit any generation. Multigenerational projects fit this bill exactly—because all generations are better-off than they would have been without that intergenerational cooperation. Indeed, by definition, every feasible *active* multigenerational project must meet this condition, because it relies on the voluntary cooperation of each generation in its turn.

As ever in Rawlsian philosophy, Post-Cataclysm Rawlsians disagree whether the resulting principles are minor variations on Rawls's originals or something radically new. The removal of worries about future stability, the need to safeguard intergenerational meaning, and steadily increasing levels of moral imaginativeness may take Rawls's basic framework in very unexpected directions. Finite immediate Rawlsians picture this as a gradual evolution, rather than a radical divide; whereas natal Rawlsians, and especially natal *final* Rawlsians, posit a more radical future transformation of liberal egalitarian justice.

8.3 Libertarian Utopias

My second utopian tradition follow's Robert Nozick's libertarianism. For Nozick, justice is all about individual property and self-ownership rights.[12] People have rights over their own bodies and talents and over justly acquired external things. External property rights depend on history. Whether I have a right to my apple depends on how I came to possess it. Nozick recognised three possible routes to just present ownership: just acquisition, just transfer, and just rectification.

In this section, I will argue that several Pre-Cataclysm critiques of Nozick's libertarianism, considered in sequence, motivate new Post-Cataclysm libertarian utopian projects—because natal, final, or finite libertarianism can evade these critiques.

8.3.1 First Critique: No One Owns Anything

The first critique objects that Nozick's conditions for just acquisition and just transfer *have never* been satisfied; that no current possessor can point to a remotely just history; that all current holdings are thus illegitimate; and therefore, according to Nozick, that no one actually *owns* anything.[13]

This critique of actual holdings is implicit in Nozick's original text. Many of Nozick's original readers thought that he was defending *their actual* property holdings. This reading is implausible. Once Nozick has laid out the conditions for property rights, the only conclusion available to anyone with the slightest acquaintance with human history is that no one has ever owned anything. Rights

---

[12] Nozick, *Anarchy, State, and Utopia*. This section draws on Mulgan, *Ethics for a Broken World*, pp. 18–68. For overviews of literature on Nozick's political philosophy, see Mack, 'Robert Nozick's political philosophy'; Bader and Meadowcroft, *The Cambridge Companion to Nozick's* Anarchy, State, and Utopia. My discussion of Nozick's libertarianism is very abbreviated. This is partly because I want to provide a taste of many different critiques of Nozick, and also because I draw heavily on my own earlier work—to which I refer readers who seek a more detailed account of the original (Pre-Cataclysm) critiques.

[13] This first critique draws on Mulgan, *Ethics for a Broken World*, pp. 22–23.

demand a just history. Actual human history has been dominated by conquest, slavery, genocide, and ecological devastation. Initial acquisition almost never satisfied either Locke's original proviso or Nozick's replacement; most actual transfers consisted of theft, conquest, fraud, or enslavement; and previous injustices were almost never rectified. Actual human history is too unjust to justify anything.

In cases of pervasive injustice, Nozick himself suggests that we employ some *proxy* for just rectification, and that pattern-based theories of justice may offer the most promising approximations.[14] (Nozick's principal examples of pattern-based distributive theories are classical utilitarianism and Rawls's liberal egalitarianism.) Nozick objected to any pattern-based redistribution of things that people already own. But when we have no idea who owns what, we should seek a *fair distribution*; and the default is *equality*. Once equality has been established, we could then apply Nozick's principles of acquisition and transfer to future transactions.

Any actual libertarian utopia must therefore be preceded by radical redistribution. And this redistribution must *include self-ownership*. Nozick explicitly acknowledges that just transfer could give one person ownership over another. Therefore, whenever one person claims ownership of a person—either someone else *or themselves*—we have no idea whether or not this claim is just, because we have no idea whether or not it rests on a *just history*. We must redistribute the ownership of persons—and the obvious default is to give everyone self-ownership *from the outset*.

This first critique thus strongly suggests that, if there is any coherent libertarian utopia, then it must be *natal*. This reinforces my earlier claims about rectification in my introductory lecture. I argued in Section 3.7 that rectification requires a new generation who enjoy life-long rights. We cannot enjoy justice; we can only establish it for new people to enjoy.

This first critique is not peculiar to our Post-Cataclysm world. And it may seem uncontroversial. However, it is worth beginning here, because this critique lays the foundations for later critiques—which are both novel and controversial.

8.3.2 Second Critique: Your Mother Owns You

Before the Cataclysm, natal utopias could be enduring. Now they must be either final or finite. The second critique argues that any natal libertarian utopia must be a *final* utopia. It is based on Susan Okin's challenge to Nozick:

> There is nothing about a woman's production of an infant that does not easily fulfil the conditions of the principle of acquisition as Nozick specifies. "Whoever

---

[14] Nozick, *Anarchy, State, and Utopia*, pp. 230–231.

makes something," he says, "having bought or contracted for all other resources used in the process... is entitled to it." Pregnancy and birth seems to constitute a paradigm of such processes. Once she is freely given a sperm (as usually happens) or buys one... a fertile woman can make a baby with no other resources than her own body and its nourishment."[15]

In other words, mothers own their children. This conclusion is troubling for Nozick for three reasons:

1. A mother who owns her child has the same rights *as other owners*. The state must uphold her right to treat her child however she pleases. This is a very counter-intuitive result.
2. Mothers have no positive duties to their children. They owe them only what is voluntarily agreed. They can, if they choose, simply leave their children to starve. Again, this is a very counter-intuitive result.
3. Okin confronts Nozick with a vicious regress. Mothers don't come into the world unowned, any more than anyone else does. So mothers don't own themselves; and their mothers didn't own themselves; and so on. No one owns themselves. But if no one (ever) owns themselves, then no one can ever own anything else either.

Of course, Okin's critique of Nozick was already controversial before the Cataclysm.[16] I set that controversy aside here. Instead, I draw on Okin to sketch a natal final utopian project, which consists of three distinct stages:

1. The third-last generation, recognising that current holdings are illegitimate, institute a radical redistribution of all external resources.
2. The second-last generation, who inherit this new just distribution, create the last generation *and freely gift them self-ownership*.
3. The last generation enjoy their (justly created and transferred) self-ownership without the burden of having to decide either (a) whether or not to create another generation; or (b) whether or not to gift self-ownership to the next generation, if there is one.

This utopian project presupposes the intelligibility of *gifting* self-ownership. The case for the superiority of Post-Cataclysm libertarianism over Pre-Cataclysm libertarianism assumes that this gift is both (a) possible; but also (b) unlikely to be universal. Mothers who initially own their children *can* gift self-ownership to them. In an ongoing (Pre-Cataclysm) Nozickian free society, many parents *will*

[15] Okin, *Justice, Gender, and the Family*, pp. 82–83. This critique draws on Mulgan, *Ethics for a Broken World*, pp. 42–46.
[16] For an overview of the debate, see Hicks, 'On Okin's Critique of Libertarianism'.

gift self-ownership—once their children are old enough to fend for themselves. But some parents may instead retain control over their children—granting self-ownership only on very onerous terms (if at all). We cannot reasonably expect that, across a whole enduring society, self-ownership will *always* be freely gifted by all mothers in all generations. Therefore, in practice, any Pre-Cataclysm Okin-inspired Nozickian matriarchy would be (intuitively) clearly unjust.

I share Okin's intuition that it *is* clearly unjust for people to come into this world already *owned* (in Nozick's strong sense of ownership) by other people. Consistent libertarians could simply reject this intuition, and treat the fact that all people are initially owned by their mothers as a feature of Nozick's view rather than a defect. I am not aware of any Pre-Cataclysm libertarian who actually did this.

However, while we cannot suppose that all mothers always gift self-ownership across many future generations, we *can* imagine a small natal final utopia founded by like-minded mothers who all, as a condition of entering this utopian scheme in the first place, agree to gift unconditional self-ownership to their children (alongside an equal share of external resources). I think this is the most expansive libertarian utopia that *anyone* can possibly imagine.

While my new libertarian *utopia* is final, the underlying *project* of establishing it is multigenerational. It would take several generations of moral transformation to produce suitably motivated third-last and second-last generations who could then inaugurate our one-generation utopia.

My new, Okin-inspired matriarchal utopia is only plausible now, *after* the Cataclysm. There are two related reasons for this. First, as Okin herself observed, Pre-Cataclysm libertarians, with their emphasis on every potential mother's freedom to use her resources as she sees fit, found it very difficult to justly *prohibit* the creation of future people—no matter how badly those future people's lives might go. Therefore, before the last generation, there will always be some actual mothers who create new people and then treat them very badly in ways that principled libertarians cannot fault. Only in the last generation would the temptation to create a new generation of slaves entirely disappear. Second, as a matter of psychological fact, I believe it is only at the very end, when it is *impossible* to create a society that could last more than one generation, that my new final natal utopian project can attract a sufficient number of devotees to be viable. While nothing in principle prevented similar Okin-inspired experiments from occurring before the Cataclsym, it is only in our Post-Cataclysm world that they could ever actually take off.

8.3.3 Third Critique: Nozick Predicts the Future of Freedom

The third critique relates to Nozick's need, for reasons internal to his theory, to predict people's future free choices. For Nozick, I own anything that I make using things *that I own*. But how can anyone justly acquire unowned external things?[17] A productive economy demands that people can take more than they need. But they cannot take *everything*. I cannot simply 'acquire' a whole planet, an entire uninhabited island, or an unexplored continent.

The classic Pre-Cataclysm libertarian solution begins with the following constraint made famous by Locke:

> *Locke's proviso*: I can acquire an unowned resource only if I leave 'enough and as good' for others.[18]

Locke imagines a frontier world of inexhaustible resources. His model is land. Each person takes as much as they can productively farm, while leaving *enough and as good* for later arrivals. Call a resource *abundant* if this is possible; and *scarce* if not. Pre-Cataclysm thinkers regarded land, fossil fuels, water, breathable air, and food as abundant. Unfortunately, the line between abundance and scarcity is fluid. In Locke's day, it was hardly obvious that land *was* abundant. By Nozick's time, land was definitely *not* abundant. Nozick demonstrates that Locke's proviso cannot ever be satisfied if a resource is (*or will become*) scarce.[19] Suppose each person needs one unit of a resource. People outnumber units. The resource is scarce. All but one of the units have already been acquired. Unlucky Person is one of many who have no units. Unlucky Person cannot justly acquire the last unit, because they would then not leave *anything* for others. But now consider Penultimate Person, who took the second-to-last unit. They did leave one unit unacquired. But Penultimate Person did not leave Unlucky Person anything *that could be justly acquired*. Therefore, Penultimate Person also violates the proviso. The argument 'zips' back to First Person, whose acquisition of the first unit is also unjust. Nozick concludes that no one can ever justly acquire *any amount* of a scarce resource.[20] We discussed a version of this zipper argument in our pessimism debate, as it underlies many Ponzi-style arguments (cf. Section 1.5).

A crucial feature of this zipper argument is that the various people involved need not all exist *at the same time*. Unlucky Person and Penultimate Person might both be distant future people. The fact that they *will* exist—and that they will be unable to justly acquire—is sufficient to render First Person's initial acquisition unjust.

Nozick's free society depends on the just acquisition of scarce resources. If no one can justly acquire anything, then no property-based society can ever emerge. Nozick must permit *some* just acquisition. Nozick therefore provides a new proviso to replace Locke's:

---

[17] This third critique draws on Mulgan, *Ethics for a Broken World*, pp. 47–57.
[18] Locke, *Two Treatises on Government*, Second Treatise, chapter five. My discussion of Locke draws on Mulgan, *Ethics for a Broken World*, pp. 47–48, 58–61, 66–68.
[19] For Nozick's critique of Locke, and his response, see *Anarchy, State, and Utopia*, pp. 174–182.
[20] Nozick, *Anarchy, State, and Utopia*, p. 176; cf. Mulgan, *Ethics for a Broken World*, p. 49. I owe the name 'zipper argument' to Gosseries, 'What Do We Owe the Next Generation(s)?'

Nozick's proviso: I can acquire an unowned resource only if I leave others no worse-off than they would otherwise have been.

Nozick's proviso seems very demanding. Each act of acquisition must leave *everyone else* no worse-off. This suggests that acquirers must compensate everyone who misses out. This would be so onerous that it would make any ongoing system of property rights impossible. Nozick doesn't want that! Instead, he applies his proviso, not to isolated acquisitions, but to the *institution* of property—including rules of self ownership, transfer, and rectification, as well as acquisition. Even if you are worse-off as a result of this particular acquisition, you cannot complain so long as the rules that permit it benefit you *overall*.

To apply Nozick's proviso, we must ask how his proposed institution of property affects all present *and future* people. But rights and institutions have no practical effect in themselves. What matters is how people *respond* to institutions—how they *exercise* their rights. And in any free, rights-respecting society governed by Nozick's property institution it is very difficult to predict how people will behave. If human beings are genuinely free, there may be no *facts* about their future behaviour to discover. Even if there are such facts, we cannot easily discover them. At best, we can only hope to know the *probabilities* of different possible future actions. But how does Nozick's proviso work *under uncertainty*? Must I be *certain* that future people will be better-off, or can I justly acquire even though some people might be worse-off?

These difficulties are exacerbated by the fact that Nozick's proviso is explicitly anti-utilitarian. It is not sufficient to leave most people better-off, or to maximise total future well-being. I must leave *no one* worse-off. But how could I be sure of this, especially in Nozick's free society where some people are very wealthy while others might be starving or enslaved?

Nozick sidesteps these complexities by comparing his free society with a single, clearly undesirable alternative: permanent stagnation. If no one can acquire anything, then there is no incentive to improve anything, and human beings remain forever in Stone Age poverty. Pre-Cataclysm proponents of alternative property conceptions rejected this limited comparison. Why compare *only* (a) Nozick's particular scheme of property rights; and (b) a world without any property at all? What about other property institutions, such as collective ownership or individual (positive) welfare rights?

Predicting future human *behaviour* was very difficult before the Cataclysm. It is, if anything, even harder in our Post-Cataclysm world—where future people face unprecedented challenges, and where future moral behaviour depends on future ethical beliefs that may be transformed by future moral imaginativeness.

We have encountered these Post-Cataclysm difficulties in predicting the future before. Many Pre-Cataclysm principles permit procreation only when one is reasonably confident that one's future child's life will go well and/or that they will not suffer some particular avoidable harm. In particular, Weinberg's contractualism and collective consequentialism both require us to evaluate the actual risks that we impose on future people (Sections 5.2.2 and 6.3.4). We cannot do this without some ability to predict the future. Finally, as I argued in my previous lecture, multigenerational projects require confident predictions about how future people *might* exercise their moral imaginativeness and creativity—alongside confidence that they *have* imaginativeness and creativity to exercise in the first place (Section 7.2)!

If predicting the future of human behaviour is a problem for everyone in our Post-Cataclysm world, why regard this as a problem for *Nozick's libertarianism* in particular? The answer is that *Nozick's* reliance on future predictions is even more fundamental than other theorists', and even harder to avoid. Weinberg's contractualism asks you to predict what will happen *to your future child*. CC asks you to predict what life will be like *for people in general*. But Nozick expects you to predict what will happen *to every single individual future person*. This is a much more demanding standard.

In short, the third critique objects that, to apply Nozick's account of just acquisition, we must predict how future people will actually behave. As we cannot hope to predict this, we cannot apply Nozick's criteria. Therefore, no present person can ever be confident that any particular acquisition is just.

Personally, I find this third critique decisive. In a world with an indefinite human future, Nozick's proviso, like Locke's, *could never possibly* be satisfied. (Or, at the very least, no one could ever know that Nozick's proviso was satisfied, which amounts to the same thing in practice.) Nozick's problem is even more intractable than Locke's. If resources are not scarce, then we can easily tell if Locke's proviso is satisfied; whereas if there are *any future people at all*, then it is very hard to know that we have satisfied Nozick's proviso.

If we retain Nozick's proviso, then the obvious solution is *final* utopianism—which Okin has already persuaded us to adopt. In a (natal) final utopia, Nozick's property institution only has to last a single generation. This one-off prediction might be feasible, even if longer-term predictions are not.

I therefore conclude that we *could* rehabilitate Nozick's proviso—not for our whole Post-Cataclysm world, but only for the last generation. However, I argue in the next section that, once they embrace final utopianism, Post-Cataclysm libertarians have a simpler solution. Instead of rehabilitating Nozick, they can return to Locke.

8.3.4 Fourth Critique: Back to Locke: 'Leaving Enough and As Good'

As we have just see, Nozick's new proviso is very problematic. In particular, it is very hard to apply. By contrast, Locke's proviso is easy to assess. I know I have met it if each other person can still acquire something equally good.

Post-Cataclysm Lockean libertarians can now turn Nozick's zipper argument on its head. Property rights presuppose just initial acquisition; which presupposes Locke's Proviso; which can only be satisfied if the future human population is small relative to available resources. Therefore, justice requires either a small future human population or a vast increase in resources. We will consider the latter alternative in our Third Debate—in the form of the potentially vast 'resources' of a *virtual* or *digital* utopia (Section 9.10). For the moment, I focus on the former option—reducing the number of future people.

The argument here is simple. Locke's proviso *can* be satisfied if there are few future people. It *cannot* be satisfied if there are many future people. Therefore, the existence of *many* future people *is incompatible with justice*. This is a disaster for Pre-Cataclysm libertarians, who cannot justly *prevent* the creation of future people. But, in our Post-Cataclysm world, the solution is obvious. Our libertarian utopia must be finite and sparsely populated. And perhaps things go best if it is final. This Locke-inspired argument mutually supports my earlier Okin-inspired argument in Section 8.3.2. Given the need for universal voluntary gifting of self-ownership, together with radical redistribution, our third-last and second-last generations are likely to be small. Therefore, they will create a small last generation who can easily satisfy Locke's original proviso.

I conclude that, while Locke's original proviso and Nozick's replacement can both, in principle, be resurrected in our Post-Cataclysm world, Locke's proviso is preferable, as it is simpler to understand than Nozick's and easier to apply.

8.3.5 Critique Five: The Impossibility of Meta-Utopia

Nozick ended *Anarchy, State, and Utopia* with an optimistic vision of a meta-utopia where different groups pursue their own utopian experiments, and everyone is free to enter or exit these local utopias at will.[21] This meta-utopian fantasy was obviously inadequate to the global challenges that pre-occupied Pre-Cataclysm philosophers. But it enjoys renewed popularity in our Post-Cataclysm world, where large-scale coordination is less urgent.

A Post-Cataclysm pluralist fragmentation of utopian experiments might include radical non-human and trans-human options such as virtual utopias, digital utopias, and ecological utopias—alongside more conventional Rawlsian, communitarian, or libertarian utopias. Indeed, any reorientation of an existing tradition generates a *local partial utopia*, where the inheritors of a particular tradition seek to realise non-future-dependent intergenerational meaning within a broader liberal society. (The ultimate success of liberal or libertarian meta-utopian frameworks may then depend

---

[21] Nozick, *Anarchy, State, and Utopia*, pp. 297–334.

on their ability to nurture these more fine-grained sources of individual or communal non-future-dependent meaning.)

The acid test for any meta-utopia, of course, is whether it offers genuine freedom of *movement* between mini-utopias. Many critics object that, in Nozick's original meta-utopia, only able-bodied adults with 'marketable' talents possess genuine freedom to choose. The less able and less mobile must take what they are given.[22] This is where proponents of *virtual worlds* argue that the only true meta-utopia is a *virtual* environment where 'movement' between competing ideal 'societies' is costless for everyone.[23] That issue belongs to our next debate (Section 9.1). For the moment, I merely note that the possibility of a virtual meta-utopia provides another reason why the realisation of a natal final (meta-)utopia is a multigenerational project. The necessary technological infrastructure to produce a virtual meta-utopia is not yet available; and future moral imaginativeness is necessary to enable human beings to truly *flourish* in this strange new world.

I have hardly scratched the surface of Post-Cataclysm libertarianism. However, I hope I have done enough to motivate others to explore its resources, by showing that, at the very least, libertarian utopias are now *more appealing* than they were before the Cataclysm.

8.4 Post-Cataclysm Ecology

Both liberal and libertarian utopias address human flourishing. My other Post-Cataclysm utopias ground human reasons, values, and meaning in our contributions to the non-human world or in our connections to a supernatural reality.

The Cataclysm signals, not only the end of humanity, but the end of all life on Earth. All non-human terrestrial species now face imminent extinction. Pre-Cataclysm environmental philosophy placed considerable weight on long-term *intergenerational* properties such as sustainability, ecosystem equilibrium, population health, and species extinction.[24] How can ecosystems, populations, or species flourish when *every living thing* will become extinct within two centuries?

---

[22] See, e.g., Barry, 'Review of *Anarchy, State, and Utopia*'.

[23] Hailwood explores possible synergies between Nozick's experience machine and his optimistic utopian dreams, concluding that Nozick's meta-utopia actually *requires* an experience machine: 'a *Libertarian* Amsterdam of moralities is possible only as a program in the experience machine' (Hailwood, *Exploring Nozick*, p. 178).

[24] For overviews of environmental philosophy, see Brennan and Lo, 'Environmental Ethics'; Brennan and Lo, *Understanding Environmental Philosophy*. Within philosophy, prominent landmarks included Leopold's *A Sand County Almanac*, Singer's *Animal Liberation*, Jonas's *The Imperative of Responsibility*, and Taylor's *Respect for Nature*. On environmental philosophy and creativity, see especially Ebenreck, 'Opening Pandora's Box'; King, 'Narrative, Imagination, and the Search for Intelligibility in Environmental Ethics'; Brady, 'Adam Smith's "Sympathetic Imagination" and the Aesthetic Appreciation of Environment'.

Post-Cataclysm ecological utopians reimagine environmental philosophy in our Post-Cataclysm world. They adapt a range of familiar Pre-Cataclysm environmental, ecological, or conservation projects. Post-Cataclysm ecological utopians may seek to maximise non-human flourishing, minimise non-human suffering, repair human damage to non-human nature, or otherwise create a non-human utopia. What is distinctive about these *Post-Cataclysm* projects, of course, is that they also seek to bring non-human nature to a *suitable end*.

Post-Cataclysm ecological utopianism raises many questions. I will address two main ones: What (if anything) is distinctive about *Post-Cataclysm* ecological utopias? Is Post-Cataclysm ecological utopianism a *multigenerational* enterprise?

I begin with a challenge to the idea that there *is* anything distinctively Post-Cataclysm to be said here. Hedonists, in particular, will object that the most important ecological projects are totally unaffected by the Cataclysm, because they concern the flourishing, pleasure, or suffering of non-human *individuals*. Virtually all non-human organisms have lifespans shorter than two centuries. Very few currently living individual organisms would still be alive in two hundred years. Therefore, the Cataclysm itself will not kill them. Unlike human beings, non-human animals (and plants) have no sense of any future *beyond their own death*. My cat is simply uninterested in the prospect of imminent feline extinction. The Cataclysm thus cannot rob *present* individual non-human animals of anything valuable.

This hedonist critique is not limited to individuals who die before the Cataclsym. *Future* non-human organisms killed by the Cataclysm can still enjoy worthwhile lives. As well as not worrying about future extinction, most non-human animals (let alone plants) have no clear sense *of their own future*. Early death is *only* bad for them insofar as it deprives them of future pleasures.[25] Therefore, non-human animals are only harmed by the Cataclysm if their lives are worth living overall—in which case it is still good (for them) that they lived.

Hedonists conclude that the Cataclysm has no impact on present moral reasons based on non-human welfare or flourishing. We can still promote non-human flourishing. Our efforts to reduce, remove, or even eliminate animal suffering are equally unaffected. Hedonists are not alone here. Most Post-Cataclysm *sentientists* (for whom all sentient beings matter) and *biocentrists* (for whom all living beings matter) agree that individual organisms can flourish right up to the end.[26]

Indeed, non-human moral individualism—which responds to the flourishing of individual organisms—thus promises *human agents* a rare source of *unproblematically* meaningful projects even in the last generation. The meaning we

---

[25] cf. McMahan, *The Ethics of Killing*.
[26] For representative defenses of Sentientism and Biocentrism, see, e.g., Singer, *Animal Liberation* and Taylor, *Respect for Nature*, respectively. For commentary, see Brennan and Lo, *Understanding Environmental Philosophy*, chapter four.

derive from ecological projects is completely independent of the human future—because it transcends *all human interests*.

This suggests two conclusions. First, non-human lives remain a source of important reasons in our Post-Cataclysm world. Second, those reasons are unchanged. The Cataclysm has no significant impact on the *content* of individualist environmental philosophy.

I agree that non-human nature is a source of important reasons. But I deny that our reasons are unchanged. I offer two replies. First, even if the Cataclysm didn't affect the *content* of our ecological projects, it could still decisively alter their *comparative significance*. A theme of our earlier debates, and my earlier lectures, is that the Cataclysm *does* remove (or at least threaten) some of our strongest human-based reasons—namely, those that depend on the indefinite human future. If the Cataclysm removes significant human-based reasons while leaving non-human-based reasons intact, then it greatly increases the comparative significance of the latter. In particular, suppose Post-Cataclysm pessimism is correct *with respect to human-based reasons*. Our duties to (and relations with) one another are no longer sufficient for a meaningful life. Ecological projects might then come into their own as vital components of every flourishing human life. This might now be the only place we can find sufficient meaning.

The Cataclysm thus *could* impact environmental philosophy even if it left our ecological reasons untouched. However, it doesn't. On the contrary, the Cataclysm also decisively alters the balance *within* our environmental reasons. This is because it undermines our *non-individualist* ecological reasons. In particular, the Cataclysm undermines any environmental project based on healthy eco-systems and/or the preservation of 'endangered' species.[27] Pre-Cataclysm efforts to prevent (early) non-human extinctions no longer make sense. All species face imminent extinction. The most we could now ever hope is to delay extinction for a tiny fraction of a species' total lifespan. (Why would it matter if some species that has persisted for millions of years becomes extinct now *rather than in two hundred years' time?*) Other non-individualist ecological projects are similarly undermined. Ecosystem stability is no longer a coherent goal, because a stable ecosystem (by definition) is one that *will continue to flourish into the future*.

A central debate in Pre-Cataclysm environmental philosophy was how to *balance* individual reasons against holistic reasons. Individual organisms' interests competed with the health of eco-systems or the survival of species. If individual flourishing means as much as before, while we can no longer promote the health or survival of species or ecosystems, then the *balance* of environmental reasons shifts decisively. Individual flourishing is now *comparatively more*

---

[27] On eco-centrism, see, e.g., Callicott, *Thinking Like a Planet*. On the preservation of species, see, e.g., Agar, 'Valuing Species and Valuing Individuals'; and Bradley, 'The Value of Endangered Species'.

important. If we cannot pursue larger longer-term ecological goals, then it no longer makes sense (if it ever did) to sacrifice individual organisms in pursuit of those goals.

Hedonists will conclude that we should simply focus on promoting the flourishing of individual organisms, and minimising their suffering. Post-Cataclysm ecological anti-natalists, on the other hand, draw a different lesson from the collapse of ecocentric or species-preservation reasons. They picture the non-human natural world on the model of Hartmann's bleak view of human civilisation—as a sphere of individual suffering justified only (if at all) by larger ecocentric goals beyond (and distinct from) individual flourishing (Section 1.7). Nature is red in tooth and claw; animal suffering exceeds animal pleasure; in purely hedonist terms, the game is not worth the price of admission. Before the Cataclysm, all this suffering at least served a higher purpose—the emergence of healthy ecosystems, the evolution of new species, and so on. But the Cataclysm has destroyed those higher goals. Therefore, *no* future non-human suffering can possibly be justified. Insofar as we care about the non-human story, we should simply bring it to an *immediate* end. And the best way to achieve this ecological anti-natalist goal is probably either (a) to opt for immediate *human* extinction as well; or (b) to retreat into virtual worlds where humans can flourish without any need to inflict further harm on non-human individuals.

Another route to Post-Cataclysm ecological anti-natalism is via a non-hedonist account of individual flourishing. If we only consider pleasure and pain, then future non-human extinctions don't matter to individual organisms; and early deaths caused by the Cataclysm are not especially troubling (they are certainly much less troubling than early *human* deaths). However, on some ecologically based *non-hedonist* accounts of non-human flourishing, we see a very different picture. Drawing on Pre-Cataclysm explorations of the relationship between *individual flourishing* and *biological fitness*, these views argue that, while we intuitively *start* from inherited pre-evolutionary notions of what is it for this plant or that animal to flourish, Darwinian evolutionary theory tells us that individuals actually flourish if (and only if) they survive *and reproduce*.[28] The last non-humans, like the last humans, cannot flourish because they cannot nurture a new generation.

This ecological account of non-human flourishing offers the following challenge to other accounts, including hedonism. If our (human) accounts of non-human flourishing are *not* based firmly in facts about biological fitness, then they will be irredeemably anthropocentric. Who are *we* to decree that this deer's life goes well even if all her offspring are obliterated in a forest fire moments after her

---

[28] On the relationship between human and non-human flourishing, see, e.g., Bruckner, 'Human and Animal Well-Being'.

own death? Or that this plant continues to thrive even though its entire species is about to become extinct? Organisms *need* to pass on their genes. Therefore, *individuals* in the last non-human generations *do* suffer an extra harm, even if their own lives are not cut short.

Ecological anti-natalists then conclude that, as all future non-human organisms are doomed to a pointless existence—devoid of the ongoing ecological purpose that alone could justify their suffering—then we *must* bring the non-human story to an immediate end.

As usual, as a multigenerationalist, I try to have the best of both worlds. I agree that Pre-Cataclysm ecological goals no longer make sense. But I would argue that, instead of abandoning ecocentric or species-preservation projects, we must *reimagine* them. The Cataclysm *affects* ecocentric reasons much more than it affects individualist reasons. But it does *not* follow that ecocentric reasons *no longer apply*. Indeed, they now matter more than ever. We must now strive to give the terrestrial biosphere a *fitting end*.

That may sound even more implausible than my human-based multigenerational ambitions. Ecocentrism derives ethics from ecology. We extrapolate our values from nature, rather than imposing them on it. How can evolutionary biology possibly tell us what counts as a good ending *for evolution itself*? Ecocentrism places individual suffering, struggle, and death in a broader context. Individual lives gain meaning from their place in a larger whole. But what greater whole could possibly give meaning to the destruction of all life on earth? And even if we could imagine such a perspective, can we embrace it? Can it give *our lives* meaning?

I agree that the idea of a good ending for non-natural nature is very counter-intuitive. But I would reply that this is precisely why our ecological project must be *multigenerational*—because it demands unprecedented future moral transformation. And this need for future moral revolution is not unique. Environmental *individualism* also needs future moral imaginativeness. Future people must develop superior accounts of non-human flourishing that are tailored to the challenges of immediate extinction.

This brings us to my second main question: How *multigenerational* is Post-Cataclysm ecology? At one end of the spectrum lies ecological *anti-natalism*—the antithesis of multigenerationalism. If our goal is that there be no more non-human suffering, then we seek *immediate* non-human *and human extinction*. And that goal is best-pursued without future human generations.

Once we set aside anti-natalism, Post-Cataclysm ecological projects can fill the whole spectrum of multigenerational possibilities. Some ecological projects are only incidentally multigenerational: the magnitude of our ecological endeavours means that, in practice, they will inevitability take several human generations to complete. This intergenerational dimension was a perennial feature of ambitious environmental projects even before the Cataclysm.

Other Post-Cataclysm ecological projects are multigenerational because their successful implementation depends on future human *non-moral creativity*—innovations in technology and/or scientific understanding. Present people must therefore cooperate with future people, and we must strive to enhance future non-moral imaginativeness.

Another set of Post-Cataclysm ecological projects demands future human *moral creativity*—but still only incidentally. In these cases, while our goal itself makes no reference to humans, its successful *completion* depends on the multigenerational development of a new *Post-Cataclysm ecological ethic*. We must enable future people to reimagine non-human flourishing, species value, and ecosystem health in the face of immediate *non-human* extinction; or to invent new ecocentric holistic values. This ambitious moral transformation is necessary to rebut Post-Cataclysm ecological anti-natalism.

Some multigenerational projects are multigenerational in a stronger sense. If our ecological projects made no reference to humans, then they could (in theory) be completed by inanimate robots rather than future humans. Our projects could then only ever be incidentally multigenerational. But some vital ecological projects *intrinsically* involve human agency. Robots can (in principle) promote future non-human flourishing or minimise non-human suffering. But suppose instead that our goals include (a) providing humans with meaningful projects; (b) enabling humans to bring the natural world to a fitting end; and/or (c) ensuring that humans rectify the wrongs that *we* have inflicted on non-human nature. In all *these* cases, robots would *not* be a satisfactory substitute for (present and future) humans. Robots cannot find anything meaningful and we cannot 'contract out' our obligation to rectify past wrongs. Human agency is essential.

If our goal is that present and future humans will find intergenerational *meaning* in a shared commitment to bring non-human nature to a satisfactory end, and if that cooperative search for meaning itself depends on future moral transformation, then our ecological project is multigenerational in the deepest sense.

8.5 Post-Cataclysm Religious Utopias

My final topic is Post-Cataclysm religious utopias—multigenerational projects aiming to create an ideal society along religious, supernatural, or transcendent lines. I draw in particular on two earlier topics—my exploration of alternatives to theism and atheism in our religion debate (Section 2.4), and my exploration of Post-Cataclysm Rawlsian utopias earlier in this lecture (Section 8.2).

I first ask whether the Cataclysm alters the range of religious (and non-religious) views that might emerge within Rawls's just society (Section 8.5.1) before asking whether our Post-Cataclysm world calls for a new religious view entirely (Section 8.5.2).

8.5.1 Reimagining Reasonable Pluralism

Post-Cataclysm Rawlsians must ensure the last generation can enjoy self-respect and meaning. This prompts a re-examination of Rawls's ideas about reasonable pluralism, religious freedom, and overlapping consensus. Can Rawls's ambitious idea of an *overlapping consensus*—where a range of competing worldviews all support the same principles of justice—still guarantee sufficient meaning in the last generation? Or do the demands of *intragenerational* stability narrow the range of suitable justice-supporting worldviews?

Especially in his later work, Rawls treats *religious pluralism* as an ineliminable and desirable feature of modern liberal democratic societies.[29] Very roughly, Rawls argues that (a) liberal democratic principles of justice *must* respect religious, metaphysical, and moral pluralism; and (b) that a stable liberal democratic society *can* respect pluralism—because a wide range of reasonable moral, metaphysical, and religious worldviews are all capable of motivating self-respecting citizens to obey the correct principles of justice. In this pluralist Rawlsian utopia, everyone respects the same principles of justice, albeit for very different ultimate reasons.

Rawls's overlapping consensus doesn't just cover principles of justice. It also covers self-respect, and the ability to find meaning in one's life. Rawls's original non-pluralist opponents argued that self-respect, and especially the ability to endorse one's own conception of the good, requires genuinely *transcendent* values, which in turn demands a religious worldview.[30]

I am interested in a Post-Cataclysm version of this anti-pluralist argument. Even if they could ground *future-dependent* meaning before the Cataclysm, can the Pre-Cataclysm secular worldviews that Rawls wants to include within his overlapping consensus possibly ground *non-future-dependent* intergenerational meaning in the last generation? If they cannot, then no plausible last generation overlapping consensus can include such views.

Religious Rawlsians insist that only religious worldviews which ground genuinely *transcendent* meaning *in God* can meet the original Rawlsian self-respect test at humanity's end. Everyone in a Rawlsian liberal society must be raised to put their trust in God. Religious Rawlsians need not reject Rawls's overlapping consensus altogether. They will not advocate some crude theocracy where a single religion is imposed on everyone. Instead, they favour a reasonable pluralism of diverse religious worldviews—each building self-respect and a sense of justice on some supernatural foundation or other.

---

[29] Rawls, *Political Liberalism*, especially pp. 58–66 on 'reasonable comprehensive doctrines'.
[30] On the place of religion in Rawls's theory of justice, see, e.g., Dombrowski, *Rawls and Religion*; Bailey and Gentile, *Rawls and Religion*.

As ever, anti-natalists draw a very different conclusion. They argue that *no* possible worldview (whether secular or religious) passes the self-respect test; and therefore that we must not continue our liberal society. Anti-natalists reject both secular and religious searches for meaning. Secular worldviews cannot replace lost future-dependent meaning; while religious worldviews cannot survive the scrutiny and doubt that are inevitable in a liberal society—especially as religious worldviews struggle to make sense of the Cataclysm itself (Section 2.3)!

Against both religious Rawlsians and anti-natalists, *secular* Rawlsians, while agreeing that our *final generation overlapping consensus* cannot include any worldview that ties self-respect to the human future, will insist that this still leaves open a range of non-future-dependent alternatives. Perhaps the Pre-Cataclysm secular/religious dichotomy is a distraction in this context. After all, every acceptable worldview must provide *some* substitute for the human future—whether it relies on some transcendent ultimate reality or on the human past or present. Religious Rawlsians will *then* reply that, because no suitable *secular* substitute is currently available, our only *actual* present options are *religious* pluralism and anti-natalist despair.

As a multigenerationalist, I seek to break this deadlock. I argue that, even if they are not presently available, secular substitutes could *become* available *before the last generation*. The development of those future secular substitutes must become the goal *of our present multigenerational project*. For instance, as I have suggested many times, the last generation might derive non-future-dependent intergenerational meaning by helping to give the human story a good ending.

This line of argument reinforces my earlier remarks about the demandingness of Post-Cataclysm Rawlsian principles of justice (Sections 8.2.1 and 8.2.3). The desire to give the human story a good ending will also help to motivate liberal citizens to obey very demanding redistributive principles of justice—if such redistribution turns out to be necessary to the establishment of a perfect final utopia.

My main claim is that any Post-Cataclysm Rawlsian utopia—whether secular, religious, or pluralist—must be multigenerational. The shift from Pre-Cataclysm secular pluralism to Post-Cataclysm religious pluralism would take several generations—and it would surely require quite a lot of moral imaginativeness!

Even if we don't seek a purely religious utopia, I don't think we will end up with anything identical to Rawls's original overlapping consensus. Even if our natal final utopia contains something analogous to Rawls's original mix of religious and secular worldviews, our final overlapping consensus will be very different from his. Parties to the final original position want to ensure that everyone in society has access to intergenerational meaning. Insofar as intergenerational meaning requires the reimagining of future-dependent traditions, parties must therefore design a society where moral imaginativeness will flourish. Therefore, other things equal, the parties to the final original position favour principles and institutions that promote moral imaginativeness. Fortunately, as I argued in my fifth lecture on moral transformation, all the available evidence suggests that this desideratum *reinforces* Rawls's claims about the ideal liberal democratic society, rather than conflicting with them—because free, equal, democratic societies are also the best environment for future moral progress and transformation (Section 7.3).[31]

8.5.2 The Content of Religious Utopias

Religious Rawlsians make two distinctive claims. As *Rawlsians*, they presume some kind of reasonable pluralism. Our Post-Cataclysm utopia will contain many different worldviews and conceptions of the good. As *religious* Rawlsians, they insist that our Post-Cataclysm utopian overlapping consensus contains only *religious* worldviews, because secular worldviews cannot ground self-respect and a sense of justice at humanity's end.

Post-Cataclysm non-Rawlsian religious utopians go further. They imagine future utopias governed by a single religious worldview that delivers *transcendent* meaning even in the last generation. Secular intergenerational meaning is not enough. At humanity's end, people will need something beyond their dying world.

Both pluralist religious Rawlsians and monist religious utopians respond to the Post-Cataclysm anti-natalist challenge by appealing to religious worldviews. But what are these religious worldviews? And how exactly do they ground transcendent meaning, self-respect, and a sense of justice?

These are very large questions. I cannot hope to answer them adequately here. One obvious short cut is to identify the religious worldviews in our future religious utopia with existing religious traditions such as Christianity; and then to point the reader to the vast Pre-Cataclysm literature on the connections between God and morality, self-respect, meaning, and justice. This would lead back to familiar Pre-Cataclysm debates between theists and atheists that we addressed in our Second Debate.

This approach suits a utopian project where founders do the metaphysical or religious heavy-lifting—laying the religious foundations within which later generations will build.

My approach is both more ambitious and more tentative. I don't know what religion our future utopians will endorse. But I doubt it bears much resemblance to anything available today. My starting point is dissatisfaction with both Pre-Cataclysm theism and Pre-Cataclysm atheism. The lesson I draw from our earlier religion debate is that both sides are in trouble (Section 2.4). After the Cataclysm,

---

[31] cf. Buchanan and Powell, *The Evolution of Moral Progress*, chapter six; Mulgan, 'Moral Imaginativeness, Moral Creativity and Possible Futures'.

it is much more difficult for atheists to find life meaningful and immerse themselves in satisfying and fulfilling projects. Without the indefinite human future, it is much harder for individuals to commit wholeheartedly to pursuing *any* conception of the good. Therefore, the foundations of any just society are much less secure. Whatever its principles of justice, our utopia needs self-respecting people living meaningful lives.

On the other hand, I also think that traditional Pre-Cataclysm theism is in trouble, because the Cataclysm puts pressure on theism's ability to reconcile the existence of a benevolent omnipotent God with the sub-optimal world in which we find ourselves. This problem may be psychological rather than theoretical—as the Theist speaker argued in our Second Debate. But utopian planning must deal in psychological realities.

I conclude that we cannot simply bequeath our inherited Pre-Cataclysm religious worldviews, and then complacently assume that future people (especially the last generation) will find them fit for purpose. Instead, we must equip the remaining Post-Cataclysm generations with religious and metaphysical *imaginativeness* to complement their moral imaginativeness. They will need to build a new worldview to give them sufficient self-respect and meaningfulness to build their own just society. As with moral transformation, this worldview will not be entirely new, but rather a reinvention or synthesis of existing views.

As with any multigenerational project based on future transformation—which now includes metaphysical or religious transformation as well as moral transformation—I cannot describe this final religious utopia in much detail. But I will make some predictions. Insofar as religious transformation mirrors moral transformation, we can be confident that our future religious utopia remains an open, pluralist, liberal society—because only in such a society can the necessary degree of imaginativeness emerge and flourish. We also know that, however radical they are, future people must work with existing materials. We expect a *transformation*, not some radical creation *ex nihilo*. We can predict that future people will build on Pre-Cataclysm religious and philosophical ideas, perhaps combining emerging alternatives to theism and atheism with analogous work within other (non-Western, non-monotheistic) religious and philosophical traditions. We can also predict that, insofar as the motivation for future transformation is dissatisfaction with both Pre-Cataclysm atheism and Pre-Cataclysm theism, future people will particularly explore alternative sources of transcendent meaning and value that are not undermined by imminent (or, in their case, *immediate*) human extinction.

One option, as I argued at the end of our religion debate, is non-human-centred cosmic purpose, where the universe is about something but it is not about us. This austere view could lead back to an ecological utopia where we find meaning, even at humanity's end, by serving non-human nature. Or it could lead to a utopia build around the contemplation or imitation of values beyond both humanity and the non-human terrestrial world. One inspiration here is Hartmann's stark division between human happiness and cultural progress (Section 1.7). Non-human-centred purposes go further even than Hartmann, as their motivation for future cultural progress transcends all human concerns.

Our present task is not to predict the content of future religious transformation. We lack Nozick's faith in our own powers of prediction! Our task is to initiate a multigenerational utopian project. I make no precise predictions. I claim no certainty that any future utopia will, or even could, emerge. However, launching any multigenerational utopian project built on future religious and moral transformation does require two kinds of reasonable confidence. We must be confident that future moral and religious transformation is possible and that we can promote it. If our future utopia is impossible, or if we cannot hope to make it more likely, then it serves no useful purpose.

I believe we can reasonably be confident that future religious transformation is possible—at least if future moral transformation is also possible. Religions have transformed themselves in the past—often in response to new information, changing social circumstances, or moral transformations. If theism can survive Galileo, Darwin, the industrial revolution, and several hundred years of moral progress, then it can probably survive imminent human extinction. We can also reasonably be confident that if we can promote future moral transformation, then we can also promote future religious transformation. We can make a future religious utopia more likely.

I conclude that present people can reasonably put their faith in future moral and religious transformation, even if we can only guess what the future might be like. The real lesson is that we should not choose one utopian tradition over others—whether secular or religious, liberal or libertarian, individualist or ecocentric. Our best gift to future people is to leave *their* possible futures as open as possible. We don't know what they will find meaningful, valuable, or true. So we should not constrain their thinking. I return to the need for openness in my defense of multigenerational virtualism in our final debate.

Philosophy for an Ending World. Tim Mulgan, Oxford University Press. © Tim Mulgan 2024.
DOI: 10.1093/9780191946479.003.0008

9
Third Debate
Virtual Endings and Digital Futures

Presentist: In our Post-Cataclysm world, there is increasing interest in *virtual futures* where people abandon the real world altogether and spend their entire lives plugged into Nozickean experience machines that perfectly simulate any possible human experience.[1] These virtual futures raise many questions. Are they feasible? Are they desirable? Are they worth the cost? Or does every virtual world lack something vital for human flourishing? Our question, of course, is how the Cataclysm affects Pre-Cataclysm philosophical debates about virtuality. I argue that the virtual future is now more desirable than ever. Imminent human extinction—and the imminent destruction of the Earth—reduces the attractions of physical reality. By contrast, the value of the goods available *within* a virtual world is undiminished. *We* (in the present generation) can escape from imminent human extinction by retreating into our own virtual worlds. And we can raise new generations who enjoy a completely virtual environment. Over two centuries, we could make enormous strides in virtual reality technology. Perhaps this should be our legacy to the last humans.

Post-Cataclysm Pessimist: I will argue, on the contrary, that the Pre-Cataclysm case against experience machines and virtual futures remains compelling. There is no satisfactory virtual substitute for the lost *real-life* human future. Reflection on the inadequacies of virtual futures leads us back to Post-Cataclysm pessimism.

Theist: I will argue that, because true human meaning is found only in connections to transcendent reality, and because such connections remain available in virtual worlds, the virtual future is our best hope in a Post-Cataclysm world—but only if something like theism is true.

---

[1] Nozick originally presents the experience machine in Nozick, *Anarchy, State, and Utopia*, pp. 42–45. Nozick also discusses the experience machine in later works: Nozick, *Philosophical Explanations*, p. 595; Nozick, *The Examined Life*, pp. 104–118; Nozick, *Invariances*, pp. 299–300; Nozick, 'The Pursuit of Happiness'. My discussion of experience machines and virtual futures is especially influenced by Chalmers, *Reality+*, especially chapter seventeen; De Brigard, 'If You Like It, Does It Matter If It's Real?'; Feldman, 'What We Learn from the Experience Machine'; Hewitt, 'What Do our Intuitions about the Experience Machine Really Tell Us about Hedonism?'; Kawall, 'The Experience Machine and Mental State Theories of Well-Being'; Kraut, *The Quality of Life*, part three, pp. 79–147; Silverstein, 'In Defense of Happiness: A Response to the Experience Machine'; Tollefsen, 'Experience Machines, Dreams, and What Matters'; Weijers and Schouten, 'An Assessment of Recent Responses to the Experience Machine Objection to Hedonism'.

Escapist: I will defend a specific virtual future—a digital world where, thanks to the exponentially faster pace of digital life, an indefinite number of human generations can flourish before omega rays hit. I argue, along familiar Pre-Cataclysm long-termist, expected-utility-maximising lines, that we should pour all our efforts into digital futures, no matter how problematic or unlikely they appear.

Multigenerationalist: Unsurprisingly, I will defend a *multigenerational* virtualism, where our best present option is to launch a multigenerational project designed to create the best possible virtual future at humanity's end. A virtual world would be best *for the last generation*, even though if it would not be good for us. Insofar as the desirability of the virtual future depends on one's actual desires, values, and attachments, that future is only valuable to a *new* generation with new virtual-friendly values.

Presentist: Our debate proceeds as follows. In Section 9.1, I outline my argument that the virtual future is more appealing now than before the Cataclysm.

Post-Cataclysm Pessimist: In Section 9.2, I outline the Pre-Cataclysm case against virtual futures. I argue that it still holds true today.

Presentist: In Sections 9.3 and 9.4, I reply that practical objections to experience machines and virtual futures have less weight after the Cataclysm than they did before.

Multigenerationalist: In Section 9.5, I defend multigenerational virtualism, arguing that attachment-based objections to experience machines support a virtual *future*. Virtual worlds can be good for future people, even though they would not be good for us. (I extend this argument in Section 9.7.)

Theist: In Sections 9.6, I argue that, from the perspective of transcendent metaphysics, virtual futures are preferable to empirical reality, because they offer a deeper connection to ultimate reality. I also argue that the transcendent case for virtual futures is more powerful after the Cataclysm than it was before.

Post-Cataclysm Pessimist: In Section 9.8, I defend Nozick's freedom-based objection to virtual futures. I argue that it is more powerful now than before the Cataclysm.

Presentist: In Section 9.9, I defend the most radical virtual future—Nozick's original solitary experience machine. I argue that, while it was unpalatable before the Cataclysm, this extreme option may now be necessary to avoid despair at humanity's end.

Escapist: Finally, in Section 9.10, I argue that, to maximise expected future wellbeing after the Cataclysm, we should pour all our efforts into enabling future people to escape into *digital* futures.

9.1 The Case for Virtual Futures

Presentist: The starting point for Pre-Cataclysm philosophical discussion of virtual futures is Robert Nozick's famous experience machine: 'Suppose there were an experience machine that would give you any experience you desired. Superduper neuropsychologists could stimulate your brain so that you would think and feel you were writing a great novel, or making a friend, or reading an interesting book. All the time you would be floating in a tank, with electrodes attached to your brain. Should you plug into this machine for life, preprogramming your experiences?'[2]

I defend the virtual future, *not Nozick's original experience machine*. In particular, I generally prefer an *interpersonal* virtual future—where different people share the same virtual space—to Nozick's passive solipsist experience machine. When they first encounter this thought experiment, modern students, accustomed to multi-participant online worlds, naturally imagine some *interpersonal* experience machine—some *shared virtual reality*—rather than Nozick's solipsist original. And many think *this* 'experience machine' would be fully satisfactory. In this interpersonal virtual future, we can interact with other *people*—but we cannot enjoy bodily interactions with other people or with any other aspect of the physical world.

Nozick wrote before personal computers, the internet, mobile phones, and virtual reality. His original discussion concerns a solitary experience machine. However, in 2000, Nozick explicitly rejects interpersonal experience machines: 'even if everyone were plugged into the same virtual reality, that wouldn't be enough to make its contents real'.[3] On the other hand, in a very different context, Nozick comes very close to *endorsing* an interpersonal virtual future. Some Pre-Cataclysm commentators argued that the meta-utopian fantasy that closes *Anarchy, State, and Utopia* is best interpreted as a shared virtual world—a deliberately unrealistic libertarian paradise where everyone is an able-bodied, self-reliant adult who can effortlessly emigrate from one non-state to another until they find the one that best serves their quest for self-realisation—while the machinery that keeps this meta-world running carries on (mysteriously and unobtrusively) in the background (Section 8.3.5).[4]

---

[2] Nozick, *Anarchy, State, and Utopia*, pp. 42–45, at p. 42.
[3] Nozick, 'The Pursuit of Happiness'. For critical discussion, see: Chalmers, *Reality+*, chapter seventeen.
[4] cf. Nozick, *Anarchy, State, and Utopia*, part three; Hailwood, *Exploring Nozick*, p. 178. A similar meta-utopia is imagined in Greg Egan's novel *Diaspora*, where uploaded humans and digital AIs choose between virtual societies whose operating rules and underlying real-world machinery are somehow-or-other already secured and more or less unchangeable. The closest real-world analogue of Nozick's meta-utopia might be the life choices of tenured professors at wealthy private universities whose investments and security are guaranteed (in the 'real world' outside this league of ivory towers) by a powerful State funded by other people's taxes.

Interpersonal and solitary virtual worlds raise different philosophical issues. I propose to focus primarily on the interpersonal variant, as I think it is the most popular in our Post-Cataclysm world. However, towards the end of our debate, I will defend a more radical solitary experience machine (Section 9.9).

Nozick's imaginary experience machine *perfectly* replicates *any possible experience*. In practice, the *best available* virtual future need not be a *perfect* experience machine that is phenomenologically indistinguishable from the 'real thing' and preserves *all* the values of the 'real' world. The virtual future is superior to available alternatives so long as, even if something valuable is lost in the transition to the virtual, more is gained.

The appeal of experience machines is obvious. *Ex hypothesi*, they offer a broader and more enjoyable range of experiences than anything available outside the machine. Much of this comparative advantage is practical. Virtual futures cost less, consume fewer real-world resources, remove unnecessary competition for both experiences and resources (for instance, everyone can experience the thrill of winning an Olympic gold medal), and offer the same full range of pleasures to everyone regardless of disability, illness, exclusion, or prejudice. For *some* people, many very ordinary human pleasures are *only* available within the machine. And some pleasures are only possible for *anyone* if they are inside a machine. Outside the machine, not everyone enjoys the pleasure of walking or seeing; and no one enjoys the pleasure of using their own wings to fly.

We can all agree that, *if* some credible virtual future is available, then each person's *experiences* are better—*qua experiences*—within it. For hedonists, this is decisive. If experience is *all* that matters, and if the experience machine offers superior experiences, then it is better. Even for non-hedonists, this comparative superiority is very significant. The experience machine doesn't only appeal to hedonists. Insofar as everyone values pleasurable experiences to some degree, everyone has some positive reason to prefer the virtual.

The distinctive feature of hedonism, for our present purposes, is that it focuses entirely on the internal features of our experiences. Well-being is entirely a matter of what our experiences are like for us. Hedonism thus represents a broader class of *experientialist views*, where well-being may depend on features of our experiences beyond pleasure and pain.[5] While I recognise the importance of non-hedonist experientialist views, I retain the term 'hedonism' simply because it is more familiar, and because the distinctions between different experientialist views are not directly relevant to our debate.

My first claim is that these Pre-Cataclysm reasons *to* choose an experience machine, or any suitable virtual future, retain their original force today. The only

---

[5] Kraut offers this definition of experientialism: 'Experientialism...holds that: (A) well-being is composed of many goods; (B) all of them are experiential; but (C) pleasure is only one element of good experiences' (Kraut, *The Quality of Life*, p. 4).

remaining question is whether the best virtual future has deficiencies that outweigh its comparative advantages. Pre-Cataclysm anti-virtualists listed many alleged deficiencies of Nozick's original experience machine. My second claim is that, while the reasons supporting virtual futures remain unaffected, the main Pre-Cataclysm *objections* to experience machines are now less compelling than before the Cataclysm. The virtual future is thus more desirable now than ever. (I return to this second claim in Section 9.3.)

9.2 Nozick's Anti-Hedonist Argument

Post-Cataclysm Pessimist: I will now set out the case against virtual futures. Like many good thought experiments, Nozick's works by prizing apart things that typically go together. If pleasure is entirely cut adrift from achievements, personal relationships, and any connection to the world outside my head, then we see clearly whether or not the *absence* of these things matters *in itself*. Nozick argues that it is a mistake to choose the experience machine. Experience is not the only thing that matters. We want to *do* things, not merely to have the illusion of doing them. And we need a connection to some reality that is deeper than the imagination of a video game designer.

Nozick's thought experiment was so influential because many Pre-Cataclysm people shared his reaction that something vital *is* lost if one spends one's entire life in a virtual world—however perfectly it replicates the real thing.

Nozick's discussion is tantalisingly brief, and his dialectical purpose is unclear. However, one popular Pre-Cataclysm interpretation presents Nozick's thought experiment as a *reductio ad absurdum* of any hedonist, internalist, experientialist, or mental state account of human well-being.[6]

The resulting argument against hedonism is very straightforward. By definition, life in any experience machine is phenomenologically indistinguishable from the 'real thing'. Therefore, hedonists must find the experience machine unobjectionable. However, it is clearly a prudential mistake to enter an experience machine. Therefore, there is more to human flourishing than the quality of one's experiences. Therefore, hedonism is false.

I would add a Post-Cataclysm pessimist *explanation* of hedonism's failure. We now recognise very clearly that what matters most are connections to realities outside the experience machine—and especially connections to other

---

[6] cf. Feldman, 'What We Learn from the Experience Machine'. For summaries of the way that Nozick's experience machine dominates recent evaluations of hedonism, see, for instance: Chalmers, *Reality+*, p. 314; Cogburn and Silcox, 'Against Brain-in-a-Vatism'; Hewitt, 'What Do our Intuitions about the Experience Machine Really Tell Us about Hedonism?' p. 332; Kawall, 'The Experience Machine and Mental State Theories of Well-Being', p. 381; Kraut, *The Quality of Life*, footnote 8, p. 42; Silverstein, 'In Defense of Happiness: A Response to the Experience Machine', p. 282.

human beings, to human traditions, and to the non-human natural world. Therefore, we now see more clearly *why* life in the experience machine would be unsatisfactory.

Presentist: Nozick presents a powerful argument. In reply, hedonists must either deny that hedonism recommends the experience machine or deny that the experience machine is deficient. Many Pre-Cataclysm hedonists did both. They reject Nozick's *original* experience machine, and then argue that any virtual future that hedonism *did* recommend would be unobjectionable.

It is helpful to distinguish *practical* and *philosophical* objections to the experience machine. Pre-Cataclysm *hedonists* deployed practical arguments to explain why it is rational to reject the experience machine *even if hedonism is true*. In reply, Pre-Cataclysm *anti-hedonists* deployed philosophical objections to demonstrate that hedonism cannot actually capture what is missing in (even the best) experience machines. Let's begin with practical objections.

9.3 Practical Objections to the Experience Machine

Presentist: Nozick notoriously invites us to put aside all practical problems, worries, or concerns about the experience machine. Nozick's Pre-Cataclysm hedonist opponents object that this is easier said than done, and that practical concerns are sufficient to explain our intuitive reluctance to plug into the experience machine.[7] Therefore, that reluctance tells us nothing about the plausibility or otherwise of hedonism, nor about any other philosophical controversy.

One central practical worry is the fear of losing control. Anyone encountering Nozick's thought experiment for the first time naturally worries about *leaving a machine in charge of their life*. This worry is exacerbated in a *virtual future* where everyone else is also plugged-in. Who keeps the machines running? What happens if something goes wrong?

It is thus perfectly reasonable *even for a committed hedonist* to remain reluctant to enter any actual experience machine. Hewitt expresses this reluctance forcefully, 'in order for it to be clearly a good idea for us all to plug into the experience machine, we will have to have created machines that are better problem solvers than we are.... And perhaps an intuition about our own superiority in dealing with the external world is part of what causes us to reject putting our lives in the hands of a machine.'[8]

---

[7] e.g., Hewitt, 'What Do our Intuitions about the Experience Machine Really Tell Us about Hedonism?' p. 332; Kraut, *The Quality of Life*, part three, pp. 79–147; Silverstein, 'In Defense of Happiness: A Response to the Experience Machine', p. 282.

[8] Hewitt, 'What Do our Intuitions about the Experience Machine Really Tell Us about Hedonism?' p. 340.

Post-Cataclysm Pessimist: This practical objection surely *remains* decisive. We don't have universal problem-solving machines either. Nor can we assume they will be available in two hundred years' time. Therefore, whatever its *theoretical* virtues, no virtual future is a viable way to actually find meaning in our Post-Cataclysm world.

Presentist: I agree that this is a serious challenge. But it is no longer a distinctive objection to *virtual* futures. Instead, this is now a challenge that must be solved *whatever we do*. In a world without a Cataclysm, each generation could reasonably assume that it would be followed by later generations *of ordinary humans* who would care for its members when they could no longer care for themselves. For Pre-Cataclysm philosophers, the search for *machines* who can care for everyone thus *only* arises in the peculiar (and imaginary) context of the universal experience machine.

Things look very different at humanity's end. By definition, *the last generation* have no successors. If their lives are not to end abruptly in middle age, then they must have *some* population of artificial carers. And those carers, like the operators of a universal experience machine, must be universal problem-solvers. Therefore, whatever future we bequeath to the last generation, we must first solve the challenge of universal problem-solving machines. But then the *virtual* future poses no *special* problem. If we can design robots who will care for the last generation in their dotage in the real world, then why not ask them to monitor experience machines instead?

Post-Cataclysm Pessimist: This may save hedonism from *its* opponents. But it won't help *optimists* in their debate with *pessimists*. Indeed, it surely does the opposite. We now have a new argument for last generation pessimism, which in turn leads back to general Post-Cataclysm pessimism—as we saw in our pessimism debate (Section 1.5). The last generation won't enjoy meaningful or enjoyable lives, because they cannot have robots to care for them. But now every earlier Post-Cataclysm generation can only flourish by imposing a terrible fate on their own descendants.

Presentist: I am more optimistic. I agree that the loss of control *is* an objection to *immediate universal* virtualism. We cannot all immerse ourselves entirely in virtual futures and completely ignore the world outside. But no one is suggesting *that*! Instead, present people should divide their time between virtual worlds and the outside world—deriving an increasing proportion of the meaningfulness and enjoyment in our lives from the former, while still taking care of one another's basic needs in the latter. I am confident that, in such a virtually oriented society, the necessary technology for robot carers will emerge before the end—because everyone in each generation will have very strong incentives to find new ways to spend more time in virtual worlds. Two hundred years is a long time. Later generations will find solutions that we cannot yet imagine.

Multigenerationalist: I think your optimism is too complacent. We cannot rely on business-as-usual technological and social development. Instead, we need a radical new multigenerational project that requires both (a) future non-moral creativity to engineer viable lifelike virtual reality that captures what really matters about human experiences; and (b) future *moral* imaginativeness to determine what *does* really matter (Section 7.2). Fortunately, there is a better solution. We can launch a multigenerational virtualist project—designed to enable the last generation to enjoy a virtual utopia. The kinds of moral transformation I explored in my earlier lectures are tailor-made for the challenges of a virtual future.

9.4 The Loss of the Human Future

Post-Cataclysm Pessimist: I turn now to a different worry about experience machines: the absence of any future people. Human reproduction, procreation, and nurturing are either impossible in any virtual future, or at least very hard to imagine.[9] Any generation placed in a virtual world will therefore *become*, more or less inevitably, the *last* generation. The experience machine thus cuts people off from any human future, thereby depriving them of all future-dependent meaning. If everyone enters the virtual world, then the human future disappears altogether.

This perennial worry about virtual futures is *more* troubling now, after the Cataclysm, because we are all much more aware of the significance of future-dependent meaning, and we are more focused on the plight of the last generation. Pre-Cataclysm philosophers could sidestep this concern. We cannot. If we embrace any virtual future, then we collapse the difference between Scheffler's immediate extinction scenarios and our own Post-Cataclysm world. This makes pessimism much harder to avoid.

Presentist: I disagree, for three reasons. First, as a hedonist, I deny that life would be too bad even if we were the last generation. Connections to future people have no intrinsic significance; they can be perfectly replaced by phenomenally indistinguishable *illusions* of future people within a virtual world; and the 'loss' of future-dependent meaning is irrelevant. The absence of future people is a *practical worry*. (If we are the last generation, then who will look after us?) But we have already discussed *that* worry.

Second, I think the loss of the human future *within a virtual world* should be *less* troubling after the Cataclysm, because we have all already lost the *indefinite* human future. A universal virtual future is therefore less different from 'real-life'

---

[9] Nozick himself does not highlight this particular problem, perhaps because, as I argued in the lecture on multigenerational utopias, his own libertarian theory of self-ownership ignores the realities of actual human reproduction and child rearing even more starkly (cf. Section 8.3.2).

than it used to be. Presentists are already comfortable with a real-life world without future people. We reject last generation pessimism. If we opt for a virtual world, then it will not be out of desperation, but only because we think it is the best available option. And we are certainly not worried by a virtual world without future people—if such a world is available.

Finally, I reject your equation of virtual future with *immediate universal virtual future*. As I said earlier, the natural response to worries about control is to inhabit both the virtual world *and the world outside*. People who are only partly immersed in virtual worlds can still procreate *outside those worlds*. And if virtual life is sufficiently rewarding (for them and their children), then they may procreate permissibly.

Post-Cataclysm Pessimist: Virtual futures also raise a new challenge for procreative permissibility. Imagine a potential parent who wants to enjoy an actual parent–child relationship, but who has the option of plugging into an experience machine and having the experience of doing so.[10] Suppose our procreative ethical principles permit procreation only when what is at stake for the potential parent is sufficiently important to justify the risks imposed on their future child. (This is true on Weinberg's theory, discussed in Chapter Five.) Hedonists—and other experientialists—will insist that nothing of value is at stake for *this* potential parent, because they can enjoy all the experiences associated with nurturing a child *without imposing any procreative risks on anyone*. Therefore, once virtual futures are in play, procreation can only be permissible if we place an implausible amount of weight on non-experiential facts. Virtual futures thus ground a new argument for Post-Cataclysm anti-natalism.

Presentist: As a hedonist, I would accept that conclusion. If we can make all present lives meaningful without creating new people, then perhaps that is what we should do.

Multigenerationalist: As I rely on intergenerational cooperation, I cannot accept this new anti-natalist argument. I would reply that we *should* reject experientialist accounts of well-being and meaningfulness. If you think you are cooperating with future people when, in reality, there are no future people at all, then your life is not going as well as you think.

Escapist: I reject Post-Cataclysm pessimism for a different reason. In my *digital* future, there *are* future people—albeit digital ones. Indeed, there are many more future generations inside the digital future than outside it. (That is the whole point!) Therefore, if you mourn the loss of future people, you should embrace the *digital* future.

---

[10] I borrow this example from Kraut, *The Quality of Life*, p. 108.

Multigenerationalist: I agree that the loss of future people is obviously much *more* troubling if we reject hedonism and recognise the *intrinsic* value of future-dependent meaning. And these two moves both appeal to multigenerationalists. We already acknowledge the significance of future-dependent meaning, because our main goal is to *recapture* it via reorientation toward non-future-dependent intergenerational meaning (Section 3.5). I also argued in my procreative ethics lectures that multigenerationalism is most plausible if we depart from hedonism— at least to incorporate posthumous harms, but also more broadly (Section 6.3.2). I think the transition to a virtual world is more challenging than presentists allow. I don't think *we* could flourish in a virtual world, or in any world without future people. But I think we could enable our descendants to flourish in a virtual world without future people. I extend this argument in the next section.

9.5 Attachment-Based Objections to the Experience Machine

Multigenerationalist: My case for multigenerational *virtualism* builds on one popular Pre-Cataclysm response to Nozick's experience machine, which argues that what really matters *to us* is whatever 'world' we are *already* immersed in. Nozick claims that it is a mistake to *enter* the experience machine. His explanation is that life outside the machine is more valuable *per se*. An alternative explanation is *rational status quo bias*:

> Imagine that you are offered a chance to lead an extremely happy and productive life which would also produce more happiness for others. However, to lead the alternative life you must leave your home, family and friends, and never see them again. Most people would refuse such an offer, just as they would refuse the offer of being placed on the experience machine.... We are not rejecting a life on the experience machine in particular. We would reject almost any other life, in the actual world or otherwise, if it requires abandoning our commitments.[11]

> People are averse to abandon the life they have been experiencing so far, regardless of whether such a life is virtual or real.... Some people may prefer to remain unplugged, not because they value reality, but because they are averse to losing their status quo.[12]

De Brigard presented Pre-Cataclysm experimental evidence to support the status quo bias explanation. Many people who would not choose to *enter* an

---

[11] Kawall, 'The Experience Machine and Mental State Theories of Well-Being', p. 383.
[12] De Brigard, 'If You Like It, Does It Matter If It's Real?' p. 44, p. 51.

experience machine would also not choose to *unplug* if they were suddenly informed that they were *already* in the virtual world.[13] We are attached to *the life we already have*, whether or not it is 'real' in any deeper metaphysical sense.

Some kinds of status quo bias are simply irrational. And the very term 'bias' implicitly suggests irrationality. However, a bias *in favour of one's existing attachments* seems perfectly reasonable.[14] And, of course, a bias toward one's existing attachments is central to the Scheffler-inspired emphasis on future-dependent intergenerational meaning that is one of multigenerationalism's central motivations (Sections 1.4 and 3.5)!

For Nozick, our reluctance to enter the experience machine grounds an objection to the experience machine. Once we recognise the role of rational status quo bias, any reluctance-based objection is turned on its head *for a generation who already inhabit a virtual world*. If the last generation are born and raised in a virtual world, then *their* status quo bias will *favour virtualism*. They will not regard their world as a second-best inferior option; and—more importantly—it will not *be* second-best *for them* (even if it *would* be second-best *for us*).

A central theme of my multigenerationalism lectures was that, while immediate extinction would be bad *for us*, this is primarily a function of our particular desires, preferences, attachments, values, and traditions, rather than anything essential to human flourishing per se. Over two centuries, we could reorient our inherited future-dependent traditions and values so that, in the last generation, well-being and meaning are no longer tied to any human future.

The badness of life in an experience machine *for us* is primarily a function of our *reality-oriented* attachments, values, and traditions. Perhaps *our* flourishing *does* demand something that is missing within the machine. But over two centuries, we could reorient our inherited reality-dependent values, so that well-being and meaning are no longer tied to any connection to the world outside the machine. The value that *we* would lose in a virtual world is recaptured for the last generation via virtual reorientation of our own reality-saturated values.

Of course, this virtual reorientation will not be easy. That is why our virtual project is multigenerational. And *any* multigenerational reorientation is risky. Before the Cataclysm, when future-dependent, reality-dependent meaning was unproblematically available, multigenerational virtual reorientation was perhaps too risky. But in our Post-Cataclysm world, we cannot continue the safe business-as-usual option of future-dependent, reality-dependent traditions. If we are to salvage *intergenerational* meaning, then we need *some* radical reorientation. Virtual reorientation is *now* worth the risk.

---

[13] De Brigard, 'If You Like It, Does It Matter If It's Real?' pp. 44–50.
[14] cf. De Brigard, 'If You Like It, Does It Matter If It's Real?' p. 54.

Theist: What exactly is the connection between *future*-dependent meaning and *reality*-dependent meaning? Why would the loss of the human future affect the desirability of virtual worlds?

Multigenerationalist: I think the connection is this. *Our* inherited values are both future-dependent and reality-dependent. We find meaning in projects located in the empirical world (the world *outside* the machine) that include future people who will live in that empirical world. Future people, living at humanity's end, will need radically different values. For them, meaning must be divorced from connections to (further) future people. They much therefore consider radical alternatives. One such alternative is to ground meaning in something that is beyond the empirical world altogether.

However, I also don't think this link between future-dependence and reality-dependence is merely an historical accident. Whenever human beings look beyond themselves, they naturally fix on three things: the empirical world, other people, and the supernatural. If I want some kind of meaning that transcends myself, and I insist on side-lining possible supernatural sources of meaning, then I am left with the empirical world and other people. If *we* (the present generation as a whole) want something that transcends our generation, then we are left with the empirical world and future people. Reality-dependence and future-dependence go hand in hand. Our experience of other people occurs within the empirical world. Our expectations regarding future people also relate to the empirical future. It is not surprising that we run the two kinds of self-transcendence together. Therefore, it is not surprising that, once we start to radically rethink one kind of dependence, we find ourselves also questioning the other kind of dependence.

Presentist: I agree that perhaps the best way to deal with imminent extinction is to abandon all connections to future people. Indeed, in Section 9.9, I explore the possibility that we must abandon all connections to other people (including present people)—because concern for other present people leads inevitably to concern for future people, which leads to despair when there can be no future people. But I don't agree that we need future moral transformation, as we already have a sufficient stock of self-contained, present-focused sources of meaning to fall back on.

Multigenerationalist: I disagree. I conclude instead that the project of building a virtual future offers our generation's best hope of present meaning. Drawing on my earlier taxonomy of multigenerational utopias, I argue that the best virtual future is natal and final, but that its *realisation* is a multigenerational project (Section 8.1). The last generation will be born into a virtual future, so their values, desires, and attachments will be tailored to that world.

Presentist: I don't find the status quo bias argument very persuasive. I think our reluctance to enter experience machines is more practical. Once our legitimate practical concerns are addressed, I don't think we need any radical moral transformation to recognise the value of escaping into virtual worlds. After all, hedonists have already achieved that 'transformation'!

Post-Cataclysm Pessimist: I agree that future moral transformation is necessary. *We* could not thrive in a virtual world. But I don't think this necessary future moral transformation is *feasible*. We cannot reasonably be confident that launching your multigenerational virtual project would achieve anything useful. The moral transformation involved is too far removed from any previous example of moral progress. Historical moral progress expanded our circles of moral concern, introduced new moral norms, and adapted slowly to changing circumstances. Abandoning our attachment *to the empirical world* is something very different—and *much more ambitious*.

Multigenerationalist: I'm not so sure. We do have precedents for moral imaginativeness that is not solely confined to the empirical world—in the form of hedonism (which turns inward), and various mystical traditions that turn either inward or look beyond the physical world altogether. Indeed, I think moral transformation *combined with non-empirical metaphysics* may be just what we need.

9.6 What Is Reality?

Theist: I now introduce a new dimension. I will argue that the emphasis on *reality* that underlies Nozick's objection to the experience machine actually favours *theism*, rather than Post-Cataclysm pessimism. From a theist point of view, arguments about the value of reality look very different.

I begin by asking what reality *is*. It is often said that people in experience machines lack a 'suitable connection to reality'. But what does this mean? It can't mean that there is *no* connection. There are many *actual* connections between my experiences within the machine and the world outside. For a start, my experiences are ultimately caused by that outside reality. (The experience machine is, after all, a *machine*.) And, in a deterministic universe, every individual's series of experiences (whether real or virtual) ultimately has the same cause: the Big Bang.

Nonetheless, there is a clear intuitive sense in which *something* is lacking in an experience machine—and therefore in any virtual future—because we are 'one step removed' from reality. The question is how to make sense of what we are removed *from*.

One account of what is lacking in the experience machine is *epistemic*. In epistemology, experience machines, virtual realities, dream hypotheses, and Evil

Demon scenarios all have a sceptical dimension. The central question for epistemologists is: How do I know that I am not now already immersed in the machine or dream? In these sceptical scenarios, I am (*ex hypothesi*) *unaware* of the actual causal chain that leads to my experiences.

Unfortunately, this epistemic gap cannot be the whole story, for two reasons. First, *comparative* ignorance is not an *essential* feature of virtuality. Knowledge of causal connections is hardly ubiquitous in the 'real' world either. In principle, I could be as well informed about the causal history of my experiences inside the machine as I am in the world outside. Second, *ignorance* of (causal) connections to ultimate reality presumably only matters *if those connections themselves matter*. I therefore focus on asking whether they *do* matter. Setting aside scepticism and deception, I stipulate a virtual future where people *are* aware of their virtual situation. We can then concentrate on the intrinsic (dis)value of virtuality itself. If my experiences are caused by an experience machine, and I am aware of this, do I *still* lack an appropriate connection to reality? If so, what exactly is missing?

The main Pre-Cataclysm reply to any objection that, within the experience machine, I lack a valuable connection to 'reality' is hedonist. All connections to any reality beyond my immediate sensations have only *instrumental* value, which is fully replaceable in a virtual future. Therefore, nothing is lacking in the experience machine.

A less-explored reply appeals, not to hedonism, but to views at the opposite end of the spectrum—austere, non-empirical, achievement-oriented accounts of human values. Real value is not found in the empirical, physical, or natural world, but in *transcendent* achievements that are equally available (and perhaps more readily accessible) inside an experience machine. I will now develop this *second* reply. It is the natural reply for theists, and it is now more plausible after the Cataclysm.

The Pre-Cataclysm *philosophical* literature often presents the virtualist as a 'hedonist' in the vulgar sense—a shallow, pleasure-seeking, present-sensation-focused egoist. By contrast, the most beguiling virtual worlds imagined by Pre-Cataclysm *speculative fiction* were often highbrow aesthetic—even ascetic—realms of abstract disembodied intellectual pursuits where pure mathematics shades into mysticism. (Consider the digital heroine of Greg Egan's *Diaspora*, who eventually abandons her search for knowledge of the physical universe to immerse herself in the eternal world of mathematics.)

Post-Cataclysm Pessimist: I reply that the reality that *matters* is *empirical reality*—including our relations to other persons. That is what is lost in the experience machine.

Theist: By contrast, many philosophical and religious traditions who agree that reality is better than illusion also reject the world 'outside' the experience machine as merely another illusion. Consider Plato's cave, the Neo-Platonic image of the empirical world as a dream, Buddhist doctrines of the gap between ultimate and conventional truth, Hindu concepts of pervasive illusion or maya, and so on. Within these traditions, both the experience machine and the world outside it exist *within* the world of illusion. Empirical reality therefore has no comparative advantage. Why would a dream within a dream be any less valuable than the dream itself? Kraut puts the point well: 'For upholders of the Platonic and the idealist tradition, the loss of the body that Nozick contemplates by way of the experience machine would not be a loss of anything worthwhile.'[15]

9.6.1 Three Contrasting Worldviews

Theist: I find it helpful to contrast three competing accounts of reality: solipsist, empiricist, and transcendent:

- *Solipsism*: Only my own individual experience is real. This reality is accessible within the experience machine. Admittedly, solipsism is not a popular *metaphysical* view, but some kinds of hedonism are *evaluatively solipsist*. Nothing has value to me except insofar as it enters into my experience.
- *Empiricism*: The world immediately outside the experience machine is the ultimate reality.
- *Transcendence*: The everyday world is a mirage, an illusion, a dream—at best an echo, shadow, or distortion of *ultimate reality*. There is some deeper reality behind or beneath empirical reality. And that ultimate reality is *not* the empirical world of our everyday experience. Idealists, Neoplatonists, some mystical Western theists, and many Hindu and Buddhist philosophers defend a transcendent metaphysics. We must then ask whether, in the experience machine, my separation from empirical reality makes it harder (or easier) to connect with ultimate reality.[16]

The reality-based objection to the experience machine presupposes an empiricist metaphysic. The ultimate reality is *just* outside the machine—and I will encounter it directly if I stay outside. Within the experience machine, I lack some valuable connection to *this* ultimate reality that *is* available if I step *outside* the machine.

---

[15] Kraut, *The Quality of Life*, p. 87.
[16] My brief discussion of what I call 'transcendent metaphysics' is particularly influenced by British Idealism, Neoplatonism, and contemporary work on alternative conceptions of God. On British Idealism and Neoplatonism see, respectively, Mander, *British Idealism*; Clark, *Plotinus*. On alternative concepts of God, see Buckareff and Nagasawa, *Alternative Concepts of God: Essays on the Metaphysics of the Divine*; Diller and Kasher, *Models of God and Alternative Ultimate Realities*; Gasser and Kittle, *Personal and A-Personal Aspects of the Divine*; Mulgan, *Purpose in the Universe*.

But empiricism is not the only philosophically respectable option. And I would argue that it is the worldview *least* suited to our Post-Cataclysm world. Solipsist or transcendent alternatives may now have more appeal, especially to the last generation.

Metaphysical solipsism is very much a minority view. The real alternative to empiricism is transcendent metaphysics. If this is the correct picture, then the reality-based objection is certainly weakened. Indeed, a more plausible argument runs in the opposite direction—*from* transcendence *to* virtualism. If the world *immediately outside* the experience machine is no *more* real (i.e., no closer to ultimate reality) than the world *within* the experience machine, then a person's *valuable* connection to reality cannot be greater outside the machine than inside it.

If empirical reality is merely an illusion, then connections to empirical reality seem very unlikely to have any non-instrumental value. Insofar as *any* connection to *reality* matters in itself, it will be the ultimate, deeper, non-illusory reality that counts. *Modest* transcendent virtualists will now conclude that the world immediately outside the machine has no comparative advantage. *Ambitious* transcendent defenders of virtual worlds will go further. The virtual world is not only not deficient. It is *superior* to the world outside—because it offers a more reliable window onto ultimate reality itself. Perhaps we *need* the experience machine to enable us (i) to *recognise* that all empirical reality is an illusion; and (ii) therefore (hopefully) to *escape* from it. Immersing ourselves in a virtual world may open our eyes to some deeper underlying ultimate reality. In particular, *knowing* you are in an experience machine prompts reflection on reality and illusion—and the distinction between dream and waking—that leads to metaphysical enlightenment and a realisation of what 'really' matters. More mundanely, an experience machine might enable us to discover ultimate reality simply by freeing us from the distractions of empirical reality. (Perhaps the most valuable experience machine would be a sensory deprivation tank.)

Mystical virtualists present the virtual world as the best place to seek connections to *divine* reality. A religious person might retreat into a virtual world *in order to focus all their attention on the contemplation of God*. Indeed, many contemplative traditions *do* recommend a retreat from 'the world'. It is mere secular prejudice to insist that, when contemplatives deliberately turn their back on the empirical world, they must be making some evaluative or deliberative *mistake*.

In Western philosophy, the classic transcendent metaphysic is the Idealist tradition, going back at least to Plato. In Pre-Cataclysm, post-Idealist, 'analytic' philosophy, the Dream Hypothesis—the hypothesis that 'all this' is a dream—is treated as a (false) sceptical hypothesis.[17] The philosophical puzzle is to explain

---

[17] I have found Valberg's analysis of dreaming especially useful (Valberg, *Dream, Death, and the Self*).

why we can be confident that the Dream Hypothesis is false. At the opposite end of the metaphysical spectrum, Neoplatonists regard the Dream Hypothesis as a very significant metaphysical *truth*. For instance, Plotinus explicitly likens metaphysical enlightenment to waking from a dream, or sobering up from a drunken stupor: 'It is as if people who slept through their life thought the things in their dreams were reliable and obvious, but, if someone woke them up, disbelieved in what they saw with their eyes open and went to sleep again.'[18]

For Neoplatonists, the solution is simple. If you asleep, then you need to wake up: 'What is needed is to wake up entirely from the body, as Plotinus said he had "often" done.'[19] From this perspective, philosophy's central task—both therapeutic and theoretical—is to awaken us from our empirical slumber. We need to recognise that the world 'outside' the experience machine is no more *real* than the world inside it. Perhaps the more obvious illusion of the virtual world is a vital first step—the jolt we need to wake us up.

A common theme of all transcendent metaphysics is that *knowledge* of ultimate metaphysical truth is valuable (or, indeed, *invaluable*). Unless we know what reality is ultimately like, we remain attached to meaningless, transitory illusions. We cannot flourish without connections to ultimate reality.

Post-Cataclysm Pessimist: I concede that, *if* we accept some transcendent metaphysical picture, *then* reality-based objections to experience machines and virtual futures are weakened. But that is a very big if! For many empiricists, naturalists, materialists, or physicalists, transcendent metaphysics is simply incredible—and certainly undermotivated by any empirical evidence or philosophical argument. Without a compelling independent theoretical case for the revival of Idealism, this defense of the virtual future is a dead-end.

I also don't think your argument has any dialectical force *in our underlying debate between optimists and pessimists*. What you call 'transcendent metaphysics' is just theism by another name. I agree that, if theism is true, then pessimism is in trouble—because God will no doubt find *some* way to give humans meaningful lives, perhaps by giving us valuable connections to ultimate reality. The first step in any case for Post-Cataclysm pessimism is the rejection of theism—and transcendent metaphysics along with it.

Furthermore, as I argued in our religion debate, I think the philosophical case against theism is even stronger now that before the Cataclysm (Section 2.3). Therefore, prima facie, your present appeal to transcendent metaphysics is also *less* persuasive than it was.

---

[18] As translated by Clark, *Plotinus*, p. 71. As Clark explains: '"Sleep" in this context, meant a failure to engage, even to wish to engage, with the real situation. Being asleep and dreaming, we are content with what appears, without asking whether it is true' (Clark, *Plotinus*, p. 226).

[19] Clark, *Plotinus*, p. 228.

Theist: I think the opposite is true. The case for transcendent metaphysics is stronger now—for the same reason that the case for theism is stronger. I will now present two brief arguments for transcendent metaphysics—one theoretical, the other moral or practical.

9.6.2 A Theoretical Argument for Transcendent Metaphysics

Theist: I agree that, if transcendent metaphysics simply *is* theism, then I haven't advanced our overall dialectic much beyond the point we reached in our religion debate. But I think there is more to be said. As I see it, transcendent metaphysics is not identical to theism. Rather, the idea of transcendent metaphysics is orthogonal to the theism–atheism divide. Some proponents of transcendent metaphysics are theists. But others are not—consider McTaggart's Idealism where ultimate reality consists of a plurality of eternal, uncreated spirits none of whom is a creator God; or those forms of monist Idealism in Indian philosophy that recognise many gods but no omnipotent creator God.[20] Furthermore, not all theists defend transcendent metaphysics. By definition, theists are not materialists. All theists recognise spirits beyond the physical universe—simply because God is such a spirit. But a theist could also recognise the independent reality of the empirical world. And many do.

From a theist perspective, I see transcendent metaphysics as one (extreme) option among many. Theists who embrace transcendent metaphysics regard the empirical world as merely a pale shadow of the ultimate divine reality. All theists agree that the empirical world is more contingent, less secure, and less valuable than the divine reality. Transcendent theists go further, and insist that it is also *less real*.

Transcendent theists emphasise contemplation, union with the divine, or communion with other spirits *even more than other theists do*. They regard this-worldly achievements and projects as largely irrelevant.

I will now defend two claims. First, within Post-Cataclysm theism, a commitment to transcendent metaphysics mutually supports an increased emphasis on contemplation and other-worldly goals. Second, reflection on experience machines and virtual futures, especially after the Cataclysm, further supports the case for transcendent metaphysics *relative to other possible theist worldviews*.

I noted in our religion debate that, since the Cataclysm, many theists have turned inward—focusing more on contemplation of eternal divine reality and less on 'good works' in the doomed human world (Sections 2.1 and 2.2). Obviously, this shift makes sense if one adopts a more transcendent interpretation of theism. If our connections to the empirical world are ultimately unreal, then they will

---

[20] On McTaggart's atheist 'pluralist' idealism, see Mander, *British Idealism*, especially pp. 369–376; McTaggart, *Some Dogmas of Religion*; McDaniel, 'John M. E. McTaggart'.

seem less important. But the reverse is also true. The contemplative turn supports a metaphysical shift. Theists turn to contemplation, not out of despair, but because they interpret the Cataclysm as evidence that this world is less important than we previously thought. The metaphysical picture that best fits the general idea that this empirical world is less important than we previously thought is transcendent metaphysics. Theists' underling motivation for a practical contemplative turn also motivates a transcendent turn in metaphysics.

But what does all this have to do with experience machines and virtual worlds? Reflecting on these possible scenarios, from a theist point of view, in light of our theist reactions to the Cataclysm, I find myself struck by the gap between the connections that *really matter* (our links to God and one another) and the connections that are lost if we leave the empirical world behind and enter an (interpersonal) virtual world. All that is lost in this transition is ephemeral connections to a fleeting empirical world. Thinking about virtual worlds thus reinforces both transcendent metaphysics and contemplative practice.

Post-Cataclysm Pessimist: As a pessimist, I am not persuaded. I don't think the metaphysical case for transcendent metaphysics, or theism, or anything else beyond empiricism is stronger now than before the Cataclysm.

Theism: To persuade anyone who remains unconvinced by theoretical arguments, I will now offer a different kind of argument altogether.

9.6.3 A Moral Argument for Transcendent Metaphysics

Theist: I have argued that, if ultimate transcendence is *true*, then the virtual future is superior to non-virtual alternatives. I moved from metaphysics to ethics—basing value claims on metaphysical ones. Moral arguments move in the opposite direction. We begin with our inescapable ethical commitments, and then seek a metaphysical picture on which those commitments make sense. This is a very common move in Idealist and Neoplatonist philosophy. From an Idealist perspective, William Mander argues that, if our primary knowledge is ethical, if we are most certain of our reality as moral beings, if 'our moral vision is non-negotiable, [then] the task of metaphysics can only be to find a worldview which fits in with this.'[21] Or consider Stephen Clark's Neoplatonic reaction to the pointless, empty universe of modern, scientific materialism: 'What would it be like to be wholly persuaded by this colder vision and to be united, in feeling and imagination, with "the view from nowhere"? ... And why, if the universe were really as indifferent to anything we value as so many moderns say, and there is no comfort in it, should

[21] Mander, *Idealist Ethics*, p. 20.

we set ourselves to realise this truth?... If reality is what moderns often claim, we have neither duty nor ability to find it out and may reasonably relax into fictions!'[22]

Moral arguments respond to a perceived gap between (a) what we *can establish* by neutral, scientific, empirical, or metaphysical argument; and (b) what we *must believe* to function (or thrive) as moral, meaning-seeking agents. Moral arguments plug the gap between the deliverances of theoretical reason and the demands of practical reason. They ground *meaning* in an otherwise meaningless universe.

Suppose we do not dismiss moral arguments out of hand. We agree that the need to find meaning can (at least) shape, colour, or influence our metaphysical commitments. As I argued in our religion debate, in our Post-Cataclysm world, where meaning is much harder to find *within the empirical realm*, all moral arguments for non-empirical metaphysical claims are now more compelling (Section 2.2). These arguments now provide a necessary antidote to pessimist despair. Therefore, the stronger the case for Post-Cataclysm pessimism, the greater the need for moral arguments.

Presentist: Of course, moral arguments are notoriously controversial. We considered them in our pessimism and religion debates (Sections 1.8 and 2.2). I was sceptical then, and I remain sceptical now. My present question, however, is what these moral arguments have to do with our present interest in virtual worlds.

Theist: Moral arguments are relevant to virtual futures in several ways. First, familiar Kantian 'practical' arguments for belief in (libertarian) free will, God, and immortality indirectly support transcendent metaphysics, because their specific metaphysical claims go beyond empirical reality.[23] This is the whole point of Kant's original arguments. As we have seen several times before, in our Post-Cataclysm world, *any* practical argument for God or immortality is strengthened by the removal of alternative routes to meaning based on the *secular* human future.

There is also a more direct moral argument for transcendent metaphysics itself, insofar as we must posit an intelligible (and moral) ultimate reality to make sense of morality. If the world only makes moral sense if there are (some) non-natural normative facts, and if non-natural normative facts cannot exist on their own—if they sit too uneasily alongside an otherwise compelling naturalistic metaphysical

---

[22] Clark, *Plotinus*, pp. 38–40.

[23] On Kant's original moral arguments, see, e.g., White, *Commentary*, pp. 267–269; Sullivan, *Immanuel Kant's Moral Theory*, pp. 142–144; Beach, 'The Postulate of Immortality in Kant: To What Extent Is It Cuturally Conditioned?'; Guyer, *Kant*, chapter six: 'Freedom, Immortality, and God: The Presuppositions of Morality'; Irwin, *The Development of Ethics*, volume three, chapter seventy-one, sections 975 to 980; Rossi, 'Kant, Immanuel: Philosophy of Religion'. On moral, practical, or Kantian arguments more generally, see Hare, *The Moral Gap*, chapter three on Moral Faith; Bishop, *Believing by Faith*; Chignell, 'Belief, ethics of'; Adams, 'Moral Faith'; Adams, *Finite and Infinite Goods*, pp. 373–389. I discuss moral arguments myself in Mulgan, *Purpose in the Universe*, pp. 301–322.

worldview—then we must posit some *other* (i.e., non-moral) non-natural facts.[24] Proponents of transcendent metaphysics argue that it is only against the backdrop of a transcendent worldview, where reality is saturated by (and founded upon) values, that non-natural moral facts can be truly at home.

If there is a good moral argument for transcendent metaphysics, whether direct or indirect, then of course this is bad news for any reality-based argument *against* virtual futures, as such arguments presume an empiricist metaphysics.

Post-Cataclysm Pessimism: So far, I think your moral arguments for transcendent metaphysics are very similar to the argument for theism that we considered in our religion debate. I still don't see how the virtual future is directly relevant.

Theist: Consideration of moral arguments also supports virtual futures more directly. The shift from (a) discovering the truth about reality; to (b) making a leap of faith to a morally necessary metaphysical position (or metaphysical diagnosis) changes the dialectical situation. We no longer have to demonstrate that the virtual life is *epistemically* superior to a life outside the machine—that it offers a greater insight into the *truth*. Instead, the virtual life may simply be an easier, safer, more reliable environment for some *practically necessary* leap(s) of faith.

Post-Cataclysm Pessimist: I don't find moral arguments persuasive. I don't think our commitment to empiricism is so easily undermined. I agree that secular sources of meaningfulness are more precarious after the Cataclysm. Optimists have more need to *hope* that theism (or transcendent metaphysics or whatever) is true. But hope has never been sufficient for reasonable belief.

Presentist: Unsurprisingly, I disagree with both of you. I don't think we must choose between transcendent metaphysics and despair. We have a credible alternative. Hedonism is true, present pleasures and activities are sufficient for meaning, and, once our reasonable practical worries are met, the virtual future will be great! However, while I don't find transcendent metaphysics very plausible, I do think your arguments give us the materials for a new disjunctive argument for virtualism that is stronger than hedonism alone. I defend that argument in the next section.

9.7 New Disjunctive Arguments for Virtual Futures

Presentist: My new disjunctive argument combines the seemingly opposite goals of immediate-pleasure-seeking hedonism and other-worldly transcendent metaphysics. Either a connection to ultimate reality is important or it is not. If it is not,

---

[24] I explore this argument at length in Mulgan, *Purpose in the Universe*, especially chapter two.

then the virtual world is not deficient. On the other hand, if a connection to ultimate reality is valuable, then the virtual world does not hinder such a connection. Indeed, it may even enhance it, precisely because the world immediately 'outside the machine' is *not* ultimately metaphysically real. By removing the distractions of the empirical world, the virtual world enables us to focus more wholeheartedly on what really matters—which is *either* the feel of our experiences *or* the prospect of some valuable connection to ultimate reality.

Multigenerationalist: And I would offer another yet disjunctive argument. Either a connection to ultimate reality is valuable, or it is not. If it is, then, as the theist has just argued, the virtual world is superior to the world outside the machine, because virtualism offers a more reliable route to knowledge of ultimate reality. On the other hand, if a connection to ultimate reality has no intrinsic value—and everything that matters to us is internal to whatever reality *we experience*—then we have a new argument for *natal multigenerational* virtualism. We should *not* seek a virtual world *for ourselves*. Any generation born *outside* the machine will struggle to adapt to life within it. But a generation born *within* the machine—for whom the virtual *is* their 'everyday reality'—would equally struggle to live outside the machine.

My original status quo-based argument for natal virtualism did not presuppose any particular metaphysic (Section 9.5). That argument goes through even if the (empirical) world (directly) outside the experience machine *is* the ultimate reality. But transcendent metaphysics obviously strengthens that earlier argument. If transcendent metaphysics is true, then the world directly outside the experience machine is *not* the ultimate reality. If we combine this metaphysical worldview with a rational status quo bias, then connections to empirical reality can only derive non-instrumental value *from our attachment to them*. If our descendants lack that attachment, then the virtual future will not be deficient for them at all.

My case for *natal* virtualism is also strengthened by any plausible *moral* argument for transcendent metaphysics. Many philosophers find that our current 'ordinary' non-virtual environment renders *any* leap of faith—any leap beyond the empirical—simply unbelievable. For anyone already living outside the machine, the pull of empirical reality may be too strong for metaphysical leaps—even ones that are practically necessary to avoid existential despair. Post-Cataclysm pessimism appeals to so many people precisely because we cannot shake our dependence on the empirical world.

Of course, if we could *demonstrate the truth* of some transcendent metaphysical claim, then believability might not matter. And, if there were such a proof, then we could presumably discover it either inside or outside the machine. But the whole starting-point of a *moral* argument is that there is no such decisive demonstration—no compelling theoretical proof of any controversial metaphysical claim.

I conclude that any desirable virtual utopia must be *natal*. It is too late for people who have grown up outside the machine. We are already too attached to the empirical. For too many of us, any transcendent metaphysic is simply too unbelievable. We cannot make the necessary leap of faith to replace empirically grounded, future-dependent meaning with non-future-dependent, *transcendent-reality-based*, intergenerational meaning. Only a new generation, immersed from the beginning in a virtual world, and knowing no other, can take that necessary leap.

I believe that our present disjunctive argument *mutually supports* moral arguments. In other words, locating it *within* our overall disjunctive argument for virtualism also strengthens any moral argument that we already have. If our leaps of faith occur within one fork of that argument, then we can help ourselves to controversial anti-hedonist premises. We need not prove that transcendent metaphysics is a practical necessity per se. We only need to claim that transcendent metaphysics is a practical necessity *for everyone who believes that intrinsic values beyond immediate experiences are essential for a meaningful human life*. (This includes Post-Cataclysm pessimists themselves!) This is a much less ambitious leap. Empiricism thus finds itself caught between hedonist evaluative parsimony, on the one hand, and transcendent metaphysics, on the other.

9.8 Freedom in the Experience Machine and Beyond

Post-Cataclysm Pessimist: I now present another argument against the experience machine. One common interpretation of Nozick's own critique of his experience machine says that what is really lacking in any virtual future is *freedom*.[25] This anti-virtualist argument is now more compelling that ever, because it is especially powerful against the fully immersive final *natal* virtual future you all need to defend in the last generation.

I begin by asking what Nozick is really doing. Out of context, Nozick's very brief discussion of the experience machine looks like a simple counterexample to hedonism. But this is not the whole story. Nozick first introduces the experience machine after a discussion of the differences between humans and non-human animals. The broader context in *Anarchy, State and Utopia* is Nozick's various attacks on utilitarianism, pattern-based theories of justice, state control, and centrally planned social and economic systems.[26] Seen in this light, the thought

---

[25] For introductions to the vast literature on free will, see, e.g., Fischer et al., *Four Views on Free Will*; O'Connor and Franklin, 'Free Will'; McKenna and Coates, 'Compatibilism'; Vihvelin, 'Arguments for Incompatibilism'; Clarke, Capes, and Swenson, 'Incompatibilist (Nondeterministic) Theories of Free Will'. On free will in experience machines, see Chalmers, *Reality+*, p. 320.

[26] Nozick's discussion of the experience machine in later works supports this interpretation. In *Philosophical Explanations*, Nozick's sole reference to the experience machine is in the context of 'transcending limits': 'The experience machine, though it may give you the experience of transcending

experiment is designed to teach us both (a) what separates us from non-human animals; and (b) why all non-libertarian political and economic systems are so objectionable.

While the subsequent literature focuses almost exclusively on the experience machine, Nozick also critiques two other imaginary machines: a *transformation* machine that turns us into the people we want to be; and a *results* machine that produces any desired result.[27] All three machines (experience, transformation, results) are objectionable for the same reason—they each do something for us that we need to *do for ourselves*.

Nozick's real worry is thus not about experiences, but about *machines*. Machines are deterministic, preprogrammed, predictable, and limited to the imagination of their creators. A machine imposes its values on us, rather than allowing us to discover our own values. It prescribes our future, rather than allowing us to invent that future for ourselves. Even if we choose to enter the machine, and choose our own preprogrammed pattern of experiences, we are limiting our future selves. The defining feature of life within the experience machine is its *passivity*. We don't *do* anything; we merely *receive* experiences.

Freedom is Nozick's primary concern throughout *Anarchy, State and Utopia*. Inside the experience machine—inside *any* machine—there is no freedom. The world of the machine is a world without freedom. Nozick objects that utilitarians, planners, patternists, and other non-libertarians treat the human world as if it were predictable, calculable, causally closed—in other words, as if it were a machine. The freedom to obey the machine is no freedom at all. If our lives are lived for us—by the experience machine, by the unrelenting demands of utilitarian morality, or by the forced taxation and redistribution of the non-minimal state—then they are not really lived at all.[28]

For Nozick, the experience machine's most obvious deficiency is *passivity*. Once inside the machine, the person does nothing—they choose nothing, they perform no actions, they merely passively experience a series of (hopefully pleasurable) sensations. Nozick suggests that this passive state is *not* how humans flourish.

---

limits, encloses you within the circle of just your own experiences' (Nozick, *Philosophical Explanations*, p. 595). This clearly supports the interpretation I offer here. In *The Examined Life*, while Nozick's discussion of the experience machine primarily relates to the value of connections to reality, he also emphasises the importance of openness and control (Nozick, *The Examined Life*, pp. 104–118—see, especially, pp. 115–118). Finally, Nozick also mentions the experience machine in *Invariances*. This discussion does occur in a discussion of the function of self-consciousness, focused on the value of connections to reality: 'if the function of conscious awareness is to enable our actions to conform more closely to aspects of the world, then conscious awareness cannot be valuable without its also being valuable to have actions conform more closely to aspects of the world' (Nozick, *Invariances*, pp. 299–300). This suggests that reality is Nozick's main concern. However, Nozick then asks; 'But what if something once did have a function but that function now is vestigial, or is no longer adaptive, or is no longer needed?' (Nozick, *Invariances*, p. 300). This is the very question that virtualists ask!

[27] Nozick, *Anarchy, State, and Utopia*, pp. 44–45.
[28] cf. Tollefsen, 'Experience Machines, Dreams, and What Matters', p. 158.

Presentist: One obvious response, for a *hedonist*, is simply to bite this bullet. Human freedom, choice, and agency only ever have instrumental value. Freedom is valuable only insofar as it produces pleasurable sensations. Outside the machine, we need freedom of choice to reliably obtain pleasure. But inside the experience machine, where pleasure is guaranteed, *normally* valuable human freedom ceases to have any value at all. Therefore, no valuable freedom is lost.

Theist: Sadly, this reply is not available to me. While hedonists can simply deny the intrinsic value of freedom, theists cannot easily do so. We need freedom to construct plausible theodicies.[29] Therefore, I have to agree with Nozick that any purely passive life *is* deficient.

Multigenerationalist: So do I. While the hedonist bullet-biting move was one important strand in my overall disjunctive argument for virtualism, I am also committed to exploring alternatives that respect Nozick's non-hedonist values. As I noted in Section 9.5, I also argued in my procreative ethics lectures that multigenerationalism is most plausible if we depart from hedonism in several ways (most obviously to recognise significant posthumous harms)—Section 6.3.2. I therefore also concede (for the sake of argument) that any purely passive life *is* deficient.

Post-Cataclysm Pessimist: The obvious non-hedonist solution is to locate genuine human choice *outside the machine*—when we decide to enter the experience machine. The *experience* machine is then a special case of Nozick's *transformation* machine, where you choose who you will be. Of course, this would be a very limited freedom. But perhaps the most valuable freedom is not an everyday event. For instance, Peter van Inwagen argues that true human freedom is very rarely exercised—most people make only a handful of genuinely free choices in a lifetime.[30] Someone who spends *the rest of their adult life* experiencing the consequences of a single decision to enter an experience (or transformation) machine might thus exercise as much valuable human freedom as someone else living a 'normal' human life outside the machine—whose life is similarly spent working out the consequences of one momentous decision.

This is where our Post-Cataclysm context bites. This appeal to extra-machine freedom *cannot* work *for people who are born into the virtual future*. These people can only ever be free *within the machine*. Even if future people can choose some details of their virtual world, they cannot choose it *in preference to some desirable non-virtual alternative*. They may *prefer* their virtual world. And, indeed, we may seek to ensure that they *do* prefer it—because this would be better for them. But they have not *chosen* it. Anyone who thinks it is a prudential mistake to enter the

---

[29] On free-will-based theodicies, see Oppy, 'Arguments from Moral Evil'; Dougherty, *The Problem of Animal Pain*; van Inwagen, *The Problem of Evil*; Mulgan, *Purpose in the Universe*, pp. 233–360.

[30] Van Inwagen, 'When Is the Will Free?'; Van Inwagen, 'When the Will Is Not Free'.

experience machine—*because one loses one's valuable freedom within it*—is likely to find your future virtualist utopia especially troubling. If Nozick's original experience machine is unacceptably passive, then any virtual future must be even more passive.

If their world is as passive as Nozick's original experience machine, then people living in a virtual *future* will be even less free than in Nozick's original scenario. If you recognise the value of freedom, and if you claim that nothing of value is lost at humanity's end, then you can only defend your *natal* virtual future by claiming that there is genuine choice *within* the machine. Contra Nozick, you must show that a credible virtual future contains significant decision-making.

Multigenerationalist: And why not? People do make real choices in dreams, in virtual realities, or inside other illusions. These choices are no less metaphysically free than non-virtual equivalents.

Post-Cataclysm Pessimist: One way to cash out the freedom-based objection is to note that interactions within an experience machine are too predictable. They lack the open-endedness of real life.

Multigenerationalist: To evaluate this objection, we must first distinguish two kinds of predictability: predictability to inhabitants and predictability in principle. We might worry that the machine itself is too predictable *for its inhabitants*— that living in a virtual future is like playing chess against an unsophisticated programme. However, I think *this* worry is easily addressed, for two reasons. First, even fully preprogrammed machines are not necessarily predictable *by human beings in real time*. We already have virtual environments that surprise even the most experienced users—not to mention checkers/chess/Go programmes whose only predictable feature is that they always defeat any human opponent! And the best virtual future available in two centuries could be effectively impossible to predict from the inside. Second, if our virtual environment is *interpersonal*, then each person's fate depends on *other people's free choices*— which are certainly not predictable in this sense. (At least, other people are no more predictable inside the machine than they are outside it.)

Post-Cataclysm Pessimist: I agree that this worry about predictability is not too serious. However, another predictability worry is much harder to avoid: *predictability in principle*. If a machine is, by definition, a closed deterministic system, then there can be no genuine choice within it.[31]

Presentist: Only incompatibilists worry about this kind of predictability. If we are *compatibilists*—for whom genuine, valuable, human free will is compatible with a completely deterministic universe—then it is hard to see what all the fuss is

---

[31] On predictability in virtual reality, see Chalmers, *Reality+*, p. 313.

about.³² For the compatibilist, free will is found even in a determinist empirical world. After all, historically, the point of compatibilism is that we can enjoy free will *even if the empirical world itself is a machine*.³³ Therefore, there is no reason why someone in a virtual world could not possess free will. If what is truly valuable *can* be found in a deterministic, predictable, preprogrammable world, then we are still free in the way that truly matters, even if we *are* cogs in the machine.

Compatibilism is designed to reconcile us to a universe where the only freedom available to us is compatible with determinism. So long as my actions are caused by desires that I endorse, then I am free.³⁴ For the compatibilist, if there are barriers to genuine virtual freedom, then they are, in Parfit's terminology, merely *technical*.³⁵ Two hundred years is a long time in technology. Perhaps, by the last generation, we will know how to generate valuable (compatibilist) free will within a suitably designed virtual world.

Escapist: I would take your compatibilist argument a step further. Even the artificial constructs who exist *only* in the experience machine (such as non-player characters in a virtual game world) can enjoy valuable free will. This claim is central to my later defense of digital futures (Section 9.10). And if digital creatures in a purely digital world are free, then surely humans plugged into a shared virtual world are also free!

Post-Cataclysm Pessimist: By contrast, I regard the fact that it acknowledges the 'freedom' of digital constructs as a *reductio ad absurdum* of compatibilism. Nozick's objection, in effect, is that once we are trapped within the machine, we have no greater free will than the artificial creatures *of* the machine—*because* our experiences are preprogrammed and pre-determined. If compatibilism cannot even see what the problem is, then we must reject compatibilism. Its approval of the experience machine is a *reductio ad absurdum* of the very idea of compatibilist free will.

My Nozick-inspired free-will argument against the experience machine presumes a libertarian or incompatibilist *metaphysic* of freedom.³⁶ Genuine, valuable, human freedom is not compatible with determinism. And, outside the machine, humans *do* possess this incompatibilist freedom. Nozick himself

---

³² On compatibilism, see, e.g., McKenna and Coates, 'Compatibilism'.
³³ Many early modern formulations of the free will debate explicitly imagine the determined world as a machine: 'the image of the world as an edifice designed and built by an infinitely knowing maker was a commonplace in the 17th century understanding of the cosmos' (McClure, *Judging Rights*, p. 27). Of particular relevance in Nozick's case is the prevalence of this image in Locke, whose political philosophy is one foundation for Nozick's libertarianism, as we saw in Section 8.3.3: 'Locke often likened this universe to a magnificent and timeless machine' (McClure, *Judging Rights*, 31).
³⁴ There are, of course, many other formulations of compatibilism—but the differences between them are not relevant to the present debate (see, e.g., McKenna and Coates, 'Compatibilism').
³⁵ Parfit, *Reasons and Persons*, pp. 388–390.
³⁶ See, e.g., Clarke, Capes, and Swenson, 'Incompatibilist (Nondeterministic) Theories of Free Will'.

explicitly defends a libertarian model of human agency elsewhere: 'Without free will, we seem diminished, merely the playthings of external forces.'[37] The real objection is therefore that, on a libertarian account, there is no genuine free will within the predetermined world of the experience machine.

Theist: As with the value of freedom itself, I cannot dismiss your argument as easily as the presentist can. Like most theists, I want to reject compatibilism—because otherwise my options for replying to the problem of evil would be greatly reduced. I recognise the value of incompatibilist freedom. But I don't agree that incompatibilism helps your freedom-based attack on virtual worlds. On the contrary, I think true *incompatibilist* freedom is equally available within a virtual world.

The puzzle of how incompatibilist free will fits into our physicalist universe is not new. This brings us back Kant's *moral* argument for transcendent freedom—the most famous practical argument of all. And we can use Kant to turn your freedom-based objection on its head. True human freedom is no more credible in the empirical world directly *outside* the machine than in the virtual world itself. Kant argues that, because (i) the empirical world is deterministic; and (ii) genuine human freedom is incompatible with determinism; and (iii) all human value and morality presuppose genuine human freedom; therefore (iv) we must posit *transcendental freedom*. We must believe that we are noumenal beings whose freedom (somehow) transcends the empirical world both inside *and outside* the machine.

If we agree with Kant both (i) that it is impossible to fit incompatibilist freedom into a empiricist worldview; and (ii) that valuable human freedom is *transcendent*; then why should we believe that *that particular kind of freedom* is more accessible when we step outside the machine? After all, even outside the machine, *we are still imprisoned within the phenomenal/empirical world*.

Indeed, I think the theist defense of virtualism can be more ambitious. I go beyond parity and claim superiority. In terms of realising our true freedom, the virtual world is *better* than the world outside. Although the empirical world is just another machine, it is *less obviously* a machine. The *obviously* deterministic, *obviously* unfree experience machine is better than the apparent-but-illusory 'freedom' of the empirical 'real' world. In the experience machine, I cannot deny my empirical unfreedom. I cannot doubt that I am trapped in a predictable determinist machine. I must look elsewhere—seeking true (noumenal, transcendental) freedom somewhere *beyond* the world of appearances. Only by looking beyond both the experience machine and the machine outside it can we realise our transcendent non-empirical nature, as we must do if we are to *do* (or even *deliberate about doing*) anything at all.

---

[37] Nozick, *Philosophical Explanations*, p. 291.

Virtual reality helps us to believe in a transcendent metaphysic of the self. And we need that transcendent metaphysical picture, not so much because it is *true*, but rather because, without it, our lives cannot be meaningful *even from the inside*. We must believe that we are free. We discover that we can only be free if we are not living in a machine. (This is Nozick's real lesson for us.) We then discover that, in the relevant sense, the empirical world outside the machine is itself a machine. (This is the *practical* lesson that Kantians have always drawn from the interminable metaphysical debate over free will.) We conclude that we are only free if our true selves are not limited to the empirical world. Therefore, to believe that we are free, we must believe that we are noumenal or transcendent beings. We must reject empiricism in favour of some transcendent metaphysic.

This obviously mirrors my earlier metaphysical arguments (Section 9.6). Transcendent metaphysics and transcendental freedom are mutually supportive. On the one hand, we need transcendent metaphysics to ground our individual transcendental freedom. If this world is merely a deterministic machine, then nothing here matters. Things only matter if both (a) there are free (non-physical) *agents* for whom things can matter; and (b) there is a metaphysically transcendent *place* where those agents can freely act. Therefore, if we must believe in transcendental freedom, then we have practical reasons to embrace transcendent metaphysics.[38]

Transcendental freedom thus supports transcendent metaphysics. Conversely, if we are already committed to transcendent metaphysics, then we will find any *non-transcendental* account of free will unsatisfactory. Compatibilism will appear as a second-best option—to which naturalists are reluctantly driven because their metaphysical worldview excludes *true* (incompatibilist) human freedom. If we already accept transcendent metaphysics, then we have no good reason to settle for second best.

Multigenerationalist: I now offer yet *another* disjunctive argument for virtualism. Once again, the case for virtualism is strongest at the two extremes. If valuable human freedom is compatible with determinism, then it can, in principle, be enjoyed even by *artificial* beings who exist only inside an experience machine. (And therefore, a fortiori, valuable freedom is also available to human beings plugged into experience machines.) At the other extreme, if true human freedom requires a world entirely beyond the empirical, then *either* it is available *neither* in the empirical world *nor* inside the experience machine, *or* it is available in *both*.

Post-Cataclysm Pessimist: I concede the Kantian *conditional* claim that, *if* the empirical world is a predictable, programmable machine, *then* our empirical freedom is no better than freedom within a human-designed machine. But this

---

[38] See, for instance, Mander, *Idealist Ethics*, p. 227, on the Post-Kantian Idealist expression of this thought.

equation of *naturalism* with *mechanism* is extremely controversial. Not all Pre-Cataclysm naturalists regarded the natural world as a deterministic machine. Instead, I think the most serious threat to virtualism comes from *naturalist incompatibilism*, where our freedom is that of biological animals whose behaviour is not entirely determined by prior causes, instincts, or anything else outside our present agency. For instance, consider Helen Steward's account of free will as a *biological phenomenon*.[39] Animals have evolved as *self-movers*: entities able to 'settle' certain facts about themselves and their world through their decisions and choices. (This is evolution's actual solution to the problem of enabling creatures to negotiate very complex environments.) Animals are free, and we are free *because we too are animals*. This view clearly supports Nozick's freedom-based attack on experience machines. If our physical or biological nature is central to our freedom, then we are *not* free when our bodies lie inert inside the machine.

Multigenerationalist: I agree that naturalist biological incompatibilism is the most challenging view for proponents of virtual worlds. Of course, Steward's account is itself controversial.[40] Defenders of virtuality could simply reject it. However, as I want my case for multigenerationalism to beg as few philosophical questions as possible, I propose to grant that Steward's account of free will *was plausible before the Cataclysm*. But I would then argue that it is much less plausible *now*. Indeed, all Post-Cataclysm non-pessimists must reject it.

In our Post-Cataclysm world, where there is no human future—where normal biological flourishing is cut short—any *biological* account of human flourishing inevitably leads to *last generation pessimism*. (I drew a similar lesson, in relation to non-human flourishing, in my discussion of ecological utopias in my final lecture—Section 8.4.) *Animals* flourish by survival and reproduction. In the last generation, humans cannot truly flourish qua animals. If the last humans are to flourish, then they must do so, not as biological organisms, but as rational persons whose values transcend their (doomed) animal nature.

The intuitive appeal of Steward's biological picture of free will grounds yet another argument for *multigenerational natal* virtualism. If our *current* conception of ourselves (and of our present freedom) is biological, then *we* will have difficulty adjusting to a virtual world. Insofar as *our* self-image, our attachments, and *our valuable freedom* are all tied to our physical, embodied, evolved, biological, animal nature, then entering any experience machine would be a great loss *to us*—in the same way that immediate extinction would be bad *for us*. Both the virtual environment and immediate extinction cut us off from what matters to us. Our valuable freedom must be reality-based and future-directed. But our naturalist, biological self-image—our view of ourselves as animals who look to an

---

[39] Steward, *A Metaphysics for Freedom*.
[40] For critiques of Steward's novel incompatibilism, see, e.g., Broadie, 'Agency and Determinism in *A Metaphysics for Freedom*'; and Levy, 'Are We Agents At All? Helen Steward's Agency Incompatibilism'.

empirical future beyond our own lifespan—is not immutable. Not all humans have shared this self-image, and our descendants could leave it behind. The last generation could focus on other aspects of human freedom, far removed from (and therefore available without reference to) any non-human animal's mundane choices between different means to its predetermined ends.

Reflecting on Steward's naturalist incompatibilism thus helps us to see both (a) why we might *think* that valuable freedom is under threat in our Post-Cataclysm world; but also (b) how we could escape that threat and ensure that *truly* valuable freedom will be *more* available in a natal virtual future.

I conclude that, while Kant's transcendental freedom supports multigenerational virtualism by supporting transcendental metaphysics, Steward's naturalist incompatibilism also supports multigenerational virtualism in a very different way. Whatever its credibility before the Cataclysm, Nozick's freedom-based objection to virtual futures is no longer persuasive.

9.9 In Defense of Virtual Solipsism

Presentist: I now defend a radical alternative. So far, we have focused on interpersonal virtual futures. I return now to Nozick's original solitary experience machine. This *solitary* virtual future in not a sceptical or solipsist scenario. I know that other people still exist inside *their own* self-contained solitary experience machines. What is missing is not the independent value of their lives, but any connection to *me*.

I first argue that connections to other people are *unnecessary*. My argument is disjunctive, in a very familiar way. The first prong is hedonist. If hedonism is correct, then, other people are only instrumentally valuable. They only matter to me insofar as they affect my experiences. In a non-virtual environment, interpersonal relations are instrumentally valuable in many ways. We pity people whose lives are completely virtual (or who live surrounded by automata or slaves), because we think their inability to 'play well with others' threatens their future happiness *outside the machine*. But if your life will never contain interpersonal interactions—if you will permanently inhabit a solitary experience machine (or you are the last living human)—then your lack of interpersonal skills does not matter.

If hedonism is true, then the solitary experience machine is not deficient. On the other hand, if hedonism is false, then genuine connections to independent value are central to human flourishing. I need *some* interactions with external things that I cannot control; some external moral constraints on my behaviour; and some projects whose objects have independent value. Connections to other people offer *one* route to human flourishing—other people do have independent value. But the solitary experience machine offers other more reliable connections to the transcendent values of mathematics, mysticism, or supernatural ultimate reality (God, the Absolute, or cosmic purpose).

Theist: A more radical possibility is that *truly* valuable interpersonal relations remain available *even within a solitary experience machine*. For some theists, the most valuable interpersonal relationship is between the individual *and God*. And *this* relationship is most easily available (and perhaps *only* available), if one withdraws from the ordinary, empirical, interpersonal world entirely. Many theist contemplative traditions recommend retreat from both empirical reality *and interpersonal interaction*. If I can encounter God in a solitary virtual world, and if God is personal, then I *do* enjoy the most valuable personal relationship.

Presentist: The solitary experience machine, while strange and counter-intuitive, is not absurd. Our Post-Cataclysm situation itself is also strange. We are the first generation to seriously ask *how humanity should end*. Perhaps we should heed the words of Nozick himself in another context: 'someone who proposes a non-strange answer shows that he did not understand this question'.[41]

This leads me to my *second* claim: that solitary virtualism is especially appealing *for the last humans*. In a nutshell, my worry is that *any* connection to other people is too dangerous for the last generation. Normal human relations—even those between hedonists seeking pleasurable experiences or contemplatives exploring transcendent ultimate reality—inevitably bring concern for other people, which in turn brings concern for the future of humanity, which (in our Post-Cataclysm world) can only end in tears.

Connections to other present people are hollow without connections to future people. It is simply too hard—whether psychologically or conceptually—to separate the two. Therefore, the last generation cannot derive meaning from connections to other people. They can only thrive by *not* caring for other present people, and pursuing instead either (a) purely pleasurable sensations; or (b) solitary projects focused on impersonal values.

Post-Cataclysm Pessimist: As ever, I am prepared to concede, for the sake of argument, that this radical transformation may be *necessary*. But I would then deny that it is *possible*. Can we really separate ourselves so radically from others?

Multigenerationalist: This debate is grist to my multigenerationalist mill! Separating *ourselves* from other people would be extraordinarily difficult. We *are* hardwired to care about others. Something drastic is required. We must remove all temptation to care for others—by removing others altogether. Perhaps the last generation can *only* thrive *inside a solitary experience machine*. Multigenerational solitary virtualism would then emerge as humanity's last best hope. The closer the

---

[41] Nozick, *Philosophical Explanations*, p. 116. The question Nozick had in mind was: Why is there something rather than nothing?

ties between present people and future people—the harder it is to break our dependence on other people—the more necessary the solitary experience machine becomes.

As ever, I insist that what is valuable to us depends, in part, on our values, attachments, and worldviews. This is especially true for values dependent on our self-image. If we identify ourselves as physically embodied animals, then our interpersonal interactions within the empirical world do matter in themselves, and something of real irreplaceable value is missing in an interpersonal virtual future—let alone a solitary one! By contrast, if future humans come to regard themselves as rational souls trapped in inferior physical prisons, then the physical interactions of their animal bodies will not matter at all. For instance, if the last generation are raised to believe in McTaggart's Personal Idealism, where the ultimate reality is an irreducible multiplicity of spiritual (non-physical) entities, then the most valuable thing *for them* will be interaction with other spirits, and they will insist that such interaction is no more problematic in a virtual environment.[42] Alternatively, if the last generation are raised as *Absolute* Idealists—for whom all distinctions between individuals are illusory—then they will be perfectly at home seeking union with the Absolute in a solitary virtual future.[43]

This solipsist experiment involves the most intimate and difficult reorientation of any multigenerationalist project. Such a radical reorientation of humanity's self-image could never be completed within a single generation. It would take several generations to train human beings to transcend the doomed empirical world. The greater our current attachment to that world, the more challenging the necessary reorientation, and therefore the longer it would take. Any plausible virtualism must be multigenerational. And given the difficulties involved, the best multigenerational virtualism will be accelerating and agnostic—leaving intermediate generations to determine the exact nature of the natal, final, virtual utopia.

Post-Cataclysm Pessimist: As ever, I don't think we can reasonably be confident that this is possible, even with two hundred years of moral transformation!

Multigenerationalist: One strength of multigenerationalism is that it doesn't have to decide all these issues in advance. We can trust future people to sort out the competing merits of empiricism and transcendence, hedonism and its rivals, theism and atheism, and so on. And future people will also decide whether the best final natal utopia is virtual or not—and whether a virtual utopia should be interpersonal or solitary. Our job is to leave them as well-equipped as possible to realise whatever utopia brings the human story to its best possible end.

---

[42] On McTaggart's atheist personal idealism, see Mander, *British Idealism*, especially pp. 369–376; McTaggart, *Some Dogmas of Religion*; McDaniel, 'John M. E. McTaggart'.

[43] cf. Mander, *British Idealism*, chapters five and eleven.

We should also remember that multigenerationalists do not defend virtual futures *no matter what*. If all virtual futures are impossible, then we must seek meaning elsewhere. Active multigenerationalism insists that we should leave it to future people to determine, not only the design of the final, natal virtual utopia, but whether that utopia should be virtual at all. It is reasonable to hope that they will be able to judge these things better than we ever could.

Escapist: By contrast, I think we already *know* exactly where the future must go.

9.10 Escaping to a Digital Future

Escapist: Our symposium has proceeded on the assumption that imminent human extinction is unavoidable. I question that presumption. I don't deny that our planet and everything on it will be destroyed in two hundreds years. I also agree that, when that happens, humanity will become extinct. However, we could still enjoy an indefinite human future *before omega rays hit*, by escaping to a *digital world*.[44]

I argue that our overriding moral priority is to do everything we can to maximise the probability of a good digital future. My argument is simple.

1. *Overwhelming Value*: The good digital future is astronomically more valuable than any other possible future in our Post-Cataclysm world.
2. *Possibility*: The good digital future is possible.
3. *Impact*: Our actions can affect the probability of a good digital future. We can make it more (or less) likely.
4. *Normative Premise*: If one possible future is astronomically more valuable than all others, and if we can increase the probability of that future, then we should devote all our efforts to maximising that probability.
5. *Conclusion*: Therefore, we should devote all our efforts to making a good digital future as likely as possible.

I begin with definitions. A *digital future* is any world inhabited by vast numbers of digital beings. Digital beings can be uploaded copies of human minds, uploaded

---

[44] There is a huge literature on digital futures—and on the nature, agency, consciousness, and value of digital beings. Chalmers, *Reality+* is a very readable, up-to-date overview of philosophical issues. My thinking about digital futures is especially indebted to Agar, *Humanity's End*; Agar, 'On the Prudential Irrationality of Mind Uploading'. For general philosophical discussion, see Blackford and Broderick, *Intelligence Unbound*; Bostrom, *Superintelligence*; and Hauskeller, *Better Humans?*, pp. 115–132. Some philosophically rich fictional presentations are Bayley, *Soul of the Robot*; Egan, *Diaspora*; Egan, *Permutation City*; MacLeod, *The Star Faction*; Naam, *Nexus*; and Walton, *The Just City*. I have discussed digital futures briefly in Mulgan, 'How Should Utilitarians Think about the Future?' section 8: 'Moral Philosophy, Superintelligence, and the Singularity'. My discussion of digital futures is particularly quick. I only sketch one argument in favour of digital escapism, and then sketch some Post-Cataclysm responses. Anything approaching a full treatment would take us too far afield.

copies of non-human minds, artificial entities, or hybrids of the three. Digital beings exist as software programmes running on machines of some kind. I distinguish three broad classes of digital future:

1. *Good Digital Futures*: Digital beings (on average, on the whole) enjoy good lives that contain at least some of the things that makes human lives valuable, worthwhile, meaningful, or morally significant. Consider two examples. If pleasurable experience is what matters, then a good digital future is one where most digital beings enjoy pleasurable experiences. If complex self-organising pattern is what matters, then a good digital future is one where most digital beings instantiate valuable patterns.
2. *Bad Digital Futures*: Digital beings (on average, on the whole) have lives that contain some things that makes human lives dis-valuable. For instance, if painful experiences are bad, then a world where most digital beings experience unrelenting agony is a bad digital future.
3. *Neutral Digital Futures*: Digital beings exist. However, their lives are neither good nor bad. In principle, digital beings *could* have potentially valuable lives that just happen to hit the zero level between good and bad. However, a much more likely neutral digital future would contain digital lives that lack some necessary condition for mattering either way. For instance, if consciousness is a precondition for good or bad lives, and if no digital being is ever conscious, then the digital future is a valueless void.

I claim that a good digital future, where digital beings enjoy good lives, is possible; that we can make it more likely; and that we should devote ourselves to making *it* happen.

To defend my Overwhelming Value premise, I draw on Pre-Cataclysm discussion of digital futures. The speed and efficiency of digital processing mean that digital 'lives' are much faster and much less resource-intensive than biological human lives. Therefore, digital futures can contain many more beings with potentially valuable lives than any possible *non-digital future*.[45] Even if total well-being is not the only thing that matters, it must count for something. If one possible future contains astronomically more total well-being than another, then the former is astronomically more valuable—unless other things are *very* unequal. Therefore, *any* plausible axiology will judge a good digital future to be astronomically more valuable than any non-digital future.[46]

Before the Cataclysm, debates about overwhelming value were complicated by the fact that some possible non-digital futures also promised vast numbers of flourishing future lives. (Biological humans *could* have colonised the galaxy for billions of years.) After the Cataclysm, the case for my Overwhelming Value premise is

---

[45] Bostrom, *Superintelligence*, pp. 53–54.   [46] cf. Greaves, 'Population Axiology'.

much stronger. No non-digital future now offers more than a (comparative) handful of valuable lives. Only digital futures can possibly deliver anything more.

From our Post-Cataclysm perspective, the most striking thing about digital futures is that they can contain, not only vast numbers of valuable *lives*, but also vast numbers of *future generations*. In a non-digital future, the *subjective* human future can only last beyond two hundred years. We are limited to the number of generations we can fit into two centuries. By contrast, if our descendants are digital beings, then the human future could contain an enormous number of future generations. If digital beings think, act, and live a thousand times faster than biological humans, then a digital future could contain the equivalent of 200,000 years' worth of human generations. If digital beings are a million times faster than biological humans, then it could contain the equivalent of 200,000,000 human years.

As we saw in our First Debate, *the* central argument for Post-Cataclysm pessimism is that, without an indefinite human future, life is *now* meaningless. Digital technology reinstates that indefinite future. A digital future can deliver at least as many future (digital) generations as Pre-Cataclysm people anticipated in the non-digital, Cataclysm-free world they thought they inhabited. Therefore, every argument for Post-Cataclysm pessimism is, in effect, an argument for embracing the digital future.

I must now show both (a) that a good digital future is *possible*; and (b) that we can make it *more probable*. I deliberately adopt a very low standard of possibility. When I say that a good digital future is possible, I mean *epistemically possible*. For all anyone knows, this *might* happen. I concede that it is also true that, for all anyone knows, good digital futures *may* be technologically, metaphysically, or axiologically *impossible*. It may not be possible to perfect the necessary technology within two centuries. It may be metaphysically impossible for any digital being to be conscious.[47] The truth about ethics may make it impossible for digital lives to be either good or bad. However, nobody *knows* that these things are impossible. Digital futures are (epistemically) technologically possible. For all anyone knows, the necessary technology will arrive sometime in the next two hundred years. Good and bad digital futures are (epistemically) metaphysically and axiologically possible. For all anyone knows, digital beings *can* be conscious, sentient, self-aware, rational beings whose lives matter as much as ours do.[48] It is merely 'substratist' prejudice to *presume* that only carbon-based lives can possibly matter.

---

[47] On the possibility of digital consciousness, contrast Hofstadter, *I Am a Strange Loop* (who regards consciousness as simply a matter of patterns of information processing that machines could easily replicate) and Searle, *The Mystery of Consciousness* (who insists that consciousness is an emergent feature specific to our biology). A very good recent overview of that debate is Chalmers, *Reality+*, chapter fifteen.

[48] On digital agency, see Boden, 'Creativity and AI: A Contradiction in Terms?'

I do not presume atheism. Theists can embrace digital futures. For all anyone knows, digital beings can have souls, be made in the image of God, contemplate cosmic purpose, or do whatever else theists regard as important in human lives. Digital beings might even be better at these things—especially if the universe's purpose is not itself human-centred.

I adopt a similarly low threshold when I claim that we *could* increase the probability of a good digital future. *Any* increase in the *epistemic* probability of a good digital future will do—no matter how slight the increase or how low the resulting probability. If we can raise the epistemic probability of a good digital future from 0.01 per cent to 0.02 per cent, then that is more than sufficient for my purposes.

We *can* affect the probability of a good digital future. In the first place, whether or not there is *any* digital future depends on what present people do. If we *universally* abandon all computer technology forever, or opt for immediate voluntary extinction, then no digital future can arise. We *could* reduce the probability of a good digital future to zero. Conversely, if we devote more resources to exploring the necessary technology, then we make *some* digital future more likely. The more resources we devote to this, the more likely some digital future becomes.

Our behaviour also affects *what kind of* digital future is likely to emerge. We don't have to leave the value of the digital future to chance. We can influence the course of digital evolution. We can make it more probable that future digital beings will enjoy good lives—as opposed to value-less or bad lives. This is (overwhelmingly) our most important impact on the human future. The Pre-Cataclysm literature offered many strategies for enhancing the likelihood of friendly AIs. I don't claim that any particular strategy is likely to succeed. I only claim that, taken together, they do suggest that, if we put our minds to it, we could raise the epistemic probability of a good digital future.

Borrowing from the Pre-Cataclysm literature on moral uncertainty, I can also apply this expected-value-maximising approach to axiology itself.[49] I don't presuppose any particular axiology, such as total utilitarianism. I only claim that, on some credible axiologies, a good digital future is astronomically more valuable than any other possible future is *according to any other credible axiology*. Therefore, if we extend our expected value calculations to include uncertainty *about axiology*, then the expected value of any policy that raises the probability of a good digital future exceeds the expected value of any alternative policy *even if axiologies that deliver an astronomical difference in value are themselves very unlikely to be true.*

I can operate with such weak claims about possibility and probability because my *Normative Premise* is very ambitious. It claims that, when something astronomically valuable is at stake, and we can make it more probable, then this must be our overriding moral priority. Period. Analogous Pre-Cataclysm arguments

---

[49] On this approach to moral uncertainty, see, e.g., MacAskill, Bykvist, and Ord, *Moral Uncertainty*.

prioritised our ability to prevent imminent human extinction and our ability to influence the far distant human future. I bring these two Pre-Cataclysm themes together. We can *only* prevent imminent human extinction by creating a digital future. The only *far distant human (or post-human) futures* are digital. We can only influence the far future by striving for a good digital future.

Post-Cataclysm Pessimist: Following the analogy with Pre-Cataclysm debates, I have one immediate objection. Your argument tacitly assumes that a digital future is more likely to be good than bad—that the expected value of digital futures is positive. By contrast, if bad digital futures are more likely than good ones, then our over-riding imperative is to prevent *any* digital future.

This suggests a new argument for Post-Cataclysm pessimism. Even if Pre-Cataclysm optimism about the (non-digital) human future was reasonable, Post-Cataclysm *digital* optimism is not reasonable. There are simply too many digital unknowns. We cannot reasonably presume that non-neutral digital futures are probably good—nor that we can make this more likely.

Escapist: I have two replies. First, I don't need to claim that we can make a good digital future more likely than a bad one. Suppose we can raise the probability that a non-neutral digital future will be good, but we cannot raise it above 50 per cent. My Normative Premise still insists that we must devote all our energies to maximising the probability that the digital future, if there is one, will be good. That is sufficient for my central claim that we must put all our efforts into good digital futures. And this is still our best (only) way to make our own lives meaningful—by devoting them to a not-entirely-futile attempt to improve the human future.

Post-Cataclysm Pessimist: This reply is too quick. Consider this bleak inversion of your argument. The worst possible future is a *bad* digital future where vast numbers of digital beings endure awful lives. This future is astronomically *worse* than any non-digital future. It is possible. Digital futures *could* be unimaginably awful. We can reduce the probability of this future. Indeed, we can *guarantee* that it *doesn't* occur. If we embrace immediate human extinction, and eschew all technological innovation, then there will be no (bad) digital future. Therefore, according to your Normative Principle, we *must* embrace immediate human extinction—no matter how unlikely the bad digital future is, and no matter how good the next two centuries could otherwise have been. That sounds like the most pessimistic argument we've heard so far!

This new pessimist argument *doesn't* assume that bad digital futures are more likely than good ones. The crucial asymmetry concerns our ability to influence probabilities. We cannot guarantee a good digital future. Nor can we make it likely that, if there is some digital future, then it will be good. We can only fiddle with relative probabilities. By contrast, we *can* guarantee that a bad digital future never happens. Therefore, we should do so.

Escapist: I reject your alleged asymmetry. I did say earlier that 'we' could prevent any digital future by universally abandoning technology and/or embracing immediate extinction. However, I was exaggerating to make a point. This remote possibility is not action-guiding. In any *actual* situation where 'we' are collectively deciding what to do, it is not true that we could prevent a digital future. Some people will always pursue digital technology—no matter what the risks. If 'we' refers to the people who are interested in doing the right thing, then we cannot actually prevent a digital future. My argument still stands. As we cannot prevent a digital future, we must make it as good as possible.

Post-Cataclysm Pessimist: So you are saying, 'Humanity *should* embrace immediate extinction. Unfortunately, some misguided people won't. Therefore, the rest of us (the vast non-crazy majority) must devote ourselves to minimising the harm they unleash!' That is not a very philosophically satisfying response.

Escapist: I agree that this is not the best reply. I said earlier that I had two replies to your new pessimist argument. My second reply embraces digital optimism. If we are optimistic about the human future at all, then we can reasonably hope that, if there is a digital future, then we *can* make it more likely to be good than bad. We can have faith that, in cooperation with future people, we can ensure that the digital future is probably good. My argument then goes through. We must devote ourselves to maximising, not only the probability that a digital future *would* be good (if there is a digital future), but also the probability that there *will be* a (good) digital future. I admit that I don't have a compelling argument for this optimism. It involves a leap of faith in human (or post-human) technological ingenuity and moral imaginativeness. But my digital optimist faith is no less reasonable than the faith of presentists, multigenerationalists, or theists.

Post-Cataclysm Pessimist: Of course, pessimists reject all these leaps of faith. And yours does seem to be the riskiest!

Presentist: My response to your argument is to reject your Normative Premise.[50] Our ethical thinking should *not* be dominated by very unlikely events that would be astronomically valuable if they did occur. It is crazy to put all our eggs in the digital future basket. We have no over-riding imperative to maximise expected value, seek astronomical value, or obsess about the far distant human future. Any reason to promote the good is constrained by other, more urgent obligations. We should not sacrifice present needs for the mere *possibility* of some (far distant) digital future. Your argument is a *reductio ad absurdum* of Pre-Cataclysm

---

[50] This reply draws loosely on the many critiques of long-termism, expected value maximisation, and other elements in my escapist's philosophical toolkit. For defenses of longtermism, see Beckstead, *On the Overwhelming Importance of Shaping the Far Future*; MacAskill, *What We Owe the Future*. For critique, see C. Adams, Crary, and Gruen, 'Future-Oriented Effective Altruism: What's Wrong with Longtermism?'; Torres, 'Against Longtermism'.

long-termism. If *that's* where those arguments lead, then we should simply reject them.

Escapist: What is new in our Post-Cataclysm world is that, without digital futures, we cannot escape Post-Cataclysm pessimism. Without an indefinite human future, our lives are meaningless. We must hope that humanity faces an indefinite future. Digital futures are the only possible indefinite futures. Therefore, we must hope that humanity faces a digital future—and that it can be a good one.

Presentist: I reply that we *can* make our present lives meaningful without an indefinite human future. We don't need digital futures—anymore than we need fantasies about future moral transformations or about gods.

Theist: I have a different objection. I deny that your good digital future is the only possible astronomically valuable human future. Every possible world is astronomically valuable—because God (who is astronomically valuable if anything is) exists in all possible worlds. Setting aside divine value, astronomical value is still ubiquitous *within the world created by God*. God can people the universe with vast numbers of valuable lives in distant galaxies, the distant past, or the distant future. Even human futures cut short by the Cataclysm have astronomical value—because individual human encounters with divine reality are themselves infinitely valuable. So I think your appeal to 'astronomical value' begs the question against theism. Despite what you said earlier, you *do* presuppose atheism.

I would also offer a theist parody of your argument. It is possible that God will create astronomical value if we do X. (This is true for many values of X—given your very permissive account of 'possibility'.) Therefore, we should do X—no matter what.

Escapist: That is not a fair parallel to my argument. We have no reason to believe that doing X (for any arbitrary X) is more likely to produce astronomical value than doing not-X. *Your* parody argument is not action-guiding. By contrast, we can be confident that, say, thinking hard about how to make AI more friendly *will* raise the probability that the digital future is good rather than bad.

Presentist: I don't think we can be so confident about that. Every resource allocation decision has opportunity costs. If we divert significant resources to digital future research, then we may make a *bad* digital future *more* likely—perhaps by raising the probability of social collapse leading to even fewer ethical restrictions on technological development. The Pre-Cataclysm literature on precautionary principles teaches us that, if you set your threshold of possibility too low, then you get no useful guidance at all.[51]

---

[51] On the Precautionary Principle, e.g., Manson, 'Formulating the Precautionary Principle'; Bognar, 'Can the Maximin Principle Serve as a Basis for Climate Change Policy?'; Sandin, 'The Precautionary Principle and the Concept of Precaution'; Turner and Hartzell, 'The Lack of Clarity in the Precautionary Principle'.

Multigenerationalist: I agree that we should consider digital futures—just as we should consider virtual futures (both solitary and interpersonal) and non-virtual futures. However, I agree with the Presentist that we should not be obsessed with digital futures. As I argued in my lecture on consequentialist procreative ethics, the most plausible forms of consequentialism abandon the act consequentialist obsession with maximising expected value (Section 6.3.4). While I see the internal logic of the Escapist's argument, I agree with the Presentist that it *is* crazy to focus all our energy on things that will almost certainly never happen. If the digital future is *likely*, and if it could be *good*, then perhaps it *is* the best bet for multigenerationalism. But we cannot make that call yet. We have no idea whether digital beings can be conscious or whether digital lives can be valuable at all. The good digital future may be a mirage. We must trust future people to make that call *better than we could make it ourselves*.

You say we should maximise the likelihood of a *good* digital future. I reply that we should launch a multigenerational project that aims, not at a good digital future, but at the best feasible future. If a *good* digital future is achievable at reasonable cost and reasonable risk, then my project will produce it. Otherwise, it won't.

Escapist: That is not sufficient. My Normative Premise demands that we aim *directly and immediately* at a *good* digital future—even if we are very likely to fail, and even if aiming at some other excellent future would certainly succeed.

Multigenerationalist: I reply that *later generations* in our multigenerational project might do just that. Either future moral transformation leads in a digital direction, or it doesn't. If it does, then later generations might single-mindedly pursue the best digital future. If it doesn't, then why should we *impose* a controversial normative premise that won't stand the test of time?

Escapist: You assume that we can leave things to later generations. But I doubt that we can. Time is critical. We face the threat of a bad digital future—and we must respond immediately. Our best option—from *my* perspective—is to launch a multigenerational project that *is* obsessed with promoting a *digital* future.

Multigenerationalist: I disagree. I think it would take enormous confidence *in our own ethical judgement* to close off future options in that way. I also doubt that your alternative multigenerational project is *permissible*—precisely because it ties our descendants into a very restricted agenda. We cannot realise a good digital future in our own lifetimes. Any escapist project must be intergenerational. (Indeed, unless all digital beings were copies of already existing humans, even a digital future that we initiated immediately would still involve intergenerational cooperation *with future digital beings*.) However, as I argued at length in my procreative ethics lectures, intergenerational projects are only permissible if we treat future people as ends in themselves. And that, in turn, means that we must invite them to voluntarily cooperate with our intergenerational agenda (Sections 5.2.1,

5.2.5, and 5.2.7). If we leave future people free to choose, then most of them will not sign up for a single-minded digital project that is likely to fail. That leaves two options—neither of which is palatable. Either we impose our agenda on our descendants, or we do not. If we do, then we fail to treat them as cooperative partners, and our creation of them is impermissible under any plausible Post-Cataclysm procreative permissibility principle. On the other hand, if we do *not* impose our agenda, then our project is likely to fail. We cannot expect our descendants to share our obsession with digital futures. If they are free to choose, most of them will opt for other non-digital projects that are more likely to actually succeed. But we cannot justify procreation by citing some cooperative project that is almost certain to fail. Therefore, the constraints on procreative permissibility I explored in my lectures rule out any *multigenerational* obsession with digital escape.

Escapist: I would reply by rejecting your procreative principles. I think we should maximise future well-being—and doing so is a sufficient justification to offer to anyone.

Conclusion

Lessons from an Ending World

I promised that adopting the perspective of my slowly ending world would shed new light on current philosophical debates by drawing out the implicit significance of the indefinite human future. Have I delivered?

Imminent human extinction raises new pessimist worries, especially by foregrounding the plight of the last generation. We saw how different philosophical arguments for pessimism highlight different ways we rely on there being *indefinitely* many future people. Imminent extinction would also unsettle debates between theism and atheism—breathing new life into familiar arguments on both sides and motivating new worldviews where God's purposes do not include the human future.

I have argued that, in a slowly ending world, terminal intergenerational projects come into their own—especially radical, ambitious attempts to reorient inherited traditions and values that currently presuppose an indefinite human future. This ambitious reorientation is feasible. It is also essential—especially given plausible constraints on procreative permissibility. Moral imaginativeness and moral transformation come to the fore in a slowly ending world, where they enable the last humans to pursue new utopian projects that differ in exciting ways from earlier utopias that were less ambitious because they were built to last.

Contemporary procreative ethics foregrounds the interests of potential parents and their possible future children—either privileging one or the other, or balancing the two. Human extinction remains firmly in the background. I argued that the human future nonetheless plays a crucial role in our justifications for both procreative permissibility and procreative liberty. Without an indefinite future, it is much harder to defeat both anti-natalism and pro-natalism—to steer a middle course between prohibition and procreative obligation.

Human extinction and virtual reality are topical issues that are usually treated separately. I drew connections between them, arguing that imminent human extinction drives the search for alternatives to our familiar empirical-reality-based, future-presuming values and projects. Without an indefinite future, people may turn either inward to their own experiences, or outward to sources of meaning that transcend the physical universe entirely. Finally, I used the prospect of escape into subjectively indefinite digital futures to offer a new perspective on familiar debates about the sanity of relentlessly maximising expected (far distant) future well-being.

So what? Why should *we* care about the possible musings of imaginary people living in a distant possible world? What does the slowly ending world say *to us*?

Uncovering the unexpected significance of the indefinite human future is interesting in itself. It is good to know what we take for granted when thinking about meaning in life, the existence of God, procreative permissibility, the nature of the just society, and the desirability of experience machines. When I started writing this book, I didn't expect anything in particular beyond some interesting new perspectives on familiar philosophical debates. As I have thought more about my slowing ending world, however, I do think an important underlying lesson has emerged. This concerns the connection between present procreative permissibility and future moral transformation. The central theme of my series of lectures on procreative ethics is that, if we faced imminent extinction, then we could only permissibly create new people if we were reasonably confident that they would have sufficient imaginativeness and flexibility to re-imagine the ethical and religious traditions we bequeath them *in ways that enable those future-dependent traditions to still make life meaningful even at humanity's end*.

We do not (so far as we know) face unavoidable imminent extinction. But we do face an uncertain future. We don't know that our descendants will soon face immediate extinction. But we do know that they will inhabit possible futures that are radically different from anything humanity has experienced before. And we do know that some of our descendants *will* face immediate extinction. Cultivating future moral imaginativeness is as urgent for us as it is for my imaginary Post-Cataclysm philosophers. We too must justify ourselves to our own descendants who must live at humanity's end. We too can only permissibly create future people if we enable them to radically reimagine the values that we know, even as we pass them on, are already no longer fit for purpose.

Bibliography

Adams, C., Crary, A., and Gruen, L., 2023, 'Future-Oriented Effective Altruism: What's Wrong with Longtermism?' in *The Good It Promises, the Harm It Does*, Carol J. Adams, Alice Crary, and Lori Gruen (eds), Oxford University Press, pp. 265–269.
Adams, M., 1999, *Horrendous Evils and the Goodness of God*, Cornell University Press.
Adams, R. M., 1972, 'Must God Create the Best?' *Philosophical Review* 81, 317–332.
Adams, R. M., 1994, *Leibniz: Determinist, Theist, Idealist*, Oxford University Press.
Adams, R. M., 1995, 'Moral Faith', *Journal of Philosophy* 92, pp. 75–95.
Adams, R. M., 1999, *Finite and Infinite Goods*, Oxford University Press.
Agar, N., 1995, 'Valuing Species and Valuing Individuals', *Environmental Ethics* 17, pp. 397–415.
Agar, N., 2010, *Humanity's End: Why We Should Reject Radical Enhancement*, MIT Press.
Agar, N., 2014, 'On the Prudential Irrationality of Mind Uploading', in *Intelligence Unbound: The Future of Uploaded and Machine Minds*, R. Blackford and D. Broderick (eds), Wiley-Blackwell, pp. 146–160.
Arnhart, L., 2005, *Darwinian Conservatism*, Imprint Academic.
Arrhenius, G., 2004, 'The Paradoxes of Future Generations and Normative Theory', in *The Repugnant Conclusion*, T. Tännsjö and J. Ryberg (eds), Springer, pp. 201–218.
Arrhenius, G., Bykvist, K., Campbell, T., and Finneron-Burns, E. (eds), 2022, *The Oxford Handbook of Population Ethics*, Oxford University Press.
Arrhenius, G., Ryberg, J., and Tännsjö, T., 2022, 'The Repugnant Conclusion', *The Stanford Encyclopedia of Philosophy*.
Audi, R., 2018, 'Creativity, Imagination, and Intellectual Virtue', in *Creativity and Philosophy*, B. Gaut and M. Kieran (eds), Routledge, pp. 25–41.
Bader, R. M., and Meadowcroft, J. (eds), 2011, *The Cambridge Companion to Nozick's Anarchy, State, and Utopia*, Cambridge University Press.
Baehr, J., 2018, 'Intellectual Creativity', in *Creativity and Philosophy*, B. Gaut and M. Kieran (eds), Routledge, pp. 42–59.
Bailey, T., and Gentile, V., 2014, *Rawls and Religion*, Columbia University Press.
Baker, J., 2008, 'Vulnerabilities of Morality', *Canadian Journal of Philosophy* 28, pp. 141–159.
Barry, B., 1975, 'Review of *Anarchy, State, and Utopia*', *Political Theory* 3, pp. 331–336.
Bayley, B., 2001, *Soul of the Robot*, Borgo Press.
Beach, E. A., 2008, 'The Postulate of Immortality in Kant: To What Extent Is It Culturally Conditioned?' *Philosophy East and West* 58(4), pp. 492–523.
Beckstead, N., 2013, *On the Overwhelming Importance of Shaping the Far Future*, Rutgers PhD thesis.
Beiser, F. C., 2016, *Weltschmerz: Pessimism in German Philosophy, 1860–1900*, Oxford University Press.
Benatar, D., 2006, *Better Never to Have Been*, Oxford University Press.
Benatar, D., 2017, *The Human Predicament: A Candid Guide to Life's Biggest Questions*, Oxford University Press.
Bishop, J., 2007, *Believing by Faith*, Oxford University Press.

Bishop, J., and Perszyk, K., 2011, 'The Normatively Relativized Logical Argument from Evil', *International Journal for Philosophy of Religion* 70, pp. 109–126.

Blackford, R., and Broderick, D. (eds), 2014, *Intelligence Unbound: The Future of Uploaded and Machine Minds*, Wiley-Blackwell.

Boden, M., 2004, *The Creative Mind*, 2nd edition, Routledge.

Boden, M., 2014, 'Creativity and AI: A Contradiction in Terms?' in *The Philosophy of Creativity: New Essays*, E. S. Paul and S. B. Kaufman (eds), Oxford University Press, pp. 224–244.

Bognar, G., 2011, 'Can the Maximin Principle Serve as a Basis for Climate Change Policy?' *The Monist* 94, pp. 329–348.

Boonin, D., 2019, *Dead Wrong: The Ethics of Posthumous Harm*, Oxford University Press.

Bosanquet, B., 1923, *The Value and Destiny of the Individual*, Macmillan.

Bostrom, N., 2013, 'Existential Risk as a Global Priority', *Global Policy* 4, pp. 15–31.

Bostrom, N., 2014, *Superintelligence: Paths, Dangers, Strategies*, Oxford University Press.

Bostrom, N., and Cirkovic, M. (eds), 2008, *Global Catastrophic Risks*, Oxford University Press.

Boyd, R., 1988, 'How to Be a Moral Realist', in *Essays in Moral Realism*, G. Sayre-McCord (ed.), Cornell University Press, pp. 181–228.

Bradford, G., 2015, *Achievement*, Oxford University Press.

Bradley, B., 2001, 'The Value of Endangered Species', *The Journal of Value Inquiry* 45, pp. 43–58.

Bradley, B., 2014, 'Objective Theories of Well-Being', in *The Cambridge Companion to Utilitarianism*, B. Eggleston and D. E. Miller (eds), Cambridge University Press, pp. 199–215.

Brady, E., 2011, 'Adam Smith's "Sympathetic Imagination" and the Aesthetic Appreciation of Environment', *Journal of Scottish Philosophy* 9, pp. 95–109.

Brandstedt, E., 2021, 'The Just Savings Principle', in *The Oxford Handbook of Intergenerational Ethics*, S. M. Gardiner (ed.), Oxford University Press.

Brennan, A. and Lo, Y.-S., 2010, *Understanding Environmental Philosophy*, Acumen.

Brennan, A., and Lo, Y.-S., 2021, 'Environmental Ethics', *The Stanford Encyclopedia of Philosophy*.

Broadie, S., 2013, 'Agency and Determinism in *A Metaphysics for Freedom*', *Inquiry* 56, pp. 571–582.

Broome, J., 2004, *Weighing Lives*, Oxford University Press.

Bruckner, D., 2021, 'Human and Animal Well-Being', *Pacific Philosophical Quarterly* 102, pp. 393–412.

Buchanan, A., and Powell, R., 2018, *The Evolution of Moral Progress: A Biocultural Theory*, Oxford University Press.

Buckareff, A. A., and Nagasawa, Y. (eds), 2016, *Alternative Concepts of God: Essays on the Metaphysics of the Divine*, Oxford University Press.

Burley, M., 2020, *A Radical Pluralist Philosophy of Religion: Cross-Cultural, Multireligious, Interdisciplinary*, Bloomsbury Academic.

Callicott, J. B., 2013, *Thinking Like a Planet*, Oxford University Press.

Caroti, S., 2011, *The Generation Starship in Science Fiction: A Critical History 1934–2001*, McFarland and Co.

Chalmers, D., 2022, *Reality+: Virtual Worlds and the Problems of Philosophy*, Penguin.

Chang, R. (ed.), 1997, *Incommensurability, Incomparability, and Practical Reason*, Harvard University Press.

Chappell, R., 2017, 'Rethinking the Asymmetry', *Canadian Journal of Philosophy* 47, pp. 167–177.

Chignell, A., 2018, 'Belief, Ethics of', *The Stanford Encyclopedia of Philosophy*.

Clark, S. R. L., 2016, *Plotinus: Myth, Metaphor, and Philosophical Practice*, University of Chicago Press.
Clarke, R., Capes, C., and Swenson, P., 2021, 'Incompatibilist (Nondeterministic) Theories of Free Will', *The Stanford Encyclopedia of Philosophy*.
Cogburn, J., and Silcox, M., 2014, 'Against Brain-in-a-Vatism: On the Value of Virtual Reality', *Philosophy and Technology* 27, pp. 561–579.
Collins, R., 2003, 'Evidence for Fine-Tuning', in *God and Design*, N. Manson (ed.), Routledge, pp. 178–199.
Comte, A., 1875–7, *System of Positive Polity*, Longmans, Green and Co.
Cooper, J. M., 2012, *Pursuits of Wisdom: Six Ways of Life in Ancient Philosophy from Socrates to Plotinus*, Princeton University Press.
Cowen, T., and Parfit, D., 1992, 'Against the Social Discount Rate', in *Justice between Age Groups and Generations*, P. Laslett and J. Fishkin (eds), Yale University Press, pp. 144–161.
Crisp, R., 2006, 'Hedonism Reconsidered', *Philosophy and Phenomenological Research* 73, pp. 619–645.
Crisp, R., 2021, 'Well-Being', *The Stanford Encyclopaedia of Philosophy*.
Crisp, R., 2023, 'Pessimism about the Future', *Midwest Studies in Philosophy* 46, pp. 373–385.
Crowe, M., 2003, *The Extraterrestrial Life Debate 1750–1900: The Idea of a Plurality of Worlds from Kant to Lowell*, Dover Publications.
Darwall, S., 2009, *The Second-Person Standpoint*, Harvard University Press.
De Brigard, F., 2010, 'If You Like It, Does It Matter If It's Real?' *Philosophical Psychology* 23, pp. 43–57.
Dick, S., 1982, *Plurality of Worlds: The Origins of Extra-Terrestrial Life Debate from Democritus to Kant*, Cambridge University Press.
Dienstag, J. F., 2006, *Pessimism: Philosophy, Ethic, Spirit*, Princeton University Press.
Diller, J., and Kasher, A., 2013, *Models of God and Alternative Ultimate Realities*, Springer.
Dombrowski, D., 2001, *Rawls and Religion: The Case for Political Liberalism*, State University of New York Press.
Dougherty, T., 2014, *The Problem of Animal Pain: A Theodicy for All Creatures Great and Small*, Palgrave Macmillan.
Dreyfus, H. L., 2009, 'Comments on Jonathan Lear's *Radical Hope*', *Philosophical Studies* 144, pp. 63–70.
Driver, J., 2014, 'Global Utilitarianism', in *The Cambridge Companion to Utilitarianism*, B. Eggleston and D. E. Miller (eds), Cambridge University Press, pp. 150–159.
Ebenreck, S., 1996, 'Opening Pandora's Box: Imagination's Role in Environmental Ethics', *Environmental Ethics* 18, pp. 3–18.
Egan, G., 2008, *Diaspora*, Gollancz.
Egan, G., 2008, *Permutation City*, Gollancz.
Everitt, N., 2004, *The Non-Existence of God*, Routledge.
Feldman, F., 2004, *Pleasure and the Good Life: Concerning the Nature, Varieties, and Plausibility of Hedonism*, Oxford University Press.
Feldman, F., 2011, 'What We Learn from the Experience Machine', in *The Cambridge Companion to Nozick's* Anarchy, State, and Utopia, R. M. Bader and J. Meadowcroft (eds), Cambridge University Press, pp. 59–86.
Fischer, J., Kane, R., Pereboom, D., and Vargas, M., 2007, *Four Views on Free Will*, Blackwell.
Frankfurt, H., 2013, 'How the Afterlife Matters', in *Death and the Afterlife*, S. Scheffler (ed.), Oxford University Press, pp. 131–142.

Freeman, S., 2007, *Rawls*, Routledge.
Gasser, G., and Kittle, S. (eds), 2022, *Personal and A-Personal Aspects of the Divine*, Routledge.
Gaut, B., 2003, 'Creativity and Imagination', in *The Creation of Art*, B. Gaut and P. Livingston (eds), Cambridge University Press, pp. 148–173.
Gaut, B., 2010, 'The Philosophy of Creativity', *Philosophy Compass* 5, pp. 1034–1046.
Gaut, B., 2014, 'Educating for Creativity', in *The Philosophy of Creativity: New Essays*, E. S. Paul and S. B. Kaufman (eds), Oxford University Press, pp. 265–287.
Goodwin, B., 1992, *Justice by Lottery*, University of Chicago Press.
Gosseries, A., 2001, 'What Do We Owe the Next Generation(s)?' *Loyola of Los Angeles Law Review* 35, pp. 293–354.
Grant, J., 2012, 'The Value of Imaginativeness', *Australasian Journal of Philosophy* 90, pp. 275–289.
Greaves, H., 2017, 'Population Axiology', *Philosophy Compass* 12.
Griffin, J., 1986, *Well-Being*, Oxford University Press.
Gustafson, J., 1981 and 1984, *Ethics from a Theocentric Perspective*, two volumes, University of Chicago Press.
Guyer, P., 2006, *Kant*, Routledge.
Hailwood, S. A., 1996, *Exploring Nozick: Beyond Anarchy, State, and Utopia*, Avebury.
Hare, J., 1996, *The Moral Gap*, Oxford University Press.
Hargrave, T., 2009, 'Moral Imagination, Collective Action, and the Achievement of Moral Outcomes', *Business Ethics Quarterly* 19, pp. 87–104.
Harman, E., 2004, 'Can We Harm and Benefit in Creating?' *Philosophical Perspectives* 18, pp. 89–113.
Harman, E., 2009, 'Harming as Causing Harm', in *Harming Future Persons: Ethics, Genetics and the Nonidentity Problem*, M. Roberts and D. Wasserman (eds), Springer, pp. 137–154.
Harrison, V., 2022, *Eastern Philosophy of Religion*, Cambridge University Press.
Hauskeller, M., 2013, *Better Humans? Understanding the Enhancement Project*, Acumen.
Heathwood, C., 2014, 'Subjective Theories of Well-Being', in *The Cambridge Companion to Utilitarianism*, B. Eggleston and D. E. Miller (eds), Cambridge University Press, pp. 180–198.
Hebblethwaite, B., 2005, *In Defence of Christianity*, Oxford University Press.
Hewitt, S., 2010, 'What Do our Intuitions about the Experience Machine Really Tell Us about Hedonism?' *Philosophical Studies* 151, pp. 331–349.
Hicks, D. J., 2015, 'On Okin's Critique of Libertarianism', *Canadian Journal of Philosophy* 45, pp. 37–57.
Hill, T. H., 2013, 'Stability, a Sense of Justice, and Self-Respect', in *A Companion to Rawls*, J. Mandle and D. A. Reidy (eds), Wiley-Blackwell, pp. 200–215.
Hofstadter, D., 2007, *I Am a Strange Loop*, Basic Books.
Holtug, N., 2012, *Persons, Interests, and Justice*, Oxford University Press.
Hooker, B., 1994, 'Rule-Consequentialism, Incoherence, Fairness', *Proceedings of the Aristotelian Society* 95, pp. 19–35.
Hooker, B., 2000, *Ideal Code, Real World*, Oxford University Press.
Hooker, B., 2003, Review of Mulgan, T., *The Demands of Consequentialism*, *Philosophy* 78, pp. 289–307.
Hooker, B., 2014, 'Acts or Rules? The Fine Tuning of Utilitarianism', in *God, the Good, and Utilitarianism: Perspectives on Peter Singer*, J. Perry (ed.), Cambridge University Press, pp. 125–138.

Hooker, B., 2020, 'The Role(s) of Rules in Consequentialist Ethics', in *Oxford Handbook of Consequentialism*, D. Portmore (ed.), Oxford University Press, pp. 441–462.
Hooker, B., 2023, 'Rule Consequentialism', *The Stanford Encyclopedia of Philosophy*.
Irwin, T., 2009, *The Development of Ethics*, Oxford University Press.
Jackson, F., 1999, *From Metaphysics to Ethics*, Oxford University Press.
James, P. D., 2006, *The Children of Men*, Random House.
Johnson, M., 1993, *Moral Imagination*, University of Chicago Press.
Johnston, M., 2010, *Surviving Death*, Princeton University Press.
Johnston, M., 2014, 'Is Life a Ponzi Scheme?' *Boston Review*, 2 January 2014.
Jonas, H., 1984, *The Imperative of Responsibility*, University of Chicago Press, 1984.
Kaczmarek, P., 2017, 'How Much Is Rule-Consequentialism Really Willing to Give Up to Save the Future of Humanity?' *Utilitas* 29, pp. 239–249.
Kavka, G., 1982, 'The Paradox of Future Individuals', *Philosophy and Public Affairs* 11, pp. 93–112.
Kawall, J., 1999, 'The Experience Machine and Mental State Theories of Well-Being', *The Journal of Value Inquiry* 33, pp. 381–387.
Kekes, J., 2006, *The Enlargement of Life: Moral Imagination at Work*, Cornell University Press.
Keller, S., 2014, 'Posthumous Harm', in *The Cambridge Companion to Life and Death*, S. Luper (ed.), Cambridge University Press, pp. 181–197.
Kieran, M., 2014, 'Creativity as a Virtue of Character', in *The Philosophy of Creativity: New Essays*, E. S. Paul and S. B. Kaufman (eds), Oxford University Press, pp. 125–144.
King, R., 1999, 'Narrative, Imagination, and the Search for Intelligibility in Environmental Ethics', *Ethics and the Environment* 4, pp. 23–38.
Kitcher, P., 2011, *The Ethical Project*, Harvard University Press.
Kraut, R., 2018, *The Quality of Life: Aristotle Revised*, Oxford University Press.
Kronfeldner, M., 2009, 'Creativity Naturalized', *Philosophical Quarterly* 59, pp. 577–592.
Lear, J., 2008, *Radical Hope: Ethics in the Face of Cultural Devastation*, Harvard University Press.
Lear, J., 2009, 'Response to Hubert Dreyfus and Nancy Sherman', *Philosophical Studies* 144, pp. 81–93.
Lear, J., 2023, *Imagining the End: Mourning and the Ethical Life*, Harvard University Press.
Leibniz, 1991, *On the Ultimate Origination of Things*, Hackett.
Lenman, J., 2000, 'Consequentialism and Cluelessness', *Philosophy and Public Affairs* 29, pp. 342–370.
Leopold, A., 1949, *A Sand County Almanac*, Oxford University Press.
Leslie, J., 1980, *Value and Existence*, Blackwell.
Leslie, J., 1989, *Universes*, Routledge.
Leslie, J., 2001, *Infinite Minds*, Oxford University Press.
Leslie, J., 2007, *Immortality Defended*, Blackwell.
Levy, N., 2013, 'Are We Agents At All? Helen Steward's Agency Incompatibilism', *Inquiry* 56, pp. 1–14.
Lewis, D. K., 1986, *On the Plurality of Worlds*, Blackwell.
Linderman, F. B., 1962, *Plenty-Coups: Chief of the Crows*, University of Nebraska Press.
Locke, J., *Two Treatises on Government*, originally published 1690.
Lowie, R. H., 1983, *The Crow Indians*, Lincoln: University of Nebraska Press.
Luper, S., 2012, 'Retroactive Harms and Wrongs', in *The Oxford Handbook of Philosophy of Death*, B. Bradley, F. Feldman, and J. Johansson (eds), Oxford University Press, pp. 317–334.

Luper, S., 2021, 'Death', *The Stanford Encyclopedia of Philosophy*.
MacAskill, W., 2022, *What We Owe the Future: The Million-Year View*, Oneworld.
MacAskill, W., Bykvist, K., and Ord, T., 2020, *Moral Uncertainty*, Oxford University Press.
Mack, E., 2022, 'Robert Nozick's Political Philosophy', *The Stanford Encyclopedia of Philosophy*.
Macklin, R., 1999, *Against Relativity: Cultural Diversity and the Search for Ethical Universals*, Oxford University Press.
MacLeod, K., 1996, *The Star Faction*, Orbit.
Mander, W. J., 2011, *British Idealism: A History*, Oxford University Press.
Mander, W. J., 2016, *Idealist Ethics*, Oxford University Press.
Manson, N., 2002, 'Formulating the Precautionary Principle', *Environmental Ethics* 24, 263–274.
Martin, M., 2006, 'Moral Creativity', *International Journal of Applied Philosophy* 20, pp. 55–66.
Mawson, T. J., 2013, 'Recent Work on the Meaning of Life and Philosophy of Religion', *Philosophy Compass* 8, pp. 1138–1146.
Mawson, T. J., 2016, *God and the Meaning of Life*, Bloomsbury.
McClure, K. M., 1996, *Judging Rights: Lockean Politics and the Limits of Consent*, Cornell University Press.
McDaniel, K., 2020, 'John M. E. McTaggart', *The Stanford Encyclopedia of Philosophy*.
McGrew, T., McGrew, L., and Vestrup, E., 2001, 'Probabilities and the Fine-Tuning Argument: A Sceptical View', *Mind* 110, pp. 1027–1037.
McKenna, M., and Coates, D. J., 2021, 'Compatibilism', *The Stanford Encyclopedia of Philosophy*.
McKim, R., 2008, 'On Religious Ambiguity', *Religious Studies* 44, pp. 373–392.
McMahan, J., 2001, *The Ethics of Killing*, Oxford University Press.
McMahan, J., 2013, 'Causing People to Exist and Saving People's Lives', *Journal of Ethics* 17, pp. 5–35.
McTaggart, J., 1906, *Some Dogmas of Religion*, E. Arnold.
Mellor, H., 2003, 'Too Many Universes', in *God and Design*, N., Manson (ed.), Routledge, pp. 221–229.
Metz, T., 2013, *Meaning in Life: An Analytic Study*, Oxford University Press.
Metz, T., 2017, 'Meaning in Life', in *The Palgrave Handbook of the Afterlife*, Y. Nagasawa and B. Matheson (eds), Palgrave Macmillan, pp. 353–370.
Metz, T., 2019, *God, Soul and the Meaning of Life*, Cambridge University Press.
Metz, T., 2021, 'The Meaning of Life', *The Stanford Encyclopedia of Philosophy*.
Mill, J. S., 1969, 'Auguste Comte and Positivism', in *The Collected Works of J. S. Mill*, vol. 10, J. M. Robson (ed.), University of Toronto Press, pp. 261–368.
Mill, J. S., 1977, *On Liberty*, in *The Collected Works of J. S. Mill*, vol. 18, J. M. Robson (ed.), University of Toronto Press, pp. 213–310.
Moody-Adams, M., 1999, 'The Idea of Moral Progress', *Metaphilosophy* 30, pp. 168–185.
Moore, A., 2013, 'Hedonism', *The Stanford Encyclopedia of Philosophy*.
Mulgan, T., 1994, 'Rule Consequentialism and Famine', *Analysis* 54, pp. 187–192.
Mulgan, T., 2001, *The Demands of Consequentialism*, Oxford University Press.
Mulgan, T., 2004, 'Two Parfit Puzzles', in *The Repugnant Conclusion. Essays on Population Ethics*, J. Ryberg and R. Tannsjo (eds), Kluwer Academic Publishers, pp. 23–45.
Mulgan, T., 2006, *Future People*, Oxford University Press.
Mulgan, T., 2009, 'Rule Consequentialism and Non-Identity', in *Harming Future Persons*, M. Roberts and D. Wasserman (eds), Springer, pp. 115–134.

Mulgan, T., 2011, 'Review of Johnston *Surviving Death*', *Analysis* 71, pp. 755–765.
Mulgan, T., 2011, *Ethics for a Broken World: Reimagining Philosophy after Catastrophe*, Acumen.
Mulgan, T., 2014, 'Ethics for Possible Futures', *Proceedings of the Aristotelian Society* 114, pp. 57–73.
Mulgan, T., 2015, 'Utilitarianism for a Broken World', *Utilitas* 27, pp. 92–114.
Mulgan, T., 2015, *Purpose in the Universe: The Moral and Metaphysical Case for Ananthropocentric Purposivism*, Oxford University Press.
Mulgan, T., 2016, 'Can the Best Possible World Contain Death?' in *Death and Anti-Death*, C. Tandy (ed.), Ria University Press, pp. 113–168.
Mulgan, T., 2017, 'Beyond Theism and Atheism: Axiarchism, Platonism, and Ananthropocentric Purposivism', *Philosophy Compass* 12.
Mulgan, T., 2017, 'How Should Utilitarians Think about the Future?' *Canadian Journal of Philosophy* 47, pp. 290–312.
Mulgan, T., 2017, 'The Moral Significance of Extra-Terrestrial Life', *Aeon*, published online 5 December 2017. https://aeon.co/essays/how-the-discovery-of-extraterrestrial-life-would-change-morality
Mulgan, T., 2018, 'Answering to Future People', *The Journal of Applied Philosophy* 35, pp. 532–548.
Mulgan, T., 2018, 'Moral Imaginativeness, Moral Creativity and Possible Futures', in *Creativity and Philosophy*, B. Gaut and M. Kieran (eds), Routledge, pp. 350–368.
Mulgan, T., 2019, 'Alternatives to Benevolent Theism: Ananthropocentric Theism and Axiarchism', in *New Directions in Philosophy of Religion*, P. Draper (ed.), Routledge, pp. 129–145.
Mulgan, T., 2019, 'Corporate Agency and Possible Futures', *Journal of Business Ethics* 154, pp. 901–916.
Mulgan, T., 2020, 'What Exactly Is Wrong with Human Extinction?' in *Proceedings of the International Society for Utilitarian Studies*, C. Schmidt-Petri and M. Schefczyk (eds), KIT Scientific Publishing, pp. 267–283.
Mulgan, T., 2020, *Utilitarianism*, Cambridge University Press.
Mulgan, T., 2021, 'Consequentialism as an Intergenerational Ethics', in *The Oxford Handbook of Intergenerational Ethics*, S. Gardiner (ed.), Oxford University Press.
Mulgan, T., 2022, 'Could We Worship a Non-Human-Centred Impersonal Cosmic Purpose?' in *Personal and A-Personal Aspects of the Divine*, G. Gasser and S. Kittle (eds), Routledge, pp. 285–302.
Mulgan, T., 2022, 'From Brad to Worse: Rule Consequentialism and Undesirable Futures', *Ratio* 35, pp. 275–288.
Mulgan, T., 2022, 'Moral Philosophy, Superintelligence, and the Singularity', draft manuscript.
Murphy, C., 2010, *A Moral Theory of Political Reconciliation*, Cambridge University Press.
Murphy, M., 2019, 'Theological Voluntarism', *The Stanford Encyclopedia of Philosophy*.
Naam, R., 2012, *Nexus*, Axon.
Nagel, T., 2012, *Mind and Cosmos*, Oxford University Press.
Nozick, R., 1974, *Anarchy, State, and Utopia*, Basic Books.
Nozick, R., 1981, *Philosophical Explanations*, Oxford University Press.
Nozick, R., 1989, *The Examined Life: Philosophical Meditations*, Simon and Shuster.
Nozick, R., 2000, 'The Pursuit of Happiness', *Forbes*, 2 October 2000.
Nozick, R., 2001, *Invariances: The Structure of the Objective World*, Harvard University Press.
Nussbaum, M., 1986, *The Fragility of Goodness: Luck and Ethics in Greek Tragedy and Philosophy*, Cambridge University Press.

O'Connor, T., and Franklin, C., 2021, 'Free Will', *The Stanford Encyclopedia of Philosophy*.
Okin, S. M., 1989, *Justice, Gender, and the Family*, Basic Books.
Oppy, G., 2004, 'Arguments from Moral Evil', *International Journal for Philosophy of Religion* 56, pp. 59–87.
Ord, T., 2020, *The Precipice: Existential Risk and the Future of Humanity*, Oxford University Press.
Parfit, D., 1984, *Reasons and Persons*, Oxford University Press.
Parfit, D., 1997, 'Equality and Priority', *Ratio* 10, pp. 202–221.
Parfit, D., 2011/2017, *On What Matters*, Oxford University Press.
Parker Pearson, M., 2023, *Stonehenge: A Brief History*, Bloomsbury Academic.
Paul, E. S., and Kaufman, S. B., 2014, 'Introducing *The Philosophy of Creativity*', in *The Philosophy of Creativity: New Essays*, E. S. Paul and S. B. Kaufman (eds), Oxford University Press, pp. 3–14.
Pettit, P., and Smith, M., 2000, 'Global Consequentialism', in *Morality, Rules, and Consequences: A Critical Reader*, B. Hooker, E. Mason, and D. E. Miller (eds), Edinburgh University Press, pp. 121–133.
Plantinga, A., 2000, *Warranted Christian Belief*, Oxford University Press.
Rawls, J., 1971, *A Theory of Justice*, Harvard University Press.
Rawls, J., 1993, *Political Liberalism*, expanded edition, Columbia University Press.
Rawls, J., 1999, *The Law of Peoples*, Harvard University Press.
Rawls, J., 2001, *Justice as Fairness: A Restatement*, Harvard University Press.
Raz, J., 1986, *The Morality of Freedom*, Oxford University Press.
Raz, J., 1999, 'Incommensurability and Agency', in *Engaging Reason: On the Theory of Value and Action*, Oxford University Press, pp. 46–66.
Roberts, A., 2005, *The History of Science Fiction*, Palgrave Macmillan.
Roberts, M. A., 2002, 'A New Way of Doing the Best We Can: Person-Based Consequentialism and the Equality Problem', *Ethics* 112, pp. 315–350.
Roberts, M. A., 2003, 'Can It Ever Be Better Never to Have Existed at All? Person-Based Consequentialism and a New Repugnant Conclusion', *Journal of Applied Philosophy* 20, pp. 159–185.
Roberts, M. A., 2007, 'The Non-Identity Fallacy: Harm, Probability and Another Look at Parfit's Depletion Example', *Utilitas* 19, pp. 267–311.
Roberts, M. A., 2011, 'The Asymmetry: A Solution', *Theoria* 77, pp. 333–367.
Roberts, M. A., 2017, *Modal Ethics*, draft manuscript. Available on her website: https://robertsm.pages.tcnj.edu/files/2018/02/Modal-Ethics-complete-draft-2017.12.28.pdf
Rossi, P., 'Kant, Immanuel: Philosophy of Religion', *The Stanford Encyclopedia of Philosophy*.
Rowe, W., 2004, *Can God Be Free?*, Oxford University Press.
Russell, B., 1945, *History of Western Philosophy*, Simon and Schuster.
Rutledge, J. C., 2021, 'Tempering the Cosmic Scope Problem in Christian Soteriology: Hylemorphic Animalism and Gregory of Nazianzus', *Religious Studies* 57, pp. 266–286.
Sandin, P., 2004, 'The Precautionary Principle and the Concept of Precaution', *Environmental Values* 13, 461–475.
Sauer, H., et al., 2021, 'Moral Progress: Recent Developments', *Philosophy Compass* 16.
Sayre-McCord, G., 2023, 'Metaethics', *The Stanford Encyclopedia of Philosophy*.
Scanlon, T. M., 1999, *What We Owe to Each Other*, Harvard University Press.
Scheffler, S., 2001, 'Rawls and Utilitarianism', in *Boundaries and Allegiances: Problems of Justice and Responsibility in Liberal Thought*, Oxford University Press, pp. 149–172.
Scheffler, S., 2010, 'The Normativity of Tradition', in *Equality and Tradition: Questions of Value in Moral and Political Theory*, Oxford University Press, pp. 287–311.

Scheffler, S., 2010, 'Valuing', in *Equality and Tradition: Questions of Value in Moral and Political Theory*, Oxford University Press, pp. 15–40.
Scheffler, S., 2013, *Death and the Afterlife*, Oxford University Press. (Includes commentaries from Susan Wolf, Harry Frankfurt, Seana Shiffrin, and Niko Kolodny.)
Scheffler, S., 2018, *Why Worry about Future Generations?* Oxford University Press.
Schuster, J., and Woods, D., 2021, *Calamity Theory: Three Critiques of Existential Risk*, University of Minnesota Press.
Searle, J., 1997, *The Mystery of Consciousness*, London: Granta.
Sen, A., 1999, *Development as Freedom*, Oxford University Press.
Sherman, N., 2009, 'The Fate of a Warrior Culture', *Philosophical Studies* 144, pp. 71–80.
Shermer, M., 2015, *The Moral Arc: How Science Leads Society toward Truth, Justice, and Freedom*, Henry Holt and Co.
Shiffrin, S. V., 1999, 'Wrongful Life, Procreative Responsibility, and the Significance of Harm', *Legal Theory* 5, pp. 117–148.
Sidgwick, H., 1981, *The Methods of Ethics*, 7th edition, Hackett Publishing Company.
Silverstein, M., 2000, 'In Defense of Happiness: A Response to the Experience Machine', *Social Theory and Practice* 26, pp. 279–300.
Singer, P., 1975, *Animal Liberation*, Cape.
Singer, P., 2011, *The Expanding Circle*, Princeton University Press.
Stephenson, N., 2015, *Seveneves*, William Morrow.
Steward, H., 2012, *A Metaphysics for Freedom*, Oxford University Press.
Stokes, D., 2014, 'The Role of Imagination in Creativity', in *The Philosophy of Creativity: New Essays*, E. S. Paul and S. B. Kaufman (eds), Oxford University Press, pp. 157–184.
Sullivan, R., 1989, *Immanuel Kant's Moral Theory*, Cambridge University Press.
Swinburne, R., 1996, *Is There a God?*, Oxford University Press.
Swinburne, R., 2004, *The Existence of God*, 2nd edition, Oxford University Press.
Taylor, R., 1986, *Respect for Nature*, Princeton University Press.
Thompson, J., 2018, *Should Current Generations Make Reparations for Slavery?* Polity.
Tollefsen, C., 2003, 'Experience Machines, Dreams, and What Matters', *The Journal of Value Inquiry* 37, pp. 153–164.
Torres, E. P., 2021, 'Against Longtermism', *Aeon*. https://aeon.co/essays/why-longtermism-is-the-worlds-most-dangerous-secular-credo
Turner, D., and Hartzell, L., 2004, 'The Lack of Clarity in the Precautionary Principle', *Environmental Values* 13, 449–460.
Tyron, E., 1998, 'Is the Universe a Vacuum Fluctuation?' in *Modern Cosmology and Philosophy*, J. Leslie (ed.), Prometheus Books, pp. 222–225.
Vainio, O.-P., 2018, 'The Argument from Scale Revisited', *Theology and Science* 16, pp. 439–446.
Valberg, J. J., 2007, *Dream, Death, and the Self*, Princeton University Press.
Van der Lugt, M., 2021, *Dark Matters: Pessimism and the Problem of Suffering*, Princeton University Press.
Van Inwagen, P., 1989, 'When Is the Will Free?' *Philosophical Perspectives* 3, pp. 394–422.
Van Inwagen, P., 1994, 'When the Will Is Not Free', *Philosophical Studies* 75, pp. 95–113.
Van Inwagen, P., 2006, *The Problem of Evil*, Oxford University Press.
Van Inwagen, P., 2008, 'How to Think about the Problem of Freewill', *Journal of Ethics* 12, pp. 327–341.
Vihvelin, K., 2022, 'Arguments for Incompatibilism', *The Stanford Encyclopedia of Philosophy*.
Walton, J., 2015, *The Just City*, Corsair.

Webb, S., 2015, *If the Universe Is Teeming with Aliens... Where Is Everybody? Seventy-Five Solutions to the Fermi Paradox and the Problem of Extraterrestrial Life*, 2nd edition, Springer.

Weijers, D., and Schouten, V., 2013, 'An Assessment of Recent Responses to the Experience Machine Objection to Hedonism', *Journal of Value Inquiry* 47, pp. 461–482.

Weinberg, R., 2002, 'Procreative Justice: A Contractualist Account', *Public Affairs Quarterly* 16, pp. 405–425.

Weinberg, R., 2015, *The Risk of a Lifetime: How, When, and Why Procreation May Be Permissible*, Oxford University Press.

Wenar, L., 2021, 'John Rawls', *The Stanford Encyclopedia of Philosophy*.

Werhane, P. H., 1999, *Moral Imagination and Management Decision Making*, Oxford University Press.

White, L. B., 1986, *Commentary on the Critique of Practical Reason*, 2nd edition, University of Chicago Press.

Wielenberg, E., 2004, 'A Morally Unsurpassable God Must Create the Best', *Religious Studies* 40, pp. 43–62.

Wolf, S., 2010, *Meaning in Life and Why It Matters*, Princeton University Press.

Wolf, S., 2013, 'The Significance of Doomsday', in *Death and the Afterlife*, S. Scheffler (ed.), Oxford University Press, pp. 113–130.

Zagzebski, L., 2004, *Divine Motivation Theory*, Cambridge University Press.

Index

Because the index has been created to work across multiple formats, indexed terms for which a page range is given (e.g., 52–53, 66–70, etc.) may occasionally appear only on some, but not all, of the pages within the range.

act consequentialism – *see also* escapism
    and collective consequentialism 172–3
    and pessimism 11–3
    and procreative ethics 123–4
    and Rawls 223–4
Adams, R 69–70
afterlife – *see* immortality
aggregation 124, 174–6, 193–5
ananthropocentric purposivism 78–81 – *see also* theism, alternatives to
anti-natalism
    defined 120–2
    and ecological utopia 241–2
    and pessimism 120–1
    and Rawls 221
    and utopia 217, 245
    and virtual future 257
    and Weinberg 146, 148
argument from evil 62–4, 77–8 – *see also* theism
argument from scale 64–71 – *see also* theism
atheism 64–77 – *see also* presentism, Post-Cataclysm pessimism, theism

balance principle 147, 149–53, 156–63 – *see also* Weinberg
Benatar, D 7, 25, 146 – *see also* anti-natalism
bridging arguments 9–10, 17–18 – *see also* last generation pessimism, Ponzi arguments, Post-Cataclysm pessimism
Buchanan, A 210–12

collective consequentialism
    and act consequentialism 172–3
    defined 169–76
    demands of 172–3, 190–7
    and feasibility 195–7
    and hedonism 175–6, 193–4
    and human extinction 187–90
    incoherence objection to 180–2
    and the last generation 180–7
    and multigenerationalism 196–8
    and posthumous harm 183–7
    and procreative ethics 169–98
    and procreative permissibility 178–9, 197–8
    and rule consequentialism 171–2
consequentialism – *see* act consequentialism, collective consequentialism
contractualism – *see* Weinberg, Rawls
counterfactual harm 136–43 – *see also* Roberts
cosmological argument 71–3, 80 – *see also* theism

Different People Choices
    and Extra People Choices 128–9, 137, 152–3, 164–6
    and Harman 127–9
    introduced 118–19
    and Roberts 136–40
    and Weinberg 152–3, 164–6
digital future 282–90 – *see also* virtual future
doomsday scenario 13 – *see also* Scheffler

ecological utopia
    and anti-natalism 241–2
    in the ending world 238–43
    and hedonism 239–42
    and moral imaginativeness 242–3
    and multigenerationalism 242–3
escapism – *see also* act consequentialism
    and digital future 282–90
    and Post-Cataclysm pessimism 11–13
evolutionary conservatism 209–11 – *see also* moral progress
experience machine – *see* virtual future
Extra People Choices – *see also* Different People Choices
    and Different People Choices 128–9, 137, 152–3, 164–6
    and Harman 127–9
    introduced 119
    and Roberts 137–9
    and Weinberg 152–3, 164–6
extra-terrestrial life 64–9 – *see also* theism

final utopia
    arguments for 217–20
    defined 216

fine-tuning argument 72-5 – *see also* theism
finite pessimism, definition of 3 – *see also* bridging argument, Ponzi argument
freedom – *see also* procreative permissibility
  Nozick on 271-3, 275-6
  and virtual future 271-9
future-dependent meaning – *see* intergenerational meaning

generation-transcendent meaning – *see* intergenerational meaning

harm – *see* posthumous harm, counterfactual harm
Harman, E
  and Different People Choices 127-9
  in the ending world 128-34
  and Extra People Choices 127-9
  and multigenerationalism 131-6
  original theory 126-8
  and procreative ethics 126-36
  and procreative permissibility 134-6
  contrasted with Roberts 137, 139
  contrasted with Weinberg 164-6
Hartmann, E 37-43
  and hedonism 38-9
hedonism
  and collective consequentialism 175-6, 193-4
  and ecological utopia 239-42
  and Hartmann 38-9
  and meaning in life 98
  and pessimism 3-5
  and virtual future 252-4, 257, 262, 279-80
Hooker, B 171-2, 178-9, 184-5, 194 – *see also* collective consequentialism

Idealism – *see* transcendent metaphysics, McTaggart
Immortality
  moral argument for 43-8, 53-61
  secular replacements for 43-8
infertility scenario 13 – *see also* Scheffler
intergenerational meaning – *see also* meaning in life
  defined 97-101
  and meaning in life 16-24, 94-104, 131-2
  and multigenerationalism 94-104
  and theism 103-4

Johnston, M 24-5, 44-8 – *see also* Ponzi argument

Kant, I 43-4, 52-4, 276 – *see also* moral argument

last generation, the – *see also* last generation pessimism
  and collective consequentialism 180-7
  and multigenerationalism 90-1, 131-2, 154
  and Nozick 232-3
  plight of 46-7, 128-31, 160-1
  and procreative permissibility 110-12
  and Rawls 221-4, 228-9
  and utopia 217-19
  and virtual future 255-7, 259
  and Weinberg 161-3
last generation pessimism – *see also* Scheffler, Post-Cataclysm pessimism
  bridging argument 9-10, 17-18
  defined 2-3
  and Lear 33-6
  Ponzi argument 24-30
Lear, J 30-7 – *see also* Plenty Coups
Leibniz, G 66, 68
liberal egalitarianism – *see* Rawls
libertarianism – *see* Nozick
Locke, J 234, 236-7
longtermism – *see* act consequentialism, digital future, escapism

McTaggart, J 266
meaning in life – *see also* pessimism
  grounding of 97-101
  and hedonism 98
  intergenerational meaning 16-24, 94-104, 131-2
  and multigenerationalism 94-106
  and Post-Cataclysm pessimism 3-9
  and posthumous harm 186
  and theism 52-61, 103-4
Mill, J S 43-4, 178, 206-7
moral argument
  for immortality 43-8, 53-61
  for transcendent metaphysics 267-9
  for theism 52-61
moral imaginativeness
  defined 204-8
  and ecological utopia 242-3
  and moral progress 212-14
  and moral transformation 202-3, 212-14
  and multigenerationalism 206-8
  and religious utopia 245-8
  and utopia 218-20
moral progress
  theories of 200-1
  arguments for 208-14
  and moral imaginativeness 212-14
  and moral transformation 200-1, 208-14
  and multigenerationalism 208-14

moral transformation
    and digital future 289
    and moral progress 200–1, 208–14
    and multigenerationalism 201–4, 208–14
    and rectification 109–10
    and religious utopia 246–8
    and virtual future 259–61
motivation restriction 148–9, 153–6 – *see also* Weinberg
multigenerationalism
    and ananthropocentric purposivism 77–81
    arguments for 84, 93–112
    basic argument for 82
    and collective consequentialism 196–8
    defined 83–4, 89–93
    and digital future 289–90
    and ecological utopia 242–3
    examples of 85–9
    and Harman 131–6
    and Hartmann 42–3
    and intergenerational meaning 94–104
    and the last generation 90–1, 131–2, 154
    and Lear 36–7
    and meaning in life 94–106
    and moral imaginativeness 206–8
    and moral progress 208–14
    and moral transformation 201–4, 208–14
    and posthumous harm 106–8, 183–7
    and procreative permissibility 110–2, 114–16
    and Rawls 224–8
    and rectification 107–10
    and religious utopia 245–8
    and Roberts 141–3
    and theism 103–4
    and utopia 217–20
    and virtual future 258–61, 270–1, 280–2
    and Weinberg 154–6, 160–8

natal utopia
    arguments for 216–17
    defined 216
Neoplatonism 264–5, 267–8
non-identity problem 118–19, 126
Nozick, R
    and the experience machine 251–4, 271–3, 275–6
    and freedom 271–3, 275–6
    and the future 233–6
    and the last generation 232–3
    and libertarian utopia 230–8
    and Lockean proviso 233–6
    and meta-utopia 237–8
    and scarcity 233–6
    and self-ownership 231–3

Okin, S M 231–3

Parfit, D – *see* aggregation, Different People Choices, non-identity problem, repugnant conclusion
perennial pessimism, definition of 3
pessimism – *see also* last generation pessimism, Post-Cataclysm pessimism, finite pessimism, perennial pessimism
    and anti-natalism 120–1
    and hedonism 3–5
    varieties of 1–9
Plenty Coups 30–7, 202, 205–7
Ponzi arguments 24–30 – *see also* last generation pessimism, Post-Cataclysm pessimism
Post-Cataclysm Pessimism
    and act consequentialism 11–13
    and atheism 62–77
    defined 2–5
    and digital future 286–7
    and escapism 11–13
    and Hartmann 37–43
    and Johnston 43–8
    and last generation pessimism 9–10
    and Lear 30–7
    and meaning in life 3–9
    and multigenerationalism 95–7
    and Ponzi arguments 24–30
    and presentism 20–4
    and Scheffler 13–24
    and virtual future 253–61, 271–6
posthumous harm
    and collective consequentialism 183–7
    and meaning in life 186
    and multigenerationalism 106–8, 183–7
    and pessimism 5–7
    and rectification 107–8
posthumous interests – *see* posthumous harm
Powell, R 210–12
Presentism
    defined 20–2
    and Post-Cataclysm pessimism 20–4
    and theism 59–61
    and virtual future 251–7, 279–82
procreative asymmetry 124–5 – *see also* procreative permissibility
procreative ethics – *see also* procreative permissibility
    and act consequentialism 123–4
    Pre-Cataclysm 116–25
    and collective consequentialism 169–98
    and Harman 126–36
    and Roberts 136–43
    and Weinberg 144–68

procreative obligations – *see* pro-natalism, procreative permissibility
procreative permissibility
   and act consequentialism 123–4
   and collective consequentialism 178–9, 197–8
   constraints on 114–16
   and Harman 134–6
   and the last generation 110–12
   and multigenerationalism 110–2, 114–16
   and pro-natalism 122–3, 190
   and Roberts 142–3
   and Weinberg 145–7, 166–8
pro-natalism
   defined 122
   and procreative permissibility 122–3, 190

Rawls, J
   and act consequentialism 223–4
   and anti-natalism 221
   and the last generation 221–4, 228–9
   and multigenerationalism 224–8
   and Post-Cataclysm utopia 220–30, 243–6
   and redistribution 222–4
   and religion 243–6
   and Weinberg 147–8, 161–3, 222, 229–30
rectification for historical injustice 107–10, 231
repugnant conclusion 174–6 – *see also* aggregation
Roberts, M
   and Different People Choices 136–40
   in the ending world 140–2
   and Extra People Choices 137–9
   contrasted with Harman 137, 139
   and multigenerationalism 141–3
   original theory 136–40
   and procreative ethics 136–43
   and procreative permissibility 142–3
rule consequentialism – *see* collective consequentialism

Scheffler, S
   doomsday scenario 13
   infertility scenario 13
   and intergenerational meaning 95–7, 100–1
   and Lear 33–5
   and Post-Cataclysm pessimism 13–24
Steward, H 278–9

theism
   alternatives to 78–81, 246–8
   cosmological argument 71–3, 80
   argument from evil 62–4, 77–8
   and extra-terrestrial life 66–9
   fine-tuning argument 72–5
   impact of Cataclysm on 50–2
   and intergenerational meaning 103–4
   and meaning in life 52–61, 103–4
   moral argument for 52–61
   and multigenerationalism 103–4
   and presentism 59–61
   argument from scale 64–71
   strengthened by Cataclysm 52–61
   and transcendent metaphysics 265–7
   and virtual future 261–9
   weakened by Cataclysm 61–77
transcendent metaphysics
   moral argument for 267–9
   and theism 265–7
   theoretical arguments for 266–7
   and virtual future 263–9

utilitarianism – *see* act consequentialism, collective consequentialism
utopia
   and anti-natalism 217, 245
   ecological 238–43
   in the ending world 215–48
   final 216–20
   and the last generation 217–19
   and moral imaginativeness 218–20
   and multigenerationalism 217–20
   natal 216–17
   and Nozick 230–8
   and Rawls 220–30
   religious 243–8
   typology of 215–20
   and virtual future 260, 270–1, 278–9

virtual future
   and anti-natalism 257
   arguments for 251–3, 269–71
   attachment-based objection to 258–61
   in the ending world 249–90
   and the experience machine 251–2
   and freedom 271–9
   and hedonism 252–4, 257, 262, 279–80
   and the human future 256–8
   and the last generation 255–7, 259
   and multigenerationalism 258–61, 270–1, 280–2
   and Post-Cataclysm pessimism 253–61, 271–6
   practical objections to 254–6
   and presentism 251–7, 279–82
   solitary versus interpersonal 251–2, 279–82
   and reality 261–9

and status quo bias 258–61
and theism 261–9
and transcendent metaphysics 263–9

Weinberg, R
and anti-natalism 146, 148
balance principle 147, 149–53, 156–63
and contractualism 144, 161–3
and Different People Choices 152–3, 164–6
in the ending world 153–66
and Extra People Choices 164–6
contrasted with Harman 164–6
and the last generation 161–3
motivation restriction 148–9, 153–6
and multigenerationalism 154–6, 160–8
original theory 144–53
principles of procreative justice 147–8
and procreative ethics 144–68
and procreative permissibility 145–7, 166–8
contrasted with Rawls 147–8, 161–3, 222, 229–30
well-being – *see* hedonism, meaning in life, posthumous harm